RICHARD L. NORGAARD

*University of Texas*

DONALD E. VAUGHN

*Louisiana State University*

# Cases In Financial Decision Making

PRENTICE-HALL, INC.

*Englewood Cliffs, New Jersey*

LIBRARY OF CONGRESS CATALOG CARD NO. 67-22095

PRINTED IN THE UNITED STATES OF AMERICA

Current Printing (last digit)
10  9  8  7  6  5  4  3  2

C

PRENTICE-HALL INTERNATIONAL, INC., *London*
PRENTICE-HALL OF AUSTRALIA, PTY. LTD., *Sidney*
PRENTICE-HALL OF CANADA, LTD., *Toronto*
PRENTICE-HALL OF INDIA (PRIVATE) LTD., *New Delhi*
PRENTICE-HALL OF JAPAN, INC., *Tokyo*

# Preface

The cases in this book mark a departure from the scope of cases in previously published case books. The span of case difficulty is greater than that of other case books, and this allows the book to be used by both students who are inexperienced and those experienced in case work. This can be especially helpful in finance courses in which the cases are supplementary to text material and the instructor does not want to thrust the student directly into the rigors of the case method.

We have been experimenting with the use of various forms of cases for several years. In these experiments we have found that the full case and the comprehensive case can be handled very successfully by the undergraduate providing he has previously learned to handle cases properly. We have seldom found either undergraduates or graduates who have done a good job with difficult cases if they are only exposed to a very few cases during a term. Courses taught primarily through a text with only a few cases interdispursed seldom give students enough training in case procedure. In these courses emphasis can be placed on case problems and simplified cases. In courses where the term is divided equally between cases and lectures, and where the student is forced into the case method rapidly, the student should be able to successfully handle any case in this book provided he is allowed to progress from the easy cases to the more difficult ones.

We have found in most business schools where cases are used in the basic finance course that the cases are only a portion of the course. Under these circumstances students normally require considerable incentive if they are to put the necessary time into case preparation. Although the weight in grading can emphasize case work, we have seldom found grades the important incentive. Only a few students are completely grade oriented; most students will rebel if they believe they are being forced. The best incentive we have found is group desire.

Where the students doing case work start functioning as a group, they become very successful in their case work and enjoy it immensely. Further they do not believe they are overworked—even if on occasion they may be. Engendering a desire on the students' part for group action has proved to be the best enforcer for good work on the part of each student. We have found various methods for doing this, but each group is a little different. The instructor must make clear that cooperation between students is not only encouraged but necessary and that students must take initiative in this area even though their past training has led them to believe that cooperation is akin to cheating. They must realize that this is not the situation in the case method.

The courses which both we and our students have found tremendously rewarding were those which the *I* was replaced with the *we*. This did not destroy competition, it just changed its direction. The competition was with students in other classes or even with the nebulous but well known *they*. In an experiment involving four hundred students, we found that, when tested on an unbiased test, students who learned cooperatively through cases did considerably better than other students who had basically learned through text and lecture material. Cooperative learning appeared to make the difference.

The introduction to this book explains the use of the cases in the book and also gives a brief history of the case method. Students should find it most helpful in their case work. The introduction was written because of the general lack of knowledge about how cases began in business administration, and how they are to be handled and used. Surprisingly little has been written in this area even though the importance of the case method in teaching in business schools has materially expanded in the past few years.

Many people helped us in making this book possible. This is always more true of a case book than a text book. If it were not for the various business firms who gave generously of their time, few cases would ever be produced With the exception of the case problems, all cases represent actual and sometimes confidential material which had to be released by the appropriate executive officer. In addition we wish to express our appreciation to Professor Kenneth Olm for allowing us to adapt the "Houston Corporation," and to the Board of Regents of the University of Texas for allowing us to publish the following copyrighted cases: *Rente High Appartments, Continental Oil Company, Houston Petroleum Corporation,* and *Hillside.* We also acknowledge with thanks the contributions of Dr. James E. West, State University of New York; Professor Eli Schwartz, Lehigh University; Professor Robert Daines, Brigham Young University; and Professor Stephen H. Archer, University of Washington.

All cases in this book were prepared as the basis for group discussion and are not intended to illustrate either effective or ineffective handling of an administrative situation, nor are they intended to supply information of direct value to competitors of firm's supplying case material.

RICHARD L. NORGAARD

DONALD E. VAUGHN

# Contents

## Part IV
### SHORT AND INTERMEDIATE TERM FINANCING
129

## Part V
### LONG-TERM FINANCING
169

## Part VII
## SPECIAL PROBLEMS
## 269

## Part VIII
## COMPREHENSIVE CASES
## 317

## APPENDIX
## 365

# An Introduction To The Case Method

This introduction is presented so that the student and instructor can gain the maximum benefit from the cases presented in this book even though they may not have had previous case experience. For this purpose we will present a brief history of the development of cases, examine the intended uses, benefits, and limitations of cases, and then look at the role of the instructor. We should like to emphasize first that there is no one case method nor is there only one way for the case leader to conduct the case discussion. Varying the leadership of cases builds student interest and increases the dynamic experiences for the participants. That case method which appears best to fit the business situation should be utilized by the case leader.

The lecture method requires the instructor to impart a vast body of facts, principles, or definitions to the students. The case method, on the other hand, stresses maximum involvement and participation, sharing of ideas, and the development of the ability to make decisions in realistic situations on the part of the students and an almost passive attitude on the part of the case leader (instructor). The case method places little premium on the ability to memorize facts, for the emphasis is directed toward the development of a reasonable recommendation as to a course of action for a given situation or problem.

## The Evolution of The Case Method

Although hundreds of colleges and universities are now employing the case method of instruction in their business administration schools and casebooks are available in most areas of study, the Graduate School of Business Administration at Harvard University is credited

1

with the initial sponsorship of the case method. From the founding of the school in 1908 until about 1924, the number of courses at Harvard Business School which employed the case method expanded until case instruction evolved as the predominate approach. By the latter date, almost all the courses in the Harvard Business School curriculum used the case method to some degree. At present a majority of the courses continue to be developed around the case method approach, although many of the professors present short "lecturettes" on subjects which appear to be particularly troublesome to the students.

A number of programs for faculty have generated additional interest in the case method. Since 1955 Ford Foundation grants have sponsored a Visiting Professors' Case Method Program at Harvard. The operation of the Southern Casewriters from 1960 through 1964 under a Ford Foundation grant also provided some monetary support for the development of interest in the writing and usage of the case method. The Intercollegiate Case Clearing House at Harvard University provides a free exchange of case material ideas to interested professors, and multiple copies of the cases may be obtained for a nominal cost. Hopefully additional monetary grants from endowment funds will continue to sponsor worthwhile programs designed to narrow the breach between the academic and the business communities because the development of actual business situations into a form which may be utilized in the classroom to promote a dynamic learning experience is of tremendous value to the student, the professor, and the businessman.

### Preparation of Cases

For the student and instructor, the primary task in a case is finding an acceptable solution. However, let us look first at how cases are developed. The steps usually followed in the field research and casewriting include the following: (1) initial contact with an officer of the firm in order to locate a problem; (2) interviews with company personnel in order to become completely familiar with the problem situation; (3) gathering of materials and writing of the case; (4) classroom testing of the case; (5) revision of the case; (6) obtaining a release from the firm officer for publishing the materials.

Numerous methods may be used in locating a case situation, but some personal relationship between the casewriter and the businessman to be interviewed usually results in more cooperation between the researcher and the company personnel. The researcher may find that he will need to contact numerous businessmen before he can locate a business problem which appears to offer a good potential case. Listening to the president, or to some other senior officer of the company, relate something about the history of his firm, new products which are currently being developed, personnel problems which may be present, or financial alternatives which are open to the firm often gives the casewriter a glimpse of a case problem. In the initial contact, the researcher can usually tell whether his contact will be helpful and release the case once it is written. The casewriter may wish to assure the businessman that the data will be kept strictly confidential, that the case will be disguised, and that the case will not be distributed for classroom use until it has been released by the firm's officer. This technique often leads to better cooperation and to releases of the data, but undisguised cases are to be preferred if the company executive will release the undisguised materials.

After the initial interview with the company executive (the president or chairman of the board is preferred) and the location of a case situation, the officer may assign a junior officer to work with the researcher. When he begins to assemble his case material, the casewriter may find that he needs to make another visit to the business firm in order to obtain other facts. If the company president does not object to the use of the case material for classroom use, the case may be classroom tested. A written release for the final draft of the case should be obtained from a senior officer of the firm before the case is listed with the Intercollegiate Case Clearing House or published; otherwise, a lawsuit may be forthcoming from the business firm or from one of the principals mentioned within the case.

### Essence of the Case Method of Instruction

The two extremes in the approach to teaching are the lecture method and the case method. In using the lecture method, the professor imparts a vast body of knowledge to the students and requires that the students learn (or memorize) the data and transmit it to him on an exam. The case method presents the student with some facts surrounding a given situation and requires that the students think realistically about the problems involved and recommend an appropriate course of action to be taken under the conditions existing in the case. Various degrees of the so-called "discussion method" of teaching fall between these two extremes.

Teaching students at the Harvard Business School follows a distinct pattern. Since only some 7 per cent of the M.B.A. students entering the school have undergraduate degrees in business administration, the majority have very little theoretical background of business facts on which to make their decisions. Very little time is devoted to the lecture method, although short lecturettes (a few minutes in length) on technical topics may be given from time to time and outside reading assignments are frequently used by the individual professors.

The first-year student at Harvard Business School enrolls in seven case courses, each requiring about three hours of weekly class time. Since he is expected to read the case materials and reach a logical decision as to the course of executive action to be taken in each case situation, all without benefit of theoretical courses in the subjects, he often encounters a period of frustration. After a while, hopefully, this turns to enthusiasm, aggressiveness, and an improved decision-making ability.

The student who is first introduced to the case method slowly learns that little premium is attached to the memorization of vast stores of information. The emphasis is placed on decision making after considering the surrounding circumstances. Many students spend hours searching the library for a formula or for an identical situation on which to solve their case problem. One rarely exists. Having no "one right answer" to a case situation is often perplexing to the student, but after he learns that the professor is interested not so much in what is recommended but the reasons for the suggested course of action, he becomes more willing to participate in the class discussion.

Professors use many different techniques in introducing their students to the case method. Some professors use the case method in undergraduate courses, integrating the method with the lecture and/or discussion method. For example, some ten to twenty cases may be utilized in business finance, money and banking, bank management, financial institutions, investments, and other undergraduate finance courses. One or two cases with fairly broad financial coverage may be integrated effectively within each major area of a finance course. While the students may at first be reluctant to participate in discussion, some lead questions for outside preparation often prove stimulating.

At the graduate level, a majority of the class time should be spent in case discussion. Although many students desire some reading references on which to base their decisions, usually they can easily find reference material which presents the theoretical concepts covered in most actual case situations.

Each student is urged to make an individual preparation for his case, but the discussion of the problem by a small group prior to the class meeting may uncover some points of interest which will permit further pursuits during the class. Also, discussion with the small groups and sounding out the ideas may stimulate some students to speak in the classroom who would not do so otherwise. If the discussion of a case situation continues after the class is dismissed, the instructor knows that the learning process is continuing and has not ended with the final bell.

When the student receives a case assignment, he should read the case for general impressions, preferably a few days before the scheduled class meeting. He should consider the overall situation presented within the case, and jot down a number of problems which are present. He should then endeavor to determine solutions for the subproblems and reach a decision as to the course of action to be taken by the business executive within the case. He can put himself in the place of the central figure in the case, assume that the other members of the informal subgroups are his subordinates, and obtain their ideas about various aspects of the case situation. The amount of case analysis depends upon the desires of the professor as well as the type of case being analyzed; however, the student should prepare enough notes about the case so that he may refer to them for last minute review and as a basis for class discussion.

Although the Harvard Business School operates its first-year basic case courses with about ninety-five students in each section, a majority of the other institutions which use the case method do not have such large case classes. Some twenty to thirty students contribute to a more lively discussion than does a small class of ten or less. When a class is larger than fifty, each student may not be able to participate as often as he desires. Active participation by ten to fifteen good students is required in order to keep the tempo moving. A small class limits the number of participants, often leaving the discussion flat and unenthusiastic. A few hard-working, aggressive students in a class of twenty-five or thirty will have a stimulating effect upon the other students, and within a few class meetings almost every student will be contributing to the conversation. When a student is reluctant to contribute, he should be encouraged to do so.

### The Role of the Case Leader

This section deals primarily with the instructor. While on the surface this appears to be appropriate for instructors only, this is an illusion. The student should appreciate what the instructor is trying to do. Because the cases in this book are written for students at the undergraduate and first-year graduate level, most students will have had little or no previous exposure to cases and will have little confidence in their ability to make a meaningful contribution to a case discussion. Thus, the role of the instructor will be particularly trying until the students understand what the instructor is attempting to accomplish. It is our opinion that the students cannot expect the instructor to impart all necessary motivation. The students must supply much of the motivation, interest, and information themselves even in the earlier case discussions. It is the student's class, the instructor is merely an adjunct. To see this problem clearly, let us state the purpose of case development. The purpose of the case method is to impart techniques to the students for handling decision-making problems. These techniques should come from the students themselves as they attempt as a group to reach a meaningful conclusion in a particular business situation.

The role of the case leader is not to impart knowledge but rather to lead students to a logical approach to the case under discussion. The recommended course of executive action should be reached by the students alone. The case should not be the foundation from which a lecture is launched. Such a lecture method achieves very little because the students are not active participants, they do not become emotionally involved, nor do they have a dynamic learning experience. Many educators believe that the latter is necessary before the student can obtain a lasting benefit from his classroom endeavor. A case is also very dull and uninteresting when the leader gives a brief presentation of the major facts of the case and tells what he thinks should be done. Little is learned by the students from such an experience, and the case leader will frequently exhaust his supply of comments when the period is but half over.

The case leader should strive for maximum involvement, or participation, by every member of the class. This point should be emphasized at the beginning of each case course and should perhaps be reemphasized if the discussion appears to stall. A seating chart with a daily recording of symbols such as *C*, *Q*, *S*, and the like, denoting contribution, question, and schedule, respectively, will stimulate discussion from the students. When they feel that they are receiving a grade for their efforts, shy students are encouraged to join the discussion. The chart may be discontinued after a few weeks when the professor is better acquainted with his students and when all the students have begun to participate.

Perhaps the most difficult task for the professor who utilizes the case method of instruction is that of evaluating the progress being made by his students. Case exams may be given in case courses rather than some other type of test. Since some three to four hours are required for the student to read and adequately evaluate a complex case situation, the exams may be limited to a mid-term and a final. Some professors prefer to assign one case write-up to be completed outside of class and another to be completed in class as the mid-term or final. This technique does not penalize the slow student as much as requiring that all the work be done in class. One shortcoming to this approach, however, is that the outside work may be a joint project rather than each student's independent thinking.

The grading weights given to class participation, written assignments, and examinations will vary from class to class. Typically, class participation is weighted heavily, perhaps as much as 80 per cent of the final grade. Some professors, conversely, consider written and oral participation to be of equal value. Where the professor permits graduate students to lead a case, he may evaluate the overall involvement of the class, or the amount of class participation and response given by the class as a basis for assigning a grade to the case leader for that particular assignment.

The method of approach for case leadership varies with each group of students and for each case; however, some illustrations of various techniques may be helpful for the student who needs to understand the goals of the instructor. The case leader will probably strive for maximum participation by the students from the very beginning. He may attempt to set the students at ease by assuring them that there is no one "correct" answer to most cases and that he is more interested in the reasons why the students arrived at a certain recommendation rather than the suggestions themselves.

While many cases can be handled adequately in a fifty-minute period, by adequately prepared classes, some cases require more class time for reaching a logical decision. Preferably students should reach some consensus during a given class period, but the case need not be thoroughly discussed in that time. Some of the more complex cases in this book require two or three hours of discussion for exhaustive coverage. If a student occasionally directs the case discussion to an area which does not appear to help in finding a solution, other members of the class should try to turn the discussion in the proper direction. Where the case discussion leads to some interesting factors, however, the instructor may encourage the students to explore side areas even though this may mean that a solution to the case will not be reached within the desired time.

The case leader may find that his primary jobs are to keep the conversation rolling and to write the student's remarks on the blackboard. The professor may mark off the blackboard into sections devoted to such topics as: (a) major problems involved; (b) data necessary to reach decisions; (c) presentation of schedules and exhibits; and (d) planned courses of action. The students are encouraged to suggest the problems involved in the case under consideration. Then an attempt is made to determine what supporting factual data would be helpful in reaching a logical course of action. Students may volunteer to place their exhibits or computations on the blackboard, or the professor may use an opaque projector for placing the student's quantitative data before the class. When numerous courses of action are open to the executive, the advantages and disadvantages of each should be considered.

The cases which merely present one problem for consideration and which appear to call for a negative or positive course of action, such as a review of a credit request by a marginal credit applicant, may be handled in an entirely different manner from the more comprehensive cases. For example, the case leader may wish to pursue the student's reasoning with regard to the following: (a) strengths of the credit applicant; (b) weaknesses of the borrower; (c) loanable funds available; (d) benefits to the lender in making the loan; and (e) risks involved in making the loan. Students will usually respond much better to a short question, such as one of the above, than to a long, complicated question. In fact, five or ten students may respond to each of the questions above. In this way the students are each sharing their ideas, and the interest is usually much keener than in a lecture section. One reason for the interest is, that as the list increases in length, adding to the items becomes increasingly difficult. The student reads and rereads the blackboard list in an attempt to discover other possible strengths of the borrower which have been overlooked, thus storing ideas expressed during the case discussion for future reference.

Some cases are designed to illustrate a course of action to be taken by a credit committee or by the board of directors of a corporation. Appointing some of the students as committee or board members and letting the balance of the students be observers may prove interesting. This method, however, does not solicit the comments of all the class members and is probably a less effective learning technique than the use of one case leader. In order to broaden the participation, the students not serving on the panel or board may take the role of stockholders of the firm and direct questions to the chairman of the committee or board of directors.

Although probably the professor should lead all the cases in an undergraduate course, he may find it stimulating and a worthwhile learning and training experiment to require that each graduate student be responsible for leading one case or for a group to share in the leadership. Many of the graduate students are training for the academic profession, and no experience in the use of the case method is more valuable than becoming completely involved. When the student serves as the case leader, the professor may wish to give him some instructions or ideas before the class begins. The professor should be prepared to assume case leadership should the student falter or fail to get the desired response from the class. We suggest that the professor be the case leader for a period of sufficient length to completely familiarize the student with the desired role of the case leader.

## Class Nonparticipation

Infrequently a class will not respond to the questions asked by the instructor. This represents more of a breakdown in the class than a weakness in the instructor. The students must realize that they are a group, placed together to solve a problem. While the students may not know each other, they still must work together. Each must assume the responsibility of reaching a solution. Members who do not cooperate are letting everyone down, and in these instances the case leader may be forced to take special action. He may ask, "What's wrong with the class?" He is usually met with silence, or some student may point out that a majority of the students have just completed a mid-term exam and did not have time to prepare the case analysis adequately. A ten- or fifteen-minute break from the discussion while the student familiarizes himself with the facts of the case may be a more profitable method for solving the problem than to dismiss the class or continue it with little interest on the part of the students. If lack of response occurs frequently, something may be wrong with the approach of either the students or the case leader. Perhaps the class is not at ease, and the student is afraid to voice his suggestions or opinions. The professor must try to overcome the students' reluctance to participate. When the students repeatedly refuse to prepare adequately, the case leader should require that a written analysis of each case be submitted at the end of the class period.

## Limitations of the Case Method

The use of the case method is limited primarily by the lack of confidence of the participants. It is up to each student to overcome this. The enthusiasm and ingenuity of the case leader, of course, are quite important but not crucial. At least one student leader should emerge in each class. Some classes may have several. A properly working class needs no instructor once it has been thoroughly indoctrinated in the case method because the role of the leader will always be assumed by someone. The major problem in not having the professor is in the competition for leadership which may occur among students. Numerous business administrative faculties have voiced their inabilities to use the case method effectively with undergraduate students, particularly those in basic courses. This may be the result of lack of response from the immature students. The use of the discussion method in presenting the theoretical concepts in a basic course will help to pave the way for the case method. When the lecture method has been the predominant method of instruction, the student often has difficulty making valuable contributions in a case discussion.

## Written Case Reports

Instructors will periodically require that cases be written. The principal difference between a case prepared for use in class and one prepared for submission to the instructor is the form and organization. The student should devote the same amount of time to the analysis of the case in either event. Typically, a written case presentation should be concise, for it should be based on analysis and facts presented in a quantitative manner. The written portion of a case should normally be limited to two or three pages. The analysis of data should be placed at the end of the case and can be referred to for substantiation of points which the student has made in the written portion of the case. Although several methods of presentation are quite acceptable, the student may find his thinking aided through the use of the decision-making approach. This involves dividing the presentation into four parts as follows:

1. *Statement of the problem.* Each case has a primary problem. This must be determined and stated in clear, concise language. Special peripheral problems may exist which cannot be included in the main statement, and these may be listed also.
2. *Alternative solutions to the problem.* Any given business problem will have numerous possible solutions. The student should name as many of them as he can even though some may appear to be "far out." Imagination is very important here, and it is at this point where the better students can show their mettle.

3. *Evaluation of alternatives.* Once the alternatives have been stated, they must be evaluated. This must be done on an analytical basis. The facts presented in the case or available to the student from other sources should be used here to present factual analysis of the alternative.

4. *Choice of the best alternative.* Occasionally, after a thorough evaluation, the choice is obvious. Unfortunately, that type of analysis is seldom possible, so that some uncertainty will usually be present in any choice. Normally only a modest amount of justification is necessary at this point in specifying one alternative as better than another. The major work should have been accomplished prior to this step.

### Case Coverage

The cases included in this casebook are intended for both undergraduate and graduate students in business finance. Undergraduates should be forewarned, however, that these cases are not easy and cannot be put aside to do later. There is a considerable degree of variation in case difficulty. Some are relatively easy and others quite difficult, but none of the cases can be properly handled by a student who merely reads the case and jots down a few facts. Undergraduates must be prepared to meet some cases which tax their abilities. In fact, some of the cases are not solvable by one student alone. If the student remembers that many cases have a wide variety of solutions and that there is no "right" solution, it may help his peace of mind.

The cases in this book are taken from actual business situations, but some of the short problems are hypothetical. In writing these cases, some of the data were such that the involved firm did not choose to be directly identified with the material; consequently, we have changed the name and situation of the firm and modified the financial data. In these cases, however, the essence of the case has been retained intact, and the thoughts and actions of the involved executives are as they were in the business situation. Where the cases are undisguised, some students determine what the company actually did in the specific situation. In most cases, this type of detective work can prove more harmful than useful. Knowing what the company actually did may prove a tremendous handicap in developing a thorough analysis. In some of these cases we disagree with the decision made by the responsible executive.

Approximately half of the cases in the book are general in nature and require only modest computations. These cases are designed for stimulating class discussion on various phases of business principles, ethics, operations, and responsibilities. The student must delve into his own background in order to solve these cases. He should be prepared to find other students who are in violent disagreement with him. The other cases are quantitative and require computations, including a knowledge of present value, cash flows, trend and ratio analysis, simple mathematics, and statistics. The quantitative cases are so constructed that no meaningful solutions can be reached without doing the necessary computations and analysis. The better student will apply the techniques he has learned in other courses in the development of this type of case solutions. The case problems and certain simplified cases have questions which are for the benefit of students in approaching the case method. Most cases, however, do not have questions and the student will have to determine the important questions (problems) as a part of solving the case.

The cases in this book progress from easy to difficult within each section. Where cases are labeled comprehensive, the student should seek more than one problem, and a thorough analysis will be necessary in order to find and evaluate the appropriate alternatives. Generally, all information necessary for an adequate solution is included in the cases.

*Part  I*

# FINANCIAL PLANNING

## Analyzing Statements

The Sanderson Machine Tool Company was organized in 1947 by Mr. O. D. Sanderson who had formerly managed the tool division of a large industrial equipment company. Although the company had grown rapidly at first, a leveling off period had occurred, and Mr. Sanderson felt it was time to expand again.

In anticipation of such an expansion, Mr. Sanderson had had a major market study made. The study indicated that the expansion program was justified, and that if fixed assets would be increased by 50 per cent, sales of $22,500,000 could be realized by 1970. If the expansion were not undertaken, the belief was that sales would drop or at least not expand.

### QUESTIONS

1

1. Mr. Sanderson has asked you to give an unbiased opinion of the firm's past financial policies. Using ratio analysis, make up a report on the firm's policies and position.

2. Determine the amount of fixed and working capital funds needed for the expansion.

3. What action do you suggest Mr. Sanderson take regarding his financial policies?

SANDERSON MACHINE
TOOL COMPANY

**FINANCIAL DATA**

**Comparative Balance Sheets**
**(In Thousands)**

| | 1963 | 1964 | 1965 | 1966 | Common Size 1965 | Common Size 1966 |
|---|---|---|---|---|---|---|
| *Current assets* | | | | | | |
| Cash & securities | $2,475 | $3,513 | $2,793 | $2,468 | 15% | 14% |
| Receivables | 3,500 | 2,500 | 3,250 | 4,000 | 18% | 22% |
| Inventories | 2,000 | 3,875 | 4,500 | 4,600 | 25% | 25% |
| Prepaid expenses | 100 | 125 | 150 | 100 | 1% | — |
| Total | $8,075 | $10,013 | $10,693 | $11,168 | | |
| *Tangible assets* | | | | | | |
| Machinery and equipment, net | $6,500 | $6,000 | $5,500 | $5,000 | 30% | 28% |
| Buildings | — | — | — | — | — | — |
| *Intangible assets* | $2,000 | $2,000 | $2,000 | $2,000 | 11% | 11% |
| Total assets | $16,575 | $18,013 | $18,193 | $18,168 | 100% | 100% |
| *Current liabilities* | | | | | | |
| Accounts payable | $1,500 | $3,000 | $3,000 | $2,500 | 16% | 14% |
| Notes payable (5%) | 500 | 100 | 100 | 100 | 1% | — |
| Total | $2,000 | $3,100 | $3,100 | $2,600 | | |
| Common stock (par $50)* | $10,000 | $10,000 | $10,000 | $10,000 | 55% | 55% |
| Retained earnings | 4,575 | 4,913 | 5,093 | 5,568 | 28% | 31% |
| Total | $16,575 | $18,013 | $18,193 | $18,168 | 100% | 100% |

**Comparative Income Statements**

| | 1963 | 1964 | 1965 | 1966 | 1965 | 1966 |
|---|---|---|---|---|---|---|
| Sales | $15,000 | $15,000 | $15,000 | $15,000 | 100% | 100% |
| Expenses other than interest | 13,625 | 13,870 | 13,495 | 13,720 | 90% | 91.5% |
| Interest expense | 25 | 5 | 5 | 5 | — | — |
| P.B.T. | $1,350 | $1,125 | $1,500 | $1,275 | 10% | 8.5% |
| Tax | 675 | 562 | 750 | 637 | 5% | 4.25% |
| P.A.T. | 675 | 563 | 750 | 638 | 5% | 4.25% |
| Dividends | 337 | 281 | 375 | 319 | 2.5% | 2.13% |
| Retained earnings | 338 | 282 | 375 | 319 | 2.5% | 2.13% |

*200,000 unregistered shares issued and outstanding. Shares held by 200 shareholders.

**Average Price Earnings Ratios for Companies
In Industry Based on Their Equity-Debt Ratio**

| Equity-Debt Ratio | Price Earning Ratios | |
|---|---|---|
| | 1965 | 1966 |
| 100—0 | 9.0—1 | 9.0—1 |
| 90—10 | 10.5—1 | 10.5—1 |
| 80—20 | 18.0—1 | 18.0—1 |
| 70—30 | 20.0—1 | 20.0—1 |
| 60—40 | 17.0—1 | 15.0—1 |
| 50—50 | 9.0—1 | 9.0—1 |

# Financial Planning

**2**

In 1958, Mr. Francis X. Jones, in partnership with two friends, started a small business to make and distribute badges, buttons, and miscellaneous novelties to colleges for sale at football games. Although the venture was reasonably successful, Jones was unhappy with the partnership, and in 1961 he left to form his own business, Nifty Novelties. The main product that Jones decided to sell was small plastic toys for Christmas and Easter. Because he had almost no money, Jones was forced to live frugally for the first two years; but the product did catch hold and Jones was soon in a strong competitive position.

The toys were made from polyethelene which Jones purchased as scrap from local plastic users. Because he was able to utilize low-cost scrap, his raw material costs were very small, and he was able to realize a satisfactory margin on his toys. At first Jones had to travel extensively in order to get the product into stores, and he had to work on another part-time job in order to keep his business going financially. As the product sold, however, Jones commissioned manufacturers' representatives across the country to handle sales in specific areas; and by 1965, Jones no longer made any sales trips except to toy fairs and toy conventions.

Unfortunately Jones soon found his market approaching the saturation point. Because of his low cost he was able to keep out competitors; at the same time he was too small and financially weak to try manufacturing larger plastic toys which would have broadened his market and increased substantially his sales and profits. As a result he attempted to cut his expenses and to take the sales increases normally expected from an increase in population and disposable personal income. For future expansion Jones decided to develop new products of his own on which he could obtain a patent, while letting the present business supply him with funds for research.

In 1966 Jones developed a "flying saucer," made almost entirely from plastic, which he believed would sweep the market. A large Chicago wholesale distributing firm had indicated that they would be pleased to distribute the saucer at a price of $3.98 per unit. Jones believed that total sales of the saucer might be as much as $250,000 in the first year, and he estimated that the rate of earnings on net worth after the expansion would be equal to the

## EXHIBIT I

### Francis X. Jones
### D/B/A Nifty Novelties
### Comparative Income Statement

|  | 1966 | 1965 | 1964 | 1963 | 1962 |
|---|---|---|---|---|---|
| Sales | $125,305.24 | $116,341.70 | $92,160.68 | $102,990.49 | $44,173.48 |
| Less sales returns and allowances | 428.24 | 2,515.82 | 2,342,85 | 974.03 | — |
| Net sales | 124,877.00 | 113,825.88 | 89,817.83 | 102,016.46 | 44,173.48 |
| Cost of goods sold | 73,235.44 | 63,461.82 | 43,834.90 | 57,666.10 | 22,679.06 |
| Gross profit | 51,641.56 | 50,364.06 | 45,982.93 | 44,350.36 | 21,494.42 |
| Operating expenses | 39,743.89 | 40,728.79 | 37,960.63 | 29,032.55 | 14,289.20 |
| Operating profit | 11,897.67 | 9,635.27 | 8,022.30 | 15,317.81 | 7,205.22 |
| Other income and expenses | (246.94) | (737.73) | 2,664.45 | (781.20) | — |
| Net profit | $11,650.73 | $8,897.54 | $10,686.75 | $14,536.61 | $7,205.22 |

### Expense Schedule

|  | 1966 | 1965 | 1964 | 1963 | 1962 |
|---|---|---|---|---|---|
| Advertising | $1,696.68 | $1,533.91 | $1,434.87 | $102.80 | $259.18 |
| Auto expense | 889.91 | 992.91 | 871.41 | 664.14 | 818.09 |
| Commissions | 1,204.10 | 4,006.79 | 3,852.75 | 4,808.45 | 3,381.95 |
| Interest and charges | 1,215.02 | 1,218.26 | 965.92 | 324.84 | 38.64 |
| Legal and audit | 390.00 | 473.85 | 357.75 | — | — |
| Miscellaneous expense | 1,496.48 | 3,297.89 | 2,348.55 | 2,830.67 | 1,115.60 |
| Rent and utility | 10,795.69 | 10,744.42 | 8,996.48 | 7,439.52 | 4,004.95 |
| Repairs | 1,357.48 | 707.53 | 1,062.87 | 2,084.39 | 20.61 |
| Supplies | 2,742.54 | 1,503.15 | 2,659.34 | 779.39 | 827.53 |
| Taxes | 2,917.60 | 2,727.86 | 1,813.49 | 1,386.61 | 537.92 |
| Insurance | 348.45 | 719.92 | 438.31 | 464.39 | 166.27 |
| Depreciation | 5,009.78 | 5,511.37 | 4,460.10 | 2,647.35 | 1,088.24 |
| Amortization of leasehold | 792.59 | — | 467.80 | 560.29 | 175.70 |
| Bad debts | 1,670.82 | — | — | 496.91 | — |
| Office salary | 4,200.00 | 4,224.00 | 2,127.24 | — | — |
| Freight out | 3,016.75 | 2,974.87 | 3,629.61 | 1,188.81 | 498.88 |
| Collection fee | — | 15.00 | 51.00 | — | — |
| Bank charges | — | 77.06 | 80.03 | 42.52 | 55.10 |
| Indirect labor materials | — | — | 2,343.11 | 3,211.47 | 1,262.46 |
| License | — | — | — | — | 38.08 |
| Total expenses | $39,743.89 | $40,728.79 | $37,960.63 | $29,032.55 | $14,289.20 |

present rate of earnings on Nifty Novelties' net worth. To finance the production and sale of the saucer, Jones estimated that he would need a new machine costing $50,000 plus working capital of $25,000. He was sure that he could get a loan of as much as $25,000 to finance the machine and that he could obtain an additional $10,000 from accounts payable, but there seemed to be no place to get the final $40,000. Jones was still getting his short-term funds from bank loans secured by accounts receivable financing, and there was no chance of the bank providing any more funds. One possible source of the additional funds was from an outside investor, but after some checking Jones realized that he would have to relinquish 50 per cent of the company for the additional $40,000. No other possibility seemed feasible.

After reviewing his entire situation, Jones was puzzled as to what he should do. His financial situation, although improving, was still not good,

**EXHIBIT II**

**Francis X. Jones**
**D/B/A Nifty Novelties**
**Comparative Balance Sheet**

|  | 1966 | 1965 | 1964 | 1963 | 1962 |
|---|---|---|---|---|---|
| Assets |  |  |  |  |  |
| *Current assets* |  |  |  |  |  |
| Cash | $375.64 | $278.10 | $439.64 | $2,390.31 | $2,673.67 |
| Accounts receivable | 5,201.07 | 6,278.05 | 7,208.92 | 7,582.71 | 2,898.30 |
| Inventory | 13,755.00 | 14,252.60 | 11,553.55 | 4,967.25 | 5,420.00 |
| Total current assets | 19,331.71 | 20,808.75 | 19,202.11 | 14,940.27 | 10,991.97 |
| Other assets | 2,599.67 | 2,046.80 | 2,568.70 | 3,725.00 | 3,725.00 |
| *Fixed assets* |  |  |  |  |  |
| Equipment | 28,748.46 | 30,214.14 | 29,858.42 | 23,833.04 | 4,330.15 |
| Leasehold | 6,380.99 | 5,934.93 | 6,614.21 | 2,274.26 | 1,581.33 |
| Total fixed assets | 35,129.45 | 36,149.07 | 36,472.63 | 26,107.30 | 5,911.48 |
| Prepayments | 1,099.67 | 1,029.89 | 629.29 | 494.16 | 197.26 |
| Total assets | $58,160.50 | $60,034.51 | $58,872.73 | $45,266.73 | $20,825.71 |
| Liabilities |  |  |  |  |  |
| *Current Liabilities* |  |  |  |  |  |
| Accounts payable | $13,718.25 | $19,642.27 | $19,707.43 | $9,048.70 | $4,730.69 |
| Mortgage payable | 3,500.00 | — | — | 2,121.50 | — |
| Taxes payable | 3,616.50 | 2,478.85 | 1,552.71 | 1,477.75 | 884.82 |
| Accrued sales commissions | — | 898.31 | 312.57 | 1,029.92 | — |
| Notes payable | 5,541.80 | 11,624.75 | 16,252.22 | 9,525.67 | 5,824.68 |
| Other accrued charges | — | — | 47.43 | — | — |
| Total current liabilities | 26,376.55 | 34,644.18 | 37,872.36 | 23,203.54 | 11,440.19 |
| *Noncurrent liabilities* | 10,278.03 | 8,335.00 | 8,735.00 | 9,139.46 | 5,623.20 |
| Total liabilities | 36,654.58 | 42,979.18 | 46,607.36 | 32,343.00 | 17,063.39 |
| *Net worth* | 21,505.92 | 17,055.33 | 12,265.37 | 12,923.73 | 3,762.32 |
|  | $58,160.50 | $60,034.51 | $58,872.73 | $45,266.73 | $20,825.71 |

and he was getting tired of struggling to make ends meet. The new product looked excellent to him, but he did not know whether the risk was worth it. In addition, he had recently been offered a job as a sales manager for a manufacturing firm at a salary of $12,000 plus bonuses. Although Jones enjoyed selling, he considered himself independent and wanted to stay self-employed if at all possible.

# Financial Organization

On February 5, 1966, Mr. John F. Baxter, president of PDE, Inc., of St. Louis, Missouri, and of two other associated but independent companies, was reviewing the results of operations. He noted that each of the three companies was performing in line with expectations and that the benefits which he had originally envisioned from keeping the companies completely separate were being realized. Although Mr. Baxter handled all financial matters himself, he wondered if the size of the total operations of the three companies might not warrant a centralized finance function. He had considered this idea before and had rejected it, but he thought that reviewing the matter once again might be wise.

**PDE, Inc.**

# 3

## PDE, INCORPORATED

After leaving the Air Force in 1948, Mr. Baxter started engineering school at Washington University, and during his spare time he sold aluminum windows. Soon, he was devoting full-time to sales. Shortly thereafter he founded a company, which later became PDE. PDE manufactured and sold specialized aluminum window products. By 1951, the company's sales had reached $110,000. As the name became better known and the sales organization expanded, sales rapidly increased so that by 1957, the company's sales had reached the $1,000,000 mark. By 1965, the company had sales of $1.8 million and was the largest manufacturer of aluminum window products in its primary five-state market area.

PDE operated in a highly competitive market subject to considerable cyclical fluctuations. The market was not, however, as cyclical as that of the building industry because much of its sales was based on replacing old wood-type window installations. Because of this situation profit margins were low and only the most efficient survived. Exhibits II and III show financial data for the company. By 1963 PDE's sales expansion program was threatened from a lack of long-term funds. To remedy the problem, an issue of common stock was floated. This issue was nonvoting "A" stock. By 1965 more long-term funds were needed, and, for that purpose, Mr. Baxter sold directly to the public $31,500 in convertible subordinated debentures. The issue had originally been for $250,000, but adverse market conditions and a lack of interest in new securities had prevented the type of participation in the issue which had been expected.

### Midwest Aluminum, Inc.

In addition to developing aluminum windows for residential buildings, Mr. Baxter decided to get into the commercial window, door, and curtain wall market. To do this, he believed that a separate company might offer the best overall results. Such a company would have its own financing, its own management, and its own board of directors. Employees and management would then have to rely on their own skills and ability to succeed. While the companies would be under the same president, Mr. Baxter, and would not compete directly for the same type of business, they would be a source of competition for expansion and profits, and Mr. Baxter believed that this would be very good. For this purpose, then, he formed Midwest Aluminum, Inc. in 1961.

Midwest was quite successful, and by 1965 assets were $300,000 and sales, $600,000. (See Exhibits IV and V for financial statements.)

### Precision Metals, Inc.

The third company in the group, Precision Metals, commenced operations on Oct. 1, 1965. As with the others Mr. Baxter was the president while the remaining officers were independent of either PDE or Midwest. Precision Metals extruded aluminum and milled, fabricated, and machined the extruded aluminum. During its initial months of operations it sold 30 per cent of its products to PDE and Midwest and the remaining 70 per cent to other aluminum product distributors. (See Exhibit VI.)

### The Financial Position

Each company had its own officers and accountants. Financial statements were even audited by different CPA firms. Funds were not loaned from one company to another nor was interest or principal payments guaranteed between companies. The common stock of the various companies was traded in a rather inactive market, and no broker or dealer made a specific market for any of the stock. In Mr. Baxter's opinion the use of common "B" voting stock had not appreciably affected the value and interest in the common "A" stock, since the stockholders apparently did not want to enter into management, and since this arrangement meant that present management would generally be free to run the companies most efficiently without worrying about outside raiders. Mr. Baxter felt that the stockholders purchased the stock because he was president, and that they wanted to keep the situation that way. (See Exhibit VII for details on stock.)

Currently the company was relying heavily on term loans with interest rates varying between 6 per cent and 12 per cent. Further expansion of these loans appeared doubtful in the immediate future; however, Mr. Baxter believed that this would pose no problems for his sales objectives.

### EXHIBIT I

#### Officers of PDE, Midwest, and Precision

| | PDE | Midwest | Precision |
|---|---|---|---|
| President | J. F.  Baxter | J. F.  Baxter | J. F.  Baxter |
| Vice President | R. S.  Lerner | J. C.  Smith | E. R.  Johnson |
| Secretary | E. R.  Johnson | —— | J. C.  Smith |
| Treasurer | V. C.  Kriberg | J. F.  Baxter | E. R.  Johnson |
| Assistant Secretary | T. A.  Winston* | T. A.  Winston* | —— |
| Assistant Treasurer | O. C.  Swenson* | —— | —— |

*Principally occupied in other occupations.

### EXHIBIT II

#### PDE, INC.
#### Five-Year Financial Highlight Summary

| Earnings | 1961 | 1962 | 1963 | 1964 | 1965 |
|---|---|---|---|---|---|
| Net sales | $1,492,528 | $873,929 | $1,329,540 | $1,723,570 | $1,837,925 |
| Manufacturing costs | 1,049,737 | 676,747 | 1,109,054 | 1,297,920 | 1,323,025 |
| Operating expenses | 363,545 | 195,904 | 259,179 | 342,561 | 392,791 |
| Operating income | 79,246 | 1,278 | (38,693) | 83,089 | 122,109 |
| Other income or expenses | (22,710) | 1,638 | (43,443) | (66,869) | (74,249) |
| Income before taxes | 56,536 | 2,916 | (82,136) | 16,220 | 47,860 |
| Income taxes | 27,509 | 998 | 33,500* | 6,964 | 24,115 |
| Net income | $29,027 | $1,918 | $(48,636) | $9,256 | $23,745 |
| *Other Data* | | | | | |
| Cash Dividends— preferred and Common "A" | $5,307 | $6,552 | — | — | $15,575 |
| Stock dividends— common "B" | 10,986 | — | — | — | — |
| Earnings per common share | .11 | .01 | (.11) | .02 | .05 |

*Tax refund reported.

## EXHIBIT III

### PDE, Inc.
### Balance Sheet—December 31, 1965
### (With prior year amounts for comparison)

| Assets | 1965 | 1964 |
|---|---|---|
| *Current Assets* | | |
| Cash | $30,648 | $11,290 |
| Accounts and notes receivable | 461,774 | 365,575 |
| Refund of prior years' income taxes | 5,147 | 3,980 |
| Inventories, at lower of cost or market | | |
| Raw materials | 229,267 | 186,113 |
| Work in process | 9,158 | 21,027 |
| Finished goods | 49,895 | 56,315 |
| Prepaid expenses | 11,627 | 15,971 |
| Total current assets | $797,516 | $660,271 |
| *Other Assets* | | |
| Cash surrender value of life insurance | $32,918 | $27,394 |
| Deposits | 1,125 | 1,125 |
| Total other assets | $34,043 | $28,519 |
| *Fixed assets*, at cost less accumulated depreciation of $124,486 in 1965 and $107,792 in 1964 (pledged) —Note 1 | $542,710 | $539,020 |
| *Deferred Charges* | $9,330 | $6,178 |
| *Goodwill* | $4,785 | $4,785 |
| *Total assets* | $1,388,384 | $1,238,773 |

### Liabilities and equity

| | 1965 | 1964 |
|---|---|---|
| *Current liabilities* | | |
| Notes payable (partially secured)—Note 1 | $432,067 | $349,641 |
| Accounts payable | 103,374 | 149,345 |
| Accrued liabilities | 106,788 | 64,274 |
| Total current liabilities | $642,229 | $563,260 |
| *Long-Term Liabilities* | | |
| Notes payable (partially secured)—Note 1 | $320,668 | $293,812 |
| Seven per cent subordinated convertible debentures— due 1970—Note 2 | 31,500 | |
| Notes payable—officers and employees | 15,282 | 18,500 |
| Total long-term liabilities | $367,450 | $312,312 |
| *Deferred investment ¢redit* | $3,130 | |
| *Stockholders' equity* | | |
| Class "A" common—$1 par value, nonvoting | $259,580 | $256,480 |
| Class "B" common—25¢ par value, voting | 45,750 | 45,750 |
| Capital surplus | 29,893 | 27,723 |
| Retained earnings | 40,352 | 33,248 |
| Total Stockholders' Equity | $375,575 | $363,201 |
| *Total liabilities and equity* | $1,388,384 | $1,238,773 |

**EXHIBIT III (continued)**

**PDE, Inc.**
**Notes to the Financial Statements**
**December 31, 1965**

## Note 1

Notes payable at December 31, 1965 were as follows:

| | Current | Long-term | Total | |
|---|---|---|---|---|
| Great West Life Assurance Co., Winnipeg, Canada, 6-3/8% | $9,385 | $210,904 | $220,289 | A |
| Equity Capital Co., St Louis, Mo., 12% | 8,289 | 15,328 | 23,617 | B |
| Industrial Credit Company, St. Louis, Mo., one-thirtieth of one per cent per day | 369,918 | | 369,918 | C |
| First National Bank, St. Louis, Mo.: | | | | |
| 5½% | | 25,000 | 25,000 | D |
| 8% | 16,918 | 26,769 | 43,687 | E |
| Midwest National Bank, East St. Louis, Mo., 8½% | 6,006 | 21,520 | 27,526 | F |
| Kaiser Aluminum & Sales, Inc., Skokie, Ill., 6% | 19,197 | | 19,197 | G |
| PDE Employees' Pension Trust, 7% | | 16,766 | 16,766 | G |
| Missouri National Bank, St. Louis, Mo., 6% | 2,354 | 197 | 2,551 | H |
| Gordon Anderson, Avondale Estates, Georgia, 6% | | 2,184 | 2,184 | G |
| J. R. Smidt, St. Louis, Mo., 6% | | 2,000 | 2,000 | G |

A Secured by a first mortgage on land and a factory building located in St. Louis. Additional security is provided by assignment of certain officers' life insurance policies and personal guarantee of payment by officers of the company. The loan agreement includes certain additional covenants pertaining primarily to working capital, issuance of stock, and payment of dividends.
B Secured by a second mortgage on land and new factory building located in St. Louis. Prepayment penalties apply to July 5, 1966.
C Secured by accounts receivable and inventories.
D Secured by cash value of insurance on lives of officers.
E Secured by automobiles and factory equipment.
F Secured by airplane.
G Unsecured.
H Secured by certain office equipment.

## Note 2

The 7 per cent subordinate convertible debentures were issued in $500 denominations each of which may be converted into 250 shares of Class "A" common stock. Subject to the subordination provisions contained in the indenture, the company may redeem the outstanding debentures by paying the principal and accrued interest plus a premium based on the length of time the debentures are held. At December 31, 1965, 15,750 shares of Class "A" common stock were reserved for the conversion of debentures.

### EXHIBIT IV

**Midwest Aluminum, Inc.**
**Comparative Statement of Income**
**Years Ended December 31, 1965 and December 31, 1964**

|  | Dec. 31, 1965 | Dec. 31, 1964 |
|---|---|---|
| Sales | $613,981 | $839,739 |
| Cost of goods sold | 495,520 | 724,449 |
| Gross profit on sales | 118,461 | 115,290 |
| Operating expenses |  |  |
| Selling expenses | 35,016 | 28,484 |
| General and administrative exp. | 47,878 | 42,359 |
| Total operating expenses | 82,894 | 70,843 |
| Profit from operations | 35,567 | 44,447 |
| Other income | 292 | 1,506 |
| Other deductions (Principally Int.) | (12,120) | (14,169) |
| Income before income taxes | 23,739 | 31,784 |
| Federal income taxes | 5,196 | — |
| State income taxes | 1,499 | 10 |
| Total income taxes | 6,695 | 10 |
| Net income for year | $ 17,044 | $ 31,774 |

**EXHIBIT V**

**Midwest Aluminum, Inc.**
**Comparative Balance Sheet**

| Assets | December 31 1964 | December 31 1965 |
|---|---|---|
| *Current assets* | | |
| Cash on hand and in bank | $ 2,254 | $ 3,276 |
| Accounts receivable | 117,827 | 130,699 |
| Stock subscription receivable | — | 1,000 |
| Inventories | 73,895 | 87,029 |
| Office supplies and sample inventory | 2,692 | 4,008 |
| Prepaid selling and catalog expense | 3,179 | 8,403 |
| Total current assets | 199,847 | 234,415 |
| *Cash surrender value of officers' life insurance* | — | 154 |
| *Property and equipment* | 89,105 | 108,025 |
| Less accumulated deprec. and amortization | 21,401 | 35,786 |
| Net carrying value | 67,704 | 72,239 |
| *Deferred charges* | 2,489 | 2,353 |
| Totals | $270,040 | $309,161 |
| **Liabilities** | | |
| *Current liabilities* | | |
| Installment note payable | $102,058 | $114,706 |
| Accounts payable | 83,573 | 69,716 |
| Accrued liabilities | 6,813 | 9,509 |
| Income taxes | 10 | 4,336 |
| Total Current Liabilities | 192,454 | 198,267 |
| *Long-term liabilities* | | |
| Installment notes payable—secured | 10,746 | 669 |
| Notes payable—unsecured | 5,000 | 5,000 |
| Total Long-Term Liabilities | 15,746 | 5,669 |
| *Stockholders' equity* | | |
| Capital stock | | |
| Class " B " common stock | 22,300 | 22,300 |
| Class " C " common stock | 49,050 | 81,625 |
| Stock subscribed—common " C " | — | 1,000 |
| Total Capital Stock | 71,350 | 104,925 |
| Earned surplus (Deficit) | (9,510) | 300 |
| | 61,840 | 105,225 |
| Totals | $270,040 | $309,161 |

## EXHIBIT VI

**Precision Metals, Inc.**
**Balance Sheet**
**December 31, 1965**

### Assets

*Current assets*
| | | |
|---|---|---|
| Cash | | $ 7,027.80 |
| Stock subscriptions receivable | | 27,250.00 |
| Accounts receivable | | 31,479.27 |
| Recoverable die costs | | 18,962.07 |
| Inventories | | 51,363.12 |
| Inventories of supplies, estimated | | 2,172.41 |
| Prepaid expenses | | 1,927.01 |
| Rebate receivable for equipment, estimated | | 3,000.00 |
| | | 143,181.68 |
| *Fixed assets* | $339,002.81 | |
| Less accumulated depreciation | 2,783.85 | 336,218.96 |
| *Other assets* | | |
| Organization expense | | 3,006.50 |
| Total | | $482,407.14 |

### Liabilities

*Current Liabilities*
| | | |
|---|---|---|
| Accounts payable, including amounts owing for equipment | | $119,930.09 |
| Account payable for organization expense, estimated | | 3,000.00 |
| Contracts Payable for equipment—current portion | | 30,430.02 |
| Employees' payroll deductions | | 1,934.02 |
| Accrued liabilities | | 5,078.44 |
| Total Current Liabilities | | 160,372,57 |
| *Long-term Liabilities* | | |
| Contracts payable for equipment | $316,945.79 | |
| Less unearned finance charges included in contracts | 81,551.12 | |
| | 235,394.67 | |
| Less current portion shown above | 30,430.02 | 204,964.65 |
| Total Liabilities | | 365,337.22 |
| *Stockholders' equity* | | |
| Common stock, class " A " | 118,800.00 | |
| Common stock, class " B " | 13,500.00 | |
| | 132,300.00 | |
| Less net loss for period | 15,230.08 | 117,069.92 |
| Total | | $482,407.14 |

## EXHIBIT VII

### Summary of Common Stock

---

*PDE Inc.*

| | |
|---|---|
| Class A Common | $1 par, non-voting, 6% non-cumulative, participating. 259,580 shares outstanding. |
| Class B common | $.25 par, voting, 183,000 shares outstanding. Class B common is held by Baxter, Lerner and Kriberg. |

*Midwest Aluminum, Inc.*

| | |
|---|---|
| Class B common | no par, voting, 2,676 shares outstanding, stated value $8.33 per share. |
| Class C common | no par, non-voting, 7,189 shares outstanding, stated value $11.354 per share. Class B common is held by Baxter and Smith. |

*Precision Metals, Inc.*

| | |
|---|---|
| Class A common | $1 par, non-voting, 2% non-cumulative (based on $25 selling price), participating, 4,752 shares outstanding. |
| Class B common | $22.50 par, voting. Class B common is held by Baxter, Johnson, and Smith. |

Description of participating feature on common A.

Under the terms of the non-voting stock, preferential dividends as indicated must be paid before any dividends can be paid on the voting stock. Once the preferential dividends are paid, an equal amount can be paid to the voting stock and after that any additional dividends are to be on a share-and-share-alike basis.

Common A and C do not have the preemptive right.

# Analyzing
# a New
# Business

## 4

CAPITAL JANITORIAL
SERVICE, INC.

In May, 1966, Mr. Davis and Mr. Early of Austin, Texas, were considering the acquisition of the common stock of Capital Janitorial Service, Inc. from the sole shareholder, Mr. Arant. Since the shares were not actively traded, the problem arose of determining a fair evaluation for the stock. The two prospective owners also needed to decide whether they would gain a tax advantage by electing Subchapter S of the Internal Revenue Code or whether such an election was unnecessary. Since the two buyers did not have enough cash to handle the transaction, an installment purchase plan would have to be worked out which was satisfactory to the buyers and to the seller.

During the past decade, janitorial service businesses have been formed in most cities large enough to support them. A city such as Austin with about 200,000 population with moderate a-mounts of commerical and industrial businesses will not profitably support more than two or three janitorial serv-ices. In fact, this type of business has been noted for its high failure rate.

Capital Janitorial Service, Inc. was first organized by Mr. Early, the sales manager of the present company. Mr. Early operated the firm for about 18 months as a single proprietorship. He found it extremely difficult to supervise the operations activities of the firm and to build up the volume of sales. Con-sequently, after operating the firm for more than a year at a loss, he sold his interest in the business to three indi-viduals, Mr. Arant, Mr. Bartel, and Mr. Cole, who incorporated the firm. Mr. Early continued with the business as manager. The owners were not active in the management of the firm other than making an occasional visit to the business. As the revenue and labor force grew in size, an operations manager was hired so that Mr. Early could devote full-time to sales expansion, customer problems, and general clerical and accounting work. Mr. Davis joined the firm as operations manager late in 1961, and with two managers, an active sales manager and an operations manager, revenues and profits began to rise.

Both managers worked a 50-hour week for a flat salary. The crew supervisors were hourly paid employees, while the janitorial workers were paid by the job. In early 1966, each of the managers were receiving an $850 monthly salary plus a bonus of 20 per cent of the profits. Each of their salaries were scheduled to advance to $980 a month and their bonuses to increase to 25 per cent in July, 1966. No additional changes were planned for the future. The crew supervisors received about $400 each per month and the janitorial workers each received about $50 weekly.

From incorporation in 1963 to March, 1966, Mr. Arant, Mr. Bartel, and Mr. Cole were the shareholders in the company. Mr. Arant owned 480 shares, Mr. Cole owned 480 shares, and Mr. Bartel owned 240 shares. Late in March, 1966, Mr. Cole and Mr. Bartel sold their shares to Mr. Arant at an aggregate price of $27,000. Mr. Arant had other business interests and indicated a willingness to sell his shares of stock to Mr. Davis and Mr. Early. Mr. Arant offered to sell the stock for an immediate cash payment of $6,000 with a monthly payment of $600 from February, 1967, through July, 1976. Mr. Arant agreed to retire the remaining $2,400 bank loan out of the down payment so that the aggregate asking price for the stock was $72,000.

Mr. Davis and Mr. Early were undecided whether the asking price was generous or excessive. The market value of the fixed assets was about $3,000 above their book values, so that the adjusted net worth of the firm was about $25,000, including net profits generated subsequent to the March 31, 1966, balance sheet date. During the fourth quarter of the 1965–1966 year monthly revenues were about $17,000. Mr. Davis believed that total annual revenues would increase by about $24,000 per year for the next five years. Profits were expected to increase slightly more rapidly than sales since a portion of the expenses was fixed in nature. The rate of growth in revenue was expected to be only about $12,000 per year subsequent to 1971. The firm was earning profits of about $11,000 annually before payment of the bonuses to the sales and operations managers. An additional 1 per cent of revenue could be saved by terminating the accounting service contract with Mr. Bartel (who charged 2 per cent of revenue) and employing a part-time accountant (see Exhibit III). Other economies could probably reduce expenses by an additional percentage point.

Mr. Davis believed the offer was attractive. Mr. Arant's share of the profits would amount to approximately $600 per month if he retained ownership of the stock. In addition, 40 per cent of the initial cash payments would be used to retire the bank loan. Since repayment was not scheduled to begin until six months after the transfer of ownership, the down payment would, in reality, be an advance payment of Mr. Arant's share of the profits. On the other hand, the debt incurred by the two shareholders, or by the corporation, created a substantial risk in the event that profits declined.

Mr. Arant had already expressed his desire that the transaction be considered as an installment purchase of the stock so that any gain on the shares would be taxed as a long-term capital gain. Mr. Davis and Mr. Early, however, were desirous of expensing some of the purchase price of the securities if this could be done legally. Should the shares be purchased by Mr. Davis and Mr. Early with personal funds, the corporation would be taxed on its income at the normal and surtax rates (Exhibit VII), and the shareholders would have to pay personal taxes on their taxable income. Each had $2,400 of exemptions and took the standard deduction. Neither individual had income other than from his salary and bonus.

As an alternative, Davis and Early could each receive 30 shares of stock in the corporation for the down payment with the firm acquiring the remainder on an installment debt basis. If Mr. Arant were willing to draw up an agreement guaranteeing not to start a competing firm in the same city for a definite time period, say five years, the amount paid for the stock in excess of its fair value could be capitalized and amortized for tax purposes over the cease and desist period. If the latter were done, this excess would be taxable to Mr. Arant as ordinary income. Personal assets of Davis and Early consisted of mortgaged homes, household furnishings, and small amounts of liquid assets.

For the next ten years, assuming that the business were acquired, Davis and Early planned to continue to draw their basic salaries from the firm. Their bonuses and retained earnings would be used to retire the stock acquisition debt and to build up the company's assets. If the two shareholders wished, they could elect Subchapter S of the Internal Revenue Code which permitted the stockholders to be taxed on their proportionate share of profits instead of the firm's being taxed as a corporation. This would eliminate the double taxation on distributed profits.

Mr. Davis and Mr. Early realized that Mr. Arant would desire a reply to his installment sale offer within a few weeks. If the offer did not appear attractive, a counteroffer could be made. Mr. Arant, however, did not appear overanxious to dispose of the firm so that Mr. Davis and Mr. Early were not in much of a bargaining position.

## EXHIBIT I

### Capital Janitorial Service, Inc.
### Organizational Chart

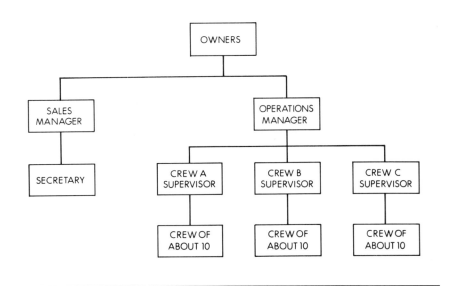

## EXHIBIT II

### Capital Janitorial Service, Inc.
### Comparative Revenue Statements

| Income | 1963 | 1964 | 1965 | 9 mos. 1966 |
|---|---|---|---|---|
| Services rendered | $ 43,721 | $ 85,688 | $142,825 | $131,644 |
| *Expenses* | | | | |
| Supervisory salaries | 6,413 | 4,868 | 14,664 | 14,669 |
| Janitorial salaries* | 20,797 | 41,640 | 68,965 | 61,909 |
| Supplies used | 2,123 | 4,381 | 8,839 | 9,320 |
| Direct costs | 72 | 229 | 182 | 250 |
| Overhead (Exhibit III) | 22,698 | 29,770 | 41,409 | 37,763 |
| Total | 52,103 | 80,888 | 134,059 | 123,911 |
| *Net Income* | $ (8,382) | $ 4,800 | $ 8,766 | $ 7,733 |

*Includes the salary and bonus paid to the operations manager and the crew supervisors.

**EXHIBIT III**

**Capital Janitorial Service, Inc.**
**Schedule of Overhead**

| Item | Year Ended 6/30/63 | Year Ended 6/30/64 | Year Ended 6/30/65 | 9 mos. Ended 3/31/66 |
|---|---|---|---|---|
| Advertising | $    — | $    58 | $    176 | $    74 |
| Amortization of leasehold improvement | 91 | 146 | 140 | 148 |
| Bad debts | 100 | 235 | 88 | 23 |
| Bank charges | 42 | 60 | 107 | 76 |
| Breakage | 110 | 126 | 43 | 118 |
| Commissions | 1,759 | 134 | — | 2,036 |
| Depr.—automotive equip. | 708 | 1,066 | 1,813 | 1,182 |
| Depr.—furniture and fixtures | 60 | 95 | 103 | 95 |
| Depr.—janitorial equip. | 702 | 1,736 | 2,465 | 1,835 |
| Employees' expense allow. | 816 | 528 | 240 | — |
| Insurance | 859 | 1,669 | 2,594 | 2,638 |
| Interest | 72 | 114 | 6 | 178 |
| Laundry | 84 | 196 | 199 | 338 |
| Legal and accounting | 1,142 | 1,187 | 3,438 | 3,892 |
| Light, heat, and water | — | 19 | 5 | 197 |
| Mileage allowance | 2,672 | 2,885 | 2,469 | 1,536 |
| Miscellaneous | 508 | 565 | 659 | 634 |
| Office salaries* | 6,684 | 8,699 | 12,320 | 9,215 |
| Payroll taxes | 2,229 | 3,119 | 6,133 | 5,472 |
| Rent | 846 | 1,008 | 1,188 | 1,044 |
| Rental of equip. | — | 58 | 25 | 16 |
| Repairs | 170 | 114 | 300 | 565 |
| Stationery, printing, and the like | 768 | 462 | 1,206 | 889 |
| Taxes and licenses | 96 | 125 | 391 | 242 |
| Telephone and telegraph | 800 | 1,410 | 1,798 | 1,114 |
| Travel | — | 262 | 185 | 136 |
| Truck expense | 1,004 | 1,934 | 1,991 | 2,832 |
| Uniform expense | 146 | 184 | 252 | 58 |
| Warehouse expense | 230 | 1,576 | 1,075 | 1,180 |
|  | $22,698 | $29,770 | $41,409 | $37,763 |

*Includes salary of the sales manager and the secretary.

**EXHIBIT IV**

**Capital Janitorial Service, Inc.**
**Balance Sheet**
**As of March 31, 1966**

| *Assets* | | | Amount | Per Cent |
|---|---|---|---|---|
| Current assets | | | | |
| Cash | | | $  3,082 | |
| Accounts receivable—trade | | | 19,706 | |
| Inventory—supplies | | | 3,174 | |
| Inventory—uniforms | | | 127 | |
| Total | | | $ 26,089 | 74.7 |
| Other assets | | | | |
| Accounts receivable—other | | | 443 | |
| Leasehold improvements | | | 49 | |
| Meter deposits | | | 120 | |
| Total | | | 612 | 1.8 |
| Fixed assets | (Cost) | (Allow. for Depr.) | | |
| Automotive equipment | 6,123 | 2,517 | 3,606 | |
| Furniture and fixtures | 1,264 | 353 | 911 | |
| Janitorial equipment | 10,222 | 6,738 | 3,484 | |
| Total | $ 17,609 | $  9,608 | $  8,001 | 22.9 |
| Deferred charges | | | | |
| Prepaid taxes and licenses | | | 216 | .6 |
| Total Assets | | | $ 34,918 | 100.0% |

| *Liabilities and capital* | | Amount | Per Cent |
|---|---|---|---|
| Current liabilities | | | |
| Accounts payable—trade | | $  1,995 | |
| Notes payable—bank | | 3,600 | |
| Due to affiliates | | 335 | |
| Due to officers and employees | | 240 | |
| Taxes payable and accrued | | 2,910 | |
| Employee withholding taxes payable | | 537 | |
| Accrued insurance | | 3,277 | |
| Accrued salaries and wages | | 3,154 | |
| Total | | $ 16,048 | 46.0 |
| Capital | | | |
| Capital stock (1,200 Shares Outstanding) | | 12,000 | |
| Retained earnings | | 6,870 | |
| Total Capital | | 18,870 | 54.0 |
| Total Capital and Liabilities | | $ 34,918 | 100.0% |

**EXHIBIT V**

**Business Service Firms**
**Corporation Income Tax Returns**
**July 1961-June 1962**
**Composite Balance Sheets**

| *Assets* | Amount | Per Cent |
|---|---|---|
| Cash | $ 619,062 | 12.1 |
| Notes and accounts receivable | 1,508,204 | 29.5 |
| Less; reserve for bad debts | (15,857) | (.3) |
| Inventories | 163,680 | 3.2 |
| Investments | | |
| State and possessions | 42,910 | .8 |
| U. S. Government | 81,680 | 1.6 |
| Other | 26,710 | .5 |
| Other current assets | 120,342 | 2.4 |
| Loans to stockholders | 9,354 | .2 |
| Mortgage and real estate loans | 7,899 | .1 |
| Other investments | 986,518 | 19.3 |
| Depreciable assets | 2,397,185 | 46.9 |
| Less: accumulated depreciation | (1,147,357) | (22.4) |
| Depletable assets | 4,511 | .1 |
| Less: accumulated depreciation | (615) | (.0) |
| Land | 70,781 | 1.4 |
| Intangible assets | 16,899 | .3 |
| Less: accumulated amortization | (3,042) | (.1) |
| Other assets | 225,945 | 4.4 |
| Total Assets | $5,114,809 | 100.0% |
| *Liabilities and capital* | | |
| Accounts payable | 824,595 | 16.1 |
| Deposits and withdrawable shares | 7,017 | .1 |
| Bonds, notes, mortgages due within year | 435,767 | 8.5 |
| Other current liabilities | 352,110 | 6.9 |
| Loans from stockholders | 157,849 | 3.1 |
| Long-term notes, bonds | 869,941 | 17.0 |
| Other liabilities | 228,322 | 4.5 |
| Total Debt | 2,875,601 | 56.2 |
| Capital stock, preferred | 57,187 | 1.2 |
| Capital stock, common | 599,841 | 11.7 |
| Paid-in capital | 293,951 | 5.7 |
| Retained earnings, appropriated | 113,988 | 2.2 |
| Retained earnings, unappropriated | 1,174,241 | 23.0 |
| Total Capital | 2,239,208 | 43.8 |
| Total Capital and Liabilities | $5,114,809 | 100.0% |

**EXHIBIT VI**

**Business Service Firms
Corporate Income Tax Returns
July 1961—June 1962
Composite Income Statements**

|  | Amount | Per Cent |
|---|---|---|
| *Receipts* | | |
| Business receipts | $7,076,516 | 95.8 |
| Other | 309,809 | 4.2 |
| Total | 7,386,325 | 100.0% |
| *Expenses* | | |
| Cost of operations | 4,027,935 | 54.5 |
| Compensation to officers | 406,712 | 5.5 |
| Rent on business property | 132,289 | 1.8 |
| Repairs | 32,139 | .4 |
| Bad debts | 15,519 | .2 |
| Interest paid | 62,405 | .8 |
| Taxes paid | 125,027 | 1.7 |
| Contributions | 4,244 | .1 |
| Amortization | 2,594 | .0 |
| Depreciation | 296,373 | 4.0 |
| Depletion | 157 | .0 |
| Advertising | 81,279 | 1.1 |
| Pension plan contributions | 59,045 | .8 |
| Other employee benefit plans | 19,534 | .3 |
| Other deductions | 1,583,103 | 21.5 |
| Total Expenses | 6,848,355 | 92.7% |
| Net Profits before Taxes | $ 537,970 | 7.3% |

## SCHEDULE VII

### Federal Income Tax Rate Table*
### Joint Return

| Taxable income (before splitting) For 1964 | | Tax | | |
|---|---|---|---|---|
| Over | Not Over | Pay | + Rate | On Excess Over |
| —— | $ 1,000 | —— | 16% | —— |
| $ 1,000 | 2,000 | 160 | 16.5% | 1,000 |
| 2,000 | 3,000 | 325 | 17.5% | 2,000 |
| 3,000 | 4,000 | 500 | 18% | 3,000 |
| 4,000 | 8,000 | 680 | 20% | 4,000 |
| 8,000 | 12,000 | 1,480 | 23.5% | 8,000 |
| 12,000 | 16,000 | 2,420 | 27% | 12,000 |
| 16,000 | 20,000 | 3,500 | 30.5% | 16,000 |
| 20,000 | 24,000 | 4,720 | 34% | 20,000 |
| After 1964 | | | | |
| —— | $ 1,000 | —— | 14% | —— |
| $ 1,000 | 2,000 | 140 | 15% | 1,000 |
| 2,000 | 3,000 | 290 | 16% | 2,000 |
| 3,000 | 4,000 | 450 | 17% | 3,000 |
| 4,000 | 8,000 | 620 | 19% | 4,000 |
| 8,000 | 12,000 | 1,380 | 22% | 8,000 |
| 12,000 | 16,000 | 2,260 | 25% | 12,000 |
| 16,000 | 20,000 | 3,260 | 28% | 16,000 |
| 20,000 | 24,000 | 4,380 | 32% | 20,000 |
| 24,000 | 28,000 | 5,660 | 36% | 24,000 |

### Business Corporations

1964

| | |
|---|---|
| Normal tax rate | 22% |
| Surtax rate | 28% (income above $25,000) |

1965 and later

| | |
|---|---|
| Normal tax rate | 22% |
| Surtax rate | 26% |

*Refer to the Appendix for other tax tables.

*Part II*

# WORKING
# CAPITAL
# MANAGEMENT

# Pro Forma
# Statements

*In Future*

# 5

TEXTRONICS, INC.

Textronics was formed in 1960 in order to produce a special vacuum tube for submarine sonar scopes. The company was formed by two electronic experts and a business manager, each of whom contributed $15,000. They enjoyed immediate success, and in their first year they received a million dollar contract from Domar Electronics for their tube. On the strength of this, they sold $155,000 of $1 par common stock with preemptive rights to their friends. Since they felt that transistors offered an excellent opportunity, they invested heavily in them and received a $1.5 million contract from a major radio producer. Because they needed more money, they sold an issue of cumulative convertible preferred in the amount of $500,000. These were $100 par, $7 dividend and convertible at $25, or one share of preferred was convertible into four shares of common. No conversion, however, took place because the stock which had been rising then started to drop. During this period, Textronics also floated a long-term loan with a bank. In the covenants of the loan the company gave the bank a first mortgage on the plant and agreed that no liens would be given on any other property. Furthermore, no dividends could be paid if profits fell below $100,000, and a minimum net working capital position of $500,000 was to be maintained. The loan was to be amortized at the rate of $100,000 a year and carried an interest rate of 6 per cent. As a result of new inventions, the vacuum tube sales were greatly lessened. The company had to rely more on transistor sales; however, with increased competition in this field the profit margins here were cut sharply. During 1965 the company spent considerable sums on research and expected to do the same in 1966. Management felt confident that 1966 would be their worst year, after which profits should return to the 1965 level or better.

**43**

**EXHIBIT I**

**Textronics, Inc.**
**Balance Sheet**
**(In Thousands)**

|                                        | 1964      | 1965      |
|----------------------------------------|-----------|-----------|
| Cash                                   | $   500   | $    65   |
| Accounts receivable (net)              | 400       | 450       |
| Inventories                            | 600       | 800       |
| Plant                                  | 1,000     | 1,575     |
| Total assets                           | $2,500    | $2,890    |
| Accounts payable                       | 300       | 500       |
| Accruals                               | 200       | 200       |
| Notes payable                          | 750       | 800       |
| Preferred stock                        | 500       | 500       |
| Common–$1 par*                         | 200       | 250       |
| Retained earnings                      | 550       | 640       |
| Total liabilities and capital          | $2,500    | $2,890    |

**Income Statement**
**(In Thousands)**

|                     | 1964    | 1965    |
|---------------------|---------|---------|
| Sales               | $3,500  | $2,500  |
| Operating expenses  | 2,755   | 2,072   |
| Interest            | 45      | 48      |
| Profit before tax   | 700     | 380     |
| Tax                 | 350     | 190     |
| Net profit          | $  350  | $  190  |
| Preferred dividend  | 35      | 35      |
| Common dividend     | 65      | 65      |
| Debt amortization   | 100     | 100     |

*Original issue: qualifies in Texas only.

Sales for 1966 are expected to increase 10 per cent; however, the operating margin is expected to go from its present 83 per cent to 99 per cent. Assume depreciation of $35,000 for 1965 and $40,000 for 1966 and no tax

**EXHIBIT II**
**Hi-Lo**

**Market Value of Stock**

|           | 1964   | 1965   |
|-----------|--------|--------|
| Preferred | 96–85  | 86–75  |
| Common    | 23–12  | 13–3   |

**Market Values**
**12/31/65**

|           | Price | E/S    | P/E Ratio |
|-----------|-------|--------|-----------|
| Preferred | 80    | $7.00  | —         |
| Common    | 3     | .26    | 5.4–1     |

rebate for losses. A/R will be reduced by $50,000 during 1966 and $150,000 of obsolete inventory will be sold for $50,000 in 1966. All other accounts will remain unchanged.

## QUESTIONS

1. Make a statement of sources and uses of funds for the year ending 1965.
2. Make a pro forma balance sheet for the year ending 1966.
3. On 1/3/67, the president of the bank asked the manager of Textronics to come in for a conference. He advised the manager that Textronics was in violation of the covenant agreements and, from the looks of things, would not be able to survive; therefore, the firm should be liquidated now. The manager disagreed. He pointed out that the high expenses involved were the result of a changing market and research which had been expensed each year, and that the benefits of this had already begun to appear. The 1967 pro forma income statement showed a return of profits to the 1965 level, and the company confidently expected it to improve even more markedly after that year. While the banker felt that some optimism was in order, he still said that the bank would not loan any more money nor would they allow a lien against the accounts receivable although he thought a 25 per cent loan against inventory might be allowed. He also said that unless Textronics could show a pro forma balance sheet with assets and current liabilities as shown in Exhibit III they would take immediate action to liquidate the firm.

   Another firm had expressed considerable interest in buying or merging with Textronics and had indicated that it would be willing to pay a fair price.

   Discuss, *evaluate*, and show your calculations for what you consider to be the best course of action open to the manager.

### EXHIBIT III

**Textronics, Inc.**
**Pro forma Balance Sheet Desired**
**as of December 31, 1967**
**(In Thousands)**

| Assets | |
|---|---:|
| Cash | $   300 |
| Accounts receivable | 500 |
| Inventories | 650 |
| Plant (net) | 1,490 |
| Total | $2,940 |

| Liabilities and capital | |
|---|---:|
| Accounts payable | 500 |
| Accruals | 200 |
| Notes payable | 800 |
| Capital | 1,440 |
| Total | $2,940 |

# Cash
# Planning

## 6

**THE UNITED
MANUFACTURING COMPANY**

The financial officer of the United Manufacturing Company, Mr. Knight, was trying to determine the probable borrowing needs for his company in early 1966 for the current year. His assistant had prepared a cash budget, by quarters, for 1966, but the finance officer believed that it should be recast by months showing the appropriate tax prepayments required under the 1966 Tax Adjustment Act. The Tax Adjustment Act of 1966 accelerated the timetable under which corporations were required to pay their estimated tax payments (Exhibit III) and placed the corporations on a strictly pay-as-they-go basis by 1967. Corporations unable to meet these payments had the privilege of requesting a time extension from their District Director of Internal Revenue, but such an extension would amount to a direct loan from the Treasury Department and would bear an annual interest rate of 6 per cent from the time of the due date until paid.

The company was a closely held, family-owned and operated corporation. During the sixty-one year history of the firm, management had passed from grandfather, to father, to son. The president was forty-six years of age. His sixty-six year old father was chairman of the board. Either, or both, were capable of running the business without the other. The president, Mr. Gray, expected his sixteen year old son to be active in the firm after the completion of his college education. In total, some sixteen members of the family owned stock in the firm, but the chairman of the board held 31 per cent, and the president owned an additional 25 per cent. The state of incorporation required cumulative voting, and the five directors were elected for a one year term, primarily from members of the family.

46

The firm produced a line of consumer nondurable goods which were considered to be necessity items. Sales did not vary more than 2 or 3 per cent during boom or recession periods, nor was any pronounced growth in the sales of the firm occurring. Although the company had been holding its own in sales volume, its investment in research and development of new products was nil. For the past five years, the sales of the company had established a definite seasonal pattern. The monthly sales were as follows: January, 7.5 per cent; February, 7.5 per cent; March, 10.0 per cent; April, 12.0 per cent; May, 15.0 per cent; June, 10.0 per cent; July, 8.0 per cent; August, 6.0 per cent; September, 6.0 per cent; October, 6.0 per cent; November, 6.0 per cent; and December, 6.0 per cent.

Sales during 1964 and 1965 amounted to $10,000,000 each year, and no change was forecasted for 1966. All sales for the firm are for credit, and the average collection period is thirty days. Production is *stable* over the year, and expenses as percentages of sales are: materials, 30 per cent; labor 24 per cent; variable overhead, 6.0 per cent; fixed overhead, $500,000 (40 per cent of which is noncash expense); and selling, delivery, and administrative expenses are 15 per cent (equally distributed). Approximately one-half the net income before taxes is required for the payment of Federal income taxes. In the determination of the 1966 prepayment dates for Federal income taxes for the corporation which operated on a calendar year basis, some 12 per cent of the estimated tax burden of the current year was to be by April 15th; another 12 per cent by June 15th; 25 per cent by September 15th; and 25 per cent on December 15th. Any balance owed at the end of the fiscal year was payable in two equal installments on March 15th and June 15th of the following year, along with the prepayment on estimated taxes. The estimated taxes payable by corporations in 1967 and subsequent years was to be on a 100 per cent prepayment basis (Exhibit III).

The December 31, 1965, balance sheet for the company appears in Exhibit I. The company had been following a 75 per cent dividend policy payout as numerous members of the family depended upon their cash dividends to meet their living expenses.

The financial officer had assigned his assistant the job of preparing a cash receipts and disbursements schedule, by quarters, to determine the probable borrowing needs of the company during the next fiscal year. After careful study of the cash budget, the financial officer also became convinced that it might not be detailed adequately to show the true borrowing need of the company when prepared on a quarterly basis. He therefore, asked his assistant to reconstruct the cash budget, by months, for the 1966 calendar year, and to correct his estimate of taxes to be paid on the four tax payment dates. The use of a 50 per cent tax rate for planning purposes appeared excessive since the corporation was actually paying taxes at the rate of 22 per cent on the first $25,000 of income and 48 per cent on the balance. Mr. Knight also instructed his assistant to prepare an estimated income statement for 1966 and a pro forma balance sheet as of December 31, 1966.

## QUESTIONS

1. As the assistant to Mr. Knight, prepare the statements requested.
2. How much borrowing will be needed, when can the loan be repaid, and what should the company do with the idle funds?

### EXHIBIT I

**Balance Sheet
as of December 31, 1965**

| | |
|---|---:|
| Cash and government securities ($100,000 min. desired cash) | $ 250,000 |
| Accounts receivable | 600,000 |
| Inventories | |
| Raw materials (3-mo. supply) | |
| Work-in-process (1-mo. cycle) | |
| Finished goods (remainder) | |
| Total | 2,000,000 |
| Fixed assets (net) | 2,150,000 |
| Total assets | $5,000,000 |
| | |
| Accounts payable (1-mo. purchases) | 250,000 |
| Taxes (1/2 1965 tax burden) | 500,000 |
| Other current liabilities | 200,000 |
| Bank loan | 550,000 |
| Capital stock | 3,000,000 |
| Retained earnings | 500,000 |
| Total liab. and capital | $5,000,000 |

### EXHIBIT II

**The United Manufacturing Company
Cash Budget
(In Thousands)**

| | Quarter of 1966 | | | |
|---|---:|---:|---:|---:|
| | 1st | 2nd | 3rd | 4th |
| Cash receipts | $2,100 | $3,700 | $2,400 | $1,800 |
| Cash disbursements | | | | |
| Materials, labor, overhead, and administrative expense | 1,700 | 1,700 | 1,700 | 1,700 |
| Selling and delivery | 250 | 370 | 200 | 180 |
| Taxes | 250 | 250 | 250 | 250 |
| Dividends | 187 | 188 | 187 | 188 |
| Total disbursements | $2,387 | $2,508 | $2,337 | $2,318 |
| | | | | |
| Beginning cash balance | $ 250 | $ (37) | $1,155 | $1,218 |
| Cash receipts | 2,100 | 3,700 | 2,400 | 1,800 |
| Less: cash disbursements | (2,387) | (2,508) | (2,337) | (2,318) |
| Ending cash balance | (37) | 1,155 | 1,218 | 700 |
| Present loan to bank | (550) | (550) | (550) | (550) |
| Minimum cash balance | (100) | (100) | (100) | (100) |
| Surplus (needed) funds | $ (687) | $ 505 | $ 568 | $ 50 |

### EXHIBIT III

#### Corporate Prepayment Income Tax Schedule

| When Sec. 6016 Filing Requirements Are First Met | Declaration Must Be Filed on or Before | Estimated tax must be paid for taxable years beginning in the following years, on the 15th day of the months (and at the percentages) listed below. [Sec. 6154(a)] | | | | | | | |
|---|---|---|---|---|---|---|---|---|---|
| | | 1964 | | 1965 | | 1966 | | 1967 and thereafter | |
| | | Mo. | % | Mo. | % | Mo. | % | Mo. | % |
| Before the 4th month | 15th day of the 4th month [Sec. 6074(a)] | 4 | 1 | 4 | 4 | 4 | 12 | 4 | 25 |
| | | 6 | 1 | 6 | 4 | 6 | 12 | 6 | 25 |
| | | 9 | 25 | 9 | 25 | 9 | 25 | 9 | 25 |
| | | 12 | 25 | 12 | 25 | 12 | 25 | 12 | 25 |
| In or after the 4th month, but before the 6th month | 15th day of the 6th month [Sec. 6074(a)] | 6 | 1-1/3 | 6 | 5-1/3 | 6 | 16 | 6 | 33-1/3 |
| | | 9 | 25-1/3 | 9 | 26-1/3 | 9 | 29 | 9 | 33-1/3 |
| | | 12 | 25-1/3 | 12 | 26-1/3 | 12 | 29 | 12 | 33-1/3 |
| In or after the 6th month, but before the 9th month | 15th day of the 9th month [Sec. 6074(a)] | 9 | 26 | 9 | 29 | 9 | 37 | 9 | 50 |
| | | 12 | 26 | 12 | 29 | 12 | 37 | 12 | 50 |
| In or after the 9th month, but before the 12th month | 15th day of the 12th month [Sec. 6074(a)] | 12 | 52 | 12 | 58 | 12 | 74 | 12 | 100 |

Source: *Federal Taxes*, Englewood Cliffs, New Jersey, Prentice-Hall, Inc., March 24, 1966, p. 4026.

# Receivables

## 7

The Aggressive Furniture Company had been selling its products to the Jones Discount House for the past four years. The supplier offered terms of 2/10, n/60 in an attempt to encourage prompt payment of the invoices. Other suppliers in the immediate geographical area offered similar terms. The account of the Jones Discount House and numerous other accounts had recently become about 30 days slow in their remittances for trade purchases. The credit officer of the Aggressive Furniture Company had become concerned about the slowness of some of these accounts and pondered the possible alternatives for correcting the situation. He did not wish to take any action which would precipitate the loss of the accounts, but he believed that some action should be planned before the problem became a more serious one involving the collectibility of some of the accounts.

As a starting point, Mr. Brown, the credit officer of the supplying firm, made a study of the fixed and variable components of his expenses. He wished to determine the profitability of each of his accounts in terms of providing net profits and in terms of absorbing a fraction of the company's fixed overhead. Since the company had excess production capacity, the loss of an account would result in the aggregate loss of fixed expense coverage and net profits.

Mr. Brown determined that at the current level of sales his fixed expenses amounted to $1,800,000; his variable expenses totaled 55 per cent of sales; and his net income before cash discounts, interest, or income taxes averaged 15 per cent.

During the past two years, the Aggressive Furniture Company had been forced to borrow from its commercial bank in order to finance the build-up of the slow accounts. The company was currently paying an interest rate of 8 per cent on the credit granted on a pledge of accounts receivables.

Mr. Brown had appealed to his slow-paying customers for discount or prompt payment, but he had been informed by many of the delinquents that they had been unsuccessful in their attempts to borrow from banks. One of the customers went so far as to say: "If you are not willing to grant us ninety-day credit, we are confident that some other manufacturer of furniture will be willing to do so." Mr. Brown believed that many of the other slow-pay accounts would be lost if pressed for prompt payment of their accounts.

During the past twelve months, the average monthly order from the Jones account had amounted to $3,000. Approximately twenty-five other accounts, with monthly purchases from the Aggressive Furniture Company ranging from $1,500 to $8,000, were following a similar pattern of slow payment. Whatever course of action the credit officer and board of directors of the Aggressive Furniture decided upon would apply to all the accounts and not just to the Jones Discount House.

Before reaching a definite conclusion as to a course of action to recommend to the board of directors of the concern, Mr. Brown wished to find answers to the following questions, thereby strengthening his defensive position with the board of directors at the next meeting.

### QUESTIONS

1. What annual contribution does the account of the Jones Discount House make toward fixed expenses?
2. How much annual profit does the account produce?
3. Assuming that an enforcement of the regular terms or the granting of credit only on C.O.D. terms to the twenty-five slow-paying accounts would result in the loss of one-half of the accounts but the prompt servicing of the balance, what course of action should be taken by the supplier?
4. Suggest a course of action to be taken by a credit officer in minimizing slow and delinquent accounts and bad debt losses.

# Receivable Policy

## 8

TONKA TOYS, INC.

On June 29, 1964, Mr. Roger S. Laurence, treasurer and chief credit manager for Tonka Toys, Inc., was wondering what action he should take regarding a recently received financial report of the Toy Center, Inc. of Buffalo, New York. The Toy Center had placed an order on April 17, for $3,000 worth of toys from Tonka Toys. In reviewing Toy Center's account, Mr. Laurence discovered that he did not have an up-to-date balance sheet, and in line with standard practice he requested this information from Dun and Bradstreet. The information supplied by the financial reporting service, however, was not up-to-date, so he wrote directly to the Toy Center and asked for their balance sheet. On June 29 he had received a report from the Toy Center which was dated March 31, 1964 (see Exhibit III). The $3,000 order had been held up pending credit acceptance, and Mr. Laurence wanted to take immediate action on this matter.

Tonka Toys was incorporated in Minnesota on September 18, 1946, and started manufacturing all-steel toy trucks. The toy line was slowly expanded to include peripheral equipment, jeeps, tractors, and some accessories. Tonka Toy's products had consistently been of high quality and rugged construction and consequently had been well received. The major impetus for the firm's success had occurred around 1959 when the firm's principal products, heavy, large, toy steel trucks, trailers, a fire engine pumper, and a hook and ladder achieved a considerable amount of popularity. Sales in 1959 were $3,200,000 with net earnings of $145,000. By 1963 sales had grown to $10,000,000 with earnings of $560,000. Pro forma sales for the period ending June 30, 1964, were expected to top $14,000,000 with profits projected at almost $800,000. Although the company had expanded its line of toys, it continued to place primary emphasis on the basic all-steel truck.

Sales for the company were made through manufacturers' representatives and jobbers, who sold to various organizations within their areas. A few large retail stores bought directly from the manufacturer. The company's production was kept relatively constant from March until the first week in December when most of the production crew was laid off. Shipments were made from March through December with peak shipments occurring around the first of October. For the coming year, Mr. Laurence predicted that accounts receivable would reach a high of $6,500,000 in October. While December had always been the big month for retail sales, the toy industry had been leaning more and more toward year-round sales. Some of Tonka Toy's products were sand box toys which could be used in the spring and summer; thus the company was slowly leveling out the pattern of production.

Credit terms in the toy industry were considerably different from the terms in other industries. Payments for the orders received and shipped from March through July 25 were due October 10. Payments for the orders shipped from July 26 through December were due January 10. All payments, therefore, were due either October 10 or January 10 at which time 2 per cent was deducted for cash payment. Any accounts paid later than these dates were automatically overdue. Anticipation discounts of 3/4 per cent per month were allowed for firms that desired to pay prior to these two dates, so that a firm could place an order for toys on July 30 and pay on December 10 deducting 2 3/4 per cent from the invoice price, or the firm could pay on January 10 and deduct 2 per cent. If it waited until January 11, it could deduct nothing.

This arrangement allowed a retail store to place two orders during the year before it had to pay for either of them. Since most firms ordered no more than twice a year, the order sizes were usually substantial. An average order was for $3,000 worth of toys. Some orders were in excess of $100,000, and some as small as $500. Minimum orders ranged from $500 to $2,500 depending on the territory and the sales representative in the territory. A single firm frequently owed as much as $150,000 to $200,000 during the year. As a result, a careful check was necessary for all customers who requested credit.

The policy of the firm was to approve a credit request wherever possible. Tonka Toys' growth rate had been maintained at 15 to 20 per cent per year, and the management felt that too conservative an approach to credit granting would restrict this growth rate. As a consequence the credit manager of Tonka Toys examined all marginal risks carefully before rejecting anyone. The firm's credit manager had noticed, however, that the number of their customers had not increased substantially. The gain that Tonka Toys had experienced in sales was the result of larger sales by its customers. This fact was especially noticeable in the area of discount houses. Discount stores had been selling a tremendous volume of toys, but their overall low profit margin had made some of them poor risks. In the past, Tonka Toys had relied on credit insurance to take care of bad risks. For the past year, however, it had been assuming its own credit losses because the cost of the insurance was excessive at high sales levels.

Each order received by the company was processed through the credit department which checked to see that up-to-date reports on the company were available and that the order was within the established credit limits of the firm. The company used several sources to check the credit acceptability of a firm, the most important of which was Dun and Bradstreet. The credit department maintained a current Dun and Bradstreet report on every account. This report gave the latest available financial statements, a history of the company, and the current information about a firm's accounts payable and bank relations. Dun and Bradstreet also placed a credit rating on each firm. When changes in a firm's conditions occurred, supplemental reports were also sent out. In addition, Dun and Bradstreet supplied a "key service" which provided, upon a customer's request, additional information on a specific account. In preparing the "key service" Dun and Bradstreet sent an analyst directly to the customer to discuss his financial statements. From this information, Dun and Bradstreet made a specific recommendation as to the firm's credit worthiness. Tonka Toys used approximately twelve such service reports a year. One disadvantage of rating services such as Dun and Bradstreet, however, was the time lag involved. Some reports currently supplied were based on information as much as one year old. A considerable change could have occurred during that period without the knowledge of the rating service.

As an additional aid in making credit decisions the toy manufacturers, through their trade association known as the Toy Manufacturers of the U.S.A., had a credit and collection committee which maintained all the services of Dun and Bradstreet with the exception of a rating book. The toy committee did not rate customers; however, they did compile a ledger indicating the credit experience that each member had had with each of its customers. Thus, Mr. Laurence was able to determine what the experience of other toy manufacturers had been with any given customer. The association also mailed a letter twice a month to all members showing those accounts which had been turned over to collection agencies. When Mr. Laurence discovered that one of his accounts was being placed with collection agencies by other manufacturers, he immediately "red flagged" the account. If any orders were pending, these were quickly checked.

Another source of credit information was the National Association of Credit Men. At the present time, however, Tonka Toys was not actively involved with this group because they supplied information similar to that provided by Dun and Bradstreet and the Toy Manufacturers' Association.

Mr. Laurence did not rely entirely on the various credit groups for financial information. On accounts where the credit firms' information appeared out-of-date or inadequate, the firm requested current balance sheets and income statements. Where any question arose about a firm's ability to pay, Mr. Laurence usually requested bank and trade references which were always checked.

Toy Center, Inc. was chartered in New York in 1952. By 1958 the company was in severe financial difficulty and filed a voluntary petition for bankruptcy under Chapter XI of the Federal Bankruptcy Act. The action was completed and dismissed during the same year. The present officers subsequently assumed control. The chairman of the Board of Toy Center, Mr. John Sampson, was also the owner of a small firm known as Sampson Manufacturing Company. By 1963 the Toy Center was divided into two divisions: wholesale and retail. Some 35 per cent of its $1 million sales was made by its wholesale division to small retail outlets in a 200-mile radius of Buffalo, New York. The remaining sales were made through retail outlets which were leased in three discount stores in the Buffalo-Niagara area. These three outlets employed thirty-five people. In addition the company leased 30,000 square feet of warehouse space where it maintained its headquarters and sales office.

Tonka Toys' past experience with the Toy Center had been good. The first orders had been received during the 1959–60 year and since that time the company had continued to maintain a satisfactory volume and had paid all accounts on time. The following sales experience was recorded:

| Year | Total Volume | High Credit | Discounted |
|------|-------------|-------------|------------|
| 1960 | $ 8,270 | $ 4,900 | yes |
| 1961 | 10,200 | 5,380 | yes |
| 1962 | 14,600 | 10,300 | yes |
| 1963 | 8,675 | 5,050 | yes |

A check by the Toy Manufacturers' Collection Committee in March of 1964 indicated that the Toy Center was either prompt or discounted all its orders. High credit for the 1963 year ranged from $24,000 for one member firm to $300 for another. Of the $24,294 owed by the Toy Center to the various members of the Toy Manufacturers' Association as of March, 1964, only $1,153 was considered to be past due. In the two cases where there were overdue accounts, however, the paying experience had been excellent. Apparently, the experience of the Toy Manufacturers' Association indicated little reason to worry about Toy Center's ability to pay.

The Dun and Bradstreet report was received by Tonka Toys on February 5, 1964. It stated that on the previous day the secretary of the Toy Center had reported that the December 31, 1963, financial statement was not yet complete and referred Dun and Bradstreet to the previous year for the latest statement available. Toy Center's Secretary indicated, however, that the sales volume for 1963 was up moderately from 1962 but the extent of the profits had not been determined. It was further noted by Dun and Bradstreet that Toy Center had substantial amounts of loans outstanding at a local bank which were secured by the personal assets of Mr. Sampson. Bank relations had been favorable.

On May 1, Mr. Laurence of Tonka Toys sent Mr. Sampson of Toy Center a letter stating that Tonka Toys had received the Toy Center's order of April 17. Mr. Laurence's letter continued:

In checking with our regular reporting service, we find that they are without current figures. It is obvious that your line-of-credit with us this year will be higher than that of 1963. Because of this, we would like to ask your cooperation by sending us a copy of your financial statements as of December 31st, 1963. As usual, your statements will be held in strict confidence for our use only. Upon receipt of this information, your order will receive our immediate attention.

On May 18, Mr. Sampson acknowledged the letter and stated that the reason an up-to-date statement had not been sent was that he had been out of the office for several weeks and that his comptroller had resigned before completing the financial reports. A new comptroller had taken over the previous week, so that in a few weeks the figures would be available and would be immediately forwarded to both Tonka Toys and Dun and Bradstreet.

Mr. Laurence received the Balance Sheet of Toy Center on June 29, dated March 31, 1964 (see Exhibit III). He knew that the balance sheet of the Toy Center included business other than toy sales, but he did not think this made any difference so far as his evaluation was concerned. Mr. Laurence did not use standard ratios in determining the credit that should be extended by Tonka Toys but analyzed each case individually. He believed, however, that a downward trend in net worth was a serious indication of grave trouble, and it was this factor which worried him about the Toy Center. The choice seemed either to ship the goods with the usual dating, to ask for cash in advance, or to send the goods C.O.D. If he asked for C.O.D. terms, the business would undoubtedly be lost.

The following points indicated that the credit should be advanced:

1. Toy Center had maintained excellent credit relations with Tonka Toys in the past. They had been prompt in their payments to other toy manufacturers.
2. Tonka Toys' emphasis on growth required them to grant credit where at all possible, even though some credit risks had to be assumed.
3. Toy Center maintained good bank and trade relations.

Conversely, there were some very disturbing points:

1. Toy Center's financial position had been deteriorating.
2. None of the financial statements supplied had been audited.
3. Income statement figures had not been disclosed.
4. Discount house operations had been experiencing a tightening in profit margins, resulting from intense competition.

Mr. Laurence knew that he would not have time to ask for any more reports, for the present order must be filled or rejected by the end of the week. He wondered if perhaps he should check some national average figures for firms of this type to see what an aggregate balance sheet looked like. He also wondered what effect the continued high level of economic prosperity would have on firms such as Toy Center. Expectations were that the 1964 Christmas would far exceed previous ones in sales. Mr. Laurence also wished to determine the profitability of the account in terms of fixed cost coverage and taxable income.

**EXHIBIT I**

**Tonka Toys, Inc.**
**Balance Sheet**
**(June 30)**

|  | 1963 | 1962 | 1961 |
|---|---|---|---|
| Cash | $ 276,445 | $ 268,408 | $ 272,022 |
| Accounts receivable, net | 2,627,123 | 2,459,483 | 1,726,828 |
| Inventories | 2,120,191 | 1,265,396 | 808,330 |
| Prepaids | 49,893 | 33,853 | 11,985 |
| Total current assets | $5,073,652 | $4,027,140 | $2,819,165 |
| Other assets | 38,229 | 35,302 | 45,134 |
| Plant, net | 1,835,060 | 1,209,310 | 652,041 |
| Total assets | $6,946,941 | $5,271,752 | $3,516,340 |
| Notes payable | 1,950,000 | 1,925,000 | 1,401,490 |
| Accounts payable | 418,382 | 376,695 | 264,215 |
| Accruals | 227,326 | 205,170 | 171,763 |
| Taxes payable | 512,688 | 539,677 | 457,139 |
| Current maturities on LTD | 328,199 | 20,788 | 19,746 |
| Total current liabilities | $3,436,595 | $3,067,330 | $2,314,353 |
| Long-term debt | 1,067,869 | 179,910 | 215,531 |
| Preferred stock | 15,600 | 15,600 | 15,600 |
| Common stock ($1 par) | 275,000 | 275,000 | 215,000 |
| Capital surplus | 580,002 | 580,002 | 4,000 |
| Earned surplus | 1,571,875 | 1,153,910 | 751,856 |
| Total liabilities and net worth | $6,946,941 | $5,271,752 | $3,516,340 |

**EXHIBIT II**

**Tonka Toys, Inc.**
**Income Statement**

|  | Year Ended June 30 | | |
|---|---|---|---|
|  | 1963 | 1962 | 1961 |
| Net sales | $9,844,619 | $8,263,989 | $6,946,798 |
| Costs and expenses |  |  |  |
| Cost of products sold | $7,102,664 | $5,970,531 | $5,099,036 |
| Selling, admin. & gen. expense | 1,441,321 | 1,125,219 | 926,602 |
| Interest expense | 95,485 | 54,094 | 63,850 |
|  | $8,639,470 | $7,149,844 | $6,089,488 |
| Earnings before taxes | $1,205,149 | $1,114,145 | $ 857,310 |
| Income taxes | 641,873 | 608,030 | 458,866 |
| Net Earnings | $ 563,276 | $ 506,115 | $ 398,444 |

## EXHIBIT III

### The Toy Center, Inc.
### Financial Statement*

|  | 7/31/61 | 12/31/61 | 12/31/62 | 3/31/64 |
|---|---|---|---|---|
| Cash | $ 2,047 | $ 74,000 | $146,032 | $ 15,383 |
| Accounts receivable net | 89,787 | 150,797 | 227,708 | 127,561 |
| Inventories | 216,448 | 174,321 | 219,721 | 292,373 |
| Total current assets | 308,282 | 399,118 | 593,461 | 435,317 |
| Fixed and other assets | 264,405 | 292,513 | 315,471 | 302,055 |
| Total assets | $572,687 | $691,631 | $908,932 | $737,372 |
| | | | | |
| Notes payable | $ 36,037 | $100,663 | $292,538 | $184,465 |
| Accounts payable | 162,238 | 185,383 | 247,492 | 93,301 |
| Accruals | 9,058 | 13,056 | 14,080 | 6,794 |
| Total current liabilities | 207,333 | 299,102 | 554,110 | 284,560 |
| | | | | |
| Long-term liabilities | 85,387 | 144,743 | 206,879† | 455,187‡ |
| Capital stock | $90,000 | $90,000 | $90,000 | $90,000 |
| Capital surplus | 189,967 | 211,178 | 211,178 | 211,178 |
| Earned surplus | | (53,392) | (153,235) | (303,553) |
| Total net worth | 279,967 | 247,786 | 147,943 | (2,375) |
| Total liabilities | $572,687 | $691,631 | $908,932 | $737,372 |

*Consolidated statement including Toy Center, Inc. and other operating companies. Toy Center had loss of $53,501 for year 1962.
†Includes $12,329 chattel mortgage; $157,500 10-yr. subordinate debentures due 1967–1973; $37,050 notes to principal stockholder.
‡Included $9,580 chattel mortgage; $410,000 10-yr. subordinate debentures due 1967–1974. Debentures are held by associated companies; $35,607 notes to principal stockholder.

# Ratio Analysis

## 9

THE INDUSTRIAL
BUILDING COMPANY, INC.

The Industrial Building Company, Inc., of Beaumont, Texas, has been incorporated since 1952 and has been an intermittent borrower from the Texas National Bank since 1957. The company had repaid its bank loans satisfactorily in the past, but as the bank credit officer was analyzing the account in June, 1965, he noted that the balance of the loan had expanded to an alarming size. He also noted that the most recent income statement reported a net loss of $27,000. Although the loan was partially secured, the credit officer felt that he should analyze the statements, obtain a current credit report, and watch the account closely in order to catch other adverse factors which might further deteriorate the collectibility of the account.

No change has occurred in stock ownership of the IBC since 1959, when one of the stockholder-officers sold his interest to an incoming officer. The three officers, president, secretary-treasurer, and vice-president were the only stockholders. The president, Mr. J. W. Johnson, age fifty-six, has been in the construction business since 1938, although he was employed by others until 1952. The secretary-treasurer, Frank McBain, age sixty-one, was engaged in the automobile business for about thirty years before he became an officer in the construction firm. He still maintains some outside activities. The vice-president, Mr. Sam K. Jones, had had nine years of experience in the insurance agency field when he joined the firm in 1959 at the age of thirty-one.

The firm has been engaged as an industrial contractor in the oil refineries and chemical construction work. It was also doing pipe fabricating. Its contracts were received through competitive bidding in the states of Texas and Louisiana. The work was being performed on a cost-plus basis so that the firm received payment every fifteen days for the work which had been completed. Some 10 per cent of the profit was held by the customer as a retainer until the job was completed.

The number of employees of the firm varied with the amount of work, but was usually between twenty-five and fifty. The company owned its own equipment, which was in good repair, and leased additional equipment as it was needed. The company owned its own warehouse of approximately 14,000 square feet and its own office space.

Although three of the four most recent balance sheets indicated small cash balances, Exhibit III disclosed that the average cash balances for the years 1962–1965 had been rather substantial. The repayments of accounts payable at the end of a month often reduced the month-end cash balance far below the monthly average. In addition to the regular demand deposit account, the firm maintained a payroll account with a balance of from $7,500 to $25,000 and a profit-sharing retirement plan account which averaged about $10,000. The former was started in 1958 while the latter was inaugurated in 1962. The bank considered the accounts to be profitable, and did not wish to precipitate any action which would endanger the loss of the customer.

The accounts receivable of the firm fluctuated rather widely over a period of time. The bank desired to have the bank loan secured with receivables equal to at least 125 per cent of the amount of the note. As the pledged accounts were collected, the amount would be repaid on the bank loan. When the customer needed additional funds, he would pledge additional accounts, and a credit would be given to his drawing account.

Investments in machinery and equipment during the past three years had been slightly less than the amount of the depreciation allowance. The investments consisted of shares of stock in two local country clubs.

The loan record of the firm is presented in Exhibit IV. During 1961, the outstanding, 30-day loan, averaged about $125,000. During much of 1962 and 1963 the loan balance was below $25,000. In 1964 the loan balance began to rise and reached a high point of $562,500 on February 28, 1965. From the end of November, 1964 until May, 1965, the collateral was not adequate to cover the account by 125 per cent. The bank had recently suffered losses on loans to other contractors and although it wished to keep the account, it wanted to guard against any loss in the event that the company got into financial difficulty.

An analysis of the income statements for the years ended February 28, 1964 and 1965 indicated some alarming features. Although sales had doubled during the period, gross profits had remained the same. Operating expenses and other expenses had remained so high that the company operated at a net loss of $27,000 in the latter year compared to a net profit after taxes of $50,000 during the preceding year. This loss had occurred during 1964–65 despite the fact that the officers' salaries had been reduced by $45,000 and no income tax liability had been incurred.

Although the account had been a profitable one for years, the bank loan officer had grown concerned over recent events. He was not sure whether the loan limit should be reduced, whether more collateral should be demanded, or whether to watch the account and hope that the situation would be improved within the near future. A study of ratios, trends, and credit report was undertaken by the bank loan officer.

## QUESTIONS

1. With the use of a ratio analysis, evaluate the financial progress (or lack of it) achieved by the firm during the past few years.
2. Would you recommend that the bank (defend with computations):

**EXHIBIT I**

**Comparative Balance Sheets**

|  | As of 2/29/62 | As of 2/28/63 | As of 2/28/64 | As of 2/28/65 |
|---|---|---|---|---|
| *Assets* | | | | |
| Cash | 4,429 | 194,768 | 5,321 | 15,019 |
| Notes receivable | 1,119,297 | 255,980 | 714,110 | 1,024,656 |
| Inventory | 23,652 | 19,761 | 525 | — |
| Prepaid items | 29,624 | 41,994 | 29,723 | 32,050 |
| Total Current Assets | 1,177,002 | 512,503 | 749,679 | 1,071,725 |
| Land and buildings | 27,495 | 27,495 | 27,495 | 27,495 |
| Machinery and fixtures (net) | 259,383 | 222,845 | 220,963 | 200,330 |
| Investments | 7,562 | 8,588 | 8,588 | 10,962 |
| Due from officers and employees | 3,604 | 2,772 | — | 11,286 |
| Cash surrender value—life insurance | 13,625 | 20,250 | 42,790 | 57,250 |
| Miscellaneous assets | 719 | 1,094 | — | — |
| Total noncurrent assets | 312,388 | 283,044 | 299,836 | 307,323 |
| Total assets | 1,489,390 | 795,547 | 1,049,515 | 1,379,048 |
| *Liabilities* | | | | |
| Notes payable—bank | 125,000 | 24,463 | 123,174 | 562,500 |
| Notes payable—other | 20,970 | — | — | 46,518 |
| Accounts payable | 439,123 | 130,233 | 289,526 | 276,612 |
| Accrued liabilities and taxes | 238,856 | 136,071 | 185,993 | 101,824 |
| Income taxes payable | 43,179 | 68,651 | — | — |
| Due officers | 20,000 | — | — | — |
| Total current liabilities | 887,128 | 359,418 | 598,693 | 987,454 |
| Deferred liabilities | 10,834 | — | — | — |
| Deferred credit to income (net of estimated costs) | 326,381 23% | 118,761 15 | 95,228 (2 | 63,134 9% |
| Capital stock—common | 125,000 | 125,000 | 125,000 | 125,000 |
| Paid-in surplus | 16,032 | 16,032 | 16,032 | 16,032 |
| Retained earnings | 8% 124,015 | 22% 176,336 | 20 214,562 | 13% 187,428 |
| Net worth | 265,047 17% | 317,368 40% | 355,594 34% | 328,460 23% |
| Total liabilities and capital | 1,489,390 | 795,547 | 1,049,515 | 1,379,048 |

100%

    a. Call the loan?
    b. Renew the loan as requested?
    c. Modify the line-of-credit?
    d. Require additional collateral?
    e. Other: specify?

3. Assume that you have the task, as a member of the bank's loan committee, of explaining the bank's decision to Mr. McBain, a member of the board of directors of the bank. Develop your answer in the form of a letter.

### EXHIBIT II

**Loan Balances and Securities Pledged
on Selected Dates**

| Date | Loan Balance | Type Collateral Pledged | | |
|---|---|---|---|---|
| | | Accounts Receivable | Retainers Receivable | Chattel Mortgage |
| 2/28/61 | $ 94,459 | $118,393 | | |
| 5/31/61 | 163,147 | 396,209 | | |
| 8/31/61 | 85,834 | 259,469 | | |
| 11/30/61 | 116,459 | 285,258 | | |
| 2/29/62 | 135,834 | 341,871 | | |
| 5/31/62 | 12,709 | 284,074 | | |
| 8/31/62 | — | — | | |
| 11/30/62 | — | — | | |
| 2/28/63 | — | — | | |
| 5/31/63 | 19,030 | — | | $19,030 |
| 8/31/63 | 14,274 | 212,835 | | |
| 11/30/63 | 9,516 | 212,835 | | |
| 2/28/64 | 79,758 | 158,481 | | |
| 5/31/64 | 145,625 | 96,641 | $ 87,326 | |
| 8/31/64 | 531,250 | 428,229 | 177,989 | |
| 11/31/64 | 531,250 | 365,055 | 146,615 | |
| 2/28/65 | 562,500 | 335,511 | 242,348 | |
| 5/31/65 | 525,000 | 277,631 | 227,604 | |

**EXHIBIT III**

**Comparative Income Statements for Years Ended**

|  | 2/29/62 | 2/28/63 | 2/28/64 | 2/28/65 |
|---|---|---|---|---|
| Completed contracts | 5,085,484 | 5,705,161 | 3,632,913 | 7,065,689 |
| Less : Job costs | 4,448,806 | 4,903,908 | 3,162,855 | 6,587,906 |
| Gross profit | 636,678 | 801,253 | 470,058 | 477,783 |
| Operating expenses |  |  |  |  |
| Salaries and bonuses—officers | — | — | 110,590 | 65,500 |
| Salaries and bonuses—others | — | — | 178,151 | 212,718 |
| Bad debts | — | — | 3,896 | — |
| Depreciation | — | — | 88,134 | 95,804 |
| Pension plan payments | — | — | 10,793 | — |
| Taxes and licenses | — | — | 15,256 | 13,072 |
| Other expenses | — | — | 135,082 | 169,689 |
| Total operating expenses | 609,708 | 763,583 | 541,902 | 556,783 |
| Net profit from operations | 26,970 | 37,670 | (71,844) | (79,000) |
| Other income | 66,705 | 75,725 | 151,877 | 76,188 |
| Total | 93,675 | 113,395 | 80,033 | (2,812) |
| Other deductions |  |  |  |  |
| Other expenses | 9,479 | 4,590 | 3,086 | (24,323) |
| Income taxes | 43,179 | 68,651 | 26,554 | — |
| Total other deductions | 52,658 | 73,241 | 29,640 | (24,323) |
| Net income to surplus | 41,017 | 40,154 | 50,393 | (27,135) |

**EXHIBIT IV**

**Average Demand Deposit Balance**

|  | Monthly Averages | | Annual |
|---|---|---|---|
|  | High | Low | Average |
| 1961 | 68,641 | 17,756 | 39,543 |
| 1962 | 242,809 | 28,140 | 128,226 |
| 1963 | 272,533 | 35,291 | 127,794 |
| 1964 | 154,482 | 26,644 | 58,064 |
| 1965 |  |  |  |
| January | 28,384 |  |  |
| February | 78,256 |  |  |
| March | 31,493 |  |  |
| April | 40,032 |  |  |
| May | 77,079 |  |  |

**EXHIBIT V**.

**Credit Report**
**May 2, 1965**
**Industrial Contractor**

| | | | | | | | |
|---|---|---|---|---|---|---|---|
| The Industrial Bldg. Co., Inc. | | | | | **1952** | | **B11/2** |
| 2408 Morrell Ave. | | | | | Trade | | Disc–PPt |
| Beaumont, Tex. | | | | | Sales | | $5,000,000 + Est |
| | | | | | Empls | | 35 |

John W. Johnson, Pres.
Sam K. Jones, V. Pres.
Frank W. McBain, Sec.-Treas.
Directors: The officers

Summary   Volume steady. Officers well regarded and capable. Condition satisfactory, trade payments as agreed.

| Trade | HC | OWE | P DUE | Terms | Apr 15 1965 | | Sold |
|---|---|---|---|---|---|---|---|
| | 2000 | | | 2–10 | Disc | | OVer 3 yrs |
| | 75 | | | | Disc | | |
| | 250 | | | 2–10 prox 30 | Disc-ppt | | 3–58 to 11–64 |
| | 6250 | 1250 | | | Ppt | | Over 3 yrs |
| | 600 | 250 | | | Ppt | | |
| | 600 | | | | Ppt | | |
| | 250 | | | | Ppt | | Over 3 yrs |

| Finance | Feb. 28, 1964 | Feb. 28, 1965 |
|---|---|---|
| Curr assets | $749,679 | $1,071,725 |
| Curr liab | 598,693 | 987,454 |
| Other assets | 299,836 | 306,073 |
| Worth | 355,594 | 328,460 |

Statement Feb. 28, 1965

| | | | |
|---|---|---|---|
| Cash on hand/bank | 15,019 | Acts pay | 276,612 |
| Receivables | 1,024,656 | Notes pay | 609,018 |
| Supplies | 32,050 | Taxes (fed and state) and | |
| | | Accrued exp | 101,824 |
| Total current assets | 1,071,725 | Total current assets | 987,454 |
| Fixed assets | 200,330 | Deferred income | 63,134 |
| Investments | 10,962 | Capital stock | 125,000 |
| Land | 27,495 | Paid-in surplus | 16,032 |
| Cash value life ins (pl.) | 57,250 | Earned surplus | 187,428 |
| Due from officers | 11,286 | | |
| Total assets | 1,379,048 | Total | 1,379,048 |

Monthly rent—owns. No contingent debts. Fire insurance on mdse and fixts and bldgs reporting form policy. Signed Apr 17, 1963 The Industrial Bldg. Co., Inc. by Sam K. Jones, V. Pres.

Interviewed April 25, 1965, S. K. Jones, V. Pres., referred to the above statement as latest available at this time.

Accounts receivable listed after reserve for doubtful accounts of $1,000. Collections satisfactory. Fixed assets $200,330 as of date of statement, listed after depreciation reserves of $550,334. Valuation of land, current market, Notes payable $609,018 comprised $562,500 in favor of a local financial institution, due Mar 15, 1965, secured by pledge of $335,511 accounts receivables and $247,348 of retainages.  $46,518 in favor of an insurance company secured by pledge of life insurance policies.  The bank reports relations satisfactory.

Cash confirmed medium five figures, receivables and retainages to continue at about $1,000,000.  Fixed assets to remain unchanged except for depreciation.  Borrowing to remain at about same level.

Volume of sales of about $5,000,000.  Cash balance small for size of sales.  Good cash flow has enabled firm to maintain a good trade credit relationship.

Operation    Industrial contractors, specializing in oil refineries and chemical construction work.  Also does small amount of pipe fabricating.  Contract work secured by competitive bid basis, throughout State of Texas and southern part of Louisiana, work performed on contract basis and lump-sum basis, subject receiving payments every fifteen days on work completed.  10 per cent withheld until completion and acceptance of contracted job (usually forty-five days).  Employees vary with amount of work on hand, averaging 35.  Location: Owns one-story frame and sheet metal building, side street, industrial section, overall premises measuring about 14,000 square feet.  Premises orderly.

History    Texas corporation chartered April 10, 1952.  Capital $125,000, 2,500 shares, $50 par.  Paid-in capital at inception, $1,250.  Original officers were Johnson, McBain, Hernendez, and Hebert.  July, 1959 Hebert sold stock to Johnson and Jones purchased stock of Hernendez.

Johnson, married, born 1910.  Employed in Boston construction work, 1938-50.  Transferred to Beaumont in 1950 where he worked until forming subject company in 1952.

McBain, married, born in Houston, Texas.  Associated with automotive Industry since high school.  Was president of an auto dealership in Houston from 1928 to 1956, whem he withdrew.  Currently a director on the board of the bank of account.

Jones, married, born 1929, Arkansas.  1950-59 operated insurance agency in Little Rock.  July 1959-present, office manager and v-pres. of subject company.

# Cash Budgeting

## 10

### RESEARCH, INCORPORATED

Mr. Donald Buck, treasurer of Research, Inc., had recently finished his semiannual projection of the company's sales for the next 12 months. From this data he expected to make an estimate of the cash requirements that the projected sales would entail. In the past he had found his cash projections had approximated the actual cash needs; however, this year he believed that his firm might get a large contract from the government, which would cause serious cash problems. Research, Inc. had experienced steady growth over the last several years, and the new year was expected to be no exception. This growth came from the firm's ability to get good government subcontracts; however, the bidding process made the amount of contracts the firm would win somewhat capricious. Recently Research's management had become interested in acquiring other firms. The combination of rapidly advancing sales, large potential government contracts, and possible acquisitions could put an impossible strain on the company's cash position if some plans were not made to anticipate the effect that these factors would have on cash and preparations were not laid for meeting the requirements when they occurred.

Research, Inc., located in Hopkins, Minnesota, was founded in 1951 as a wholly owned subsidiary of Washington Machine and Tool Co. Research's purpose was to engage in research and development for the parent company. By 1953 the company had expanded sufficiently to be housed in separate quarters from its parent company. In 1955 the manager of Research, Kenneth G. Anderson, with a few friends purchased the entire stock interest of Research from Washington Machine and Tool, and Research became a distinct and separate company. From its inception the company had engaged in research and development work, principally for the Air Force and to a lesser extent for the Navy and NASA. As the company's sales increased, the facilities were expanded, the product line improved, and the company began selling equipment to civilian buyers. By 1964, its sales were divided, 10 per cent directly to the government, 54 per cent to government prime contractors through subcontracts, and 36 per cent to civilians.

The company was organized into four divisions: Control, MTS, Precision Industries, and Monterey Research Laboratory. The Control division specialized in the design, development, and manufacture of high-performance instruments used in closed-loop systems for programming and controlling temperatures. Sales of these products had been primarily to the aerospace industry. The MTS division, which stood for materials test systems, developed products in the field of closed-loop electronic servo-controlled hydraulic systems. The Precision Industries division supplied parts for computers, missiles, and aircraft. The parts supplied were generally of a job-lot nature and were manufactured on a bid basis. The division operated in a highly competitive area. Monterey Research Laboratory, located in Monterey, California, made equipment and did research and development primarily in the field of shock programming for test conditions requiring exact duplicates of half-sine square wave, or sawtooth wave forms. From its inception, Research, Inc. had made a profit. It had also been one of the few electronics companies to pay a dividend. The company paid its first dividend in 1955 and had paid consecutive dividends since that time. Exhibits I and II show the company's financial statements.

The company had been quite successful in estimating its future sales. Generally sales had not been too cyclical, although the period from November through May had been the high-production months. This peak had come about because contracts were normally let during June, July, and August. Exhibit IV shows the company's projected sales. Mr. Buck realized that he could not project closely the fluctuations that normally occurred in sales, although he did detect a distinct secular pattern.

The company continuously bid on new government contracts and subcontracts. Its principal government contracts were all bid on a fixed basis, which meant that the company agreed to supply the prime contractor or the government with the products specified at a specific price. While such contracts were open to renegotiation by the government, Research had not been subject to that problem. The fixed-price contract had not been too popular for many bidders, and most of the bidding in this area was on the cost-plus or fixed-fee basis. Research, Inc. found that when they bid on the specific type of job in which they were experienced there were few competitors, customarily three. Thus, a look at the new contracts let by the government gave management a good idea of the amount of business they would get during the ensuing period. The fixed-price contract generally allowed Research the opportunity of applying the know-how thus acquired in producing civilian goods. It was the hope of the company that the civilian portion of their product mix would grow and that the government portion would decrease. For the next few years, however, management was not considering restricting the amount of new government contracts for they believed that their area was somewhat insensitive to a reduction in defense spending.

Sales for the fiscal year ending September 30, 1963 had been $3,750,000. Sales in the six-month period ending March 31, 1964 had reached $2,850,000, which annualized would equal $5,700,000. Mr. Buck, however, believed that this annualized rate was somewhat higher than could be expected since the first half was the higher productive period. For the year April 1, 1964 to March 31, 1965 he predicted that expected sales would reach $5,800,000, an all-time high for the company. He believed, however, that the company could well get an additional fixed-price contract in the amount of $1,000,000, which would call for delivery of goods in the months of January and February divided equally, $500,000 in January and $500,000 in February. He thought that he should somehow incorporate this in his determination of cash needs.

Although before-tax profits in the last three years had been between 7 per cent and 8 per cent of sales, Mr. Buck thought that it was reasonable to expect a 10 per cent before-tax profit during the next year. He noted that between 1957 and 1960 before-tax profits had exceeded 10 per cent by a considerable amount, and the company had now returned to this more favorable profit structure.

In examining other items in his pro forma income statement, Mr. Buck noted that other expenses, which principally included sales promotion and interest, would continue to be about 2.5 per cent of sales. The company made its civilian sales through manufacturers, representatives who operated in the principal areas of the country where prime defense contractors were located. These people received a 7 per cent commission on all civilian sales, which was paid in the month following delivery and was not included in cost of goods sold. The company's cost of goods sold included labor, which averaged 10 per cent of sales, and a burden of 150 per cent of labor. Burden included depreciation of 3 per cent of sales and R & D, which in the next period was budgeted at $150,000.

In determining the estimated cash receipts, Mr. Buck was somewhat puzzled as to how he should handle the problems of accounts receivable collections. Of the company's seventy-five customers, only one or two offered any payment problems. Bad debts over the last five years had averaged less than .1 per cent. Although one division gave terms of net 30 only, most of the non government sales were made at .25/10; net 30. While these terms were insignificant in total, many of the firm's customers took them. This was especially true of the large airplane frame and engine manufacturers who apparently had surplus cash on hand.

The government typically paid on 60-day terms, and some customers paid as late as 75 to 90 days. When Mr. Buck examined his accounts receivable collection period, he noted that it had averaged approximately 48 days. He believed this would drop to 40 days for the next year. He noted that when firms paid, they took their discount for paying in 10 days when the check actually did not get to Research, Inc. until 25 days after shipment. He reasoned that this fifteen-day delay period on checks came about because of certain inherent difficulties and frictions. For instance, if Research shipped an item one day, the item would take approximately five days to reach its destination, since most products went either to the East or West coast. A firm receiving such an item would probably take as much as five days to recognize that it had received the item. This involved time in the receiving room, time for the department requesting these goods to recognize them, and time to see that the goods were in good order. An additional five days would be required for the check to be processed and to be mailed to Research, Inc. Thus, the terms .25/10; net 30 in fact amounted to .25/25; net 45. Mr. Buck realized that this was also true of people who paid in 30 days as well as of the government that typically paid in 60 days. Exhibit III shows the percentages of accounts receivable collected in each of these periods.

The purchasing department for each of the divisions normally bought half of the necessary materials for any given order a month prior to shipment and the other half two months prior to shipment. Labor, on the other hand, was performed primarily in the month prior to the shipment. Three-fourths of the total labor on a given shipment would be expended in the month prior to shipment with one-fourth expended two months prior to shipment. The burden was accounted for in the same manner as labor. Capital expenditures were expected to average $4,000 a month except in the month of November when an addition to their present building would be completed at a cost of $8,000. The company expected to continue its present dividend, which was paid in the month of September. Mortgage payments were $2,593 a month and were included in other expenses.

Research, Inc.'s year ended September 30, thus federal income tax payments were not based on a calendar year. Large payments were due in December and March with smaller payments in June and September. Because of a change in the tax laws the payments made in the 1964 tax year would overlap payments in the 1963 tax year. This overlapping was expected to continue until 1970 when corporate taxes would be on a pay-as-you-go basis. State and local taxes were estimated at $50,000, payable in September and March. Exhibit V gives a schedule for estimated tax payments.

During February, 1964, the company's short-term borrowing had reached $600,000 at an interest rate of $5\frac{1}{2}$ per cent. This had been the peak for the year. The present line of credit was for $700,000 with a 15 per cent compensating balance. Since Mr. Buck considered $50,000 his absolute minimum cash balance, the compensating balance usually had no effect on borrowing, especially in view of the float normally associated with such a balance. In addition to the line of credit, the bank had also agreed to loan short-term funds if they were secured by accounts receivable. The bank would loan up to 70 per cent of the value of the receivables pledged.

After having collected and analyzed the data for his annual cash projection, Mr. Buck wondered whether he should consider additional permanent capital during the next year. He knew that the board of directors would be reluctant to expand short-term borrowing past $1,000,000, which meant that some other means of financing might be necessary if either a large contract were received or a cash acquisition made. During 1964 the company's stock had been selling for approximately 10 times earnings. This apparently depressed price seemed to be based on a dearth of interest by stockholders in the local over-the-counter market, and there was little likelihood of change for the next year. This meant that a direct sale of stock

**EXHIBIT I**

**Research, Inc.**
**Balance Sheet**

| Assets | 3/31/64 | 9/30/63 | 9/30/62 | 9/30/61 | 9/30/60 |
|---|---|---|---|---|---|
| Cash | $ 50,250 | 70,450 | 253,595 | 240,985 | 62,129 |
| Accounts receivable (net) | 541,174 | 506,997 | 369,053 | 232,547 | 1,301,497 |
| Inventory | 710,323 | 640,387 | 432,547 | 313,268 | 182,424 |
| Prepaid expenses | 6,020 | 6,020 | 5,044 | 2,422 | 5,710 |
| Total current assets | 1,307,767 | 1,223,854 | 1,060,239 | 789,222 | 1,551,760 |
| Land | 115,000 | 115,000 | 108,000 | 108,000 | 107,000 |
| Buildings | 626,058 | 626,058 | 477,178 | 472,792 | 469,523 |
| Machinery & Equipment | 795,865 | 745,865 | 578,589 | 580,516 | 459,480 |
| Depreciation | (543,389) | (503,290) | (423,091) | (351,331) | (271,508) |
| Total property | 993,534 | 983,633 | 740,676 | 809,977 | 764,495 |
| Total assets | 2,301,301 | 2,207,487 | 1,800,915 | 1,599,199 | 2,316,255 |
| | | | | | |
| Liabilities | | | | | |
| Notes payable | 50,000 | 185,000 | 10,000 | — | 525,000 |
| Current installment on mortgage | 15,558 | 21,655 | 18,563 | 17,833 | 15,401 |
| Accounts payable | 373,614 | 233,177 | 108,291 | 104,354 | 238,491 |
| Accrued salaries | 74,590 | 67,798 | 52,318 | 43,259 | 40,826 |
| Accrued payroll and property taxes | 47,385 | 73,839 | 34,087 | 26,771 | 25,842 |
| Federal and state income taxes | 80,000 | 131,106 | 187,883 | 81,273 | 186,560 |
| Total current liabilities | 641,147 | 712,575 | 411,142 | 273,490 | 1,033,120 |
| Mortgage payable | 161,503 | 171,061 | 188,082 | 207,983 | 226,610 |
| Minority interest | 8,017 | 3,017 | — | — | — |
| Common stock ($.10 par) | 142,905 | 142,905 | 142,905 | 142,905 | 142,905 |
| Paid-in surplus | 456,741 | 456,741 | 456,741 | 456,741 | 456,741 |
| Retained earnings | 890,988 | 721,188 | 602,045 | 518,080 | 456,879 |
| Total liabilities | 2,301,301 | 2,207,487 | 1,800,915 | 1,599,199 | 2,316,255 |

**EXHIBIT II**

**Research, Inc.**
**Income Statement**
**Years ending Sept. 30**

| | 1964* | 1963 | 1962 | 1961 | 1960 |
|---|---|---|---|---|---|
| Net sales | $2,848,800 | 3,752,993 | 3,512,954 | 2,470,634 | 3,585,900 |
| Cost of goods sold | 2,404,080 | 3,357,898 | 3,099,767 | 2,192,819 | 3,075,010 |
| Operating profit | 444,720 | 395,095 | 413,187 | 277,815 | 510,890 |
| Other expenses | 71,220 | 90,354 | 124,641 | 98,033 | 51,604 |
| Profit before tax | 373,500 | 304,741 | 288,546 | 179,782 | 459,286 |
| Income taxes | 203,700 | 154,000 | 176,000 | 90,000 | 251,000 |
| Net income | 169,800 | 150,741 | 112,546 | 89,782 | 208,286 |
| Dividends | — | 28,581 | 28,581 | 28,581 | 28,581 |
| Depreciation | — | 109,143 | 84,512 | 82,924 | 69,339 |

*6 months ending 3/31/64.

would probably be a last resort. Mr. Buck decided that he would process his material and make some definitive plan for future financing under varying conditions of expansion.

**EXHIBIT III**

**Research, Inc.**
**Percentage Distribution of**
**Accounts Receivable Collection**

| Type of Receivable | | Days | | | |
|---|---|---|---|---|---|
| | Unadjusted | 10 | 30 | 45 | 75 over |
| | Adjusted | 25 | 45 | 60 | 90 over |
| Government | | —% | —% | 100% | —% |
| Government subcontract | | 50 | 50 | — | — |
| Civilian | | 20 | 60 | 15 | 5 |

**EXHIBIT IV**

**Research, Inc.**
**Actual & Projected Sales By Months**
**(thousands)**

| | Actual Sales | | Projected Sales | |
|---|---|---|---|---|
| Month | 1963 | 1964 | 1964 | 1965 |
| January | | 564 | | 600 |
| February | | 278 | | 750 |
| March | | 865 | | 700 |
| April | 529 | | 550 | |
| May | 260 | | 300 | |
| June | 308 | | 350 | |
| July | 368 | | 400 | |
| August | 253 | | 400 | |
| September | 442 | | 450 | |
| October | 308 | | 400 | |
| November | 448 | | 450 | |
| December | 385 | | 450 | |

**EXHIBIT V**

**Schedule of Tax Payments**

| | June, 1964 | Sept., 1964 | Dec., 1964 | Mar., 1965 |
|---|---|---|---|---|
| Federal tax installments 1963 tax year* | $41,000 | $41,000 | $91,500 | $91,500 |
| Federal tax installments 1964 tax year* | — | — | 2,650 | 2,650 |
| State and local taxes | — | 25,000 | — | 25,000 |
| | $41,000 | $66,000 | $94,150 | $119,150 |

*Based on $520,000 estimated net profit before tax.

# Inventory
# Policy

# 11

## THE DRINK MORE
## COFFEE COMPANY

In July, 1963, Mr. John Green, controller of The Drink More Coffee Company of New Orleans, Louisiana, was studying the problems associated with coffee bean purchasing, desirable inventory levels, and inventory storage facilities. Prior to that date the management of the company had arbitrarily decided to maintain a two weeks' supply of green coffee beans and to keep an additional eight to ten weeks' supply on purchase order. Recent strikes by dock workers, destruction of coffee trees in South America, and prospects for rising prices of coffee beans had created a need to reevaluate the desired inventory level of coffee beans. Although the available storage capacity of the company would accommodate no more than three weeks' supply of green coffee beans, additional storage facilities could be built or leased from a public warehouse at New Orleans.

The Drink More Coffee Company had been founded some ten years earlier and was operating as a corporation. The stock of the corporation was closely held, a number of the major stockholders were officers of the firm, and the board of directors followed a 50 per cent payout dividend policy. The company's equipment was in good repair, and the debt of the firm was almost nonexistent. The production facilities would probably be adequate until 1972 or 1973 based on recent past sales trends. Although the company did not have excessive amounts of cash, it possessed unused borrowing capacity of about $500,000. Profits before taxes amounted to about $.05 per pound of coffee sold.

The basic type of raw material used in the production of finished coffee is the green coffee bean. Although more than 100 different kinds of coffee beans are bought and sold in the United States, they are divided into two general groups—Brazils and Milds. The Brazils are those grown in Brazil while the Milds are those cultivated elsewhere. The four groups of Brazil coffees, which bear the names of the ports through which they are exported, are: Santos, Rios, Victorias, and Paranas. Of the Brazilian coffees, Santos is the most popular because of its sweet clear flavor. Paranas are less popular but similar in flavor to Santos. Rios have a pungent flavor and aroma, while Victorias have a strong dirty flavor. Brazils are said to be hard or harsh in flavor, but coffee beans grown elsewhere have a soft, mellow, rich flavor. Certain of the flavor coffee beans (blenders) demand a higher price than do Brazils.

From 1960–1962, the United States was importing annually some 22 million bags of green coffee beans, each of which contained 60 kilos or 132.276 pounds. These imports amounted to about one-half of the coffee exports from the principal coffee producing countries. During this period, imports from South America declined, while increases were reported from Central America, Africa, and Asia (see Exhibits I and II). With the average coffee bean price at about $.33 per pound, U. S. imports totaled approximately $1 billion.

In mid-1963, DMCO was using about 1,400 bags of green coffee beans weekly, although sales were somewhat greater in the winter months than in the summer and fall (Exhibit IV). The company sold only one blend of coffee in both drip and regular grinds. The blend could be obtained by one of the following two mixes:

1. Santos,         70%
   Guatemalas,     10%
   Ugandas,        20%
2. Paranas,        60%
   Equidors,       20%
   Guatemalas,     20%

The mix was occasionally changed when there appeared to be a price advantage to the switch.

On July 5, 1963, the company had the following beans on hand and on order:

| Type Bean | Bags on Hand | Bags on Order | Contract Price per Pound | Due Date |
|---|---|---|---|---|
| Paranas | 2,040 | 11,000 | .32–.33 | 1,000 weekly |
| Equidors | 1,205 | 2,000 | .33–.34 | 500 bi-weekly |
| Guatemalas | 360 | 3,000 | .34–.35 | 500 bi-weekly |

The warehouse, which was adjacent to the roasting and packaging area, would house only 4,000 bags of coffee beans. Other inventory items such as rolls of paper for the manufacture of bags and storage cartons required little investment and storage space.

The company's procurement officer placed orders for green coffee beans through New Orleans brokers, usually in units of 500 bags. The order would be filled from a Brazilian warehouse (or one in another coffee producing country), carried by ships to the New Orleans docks, unloaded from the ship, reloaded on railroad cars, and transported to the company's storage facilities or public warehousing facilities. The payment for the shipment was handled by the buyer's bank on a sight draft or on a thirty-day time draft basis. Delivery time usually required three weeks from South or Central America and five weeks from Africa.

After the coffee beans arrived by rail at the company's warehouse, 20 sacks were placed, interlocking, on a 5.5 foot square wooden pallet and moved

**EXHIBIT I**

**U.S. Imports of Coffee by Countries of Origin**
**Average 1955-59, and Annual 1960 and 1961**
**(In Thousands of bags, 132.276 pounds each)**

| Continent and Country of Origin | Average 1955–59 | 1960 | 1961 |
|---|---|---|---|
| North America | | | |
| Costa Rica | 188 | 271 | 369 |
| Dominican Republic | 336 | 403 | 266 |
| El Salvador | 696 | 446 | 583 |
| Guatemala | 866 | 798 | 956 |
| Mexico | 1,154 | 1,097 | 1,253 |
| Nicaragua | 225 | 170 | 225 |
| Other | 389 | 443 | 272 |
| Total | 3,854 | 3,628 | 3,924 |
| South America | | | |
| Brazil | 8,906 | 9,261 | 8,629 |
| Colombia | 4,538 | 4,254 | 4,078 |
| Ecuador | 282 | 317 | 202 |
| Venezuela | 407 | 345 | 344 |
| Other | 152 | 422 | 426 |
| Total | 14,285 | 14,599 | 13,679 |
| Africa | | | |
| Angola | 711 | 802 | 1,024 |
| British East Africa | 572 | 934 | 1,246 |
| Congo, Republic of the | 524 | 645 | 592 |
| Ethiopia | 394 | 582 | 682 |
| Ivory Coast | 288 | 657 | 736 |
| Other | 283 | 204 | 301 |
| Total | 2,772 | 3,824 | 4,581 |
| Asia and Oceania | 90 | 49 | 201 |
| Other | 3 | — | 2 |
| Grand total | 21,004 | 22,100 | 22,387 |

**EXHIBIT II**

### Coffee Exports From Principal Producing Countries
### Average 1955-59, and Annual 1960 and 1961
### (In Thousands of bags, 132.276 pounds each)

| Continent and Country of Origin | Average 1955–59 | 1960 | 1961 |
|---|---|---|---|
| North America | | | |
| Costa Rica | 566 | 778 | 827 |
| Dominican Republic | 400 | 487 | 366 |
| El Salvador | 1,279 | 1,492 | 1,431 |
| Guatemala | 1,133 | 1,351 | 1,255 |
| Haiti | 412 | 394 | 348 |
| Honduras | 193 | 258 | 212 |
| Mexico | 1,331 | 1,384 | 1,487 |
| Nicaragua | 337 | 363 | 350 |
| Other (Cuba, Guadeloupe, Hawaii, Jamaica, Trinidad, Tobago, Panama, and Puerto Rico) | 248 | 230 | 203 |
| Total | 5,899 | 6,737 | 6,479 |
| | | | |
| South America | | | |
| Brazil | 15,027 | 16,819 | 16,970 |
| Colombia | 5,523 | 5,938 | 5,651 |
| Ecuador | 437 | 539 | 382 |
| Peru | 207 | 459 | 567 |
| Venezuela | 487 | 412 | 406 |
| Other (Bolivia, British Guinea  Surinam) | 16 | 31 | 33 |
| Total | 21,697 | 24,198 | 24,009 |
| | | | |
| Africa | | | |
| Angola | 1,312 | 1,454 | 1,864 |
| Cameroon | 348 | 509 | 546 |
| Central Africa Republic | 83 | 99 | 125 |
| Congo, Republic of the | 1,083 | 1,666 | 1,250 |
| Ethiopia | 668 | 908 | 921 |
| Guinea | 162 | 267 | 300 |
| Ivory Coast | 1,778 | 2,449 | 2,563 |
| Kenya | 403 | 470 | 541 |
| Malagasy Republic | 779 | 670 | 664 |
| Spanish Guinea | 100 | 106 | 110 |
| Tanganyika | 340 | 421 | 428 |
| Togo | 108 | 62 | 153 |
| Uganda | 1,311 | 1,982 | 2,000 |
| Other | 125 | 277 | 300 |
| Total | 8,600 | 11,340 | 11,765 |
| Asia and Oceania | 968 | 1,092 | 1,757 |
| Grand Total | 37,164 | 43,367 | 44,010 |

by a fork lift truck to the warehouse. The pallets were stacked four high so that eighty bags occupied some $30\frac{1}{4}$ square feet of floor space. Some 30 per cent of the storage area was needed for the operation of the fork lift. Use of the wooden pallets required somewhat more space than when they were not used, but the amount of human labor in handling the bags was reduced by 60 per cent.

Coffee production entailed the following: cleaning the beans; blending

## EXHIBIT III

### Green Coffee—World Supply & Distribution
### (In thousands of bags of 132.276 pounds each)

| Marketing Year | Beginning Carryover | Produc-tion | Total Supply | Net Exports | Domestic Distribution | Ending Carryover |
|---|---|---|---|---|---|---|
| 1950–51 | 9,307 | 38,093 | 47,400 | 31,593 | 8,092 | 7,715 |
| 1951–52 | 7,715 | 39,215 | 46,930 | 32,152 | 8,331 | 6,447 |
| 1952–53 | 6,447 | 41,513 | 47,960 | 32,939 | 8,275 | 6,746 |
| 1953–54 | 6,746 | 43,996 | 50,742 | 33,458 | 8,156 | 9,128 |
| 1954–55 | 9,128 | 42,188 | 51,316 | 29,219 | 8,266 | 13,831 |
| 1955–56 | 13,831 | 50,348 | 64,179 | 38,296 | 8,407 | 17,476 |
| 1956–57 | 17,476 | 45,420 | 62,896 | 36,203 | 8,452 | 18,241 |
| 1957–58 | 18,241 | 55,009 | 73,250 | 37,340 | 8,500 | 27,410 |
| 1958–59 | 27,410 | 61,665 | 89,075 | 38,977 | 9,664 | 40,434 |
| 1959–60 | 40,434 | 78,919 | 119,353 | 43,790 | 12,498 | 63,065 |
| 1960–61 | 63,065 | 65,528 | 128,593 | 44,409 | 12,689 | 68,495 |
| 1961–62 | 68,495 | 71,190 | 139,685 | 45,500 | 13,303 | 80,882 |
| 1962–63 | 80,882 | 65,550 | 146,432 | —— | —— | —— |
| 1963–64 | —— | —— | —— | —— | —— | —— |

## EXHIBIT IV

### Analysis of Current Year's Green Coffee Bean Usage
### (Based on the first week of each month)

| Date | Bags Used | Ending Inven-tory Bags in Warehouse(s) | Bags Requi-red for 8-week Supply | Addi-tional Bags | Week's Actual Supply in Warehouse | Week's Supply on Contract |
|---|---|---|---|---|---|---|
| July 7, 1962 | 1,334 | 2,465 | 10,642 | 8,207 | 1.8 | 8.8 |
| Aug. 8, 1962 | 1,229 | 3,073 | 9,832 | 6,759 | 2.4 | 7.5 |
| Sept. 9, 1962 | 1,191 | 3,506 | 9,528 | 6,022 | 2.9 | 10.0 |
| Oct. 5, 1962 | 1,487 | 3,566 | 11,896 | 8,330 | 2.3 | 7.7 |
| Nov. 3, 1962 | 1,465 | 4,090 | 11,720 | 7,630 | 2.7 | 7.8 |
| Dec. 1, 1962 | 1,509 | 3,189 | 12,072 | 8,883 | 2.1 | 8.7 |
| Jan. 5, 1963 | 1,387 | 8,507 | 11,096 | 2,589 | 6.1 | 3.4 |
| Feb. 9, 1963 | 1,682 | 4,292 | 13,456 | 9,164 | 2.6 | 9.9 |
| Mar. 2, 1963 | 1,550 | 3,674 | 12,400 | 8,726 | 2.4 | 9.6 |
| Apr. 6, 1963 | 1,462 | 2,602 | 11,696 | 9,094 | 1.8 | 9.7 |
| May 4, 1963 | 1,424 | 7,445 | 11,392 | 3,947 | 5.2 | 5.7 |
| June 1, 1963 | 1,352 | 5,946 | 10,816 | 4,870 | 4.3 | 11.2 |
| Average | 1,423 | — | — | — | 3.0 | 8.3 |

the bean types; roasting; grinding and cooling; and packaging. The beans were poured into large cleaning vats and forced by air through a shaft where gravity permitted the beans to fall and air currents removed the impurities. The process was repeated until the beans were clean and then the appropriate mix was placed in a mechanical mixer. After being mixed, a 560 pound batch of beans was dumped into a roaster where it was roasted in a revolving, metal cylinder at 400° for eighteen minutes. The coffee lost about 18 per cent of its weight as water evaporated during the roasting process. The beans were then removed from the roaster, allowed to cool for about half an hour, and then crushed to the desired grind. While the coffee was still warm, it was weighed in one pound bags and packaged mechanically by an automatic packaging machine. The bags were sealed,

**EXHIBIT V**

**Forecast of Green Coffee Storage Needs
for the Next Ten Years**

| Year | Bags to Be Stored | Present Facilities | Storage Needed |
|------|-----------|------------|---------|
| 1963 | 12,375 | 4,000 | 8,375 |
| 1964 | 12,900 | 4,000 | 8,900 |
| 1965 | 13,425 | 4,000 | 9,425 |
| 1966 | 14,000 | 4,000 | 10,000 |
| 1967 | 14,550 | 4,000 | 10,550 |
| 1968 | 15,100 | 4,000 | 11,100 |
| 1969 | 15,600 | 4,000 | 11,600 |
| 1970 | 16,150 | 4,000 | 12,150 |
| 1971 | 16,700 | 4,000 | 12,700 |
| 1972 | 17,250 | 4,000 | 13,250 |
| 1973 | 17,800 | 4,000 | 13,800 |

**EXHIBIT VI**

**Comparative Cost of Public Warehousing and Company
Owned Storage Facilities**

| Item | New Orleans Public Warehouse | Company Warehouse |
|------|-----------------|----------|
| Rent on land (per year) | | $720. |
| Building—capital outlay (per sq. ft.) | | $3.50 |
| Amortization of building (st. line) | | 10% |
| Interest cost | | 6% |
| Insurance | | |
| Building (per year) | | $200. |
| Coffee beans | 1% of Value | 1% of Value |
| Taxes | | $300–400 |
| Storage (per bag 1 mo.) | .065 | |
| Moving coffee beans | | |
| To public warehouse | .045 per CWT | |
| To company facilities | .065 per CWT | .085 per CWT |

sent down a conveyor belt, and packaged in bales of 24. One person could operate the packaging machine.

The company's manufacturing equipment consisted of: (1) the cleaning equipment, (2) the mixer, which could handle twenty-five bags of beans per hour, (3) six roasters, (4) one grinder, which could grind a batch in fifteen minutes, and (5) one packaging machine which could pack 4,000 bags hourly.

The coffee was sold to wholesalers and chain grocery stores within a radius of about 200 miles of New Orleans. Only a two- or three-day supply of the finished product was maintained so that the coffee could be delivered fresh to the wholesaler.

The company had adequate storage space to accommodate probable needs for finished goods, work-in-process, and supplies for the next ten years. If the management should decide to increase its holdings of green coffee beans above 4,000 bags, this would involve public warehousing storage in New Orleans, or the leasing of a tract of land adjacent to the coffee mill and the erection of a storage warehouse. No adjacent land was for sale, but a 100 by 200 foot plot could be leased for ten years at a cost of $720 per year. A contractor had expressed a willingness to erect a storage warehouse for $3.50 per square foot. The ownership of the building would revert to the lessor at the expiration of the lease, but an option to lease the building at that time for $2,000 annually was offered by the lessor. Other costs associated with the two storage arrangements appear in Exhibit VI. Funds could be borrowed at 6 per cent.

In an attempt to stabilize the prices of green coffee beans, which was desirable to the producer, coffee mill, and consumer, some thirty-two coffee-exporting companies having 95.1 per cent of total exports and twenty-two coffee-importing countries having 94.7 per cent of total imports had agreed in late 1962 to an International Coffee Agreement. The agreement set forth five-year export quotas for the participating exporting countries (Exhibit IX). During the six-month period prior to the coffee year (October 1–September 30), annual quotas could be adjusted to meet market demands for green coffee beans and to stabilize market prices.

During 1962, The Drink More Coffee Company had encountered no difficulty in buying Paranas or Guatemalas, but Equidors appeared to be in short supply. News of the freezing weather, frost, and forest fires which killed millions of Brazil's trees was expected to result in rising coffee bean prices during the last half of 1963. Mr. Green was not sure how long this trend would continue, but he felt that a larger inventory of green coffee beans should be considered.

## EXHIBIT VII

### New Orleans Quotations for Selected Types of Green Coffee Beans, 1952-1963*

| Year | Santos (Type 2) | | | Paranas | | | Equidors | | | Guatemalas | | | African Ugandas | | |
|---|---|---|---|---|---|---|---|---|---|---|---|---|---|---|---|
| | Ave. | High | Low | Ave. | High | Low | Ave. | High | Low | Ave. | High | Low | Ave. | High | Low |
| 1952 | 54.04 | 55.75 | 53.50 | 53.19 | 54.25 | 52.00 | 54.04 | 55.00 | 53.25 | 54.83 | 56.50 | 53.00 | 44.03 | 47.25 | 41.25 |
| 1953 | 58.75 | 66.00 | 54.50 | 57.19 | 64.00 | 53.00 | 56.78 | 63.25 | 53.00 | 55.21 | 60.00 | 53.65 | 47.59 | 51.50 | 41.75 |
| 1954 | 79.65 | 94.75 | 66.00 | 77.70 | 92.50 | 64.00 | 76.58 | 92.00 | 63.25 | N. A. | N. A. | N. A. | 57.86 | 70.00 | 46.00 |
| 1955 | 58.13 | 69.00 | 53.50 | 54.99 | 67.00 | 47.88 | 59.74 | 69.00 | 54.50 | 58.38 | 68.25 | 52.75 | 38.41 | 49.00 | 30.00 |
| 1956 | 59.49 | 62.75 | 53.63 | 53.52 | 56.25 | 49.00 | 64.39 | 72.00 | 54.75 | 67.56 | 73.00 | 60.75 | 33.59 | 35.50 | 31.00 |
| 1957 | 58.50 | 62.25 | 54.50 | 53.43 | 56.75 | 50.25 | 58.89 | 64.75 | 51.50 | 61.70 | 66.88 | 54.63 | 40.22 | 43.00 | 36.63 |
| 1958 | 49.23 | 56.50 | 41.63 | 47.29 | 53.63 | 39.00 | 47.80 | 53.50 | 39.38 | 49.11 | 55.13 | 40.13 | 37.57 | 40.50 | 30.13 |
| 1959 | 37.47 | 42.38 | 35.00 | 36.09 | 41.00 | 33.88 | 40.90 | 42.75 | 39.00 | 41.98 | 43.75 | 40.00 | 28.72 | 31.13 | 23.63 |
| 1960 | 36.97 | 38.00 | 36.13 | 35.67 | 36.50 | 34.50 | 38.11 | 40.75 | 36.00 | 40.94 | 41.63 | 38.75 | 20.18 | 23.75 | 17.38 |
| 1961 | 36.40 | 38.25 | 33.88 | 34.78 | 36.75 | 31.75 | 36.27 | 37.13 | 35.00 | 37.55 | 39.50 | 34.75 | 18.92 | 20.50 | 18.13 |
| 1962 | 34.31 | 35.25 | 33.38 | 32.68 | 33.13 | 32.00 | N. A. | 35.78 | 32.13 | N. A. | 37.13 | 33.13 | 20.63 | 23.88 | 19.63 |

*Includes all marketing costs to the port of entry. Certain of the price quotations are for N. Y. when not available from New Orleans.
Source: Pan-American Coffee Bureau.

79

**EXHIBIT VIII**

**Average Spot Coffee Prices for Green Coffee Beans**
**January, 1962 through April, 1963**

| Date | Santos (Type 2) | Paranas 4/5s | Equidors Washed | Guatemalas Good Washed | African Ugandas Native |
|------|------|------|------|------|------|
| 1962 | | | | | |
| January | 34.50 | 32.85 | N. A. | 36.08 | 19.73 |
| February | 34.43 | 32.93 | N. A. | 36.68 | 19.73 |
| March | 34.43 | 32.95 | N. A. | 36.88 | 20.08 |
| April | 34.45 | 33.08 | N. A. | 36.29 | 20.30 |
| May | 34.70 | 33.00 | N. A. | 36.25 | 20.68 |
| June | 35.10 | 32.85 | 35.34 | N. A. | 20.63 |
| July | 35.03 | 32.75 | 34.43 | N. A. | 20.50 |
| August | 34.48 | 32.63 | 33.18 | N. A. | 20.48 |
| September | 33.80 | 32.33 | 32.25 | N. A. | 20.48 |
| October | 33.45 | 32.13 | 32.38 | 33.98 | 20.48 |
| November | 33.63 | 32.23 | N. A. | 34.98 | 21.45 |
| December | 33.68 | 32.45 | N. A. | 35.60 | 23.03 |
| 1963 | | | | | |
| January | 34.13 | 32.68 | N. A. | 35.50 | 23.95 |
| February | 33.60 | 32.28 | N. A. | 35.00 | 24.98 |
| March | 33.45 | 32.13 | N. A. | 35.30 | 26.78 |
| April | 33.33 | 31.48 | N. A. | 35.28 | 26.90 |

**EXHIBIT IX**

**Export Quotas of Green Coffee Beans Under the International Trade**
**Agreement from October, 1962 to March, 1963**
**(Thousands of bags)**

| Country | October— December 1962 | January— March 1963 |
|------|------|------|
| Brazil | 4,490 | 4,348 |
| Colombia | 1,500 | 1,448 |
| Costa Rica | 190 | 303 |
| Cuba | 40 | 50 |
| Dominican Republic | 150 | 125 |
| Ecuador | 140 | 60 |
| El Salvador | 350 | 499 |
| Guatemala | 400 | 334 |
| Haiti | 110 | 135 |
| Honduras | 35 | 107 |
| Mexico | 290 | 478 |
| Nicaragua | 40 | 180 |
| Panama | 6 | 6 |
| Peru | 145 | 105 |
| Portugal | 600 | 499 |
| Other countries except U.K. | 1,054 | 1,054 |
| United Kingdom (including Kenya and Uganda) and Tanganyika | 742 | 742 |
| Total | 10,282 | 10,473 |

# Elementary Inventory Models

## 12

Mr. C. D. Wilson, treasurer of Bronson Electronics, Inc., was examining the company's April 1963 financial statements. He could see that the start-up costs of the firm's first two years of operations, coupled with rapidly expanding sales, would put an enormous load on the firm's cash position. As a consequence, every effort would have to be made to hold cash outflows to a minimum. Mr. Wilson noted that the principal use of cash during the last year had been for inventory. He believed that this would apply again to the next year, and as a result, he decided to check the inventory carefully to see if its overall size could be reduced.

Bronson Electronics was formed in February of 1962 by Charles Bronson, an electrical engineer who had been previously employed as chief electrical engineer for a large West coast electronics firm. Working on his own Mr. Bronson had discovered a new method of connecting circuits which he had patented as "Grip-tight." Grip-tight was a connector made of beryllium, copper, and gold. The firm had leased a suburban Los Angeles plant and started production in March of 1962. Its original financing came from an issue of 50,000 shares of common stock at $1.75 per share, which was made to friends of Mr. Bronson. One month later on May 2, 1962, the company executed an underwriting agreement with Kleen-Smith, a local investment banker, for the sale of 220,000 shares to the public at $2.00 per share, with the underwriter to retain .25 per share sold. The new issue met with success and was entirely taken by some 1,100 investors.

Bronson's first attempt to sell connectors was very successful. The grip-tight connector was immediately accepted by the government and was designated for use in Polaris, Zeus, and Minuteman missiles and in Naval Tactical

Data Systems. As a result, government orders began to build. High start-up costs, however, resulted in the company losing $239,259 in its first complete year of operations. This loss put a damper on advancing sales, so in order to be able to push sales Mr. Bronson had borrowed $210,000 from a local Small Business Investment Company in October, 1963. Interest on the loan was 6 per cent, and the note was to be amortized at $52,500 a year starting in 1967. The note also stipulated that the firm would maintain $100,000 in net working capital and that additional debt could not exceed 50 per cent of the present debt plus equity. As a "sweetener" for the note, Bronson issued the SBIC a stock subscription warrent to purchase up to 75,000 shares of the company's common stock at any time up to October, 1969 at a price of $2.80 per share.

In the articles of incorporation the board of directors of the company was given discretionary authority to issue stock options. In addition to the 75,000 share option given to the SBIC, the directors also gave employees options to purchase up to 41,805 shares at prices ranging from $1.93 to $4.13 per share.

During Bronson's second year of operations new connectors were developed and sales were greatly expanded. (See Exhibits I and II.) In addition to the Grip-tight connector the company also produced wire wrap connectors, building-block connectors, and tape cable connectors. By the end of fiscal 1963 (April, 1964), the company was selling 20 per cent of its product line to nongovernment buyers. Although Grip-tight still amounted to 70 per cent of total sales, management expected that their other products would take a bigger share of total sales by the following year. The only factor which would seem to slow the company's growth potential was financing. The size of the connector market in 1962 was $200 million, and in 1964 the market had been estimated to be $600 million. Mr. Bronson believed that with the aid of breakthroughs in design and miniaturization the market would continue to grow, not only in the military but in all industry.

Mr. Wilson, the company treasurer, had been given the task of making sure that the company had sufficient funds to allow sales to expand. Mr. Bronson had told him, "You worry about getting the money, and I'll worry about sales." Wilson had noted that expanding sales generally meant rapidly increasing receivables and inventories. In the first years of operations these had increased so rapidly that Wilson was afraid that he would have to use considerable amounts of outside financing regardless of the size of the present year's profits. Receivables were almost entirely government receivables, and, thus, he could do nothing to speed up payment. The increase in inventory, however, was another thing. He wanted to hold inventory levels to the very minimum in order to conserve as much cash as possible, and he wondered if there was already too much inventory.

The company had recently received a two-year government contract calling for 2,106,000 Grip-tight connectors. Delivery of the connectors was to be made daily and would be used in circuits for missiles, aircraft, and data processing systems. This order would be in addition to other orders for

Grip-tight and the miscellaneous connectors. Mr. Wilson thought that new government contracts might allow Bronson Electronics to establish a maximum inventory size for Grip-tight. Although he was uncertain about the demand for Grip-tight outside of the government's order, he thought it would be small and in fact could be ignored. When the present orders for Grip-tight were met, the only other sales for that connector would probably be through the new contract. Other connectors, however, could be expected to amount to as much as 30 per cent of sales.

In order to get an idea about the composition of the current inventory, Mr. Wilson sent for the company's production supervisor. Grip-tight was presently being produced on five automatic machines which the company owned. Five new machines had been ordered and would be installed by the end of the week but would be leased from the manufacturer. The ten machines would be sufficient to manufacture all of the necessary connectors. Because each type of connector involved different shapes and sometimes different materials, the machines had to be adjusted each time the product was changed. The supervisor indicated that the present method of production involved producing Grip-tight connectors for one month of steady production, then switching to other connectors. He explained that the reason that he produced so many Grip-tight connectors per run was that it cost $20 a machine to change from producing the one connector to producing the other connectors. The machines were typically run every day of the year except for an annual end of the year clean-up period when they were stopped for five days. Repairs under normal conditions were made at night. The firm was able to keep the machines going twelve hours a day every day because of the automatic nature of the process, in which one man could handle two machines. The supervisor indicated that a machine could be expected to produce 400 Grip-tight connectors a day under normal operation.

Mr. Wilson thought that the correct inventory policy would be one that would minimize the variable costs involved in producing and placing into inventory Grip-tight connectors while making sure that sufficient connectors would be available to meet shipping schedules. Mr. Wilson realized that setup costs were directly opposed to inventory capital costs and warehousing costs. In other words, inventory capital and warehousing costs could be decreased by having frequent production runs and a small inventory, but this, in turn, would increase the setup costs. Obviously the best plan would minimize the total for all three costs.

Inventory capital costs were considered to include the cost of funds tied up in inventory plus insurance on the value of the goods. Currently the interest rate on short-term notes was 6 per cent, and the cost of a Grip-tight connector was $3.20. Annual insurance premiums were $1.50 per $100 value of goods in inventory. Warehousing costs, which included building depreciation and maintenance, insurance, and overhead were $10 a year per box of 100 connectors.

During a production run, inventory would be produced at a rate which would be equivalent to the difference between the production rate and the selling rate. Once the production run had been completed, this inventory would be depleted by sales until production was started again. Because Grip-tight accounted for 70 per cent of the total inventory, Mr. Wilson decided just to worry about that item. He also noted that 40 per cent of inventory was raw materials and 20 per cent was goods in process. These items he thought would be handled as a separate problem if his calculations on the finished goods inventory proved valuable. For the demand, he decided to assume that Grip-tight would only be sold under the new contract, and that it would be necessary to keep two days' demand in inventory at all times in case of emergency.

### EXHIBIT I

#### Bronson Electronics, Inc.
#### Balance Sheet

| Assets | 4/30/64 | 4/30/63 |
|---|---|---|
| Current Assets | | |
| Cash | $ 30,434 | $ 80,279 |
| Accounts receivable | 91,602 | 32,849 |
| Inventories | 169,942 | 32,412 |
| Prepaid expenses | 11,935 | 4,374 |
| Total current assets | $303,913 | $149,914 |
| Property and equipment at cost | | |
| Machinery and equipment ($52,000 pledged) | 205,598 | 113,979 |
| Leasehold improvements | 17,118 | 2,198 |
| Less accumulated depreciation | (44,307) | (14,098) |
| Total property and equipment | $178,409 | $102,079 |
| Deferred expenses, less amortization | | |
| Research and development expenses | 51,142 | 43,267 |
| Other deferred expenses | 6,436 | 5,480 |
| Total deferred expenses | 57,578 | 48,747 |
| Total assets | $539,900 | $300,740 |
| *Liabilities and stockholders' equity* | | |
| Current liabilities | | |
| Accounts payable | $141,255 | $ 39,222 |
| Accrued liabilities | 35,266 | 10,059 |
| Long-term debt due within one year | 6,000 | 6,000 |
| Total current liabilities | $182,521 | $ 55,281 |
| Long-term debt due after one year | | |
| 6% note payable | 210,000 | |
| 7% contract payable, secured, due in semiannual installments to May, 1965 | 15,000 | 21,000 |
| Total long-term debt due after one year | $225,000 | $ 21,000 |
| Stockholders' equity | | |
| Common stock, $1 par value; 600.000 shares authorized, 270,317 shares issued and outstanding | 270,317 | 270,317 |
| Capital in excess of par value | 202,738 | 202,738 |
| Accumulated deficit | (340,676) | (248,596) |
| Total stockholders' equity | $132,379 | $224,459 |
| | $539,900 | $300,740 |

After collecting the data on inventory, Mr. Wilson made up a simple inventory model which he found in an operations research text book. (See Exhibits III and IV.) By placing the necessary data into the model, he hoped to find the maximum level at which inventory should be maintained. From this, he expected to determine what the size of the inventory should be, and whether he would need additional financing for the next year's inventory.

### EXHIBIT II

**Bronson Electronics, Inc.**
**Income Statement***

|  | Years Ending April 30 | |
|  | 1964 | 1963 |
|---|---:|---:|
| Net sales | $ 962,752 | $ 76,869 |
| Operating costs and expenses | | |
|    Cost of sales | 849,002 | 167,319 |
|    Selling, general and administrative | 197,076 | 151,066 |
| | $1,046,078 | $ 318,385 |
| Operating loss | (83,326) | (241,516) |
| Other (incomes) and expenses | | |
|    Interest income | (90) | (4,263) |
|    Interest expense | 8,344 | 2,006 |
| Net loss | (91,580) | (239,259) |
| Accumulated deficit at beginning of year | (248,596) | (9,337) |
| Accumulated deficit at end of year | $(340,176) | $(248,596) |

*Depreciation deducted in the above statement: 1964–$42,079; 1963–$19,784.

### Inventory During One Cycle

Let

$C'$ = Total variable cost per cycle
$C$ = Total variable cost per day
$P$ = Setup cost per production run
$I$ = Inventory capital cost per unit per day
$W$ = Warehousing cost per unit per day
$q$ = Units produced per run
$s$ = Sales demand per day
$k$ = Production rate per day
$t$ = Length of cycle in days
$t'$ = Length of production run in days

Then $t' = q/k$, and the inventory at the end of the production run would be as follows:

$$q - st' = q - s\left(\frac{q}{k}\right) = q\left(1 - \frac{s}{k}\right)$$

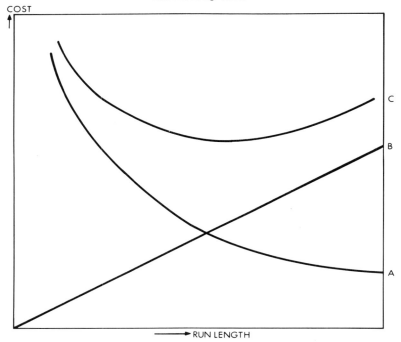

CURVE A = SETUP COSTS
CURVE B = INVENTORY CAPITAL AND WAREHOUSING COSTS
CURVE C = CURVE A AND CURVE B

This would represent the maximum inventory; average inventory would be calculated as follows:

$$\frac{1}{2}q\left(1 - \frac{s}{k}\right)$$

These two inventory relationships than could be incorporated into an expression for the total variable cost, as shown below:

$$C' = P + \frac{1}{2}Iqt\left(1 - \frac{s}{k}\right) + Wqt\left(1 - \frac{s}{k}\right)$$

or

$$C = \frac{P}{t} + \frac{1}{2}Iq\left(1 - \frac{s}{k}\right) + Wq\left(1 - \frac{s}{k}\right)$$

Noting that $t = q/s$ and collecting terms would yield the following:

**EXHIBIT IV**

**Bronson Electronics
Derivation of Optimum Run Size to Yield
Minimum Total Variable Cost**

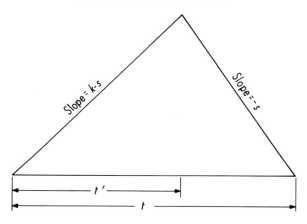

$$C = \frac{Ps}{q} + q\left(\frac{1}{2}I + W\right)\left(1 - \frac{s}{k}\right)$$

The production run size that would yield the minimum total variable cost could be obtained by differentiating the preceding expression and setting the derivative equal to zero, which would yield the following:*

$$\frac{dC}{dq} = \frac{-Ps}{q^2} + \left(\frac{1}{2}I + W\right)\left(1 - \frac{s}{k}\right) = 0$$

Then

$$\frac{Ps}{q^2} = \left(\frac{1}{2}I + W\right)\left(1 - \frac{s}{k}\right)$$

$$q^2 = \frac{Ps}{(\frac{1}{2}I + W)(1 - s/k)}$$

and

$$q = \sqrt{\frac{Ps}{(\frac{1}{2}I + W)(1 - s/k)}}$$

If the above expression were used, the maximum inventory during the cycle could be stated as follows:

$$\text{Maximum inventory} = q\left(1 - \frac{s}{k}\right) = \sqrt{\frac{Ps(1 - s/k)}{(\frac{1}{2}I + W)}}$$

---

*That a minimum has been obtained can be verified by the calculation of the second derivative.

# Cash
# for
# Evaluation

# 13

BEST MUSIC COMPANY

In May, 1962, Mr. Tenor, owner and operator of the Best Music Company of Waco, Texas, was considering the advisability of remaining in leased quarters or of building his own retail outlet. The store was being operated by Mr. Tenor, his wife, Gladys, two commissioned salesmen, and two laborers who served as deliverymen and general handymen.

The business had been operating since 1954, and sales had increased from $50,000 in that year to $180,000 in 1961. Although the proprietorship had been operated by Mr. and Mrs. Tenor at first, the increase in sales had necessitated the hiring of additional employees. The accounting work was being handled by a bookkeeping service. The firm was located in a small, downtown shop from 1954 to 1957, but as the sales of the company grew, additional display space, office space, and a repair workshop were needed. Therefore, the Best Music Company relocated from downtown to a heavily traveled street. It was moved to leased quarters which rented for $187 per month. The new location provided adequate space for three or four years, but by 1960, the company did not have enough display and storage floor space and rented a nearby warehouse at $125 per month to take care of the latter.

Although the company was merchandising sheet music, records, and miscellaneous musical instruments, the bulk of its sales was pianos and organs. The display of organs and pianos occupied approximately 75 per cent of the total display area.

In 1954 the family had assets valued at approximately $4,000. Through the usage of debt, retention of a substantial portion of the profits within the business, and careful cost control, the family's personal and business equity had increased to about $83,000 by the end of 1961.

The two salesmen were employed on a commission basis and received 10 per cent of the sales price of the merchandise which they sold. The proprietor, Mr. Tenor, spent a great deal of his time visiting schools, churches, and other organizations which had an interest in musical instruments. When a prospective customer visited the company, he would be assisted by one of the two salesmen. Although a number of the customers asked specifically to deal with Mr. Tenor, the proprietor did not actively solicit customers away from his salesmen. After a piano or organ was sold, it was tuned and delivered to the home of the purchaser. The smaller musical instruments or other merchandise were ordinarily carried by the customer. In order to minimize tuning expenses while giving professional service, Mr. Tenor employed a piano tuner on a piece basis. The tuner's services were usually required one or two days each week, and he received from $15 to $30 for tuning each instrument.

The music company permitted trade-ins on the new pianos and organs and frequently purchased used instruments which were advertised for sale. The used pianos and organs were either offered for resale at prices substantially below the new models or rented at monthly rates of from $5 to $10, depending upon the value of the instrument in question.

When a shipment of new pianos and organs arrived by rail, the two deliverymen would haul the merchandise to the music store, uncrate the items, dust and polish the instruments, and place them on the display floor. The average period of time that a piano remained in the inventory was about four months, but this varied with the price range of the items. The least expensive models turned over about every two months, while the expensive ones were on hand for four to six months. Although there was little demand for a grand piano, the owner kept one on display as an interest item. Although a grand would remain on display for perhaps two years

**EXHIBIT I**

**Best Music Company**
**Comparative Income Statements**

|  | 1960 | % | 1961 | % |
|---|---|---|---|---|
| Net sales (cash basis) | $164,505 | 100.0 | $149,152 | 100.0 |
| Cost of goods sold | 104,605 | 63.6 | 81,611 | 54.7 |
| Gross profit | $ 59,900 | 36.4 | $ 67,541 | 45.3 |
| Expenses : | — | — | — | — |
| Owner's compensation |  |  |  |  |
| Employees' wages | 12,358 | 7.5 | 19,751 | 13.2 |
| Occupancy expense | 3,844 | 2.3 | 3,750 | 2.5 |
| Advertising | 2,926 | 1.8 | 2,375 | 1.6 |
| Bad debt losses | — | — | — | — |
| Depreciation fixtures | 891 | 0.5 | 975 | 0.7 |
| All other expenses* | 20,349 | 12.4 | 24,300 | 16.3 |
| Total expenses | 40,368 | 24.5 | 51,151 | 34.3 |
| Net Profit before Income Tax | $ 19,532 | 11.9 | $ 16,390 | 11.0 |

*Tuner, Utilities, Telephone, Insurance, Auto—truck (exp., deprec.) $6200, Travel and entertainment, Legal and accounting fees, Office expense, Dues and subscriptions, Miscellaneous.

before it was sold, the profit was high. In addition, the grand was on continuous consignment and, therefore, required no investment in inventory. The other lines of pianos were sent to Mr. Tenor on sixty-day consignments. Upon the sale of an item or the expiration of the 60 days, the merchandise had to be purchased or returned to the manufacturer. Since the business was being operated on a small capital, the owner attempted to concentrate on items of rapid turnover and to minimize his holdings of slow-moving stock. Prudence and desire to meet customer demand, however, required that he maintain a fairly wide selection of merchandise which had appeal to various income groups. Other items were sold on terms of net 60.

Approximately 10 per cent of the dollar volume of sales was for cash, while the remainder was on an installment basis with a minimum 10 per cent down payment. The notes maturing in six months or less, which averaged about 10 per cent of sales, were carried by the store, and the remainder was discounted approximately equally between the bank and the piano manufacturer. The discounted notes were normally repayable in 24 equal installments and carried an add-on interest rate of 6 per cent per year. The company's bank purchased the notes at par on a recourse basis. This provided the company with an immediate flow of cash with which to pay for the pianos, organs, and the like and with which to cover its salesmen's commissions and other expenses.

In order to help finance its dealers, the piano manufacturer provided the music company with two types of credit. These were: (1) placing the merchandise on consignment for a period of sixty days; and (2) discounting customer notes. Mr. Tenor was permitted to keep the 10 per cent down

**EXHIBIT II**

**Best Music Company**
**Sales and Cash Receipts**

|  | 1960 | | 1961 | |
|---|---|---|---|---|
|  | Sales | Cash Receipts* | Sales | Cash Receipts* |
| January | $ 10,088 | $ 10,111 | $ 8,706 | $ 9,412 |
| February | 10,425 | 12,928 | 15,801 | 10,664 |
| March | 16,006 | 16,168 | 10,651 | 10,888 |
| April | 10,459 | 14,466 | 8,735 | 8,868 |
| May | 5,045 | 24,722 | 16,351 | 12,524 |
| June | 7,335 | 13,769 | 11,851 | 10,348 |
| July | 3,782 | 9,280 | 15,268 | 8,962 |
| August | 12,702 | 10,804 | 11,005 | 15,430 |
| September | 15,594 | 18,006 | 10,485 | 20,206 |
| October | 10,196 | 10,686 | 18,296 | 12,290 |
| November | 7,769 | 7,856 | 21,081 | 9,205 |
| December | 24,856 | 15,709 | 32,442 | 20,355 |
| Total | $134,257 | $164,505 | $180,672 | $149,152 |

*The company was on the cash basis of accounting for tax purposes.

payment, which paid the salesman's commission, 60 per cent of the selling price of the piano was maintained by the manufacturer to pay for the consigned items or returned to the music company where the merchandise had been purchased, and the balance of 30 per cent was maintained in an unrealized gross profit reserve with monthly payments being credited to the Best account. The interest rate of 6 per cent was passed on to the piano manufacturer.

**EXHIBIT III**

**Best Music Company**
**Development of Seasonal Index to Sales**

|  | 1958 | 1959 | 1960 | 1961 | Total | Monthly Index |
|---|---|---|---|---|---|---|
| January | $ 4,922 | $ 6,406 | $ 10,088 | $ 8,706 | $ 30,122 | 5.8% |
| February | 7,586 | 1,222 | 10,425 | 15,801 | 35,034 | 6.8% |
| March | 2,631 | 4,296 | 16,006 | 10,651 | 33,584 | 6.5% |
| April | 5,132 | 8,795 | 10,459 | 8,735 | 33,121 | 6.4% |
| May | 9,754 | 6,552 | 5,045 | 16,351 | 37,702 | 7.3% |
| June | 12,779 | 19,644 | 7,335 | 11,851 | 51,609 | 10.0% |
| July | 3,452 | 12,748 | 3,782 | 15,268 | 35,250 | 6.8% |
| August | 7,755 | 10,610 | 12,702 | 11,005 | 42,072 | 8.1% |
| September | 8,100 | 5,158 | 15,594 | 10,485 | 39,337 | 7.6% |
| October | 5,789 | 13,779 | 10,196 | 18,296 | 48,060 | 9.3% |
| November | 3,684 | 5,885 | 7,769 | 21,081 | 38,419 | 7.4% |
| December | 22,999 | 12,885 | 24,856 | 32,442 | 93,182 | 18.0% |
| Annual Total | $ 94,583 | $107,980 | $134,257 | $180,672 | $517,492 | 100.0% |

**EXHIBIT IV**

**Best Music Company**
**Forecast of Monthly Sales**

| 1962 | (a) | (b) | (c) | (d) |
|---|---|---|---|---|
| January | $ 10,875 | $ 13,050 | $ 14,500 | $ 18,125 |
| February | 12,750 | 15,300 | 17,000 | 21,250 |
| March | 12,187* | 14,625 | 16,250 | 20,312 |
| April | 12,000 | 14,400 | 16,000 | 20,000 |
| May | 13,688 | 16,425 | 18,250 | 22,813† |
| June | 18,750 | 22,500 | 25,000 | 31,250 |
| July | 12,750 | 15,300 | 17,000 | 21,250 |
| August | 15,188 | 18,225 | 20,250 | 25,313† |
| September | 14,250 | 17,100 | 19,000 | 23,750 |
| October | 17,437* | 20,925 | 23,250 | 29,062 |
| November | 13,875 | 16,650 | 18,500 | 23,125 |
| December | 33,750 | 40,500 | 45,000 | 56,250 |
| Annual Total | $187,500 | $225,000 | $250,000 | $312,500 |

*Rounded down
†Rounded up

Although local economic conditions were in somewhat of a slump in early 1962, Mr. Tenor believed it was in his best interest to relocate from his present place of business to a modern shopping area. In May, 1962 he received an offer of a 90-day option to purchase a 75 by 250 foot lot on a heavily travelled thoroughfare. The cost of the land was $750 per front foot, or $56,250. The option would cost $3,750, and Mr. Tenor had one week in which to accept or reject the offer. He estimated that a building which would meet the probable needs of the company for the next ten years could be designed and erected for a price of about $40,000. A small vacant store adjacent to the lot could be rented for $200 per month to provide additional warehousing space. The proposed store would have parking in front of and behind the building and would include a small auditorium for musical auditions.

Mr. Tenor made a visit to his bank loan officer, Mr. Mark Brand, and requested an eight-year term loan in the amount of $100,000 to cover the cost of the land and the proposed building. Although the Best Music Com-

**EXHIBIT V**

**Best Music Company**
**Balance Sheet (Selected Dates)**

| Assets | 6/30/61 | 6/30/60 | 6/31/57 |
|---|---|---|---|
| Current assets | | | |
| Cash | $ 8,071 | $ 6,447 | $ 2,105 |
| Accounts and notes receivable | 4,651 | 4,132 | — |
| Inventories (cost) | 13,125 | 13,075 | 1,292 |
| Stocks & Bonds (cost) | 2,160 | 875 | 938 |
| Life Ins. (cash-surr.) | 12,500 | 11,625 | — |
| Prepaid taxes and Ins. | 2,625 | — | — |
| Fixed assets | | | |
| Real estate (Resident) | 43,750 | 43,750 | 7,723 |
| Other personal property | 8,125 | 8,125 | — |
| Fixtures and equipment | 2,326 | 3,021 | 818 |
| Autos and trucks | 6,528 | 9,954 | 2,500 |
| Other assets | | | |
| Piano mfr's. reserve | 15,176 | 13,321 | — |
| Bank's reserve | 3,848 | 3,076 | 322 |
| Miscellaneous | — | 1,423 | — |
| Total assets | $122,885 | $118,824 | $ 15,698 |
| *Liabilities and capital* | | | |
| Current liabilities | | | |
| Accts. payable | $ 1,296 | $ 250 | — |
| Notes payable | 7,562 | 12,240 | 4,688 |
| Accrued taxes and expenses | 2,714 | 442 | 175 |
| Long-term: Mtgs. payable—real estate | 18,125 | 20,000 | — |
| Capital: Owner | 93,188 | 85,892 | 10,835 |
| Total liabilities | $122,885 | $118,824 | $ 15,698 |

pany had frequently borrowed up to $15,000 on a short-term basis and had made satisfactory repayments and had also discounted customers' install-ment notes on pianos, the banker was reluctant to grant an eight-year term loan equal to 100 per cent of the mortgage value of the property.

Mr. Brand did suggest, however, that the bank would consider the granting of a bank-SBA-participation term loan. Mr. Brand determined that the SBA had liberalized and simplified its participating loan procedure, and that where the bank was willing to initiate the loan, service the loan, and advance not less than 25 per cent of the total funds, the SBA would grant the balance of the funds. The SBA was charging an interest rate of $4\frac{1}{2}$ per cent to borrowers located within areas of high unemployment (the usual rate being $5\frac{1}{2}$ per cent), but permitted the bank to assess a higher rate of interest on its portion. As additional compensation for servicing the loan, the SBA was paying the participating bank $\frac{1}{2}$ per cent of the SBA's share of the loan principal per year.

Mr. Brand informed Mr. Tenor that it was the policy of the SBA to require that the loan be fully secured (the land and building would be adequate), that the loan be amortized monthly with equal retirement of principal plus interest, and that a decreasing term insurance policy in the amount of $100,000 be purchased by the borrower which named the bank and the SBA as joint beneficiaries. The SBA also insisted that the cash flow of the borrower from net profits and depreciation be adequate to service the debt retirement. Ten years was the maximum maturity for an SBA small business loan.

Interest rates were at relatively high levels in 1962, and Mr. Brand stated that the bank was willing to consider the loan request at an 8 per cent interest rate on their portion of the loan. The 75 per cent SBA partic-ipation would bear a rate of $4\frac{1}{2}$ per cent.

Mr. Brand requested that current financial statements, cash receipts and disbursement statements, and pro forma statements be prepared. Mr. Tenor believed that 1962 sales would be about 120 per cent of those for 1961 and that the trend would continue during the foreseeable future. The accountant prepared the requested statements which were to become a part of the loan application, which are shown in Exhibits I-IV.

Although property values had been increasing steadily since World War II, Mr. Tenor was not sure that this trend would continue. He was not certain whether renting or ownership was desirable for a small retailer. He realized, however, that he had to reach a decision within a week or lose the right to purchase the option on the tract of land. Since the option was for only ninety days, financing the building construction would have to be undertaken immediately.

## EXHIBIT VI
## Best Music Company
### Cash Receipts and Disbursement Schedule
### For 1962

| | Jan. | Feb. | Mar. | Apr. | May | June | July | Aug. | Sept. | Oct. | Nov. | Dec. |
|---|---|---|---|---|---|---|---|---|---|---|---|---|
| *Estimated Receipts* | | | | | | | | | | | | |
| From manufacturer (reserve 12/21/61 = $15,000) beginning of period | $1,500 | $1,438 | $1,375 | $1,312 | $1,250 | $1,188 | $1,125 | $1,062 | $1,000 | $938 | $875 | $812 |
| Cash sales (10% estimate) | 1,305 | 1,530 | 1,462 | 1,440 | 1,642 | 2,250 | 1,530 | 1,822 | 1,710 | 2,092 | 1,665 | 4,050 |
| Self-carried notes (6 mo. avg.) | | | | | | | | | | | | |
| Balance 12/31/61 = $5,250 assumed | 1,500 | 1,250 | 1,000 | 750 | 500 | 250 | | | | | | |
| (Assumed 10% of Sales) | | | | | | | | | | | | |
| January (1305) | 218 | 218 | 218 | 218 | 218 | 218 | | | | | | |
| February (1530) | | 234 | 234 | 234 | 234 | 234 | 234 | | | | | |
| March (1462) | | | 244 | 244 | 244 | 244 | 244 | 244 | | | | |
| April (1440) | | | | 240 | 240 | 240 | 240 | 240 | 240 | | | |
| May (1642) | | | | | 274 | 274 | 274 | 274 | 274 | 274 | | |
| June (2250) | | | | | | 375 | 375 | 375 | 375 | 375 | 375 | |
| July (1530) | | | | | | | 234 | 234 | 234 | 234 | 234 | 234 |
| August (1822) | | | | | | | | 304 | 304 | 304 | 304 | 304 |
| September (1710) | | | | | | | | | 285 | 285 | 285 | 285 |
| October (2092) | | | | | | | | | | 349 | 349 | 349 |
| November (1665) | | | | | | | | | | | 278 | 278 |
| December (4050) | | | | | | | | | | | | 675 |
| Notes discounted with bank (assumed 40% of sales) | 5,220 | 6,120 | 5,850 | 5,760 | 6,570 | 9,000 | 6,120 | 7,290 | 6,840 | 8,370 | 6,660 | 16,200 |
| Notes discounted with manufacturer | | | | | | | | | | | | |
| 10% down payment (40% sales) | 522 | 612 | 585 | 576 | 657 | 900 | 612 | 729 | 684 | 837 | 666 | 1,620 |
| (30% unrealized gross profit kept on reserve for monthly payments, other 60% = CGS paid to mfr.) | | | | | | | | | | | | |
| January | | 65 | 65 | 65 | 65 | 65 | 65 | 65 | 65 | 65 | 65 | 65 |

| | Jan. | Feb. | Mar. | Apr. | May | June | July | Aug. | Sept. | Oct. | Nov. | Dec. |
|---|---|---|---|---|---|---|---|---|---|---|---|---|
| February | | | 76 | 76 | 76 | 76 | 76 | 76 | 76 | 76 | 76 | 76 |
| March | | | | 74 | 74 | 74 | 74 | 74 | 74 | 74 | 74 | 74 |
| April | | | | | 72 | 72 | 72 | 72 | 72 | 72 | 72 | 72 |
| May | | | | | | 82 | 82 | 82 | 82 | 82 | 82 | 82 |
| June | | | | | | | 112 | 112 | 112 | 112 | 112 | 112 |
| July | | | | | | | | 76 | 76 | 76 | 76 | 76 |
| August | | | | | | | | | 90 | 90 | 90 | 90 |
| September | | | | | | | | | | 85 | 85 | 85 |
| October | | | | | | | | | | | 105 | 105 |
| November | | | | | | | | | | | | 84 |
| December | | | | | | | | | | | | — |
| Interest income (self-carried notes) est. | 75 | 75 | 62 | 62 | 50 | 50 | 50 | 50 | 50 | 50 | 50 | 50 |
| Expected Cash Receipts | $10,340 | $11,542 | $11,171 | $11,051 | $12,166 | $15,592 | $11,519 | $13,181 | $12,643 | $14,840 | $12,578 | $25,778 |
| Estimated Disbursements (assuming purchase) | | | | | | | | | | | | |
| Cost of goods sold (60% of sales × 60%)=36% | $ 4,700 | $ 5,508 | $ 5,265 | $ 5,184 | $ 5,912 | $ 8,100 | $ 5,508 | $ 6,561 | $ 6,156 | $ 7,532 | $ 5,994 | $14,580 |
| Wages | | | | | | | | | | | | |
| Commission (60% × 10%)=6% | 782 | 918 | 878 | 864 | 985 | 1,350 | 918 | 1,094 | 1,025 | 1,255 | 999 | 2,400 |
| Delivery, office salaries | 750 | 750 | 750 | 750 | 750 | 750 | 750 | 750 | 750 | 750 | 750 | 750 |
| Rent (Jan.-Aug.) | 312 | 312 | 312 | 312 | 312 | 312 | 312 | 312 | | | | |
| Loan retirement | | | | | | 833 | 833 | 833 | 833 | 833 | 833 | 833 |
| Interest on $100,000, 10 year, 5 3/8% loan | | | | | | 447 | 443 | 438 | 434 | 430 | 425 | 421 |
| Advertising | 250 | 250 | 250 | 250 | 250 | 250 | 250 | 250 | 250 | 250 | 250 | 250 |
| Other expenses (including life insurance) | | | | | | | | | | | | |
| Pro-rata (20,000) | 2,084 | 2,084 | 2,084 | 2,084 | 2,084 | 2,084 | 2,084 | 2,084 | 2,084 | 2,084 | 2,084 | 2,084 |
| Warehousing costs | | | | | | 200 | 200 | 200 | 200 | 200 | 200 | 200 |
| Personal withdrawals | | | | | | | | | | | | |
| Living expenses | 1,000 | 1,000 | 1,000 | 1,000 | 1,000 | 1,000 | 1,000 | 1,000 | 1,000 | 1,000 | 1,000 | 1,000 |
| Taxes (federal) | | | | | | 750 | | | 750 | | | 750 |
| Total cash disbursements | $ 9,878 | $10,822 | $10,539 | $10,444 | $11,293 | $16,076 | $12,298 | $13,522 | $13,482 | $14,334 | $12,535 | $23,268 |
| Receipts—disbursements | 462 | 720 | 632 | 607 | 873 | (484) | (779) | (341) | (839) | 506 | 43 | 2,510 |
| Cumulative Receipts Above Disbursements | $ 462 | $ 1,182 | $ 1,814 | $ 2,421 | $ 3,294 | $ 2,810 | $ 2,031 | $ 1,690 | $ 851 | $ 1,357 | $ 1,400 | $ 3,910 |

# Cash
# Forecasting

# 14

CAMPUS FEDERAL
CREDIT UNION

In October, 1963, the office manager of the Campus Federal Credit Union and the chairman of the investment committee were reviewing the cash position of the institution in an attempt to optimize the demand deposit balance and investment in shares of savings and loan associations.

Although the credit union had been in operation since 1939, it had experienced a great deal of growth in share and loan accounts during the years 1962 and 1963. At the end of September, 1963, the credit union had about 1,900 shareholders and about 1,100 borrowers. Loans receivable outstanding totalled $769,000 and shares aggregated $779,000 as shown by Exhibit IV.

The office was being operated by two full-time and one part-time employees. The volume of business was such that the employees were kept busy during the eight-hour, five-day week. Members of the board of directors, credit committee members, supervisory committee members, and other committee members were performing their duties without compensation. Other expenses were kept fairly low so that total operating expenses were running from 32 to 39 per cent of revenue.

The credit union had kept a high percentage of its assets invested in loans and had had relatively low loan losses. After increasing its reserve accounts by the required 20 per cent of profits, it had been able to pay a dividend of 4.8 per cent per year on share balances during the past three years and to accumulate a small amount of undivided profits.

The credit union was paying for credit insurance on its loans and term life insurance (up to $2,000 per account) on its share balances. The borrowers were paying about the same rate of interest that was being charged by banks. The rate being charged by the credit union was 1 per cent per month on loans of less than $2,000 and .8 per cent per month on loans of larger size or those which were secured by a pledge of credit union shares. The effective rates charged by banks or sales finance companies were ranging from 9.8 to 14 per cent, depending on the type and size of the loan. An extra charge was usually made by the latter types of financial institutions for credit insurance. The life insurance on shares was costing .5 per cent per year of the insured balances, so that the effective yield to the shareholder was 5.3 per cent per annum.

A majority of the members were making systematic, monthly payments through payroll deductions. Some $40,000 to $50,000 were deducted by the payroll department from the first-of-the-month payroll; a check for the total was sent to the credit union; and credit toward loan repayments and/or shares was given to each individual member. The check was then deposited in the FCU's demand deposit account, and loans were made against the balance during the next month. Other deductions from academic-year faculty and from bi-weekly payroll personnel were made at various times during the month (see Exhibit VI) totaling about $20,000 to $25,000. Similar

### EXHIBIT I

#### Campus Federal Credit Union
#### Selected Seasonal Indexes

| Month | Loans Extended | Loans Repaid | Share Debits | Share Credits |
|---|---|---|---|---|
| January | 53.5 | 83.3 | 166.9 | 117.2 |
| February | 89.6 | 90.2 | 71.4 | 99.6 |
| March | 93.5 | 101.3 | 73.4 | 94.1 |
| April | 97.9 | 96.6 | 94.8 | 84.1 |
| May | 126.3 | 98.9 | 82.8 | 98.9 |
| June | 121.3 | 104.9 | 55.2 | 117.2 |
| July | 118.5 | 126.2 | 222.2 | 116.9 |
| August | 143.8 | 124.9 | 148.5 | 100.9 |
| September | 85.2 | 87.4 | 84.4 | 87.8 |
| October | 87.0 | 96.5 | 84.5 | 93.9 |
| November | 86.2 | 89.9 | 47.0 | 89.7 |
| December | 97.2 | 99.9 | 68.9 | 99.7 |

### EXHIBIT II

#### Campus Federal Credit Union
#### Secular Trends

| Item | Index |
|---|---|
| Loans extended* | 150 |
| Loans repaid | 130 |
| Share debits | 140 |
| Share credits | 115 |

*Annual increase had been 50 per cent per year for the past five years.

procedures as outlined above were followed. The check was sometimes forwarded to the credit union within three days of the payroll date; however, it had been as much as ten days late. This had worked a hardship on the CFCU, as the bank balance was oftentimes a deficit near the end and beginning of each month.

Although the bank of deposit was honoring overdrafts, it charged $.75 per check on insufficient items. The credit union had paid as much as $15.00 for overdrafts per month during recent months, but desired to avoid this cost. The Campus Federal Credit Union officials, as well as the bank, had criticized the credit union for this overdraft practice.

The usual bank service charge was $1.00 per month plus $.05 per check written from six to 205 checks. The charges were reduced to $.04 per check for all above 205 checks issued in one month. A credit, equal to $.15 per $100 average balance, was given. The credit union issued between 300 and 400 checks per month.

When the demand deposit account built up to an unusually high figure,

**EXHIBIT III**

**Campus Federal Credit Union**

| | Month (1962-63) | Centered 12-Month Moving Total (1962-63) | Centered 12-Month Moving Average (1962-63) |
|---|---|---|---|
| Loans Extended | October | $1,021,098 | $85,092 |
| | November | 1,061,624 | 88,470 |
| | December | 1,061,970 | 88,498 |
| | January | 1,104,020 | 92,002 |
| | February | 1,135,138 | 94,595 |
| | March | 1,159,521 | 96,627 |
| Loans Repaid | October | 812,019 | 67,668 |
| | November | 844,417 | 70,368 |
| | December | 847,021 | 70,585 |
| | January | 877,822 | 73,152 |
| | February | 921,912 | 76,826 |
| | March | 939,883 | 78,323 |
| Share Debits | October | 286,859 | 23,905 |
| | November | 288,534 | 24,045 |
| | December | 292,938 | 24,412 |
| | January | 293,224 | 24,435 |
| | February | 318,543 | 26,545 |
| | March | 328,896 | 27,408 |
| Share Credits | October | 485,498 | 40,458 |
| | November | 490,577 | 40,881 |
| | December | 496,242 | 41,354 |
| | January | 493,582 | 41,132 |
| | February | 496,437 | 41,370 |
| | March | 498,154 | 41,513 |

as it did during the first three months of 1963, funds were invested in shares of savings and loan associations on which dividends of 4 or $4\frac{1}{2}$ per cent (annual rate) were paid on June 30 and December 31. Some $60,000 were transferred to local savings and loan associations early in April, 1963. Although some of the funds were needed in order to meet loan demands in May and June, it appeared more profitable to make a short-term loan from the savings and loan associations until after the dividend payment date. This type loan was made in the amount of $20,000 and was repaid in July, 1963.

Local commercial banks were competing with CFCU for consumer loans and were not eager to lend funds to the credit union. The local savings and loan associations, however, which were not making consumer loans, were willing to lend to the credit union. Rates on unsecured loans made to

**EXHIBIT IV**

**Campus Federal Credit Union**
**Comparative Balance Sheets**

| Assets | 9/30/63 | 6/30/63 | 12/31/62 | 6/30/62 |
|---|---|---|---|---|
| Loans | | | | |
| Delinquent | | | | |
| 2 months to 6 months | $ 1,773 | $ 4,747 | $ 4,709 | $ 1,111 |
| 6 months to 12 months | 4,825 | 4,742 | 2,882 | 3,059 |
| 12 months and over | 2,294 | 309 | 779 | 583 |
| Subtotals | 8,892 | 9,798 | 8,370 | 4,753 |
| Current and less than 2 mo. delinquent | 759,836 | 699,928 | 613,043 | 478,782 |
| Cash on hand and in bank | 19,038 | −13,255 | 23,237 | 2,480 |
| Bank savings account | — | — | 337 | — |
| U. S. Government obligations | | | | |
| Savings and loan shares | 28,470 | 128,072 | 71,388 | 109,988 |
| Loans to other credit unions | | | | |
| Furn., fixtures, and equip. | 3,355 | 3,119 | 3,495 | 3,797 |
| Prepaid insurance | 412 | 507 | 697 | 887 |
| Supplies | 278 | 268 | — | 100 |
| Total assets | $820,281 | $828,437 | $720,567 | $600,787 |
| Liabilities | | | | |
| Accounts payable | $ 77 | $ 77 | $ 77 | $ 77 |
| Notes payable | — | 15,000 | 20,000 | — |
| Withholding taxes payable | 460 | 338 | 315 | 255 |
| Soc. Security taxes payable | 193 | 148 | 105 | 107 |
| State withholding taxes pay. | 5 | 9 | 32 | 25 |
| Shares | 779,307 | 785,719 | 664,025 | 573,666 |
| Regular reserve | 19,810 | 15,374 | 11,762 | 8,896 |
| Spec. res. for delinquent loans | 500 | 500 | 500 | 500 |
| Undivided earnings | 6,866 | −10,746 | 2,648 | 2,648 |
| Gain or loss (current 6 mos.) | 13,063 | 22,018 | 21,103 | 14,613 |
| Total liabilities | $820,281 | $828,437 | $720,567 | $600,787 |

**EXHIBIT V**

**Campus Federal Credit Union**
**Comparative Income Statements**

|  | July—September 1963 | January—June 1963 | July—December 1962 | January—June 1962 |
|---|---|---|---|---|
| *Income* | | | | |
| Interest on loans | $18,950 | $32,540 | $28,137 | $22,125 |
| Income from investments | 406 | 1,343 | — | 1,648 |
| Other income | — | 11 | 3,504 | — |
| Total income | $19,356 | $33,894 | $31,641 | $23,773 |
| *Expenses* | | | | |
| Treasurer's salary | $   75 | $   150 | $   150 | $   125 |
| Other salaries | 2,795 | 4,548 | 3,878 | 3,554 |
| Borrowers' insurance | 1,306 | 2,242 | 1,964 | 1,493 |
| Life savings insurance | 1,039 | 1,936 | 1,688 | 1,449 |
| Surety bond premium | 95 | 190 | 190 | 190 |
| Examination fee | — | 681 | 631 | 50 |
| Supervision fee | — | 205 | — | 147 |
| Interest on borrowed money | 131 | 40 | 183 | — |
| Stationery and supplies | 206 | 446 | 397 | 745 |
| Collection expenses | — | — | — | 59 |
| Depreciation on fix. assts. | — | 375 | 303 | 266 |
| Social Security taxes | 96 | 170 | 114 | 106 |
| Other insurance | — | 22 | — | 15 |
| Recording fees, chattel lien insurance | −51 | 191 | 346 | 296 |
| Communications | 116 | 150 | 167 | 130 |
| Bank service charge | 149 | 50 | 48 | 21 |
| Notary costs | 250 | 299 | 395 | 350 |
| Misc. general expenses | 85 | 179 | 83 | 164 |
| Total expenses | $ 6,292 | $11,874 | $10,537 | $ 9,160 |
| Net earnings | $13,064 | $22,020 | $21,104 | $14,613 |

**EXHIBIT VI**

**Campus Federal Credit Union**
**Regular Payroll Deductions**
**Credited to Loan and Share Accounts**

| Dates Received | Type Payroll | Jan., 1963 | Apr., 1963 | July, 1963 | Oct., 1963 |
|---|---|---|---|---|---|
| 2–5 | Monthly (12 mo. pers.) | $39,400 | $40,400 | $45,400 | $47,600 |
| * | Bi-weekly payrolls | 6,200 | 6,600 | 6,800 | 7,300 |
|  | Bi-weekly payrolls | 6,200 | 6,600 | 6,400 | 7,300 |
|  | Bi-weekly payrolls | 6,200 | — | — | — |
| 15–19 | Academic faculty | 5,600 | 6,100 | — | 5,200 |

*Alternate Fridays beginning with January 11, 1963.

credit unions were about 6 per cent and about $5\frac{1}{2}$ per cent on loans secured by the savings and loan shares.

In October, 1963, the office manager was informed that she could draw advances against credit union payroll deductions up to $15,000. A check could be obtained on any payroll date and the amount would be deducted from the regular payroll deduction check payable to the credit union. By obtaining a part of the funds at the first and middle of the month, rather than three to ten days later, she felt that bank overdrafts could be reduced or eliminated.

In the event that the credit union's loan demand exceeded its funds available for lending, the union could borrow from other credit unions or other financial institutions at negotiated rates of interest.

Although the payroll advances would be helpful in minimizing cash balances, the office manager of CFCU believed that a six-month forecast of anticipated share and loan changes would prove helpful. The effect of these changes should then be traced to demand deposit balances, and some

### EXHIBIT VII

#### Campus Federal Credit Union
#### Investment in Savings and Loan Shares
#### September, 1962 Through September, 1963

| Date | Item | Debit | Credit | Balance |
|---|---|---|---|---|
| 9/1/62 | Balance | | | 69,988 |
| 12/31/62 | Dividends | 1,400 | | — |
| | Loan repayment + interest | | 20,021 | 51,367 |
| 1/31/63 | Deposit | 633 | | 52,000 |
| 3/31/63 | Deposit | 15,200 | | 67,200 |
| 4/30/63 | Deposit | 60,000 | | 127,200 |
| 6/30/63 | Dividends | 872 | | 128,072 |
| 7/1/63 | Share withdrawals | | 50,008 | 78,064 |
| 7/5/63 | Dividends | 406 | | 78,470 |
| 8/1/63 | Share withdrawals | | 50,000 | 28,470 |

### EXHIBIT VIII

#### Campus Federal Credit Union
#### Notes Payable
#### September, 1962 to September, 1963

| Date | Item | Debit | Credit | Balance |
|---|---|---|---|---|
| 9/1/62 | Balance | | | — |
| 11/30/62 | Loan secured with S & L shares | | 20,000 | 20,000 |
| 1/31/63 | Loan repayments | 20,000 | | — |
| 6/28/63 | Loans secured w/shares | | 15,000 | 15,000 |
| 7/31/63 | Loan repayments | 15,000 | | — |
| 8/9/63 | Bank loan (unsecured) | | 40,000 | 40,000 |
| 8/29/63 | Bank loan repayment | 40,000 | | — |

optimum demand deposit balance and temporary investment policies should be formulated.

In order to facilitate the preparation of the cash flow statement for the investment committee, the supervisory committee made a study of the share debits, share credits, loans extended, and loans repaid for the past five years. Seasonal indexes for these major types of cash inflows and outflows are given in Exhibit I. Loans extended were found to be at seasonal highs during the summer months, and loan repayments also were somewhat heavier from June through August than for other months. Because of the semiannual payment of dividends, share withdrawals (debits) were heavier in January and July than in other months. Share credits were higher in January, June, and July than in other months.

The supervisory committee had not detected a substantial cyclical effect upon cash inflows or outflows, primarily because of the tremendous secular growth rate in loans and deposits during the past five years. The general feeling of the chairmen of the supervisory and the investment committees was that loan demand declined slightly and repayments increased a small amount during a recession period. In late 1963, however, a continuation of the boom period was expected for at least another year. Neither of the financial officers were certain how long the upward growth trend would continue, but recent past trends appeared a better starting point than an outright guess. (See Exhibit II for the secular trends for the cash inflows and outflows.)

Two other factors appeared to aggravate the problem of attempting to forecast the cash inflows and outflows. The university personnel had received pay increases equivalent to about 10 per cent of their salaries beginning in September, 1963, and the effect of these pay increases upon borrowing and saving share balances was not known. In addition, the federal government was considering a personal tax cut in an approximate ratio of 20 to 25 per cent from the 1963 tax rates, and it was difficult to gauge just what effect a tax cut would have upon consumers' willingness to assume more debt, or upon the rate of savings and consumption of individuals who benefited from the tax reductions. Nevertheless, both of the committee chairmen believed that some attempt to forecast the cash inflows and outflows should be undertaken.

**APPENDIX A**

**Campus Federal Credit Union
Summary of Selected By-Laws
as of September 30, 1963**

*Shares held :* The maximum amount of shares which may be held by any one member shall be $10,000, or 2,000 shares. The minimum share balance shall not be less than $5.

*Share transfers :* Shares may be transferred from one member to another by written authorization. Shares may also be applied against loans.

*Interest rate on loans :* The interest rate on loans of less than $2,000 *shall be 1 per cent* per month. The rate on loans of greater than $2,000 or for which shares are pledged as collateral, shall be .8 per cent per month.

*Temporary investments :*  **Funds not required for general business purposes shall be invested in local savings and loan associations.** The executive committee, consisting of the president, vice-president, and the treasurer, may purchase and sell securities for the credit union, make loans to other credit unions, or borrow from other lending agencies.

*Late charge :*  **A late charge equal to 20 per cent of the interest due may be imposed upon payments which are more than five days past due.**

*Reserves :*  **At the end of June and December, the regular reserve account must be credited with not less than 20 per cent of the net profits for the period.** The remaining profits may be paid to shareholders on a share-month basis or accumulated as undivided profits.

*Type loans granted :*  **The maximum unsecured loan limit is $750, but shall not exceed one month's gross pay.** Loans secured by automobiles, furniture, credit union shares, or other acceptable collateral shall not exceed $5,000.

*Maximum terms :*  **Maximum terms shall not exceed sixty months ; new car financing shall not exceed thirty-six months ; used car financing, twenty-four months ; and single-payment loans, six months.**

*Repayment :*  **Repayment by payroll deduction is encouraged ; however, cash repayments are permitted.**

*Refinancing :*  **Refinancing, when deemed necessary and not unnecessarily risky to the credit union, may be permitted only after 50 per cent or more of a loan has been repaid.**

*Insurance :*  **Fire insurance must be carried by the borrower on homes or household items pledged.** Collision and comprehensive insurance must be carried on motor vehicles.

*Security :*  **Certificate of title, chattel mortgage, and so forth must be on file with the credit union for assets pledged as collateral for a loan.**

*Dividend payment on shares :*  **The rate of dividend payment on each whole $5 share is set by the board of directors of the credit union.** Dividends are paid on June 30 and December 31 of each year on the share-month balance of each account. (Example : For a share balance of 200, $5 shares from January-June, 1963, the semiannual dividend would be $0.2 × 200 shares per months × 6 months for a 4.8% dividend rate. Dividends per share per month equals $5.00 × .0480/12 = $.02. If the balance fell to $500 in June as a result of a share withdrawal, only one-half as much dividend would be credited to the account.) Dividends are not paid on fractional shares.

## Part III

# CAPITAL BUDGETING AND COST OF CAPITAL

The Security National Bank of Wichita, Kansas, was concerned with what to do about a potential purchase of a new IBM computer which could be used to replace the posting, monthly statement, payroll, and interest departments now operating in the bank. Using the new computer to replace the present posting machines and calculators would mean a drastic reduction in payroll in these departments. Normal employee attrition and job transfers would permit such a change without any need for discharging current employees.

The computer would cost $900,000. There would be additional costs of $50,000 for installation, $25,000 for transportation, and $25,000 for power lines and electrical work. The complete installation is expected to have a five-year useful life with a salvage value of 10 per cent of the computer's original cost. (The tax code calls for a ten-year life for tax purposes.) Depreciation is to be by the straight-line method, which is the method used by the bank for depreciating all of its assets. IBM's terms for the computer are $300,000 down and $300,000 at the end of the first and second years. The equipment that would be replaced by the computer has been fully depreciated, and the bank feels that it could be sold in the present favorable market for $50,000 net.

The bank officers estimate that the computer should save $325,000 a year before depreciation and taxes, but they realize this will be subject to the amount of business which the bank handles. In a conference, the bank officers decided that the following distribution would best reflect their estimates of the bank's activities and resulting savings for the next five years.

| Savings from Computer | Probability |
|---|---|
| 375 M | 10% |
| 325 M | 40% |
| 275 M | 30% |
| 225 M | 15% |
| 175 M | 5% |

The bank had only common stock outstanding. The liability side of the bank's balance sheet was as follows:

| | |
|---|---|
| Demand deposits | 60% |
| Time deposits | 30% |
| Capital stock, paid-in surplus and undivided profits | 10% |

The bank followed the usual pattern of charging for checking accounts; however, even so it found there is an additional expense to the bank of 1 per cent. The savings accounts earned a 4 per cent return on the average. The bank's earnings per share last year was $1, with a payout of 50 per cent. The growth of earnings per share and dividend have been 7 per cent per year for the last five years. The present market price of the stock is $15 and has not been subject to much fluctuation.

**QUESTION**

Do you recommend that the bank purchase this machine? What additional information would be of value in reaching a decision?

ABLES MANUFACTURING

Mr. James Ables, president of Ables Manufacturing, is considering the desirability of investing in a new capital addition. The asset has an initial cost of $10,000, an estimated life of four years, no salvage value, and is expected to produce $4,000 annual profit before depreciation or taxes. Mr. Ables has been told that new investments are not profitable unless the potential time-adjusted rate-of-return exceeds his weighted average cost of capital.

His capitalization plan calls for 20 per cent debt, 10 per cent preferred stock, and 70 per cent common equity at costs of 5 per cent, 6 per cent, and 15 per cent, respectively.

Mr. Ables has worked out a schedule showing the potential return on this project using the straight-line depreciation method, but he wonders whether the declining-balance method or the sum-of-the-years-digits method would produce different results.

**QUESTIONS**

1. Compute the weighted average cost of capital.

2. Compute the return using accelerated depreciation methods.

3. Should the investment be made?

**SCHEDULE I**

**Time-Adjusted Rate-of-Return Straight-Line Depreciation**

| Year | Income before Depr. | Depr. | Income after Depr. | Income Tax @ 50% | After-Tax Profits |
|------|------|------|------|------|------|
| 1 | 4,000 | 2,500 | 1,500 | 750 | 750 |
| 2 | 4,000 | 2,500 | 1,500 | 750 | 750 |
| 3 | 4,000 | 2,500 | 1,500 | 750 | 750 |
| 4 | 4,000 | 2,500 | 1,500 | 750 | 750 |
|   | 16,000 | 10,000 | 6,000 | 3,000 | 3,000 |

| Year | Cash Flow | 10% P. V. Factor | Discount | 12% P. V. Factor | Discount |
|------|------|------|------|------|------|
| 1 | 3,250 | .909 | 2,954 | .893 | 2,902 |
| 2 | 3,250 | .826 | 2,685 | .797 | 2,590 |
| 3 | 3,250 | .751 | 2,441 | .712 | 2,314 |
| 4 | 3,250 | .683 | 2,220 | .636 | 2,067 |
|   | 13,000 |   | 10,300 |   | 9,873 |

Rate=11.4 per cent

# Selecting Financing Methods

## 17

BOWL INN, INC.

In April, 1964, Mr. John Gimble and associates were considering the financial prudence of opening a twenty-lane bowling alley on a well-traveled boulevard. Mr. Gimble had been considering the merits of constructing his own building versus renting a vacant establishment. He also was uncertain as to the cheapest method for acquiring pinspotters: leasing, time-payment plan, or cash purchase. Mr. Gimble and his associates had $200,000 available for the investment and wished to earn at least an eight per cent annual return on their funds. If a lower return was probable, the associates did not want to commit their funds to this type business.

Mr. Gimble was thirty-six years of age and had been a night manager for a sixteen-lane alley for the past six years. He had read the available literature on the sport which had indicated that about 1,000 in population was needed for each bowling lane in order for the establishment to have a reasonable chance for financial success. He had also noted that some cities, such as Detroit, were supporting each bowling lane with an average of only 400 persons. Detroit was highly industrialized, however, and the auto assembly plant workers had formed more than 20,000 bowling teams. These teams, plus the outside practice of the team members, had attributed to a healthy climate for bowling establishments.

Mr. Gimble's home town already had four bowling alleys. The addition of another twenty-lane bowling alley would reduce the population to about 1,200 per lane. Although the presently operated alleys were not making spectacular profits, Mr. Gimble believed that through vigorous advertising another bowling center would prove successful. His city was heavily industrialized, a fact which attributed to the success of this venture if the management of the industrial firms

**111**

could be induced to encourage their employees to form bowling teams. A large number of young people also lived near the site of the proposed center. High school students appeared to be somewhat more interested in the sport than was true for older people. The center would be located about three miles from its nearest competitor.

Mr. Gimble has ascertained that a building suitable for his purpose could be rented for $1,500 per month. Off-the-street parking areas surrounding the building would accommodate about 50 cars. A vacant lot about 200 feet square could be purchased for $40,000 and a building constructed at a cost of $8 per square foot. Since a bowling alley requires about 1,000 square feet per lane, including office, snack bar, maintenance, and storage areas, the building cost would be approximately $160,000. It was estimated that $5,000 would be required for the construction of paved parking facilities. Additional annual costs associated with building ownership were as follows: fire insurance—$400; ad valorem taxes—$1,600; and building maintenance—$800.

Although some bowling enthusiasts were partial to Builtwell pinspotters, Mr. Gimble was more familiar with the operation of and maintenance on Ace pinspotters. Builtwell offered the equipment only on a cash or time-payment purchase plan and did not lease the pinspotters. The offering price was $8,300 per pinspotter plus sales tax of 3 per cent. Mr. Gimble believed that breakdowns in Builtwell pinspotters occurred less frequently than in Ace equipment, but that the repair time was much less for the latter. The time-payment terms were similar to those of Ace.

Ace offered its pinspotters under three plans: A cash payment of $8,600 each plus sales tax; a down payment of 25 per cent with 128 per cent of the balance amortized over 120 months (effective interest rate of about $5\frac{1}{2}$ per cent); or a ten-year lease with the rent being computed on the lines bowled. The annual rent of each pinspotter was $.10 per line up to $1,000; $.08 per line on the next 5,000 games; and $.06 per game on additional lines. An installation fee of $500 per pinspotter was assessed under the leasing arrangement. Under either the lease or ownership plans, the bowling house was responsible for maintenance. When Ace pinspotters were leased, however, a monthly Ace maintenance man called on the firm, inspected the equipment, and checked the inventory of spare parts. In the event the pinspotters had to be replaced, one week had proven adequate during Mr. Gimble's prior experience.

Other bowling alley equipment, such as the lanes, seats, score table, lockers, balls, shoes, pins, and so forth, would require an initial outlay of about $5,500 per lane. Vending machines and pinball machines were available on a concession basis. The bowling alley would receive 20 per cent of the revenue from the machines while the owner would provide the vending machines, products, servicing, and so forth. The cost of establishing a concession stand and equipping an office was estimated at $10,000. If the building were leased rather than built, an additional $10,000 renovation expense would be incurred.

Mr. Gimble had contacted several savings and loan associations and insurance companies about a loan for erecting the building. The most favorable terms he received was a twenty-year loan for 50 per cent of the cost of the land and building at a 7 per cent rate. Although the rate appeared to Mr. Gimble to be a bit high, the loan officers rated bowling establishments as high-risk ventures. The building would have an estimated useful life of forty years; the pinspotters would be amortized over ten years with a 10 per cent salvage value; and the other equipment would have an estimated life of five years.

Under either of the alternatives, lease or ownership, Mr. Gimble believed that the establishment could be opened for business by October 1, 1964. (Note: The leasing year of Ace equipment started with that date.) Mr. Gimble's estimates of games bowled per lane were 10,000 during the first year; 11,000 during the second year; 12,000 the third year; and 12,500 per year thereafter.

The charge for bowling was fairly well established in most communities: $.50 per game after 6 P.M.; $.45 per game from 6 A.M. to 6 P.M.; and $.35 for students or junior league members. Mr. Gimble's experience had indicated that the above rate schedule would produce an average of $.42 per game. A charge of $.15 for the use of shoes by each player was standard. Experience had indicated that about one-third of the players provided their own shoes and bowling balls and that the average customer bowled three games. This increased the average revenue to $.45 1/3 per line. Profits from vending machines and the concession stand were expected to be $.10 per player. An additional profit of $20,000 per year was expected from the sale of sporting goods. Mr. Gimble's estimates of variable operating expenses as per cents of bowling revenue were as follows: labor, 30 per cent; repairs, 1.5 per cent; advertising, 2.5 per cent; and other (including utilities, communications, travel, normal replacement of balls, pins, and so forth), 16 per cent. The cost of the pinspotters and housing would depend upon the decision as to whether to lease or purchase.

In addition to the funds needed to finance the acquisition of fixed assets, Mr. Gimble believed that $10,000 for working capital, including spare parts, would be adequate. He had committed his entire $20,000 savings to the venture, but he believed his associates would be willing to advance an additional $50,000 on a loan basis if the need were to arise in the future.

In order to open the establishment by October 1, 1964, Mr. Gimble needed to reach a decision within a few weeks as to the probable profitability of the venture; whether the firm should rent or buy a building; and whether to lease or buy its pinspotters.

Because of the limited amount of funds available to the enterprise, Mr. Gimble prepared Exhibit II in order to determine which of the possible combinations were feasible. He determined that the firm, with its limited access to capital, could use the following combinations: (1) rent the building, and purchase the Ace pinspotters on installment terms; (2) rent the building and lease Ace pinspotters; and (3) rent the building and obtain Builtwell pinspotters on cash terms. Although he did not have access to an amortization schedule, showing principal and interest payments under the installment-purchase plan, he decided that an estimate of interest payments based on a sum-of-the-years-digits method would yield adequate results. Under this method, he would use 10/55 of the total interest in the first year, 9/55 in the second year, and so forth through the ten-year period.

He believed that a discounted cash flow computation of the cash outflows and cash inflows for the three methods which appeared feasible should be prepared and contrasted, using the 8 per cent discount factor, to see which of the methods produced the largest excess present value of cash inflows over cash outflows.

## QUESTIONS

1. Study Exhibit III carefully and prepare similar schedules for Plan 3 and Plan 5. Which of the three is preferable?
2. What other items should be considered before reaching a decision about the business venture?

### EXHIBIT I

**Bowl Inn, Inc.**
**Estimate of Revenue and Variable Expenses**
**For the First Ten Years of Operations**

|  | 1st | 2nd | 3rd | 4th–10th |
|---|---|---|---|---|
| Estimate of games | 200,000 | 220,000 | 240,000 | 250,000 |
| Income per game | $ .45 1/3 | $.45 1/3 | $ .45 1/3 | $ .45 1/3 |
| Bowling revenue | 90,700 | 99,700 | 108,800 | 113,300 |
| Profits on vending machines, concession stand | 6,700 | 7,300 | 8,000 | 8,300 |
| Profits on sale of sporting goods | 20,000 | 20,000 | 20,000 | 20,000 |
|  | $117,400 | $127,000 | $136,800 | $141,600 |
| Variable expenses |  |  |  |  |
| (% of bowling revenue) |  |  |  |  |
| Labor          30.0% |  |  |  |  |
| Repairs         1.5% |  |  |  |  |
| Advertising      2.5% |  |  |  |  |
| Other          16.0% |  |  |  |  |
| Total          50.0% | 45,350 | 49,850 | 54,400 | 56,650 |
| Profit before expenses associated with building, pinspotters, other assets | $ 72,050 | $ 77,150 | $ 82,400 | $ 84,950 |

**EXHIBIT II**

**Comparative Cash Outlays for Various
Financing Plans for the
Bowl Inn, Inc.**

| | | Initial Cash Outlays | | |
|---|---|---|---|---|
| Plan Combination | Building | Pinspotters | Other | Total |
| 1. Rent building, cash terms on Ace pinspotters | 10,000 | 117,160 | 130,000 | 317,160 |
| 2. Rent building, installment terms on Ace pinspotters | 10,000 | 44,290 | 130,000 | 184,290* |
| 3. Rent building, lease Ace pinspotters | 10,000 | 10,000 | 130,000 | 150,000* |
| 4. Rent building, cash terms on Builtwell pinspotters | 10,000 | 170,980 | 130,000 | 310,980 |
| 5. Rent building, inst. terms on Builtwell pinspotters | 10,000 | 42,745 | 130,000 | 182,745* |
| 6. Own building, cash terms on Ace pinspotters | 102,500 | 177,160 | 130,000 | 409,660 |
| 7. Own building, inst. terms on Ace pinspotters | 102,500 | 44,290 | 130,000 | 276,790 |
| 8. Own building, lease Ace pinspotters | 102,500 | 10,000 | 130,000 | 242,500 |
| 9. Own building, cash terms on Builtwell pinspotters | 102,500 | 170,980 | 130,000 | 403,480 |
| 10. Own building, inst. terms on Builtwell | 102,500 | 42,745 | 130,000 | 275,245 |

*Feasible with available funds.

**EXHIBIT III**

**Bowl Inn, Inc.**

**Present Value of Net Cash Flows—Plan #2**

| Cash inflows | 1 | 2 | 3 | 4 | 5 | 6 | 7 | 8 | 9 | 10 | Total |
|---|---|---|---|---|---|---|---|---|---|---|---|
| Profit before fixed asset expenses | $72,050 | $77,150 | $82,400 | $84,950 | $84,950 | $84,950 | $84,950 | $84,950 | $84,950 | $84,950 | $826,250 |
| **Expenses** | | | | | | | | | | | |
| Rent | 18,000 | 18,000 | 18,000 | 18,000 | 18,000 | 18,000 | 18,000 | 18,000 | 18,000 | 18,000 | 180,000 |
| Amort. of leasehold improvement | 1,000 | 1,000 | 1,000 | 1,000 | 1,000 | 1,000 | 1,000 | 1,000 | 1,000 | 1,000 | 10,000 |
| Deprec. of pinspotters* | 15,944 | 15,944 | 15,944 | 15,944 | 15,944 | 15,944 | 15,944 | 15,944 | 15,944 | 15,944 | 159,440 |
| Deprec. of other fixed assets* | 24,000 | 24,000 | 24,000 | 24,000 | 24,000 | 24,000 | 24,000 | 24,000 | 24,000 | 24,000 | 240,000 |
| Interest expense | 6,764 | 6,088 | 5,411 | 4,735 | 4,059 | 3,382 | 2,706 | 2,029 | 1,353 | 676 | 37,203 |
| Total Expenses | 65,708 | 65,032 | 64,355 | 63,679 | 63,003 | 62,326 | 61,650 | 60,973 | 60,297 | 59,620 | 626,643 |
| Before-tax profits | 6,342 | 12,118 | 18,045 | 21,271 | 21,947 | 22,624 | 23,300 | 23,977 | 24,653 | 25,330 | 199,607 |
| Federal taxes at 22% | (1,395) | (2,665) | (3,970) | (4,680) | (4,828) | (4,977) | (5,126) | (5,275) | (5,424) | (5,573) | (43,913) |
| Investment credit | | | | | | | | | | | |
| Pins: 177,160 at 7% = 12,401 + 2,800 | 1,395 | 2,665 | 3,970 | 4,680 | 2,491 | — | — | — | — | — | 15,201 |
| Other: 120,000 at $2\frac{1}{3}$% = 2,800 | — | — | — | — | — | 2,800 | — | — | — | — | 2,800 |
| Profits after Taxes | 6,342 | 12,118 | 18,045 | 21,271 | 19,610 | 20,447 | 18,174 | 18,702 | 19,229 | 19,757 | 173,695 |
| Working capital, salvage recovery | — | — | — | — | — | — | — | — | — | 27,715 | 27,715 |
| Depreciation, amortization | 40,944 | 40,944 | 40,944 | 40,944 | 40,944 | 40,944 | 40,944 | 40,944 | 40,944 | 40,944 | 409,440 |
| Cash inflows | 47,286 | 53,062 | 58,989 | 62,215 | 60,554 | 61,391 | 59,118 | 59,646 | 60,173 | 88,416 | 610,850 |
| P.V. factor (8%) | .92593 | .85734 | .79383 | .73503 | .68058 | .63017 | .58349 | .54027 | .50025 | .46319 | |
| P.V. of cash inflows | $43,784 | $45,922 | $46,827 | $45,730 | $41,212 | $38,687 | $34,495 | $32,225 | $30,102 | $40,953 | $399,937 |
| **Cash outflows** | | | | | | | | | | | |
| Initial ..............184,290 | | | | | | | | | | | 184,290 |
| Prin. repayment | 10,247 | 10,923 | 11,599 | 12,275 | 12,951 | 13,627 | 14,303 | 14,979 | 15,655 | 16,331 | 132,890 |
| Asset replacement | — | — | — | — | — | 120,000 | — | — | — | — | 120,000 |
| Total cash outflows ..184,290 | 10,247 | 10,923 | 11,599 | 12,275 | 12,951 | 133,627 | 14,303 | 14,979 | 15,655 | 16,331 | 437,180 |
| P.V. factor (8%) ....1.00000 | .92593 | .85734 | .79383 | .73503 | .68058 | .63017 | .58349 | .54027 | .50025 | .46319 | — |
| P.V. cash outflows....184,290 | $9,488 | $9,365 | $9,208 | $9,022 | $8,814 | $84,208 | $8,346 | $8,093 | $7,831 | $7,564 | $346,229 |

*Straight-line method preferred because of the corporate income tax schedule.

# Differential
# Cash
# Flows

# 18

Progress on construction of the Rente High Apartments had been rapid through the spring and early summer of 1965. The shell had been erected and as of June 25, construction was being temporarily slowed awaiting a decision on whether a gas or an electric air conditioning system would be used in the building.

In September, 1952, Cameron Realty of Austin, Texas had purchased, for speculative purposes, a vacant lot located three blocks southwest of the University of Texas. Two years later, as the University grew, a parking problem developed around the campus owing to the increasing number of students—with automobiles—enrolling in the college. Taking advantage of this development, Cameron Realty had converted the lot into parking facilities by leveling and surfacing the ground and hiring a retired serviceman to collect fees. This arrangement had provided the company with a 5 per cent return on its investment, and the lot had consequently remained undeveloped over the years. However, with the continued rise in enrollment of the University and the increasing trend toward apartment living among the students, Mr. Cameron had decided that a more favorable return could be achieved through the construction of an apartment building on the lot.

Rente High Apartments was subsequently designed to be the ultimate in fashionable luxury. It would contain 215 units ranging in rent from approximately $200 to $400 per month with all utilities paid. The apartments would be conveniently located and ultra-modern with all the luxuries of central heating and air conditioning, separate patios, heated swimming pool, built-in kitchens, and deep-pile carpets. Demand for accommodations in this price range had been exceedingly strong among the students, and all indications were that there would be a waiting list of people desiring to move in.

In order to have the apartments available for occupancy by fall, construction had begun early in the spring, even though all plans were not complete, including the type of air conditioning system to be used. In line with the "fashionable luxury" theme, Mr. Cameron had decided that all utilities would be paid by the company, and thus he was vitally concerned in the costs of air conditioning. Two types of air conditioning systems were available. One utilized electricity and the other gas. Mr. Cameron was well aware of the fact that an electric system would cost less initially but would have higher operating costs compared to a gas system, but he was uncertain as to which would be the most advantageous in this specific building.

Consulting with the engineers at the local gas company and the city power and light department, Mr. Cameron received reports that considered basically equivalent gas and electric systems and used the same monthly consumption figures for gas, electricity, and water, but arrived at diametrically opposed solutions. After reviewing the reports thoroughly (see exhibits), Mr. Cameron thought that he had the necessary data to evaluate the two systems himself.

The total cost of the installed units would be $155,930 for the gas and $119,520 for the electric unit plus the cost of wiring the units at $30 per horsepower. Both units would have an estimated life of fifteen years with no salvage value and a double-declining-balance method of depreciation over eight years would be allowed by the Internal Revenue Service.

The city electric rates were based on both the amount of electrical energy consumed (KWH) and the peak power demand (KW) as follows:

| | |
|---|---|
| 6.0¢/KWH for the first | 50 KWH |
| 3.5¢/KWH for the next | 550 KWH |
| 2.7¢/KWH for the next | 2400 KWH* |
| 1.2¢/KWH for the next | 5000 KWH* |
| 0.6¢/KWH for all additional | KWH |

Thus, the monthly electric bill for the electric system with a peak power demand of 788 KW (see Exhibit II) would be $2,337.29 for the first 120,320 KWH plus 0.6¢ per additional KWH of energy consumed. The bill for the gas system with a peak power demand of only 188 KW would be $680.18 for the first 35,340 KWH plus 0.6¢ per additional KWH as developed in Exhibit IV.

The water rate was 30¢ per 1,000 gallons including the necessary treatment, and the monthly gas rate was on a sliding scale as follows:

---

*Add 100 KWH for each KW of peak power demand from 20 to 100 KW, and 70 KWH for each KW of peak power demand over 100 KW.

| First | 300 MCF/Mo. @ $0.34/MCF |
| Next | 700 MCF/Mo. @ $0.32/MCF |
| Next | 1000 MCF/Mo. @ $0.28/MCF |
| All addtnl. | MCF/Mo. @ $0.25/MCF |

Property taxes were expected to be 2.88 per cent and insurance 0.20 per cent of the initial investment annually on the air conditioning system. Mr. Cameron felt that the operating labor would be about the same for the life of both systems as would the maintenance expense for the first ten years. However, he felt that the electric unit with its far greater number of moving parts would require $200 more per year during the last five years of its life.

### EXHIBIT I

#### Initial Investment Estimate

| | | Gas | Electric |
|---|---|---|---|
| 1. | Chillers installed | $ 66,000 | $ 59,500 |
| 2. | Cooling towers | 18,900 | 11,400 |
| 3. | Boilers | 42,000 | 29,000 |
| 4. | Condenser water piping | 11,500 | 10,000 |
| 5. | Condenser water pumps | 3,730 | 2,360 |
| 6. | Steam and condensate piping | 6,500 | 2,360 |
| 7. | Misc. drains, traps, and pumps | 1,200 | 600 |
| 8. | Insulation | 3,500 | 2,000 |
| 9. | Condensate receiver and pumps | 2,600 | 2,300 |
| | | $155,930 | $119,520 |

### EXHIBIT II

#### Equipment Power Specifications

| Gas Air Conditioning System | Peak Power Demand |
|---|---|
| 2— 40 HP cooling tower fans | 67.44 KW |
| 2— 25 HP condensate water pumps | 42.80 |
| 2— 30 HP chilled water pumps | 50.60 |
| 2—  1 HP condensate pumps | 1.88 |
| 4—  2 HP chiller aux. | 18.12 |
| Total | 180.84 KW |

| Electric Air Conditioning System | Peak Power Demand |
|---|---|
| 2—404 HP compressors | 660.00 KW |
| 2— 25 HP cooling tower fans | 42.90 |
| 2— 30 HP condensate water pumps | 34.30 |
| 2— 30 HP chilled water pumps | 50.60 |
| 2—1/3 HP chiller aux. | 0.65 |
| Total | 788.45 KW |

Using Cameron Realty's extensive holdings in land and buildings in the city as collateral, Mr. Cameron had been able to borrow the entire capital amount necessary from a trust company. The interest rate would be $5\frac{1}{2}$

**EXHIBIT III**

**Monthly Consumption Data Worksheet**

| Electric | | | | Gas | |
|---|---|---|---|---|---|
| — | MCF | January | | 2,889 | MCF |
| 170,742 | KWH | | | 80,175 | KWH |
| 750 | M GAL | | | 1,495 | M GAL |
| — | MCF | | | 3,438 | MCF |
| 195,295 | KWH | February | | 86,560 | KWH |
| 814 | M GAL | | | 1,621 | M GAL |
| — | MCF | | | 4,779 | MCF |
| 263,946 | KWH | March | | 111,665 | KWH |
| 1,063 | M GAL | | | 2,120 | M GAL |
| — | MCF | | | 6,215 | MCF |
| 324,329 | KWH | April | | 123,386 | KWH |
| 1,216 | M GAL | | | 2,423 | M GAL |
| — | MCF | | | 8,508 | MCF |
| 414,697 | KWH | May | | 134,376 | KWH |
| 1,433 | M GAL | | | 2,857 | M GAL |
| — | MCF | | | 9,571 | MCF |
| 449,339 | KWH | June | | 130,341 | KWH |
| 1,488 | M GAL | | | 2,968 | M GAL |
| — | MCF | | | 10,756 | MCF |
| 495,323 | KWH | July | | 134,725 | KWH |
| 1,601 | M GAL | | | 3,193 | M GAL |
| — | MCF | | | 10,592 | MCF |
| 489,307 | KWH | August | | 134,544 | KWH |
| 1,588 | M GAL | | | 3,167 | M GAL |
| — | MCF | | | 9,085 | MCF |
| 431,506 | KWH | September | | 129,798 | KWH |
| 1,488 | M GAL | | | 2,888 | M GAL |
| — | MCF | | | 6,884 | MCF |
| 352,530 | KWH | October | | 128,738 | KWH |
| 1,294 | M GAL | | | 2,580 | M GAL |
| — | MCF | | | 4,152 | MCF |
| 230,081 | KWH | November | | 97,784 | KWH |
| 935 | M GAL | | | 1,864 | M GAL |
| — | MCF | | | 3,514 | MCF |
| 204,782 | KWH | December | | 94,404 | KWH |
| 884 | M GAL | | | 1,766 | M GAL |
| — | MCF | | | 80,383 | MCF |
| 4,021,877 | KWH | Totals | | 1,386,496 | KWH |
| 14,514 | M GAL | | | 28,942 | M GAL |

**EXHIBIT IV**

**Development of Electric and Gas Service Rates**

---

**Electric Air Conditioning System—788 KW power demand**

| KW | KWH @ 2.7¢ | KWH @ 1.2¢ |
|---|---|---|
| | 2,400 | 5,000 |
| 80 × 100 | 8,000 | 8,000 |
| 688 × 70 | 48,160 | 48,160 |
| | 58,560 | 61,160 |

| | Rate | Cost |
|---|---|---|
| First | 50 KWH @ 6.0¢ | 3.00 |
| Next | 550 KWH @ 3.5¢ | 19.25 |
| Next | 58,560 KWH @ 2.7¢ | 1,581.12 |
| Next | 61,160 KWH @ 1.2¢ | 733.92 |
| Additional | — @ 0.6¢ | — |
| | 120,320 KWH | $2,337.29 |

**Gas air conditioning system—188 KW power demand**

| KW | KWH @ 2.7¢ | KWH @ 1.2¢ |
|---|---|---|
| | 2,400 | 5,000 |
| 80 × 100 | 8,000 | 8,000 |
| 80 × 70 | 5,670 | 5,670 |
| | 16,070 | 18,670 |

| | Rate | Cost |
|---|---|---|
| First | 50 KWH @ 6.0¢ | $ 3.00 |
| Next | 550 KWH @ 3.5¢ | 19.25 |
| Next | 16,070 KWH @ 2.7¢ | 433.89 |
| Next | 18,670 KWH @ 1.2¢ | 224.04 |
| Additional | — KWH @ 0.6¢ | — |
| | 35,340 KWH | $680.18 |

---

per cent annually on the unpaid balance, and Mr. Cameron planned to repay the principal plus interest in ten equal annual installments.*

---

*The initial cost information was given to Mr. Cameron by the same company. The operating information was supplied by an expert from the local gas company. We should note that relative operating advantages of gas might be less if the system did not operate at capacity. While it was possible to get a more detailed analysis in this respect which might have shown both gas and electric units to operate at similar costs, Mr. Cameron did not feel the additional information was worth the cost of collection.

**EXHIBIT V**

**Plans of Repayment at $5\frac{1}{2}\%$**
**Gas System**

| End of Year | Interest Due | Year-End Payment | Money Owed After Year-End Payment |
|---|---|---|---|
| 0 | | | 161,930 |
| 1 | 8,906 | 21,483 | 149,353 |
| 2 | 8,214 | | 136,084 |
| 3 | 7,485 | | 122,086 |
| 4 | 6,715 | | 107,318 |
| 5 | 5,902 | | 91,737 |
| 6 | 5,046 | | 75,300 |
| 7 | 4,141 | | 57,958 |
| 8 | 3,188 | | 39,663 |
| 9 | 2,181 | | 20,361 |
| 10 | 1,122 | | 0 |

**Electric System**

| End of Year | Interest Due | Year-End Payment | Money Owed After Year-End Payment |
|---|---|---|---|
| 0 | | | 148,880 |
| 1 | 8,188 | 19,758 | 137,310 |
| 2 | 7,552 | | 125,104 |
| 3 | 6,887 | | 112,233 |
| 4 | 6,178 | | 98,648 |
| 5 | 5,426 | | 84,316 |
| 6 | 4,638 | | 69,196 |
| 7 | 3,806 | | 53,244 |
| 8 | 2,929 | | 36,414 |
| 9 | 2,003 | | 18,659 |
| 10 | 1,027 | | 0 |

## Cost
## of
## Capital

## 19

On February 1, 1964, Mr. John F. Thomas, treasurer of American Grain Co., was preparing a report on the company's cost of capital. His initial calculation had given him innumerable conceptual difficulties, and he was not sure his report would be given any attention. The general feeling among management was that the cost of capital concept was theoretically interesting, and, when it applied to cut-off points, that it gave a starting point for making decisions. But, since it could not be determined within rather narrow confines, refinements in measurement techniques were unimportant and should be left to academicians.

Mr. Thomas had recently become treasurer. Although he had been with the company twenty-five years, starting in the accounting and controlling area, he maintained a primary interest in finance. He had a degree from the University of Rochester, and since his graduation he had attended numerous seminars and other courses throughout the country in the area of finance and management; thus, he was well versed in the area of cost of capital.

**History**

AMERICAN GRAIN CO.

The company was organized in 1918 as the Nelson Feed Company. The company quickly expanded and by 1926 had gone into the growing and processing of grain. During this period the name was changed to the American Grain Company, and the corporate officers were moved to Buffalo, New York. The company's product line slowly changed over time so that by 1964 the principal product of the company was soya beans. The company grew soya beans both in the United States and overseas. It processed the beans and merchandised products such as margarine, Soya Delight, breakfast cereal, and various other grain-oriented products. Most of the processed products were sold overseas, particularly in Egypt and Italy. The company was fully integrated, for it owned ships used on the Great Lakes, port facilities, warehouse plants, and grain elevators. In addition, the company had recently purchased controlling interest in a medium-sized Buffalo bank.

Government regulation of agriculture and increased competition from other processors had first caused American Grain to enter the foreign market in 1948. Since that time sales had built up steadily. Some 13,000 of the firm's 24,000 employees were located in Southern Europe and Northern Africa. Until recently this area had also produced a handsome profit for the company, but the inability of the Common Market to get France to lower agriculture tariffs had resulted in a much lower profit margin for the firm's products. The present situation did not appear likely to change for a few years. In Egypt, the company had recently written down much of its investments to their present worth. These two situations caused American Grain to reduce its dividend in 1963.

### Cost of Capital Calculation

While making up the report on cost of capital, several questions occurred to Mr. Thomas. First, he wondered whether the present capital structure of American Grain led to the lowest possible cost of capital. He realized that this problem was integrally involved in the question of leverage. Although the company could perhaps increase its debt, the real problem seemed to be too much capital in relation to the amount of sales and profits. The present earnings on invested assets was 2.9 per cent. This percentage was the lowest in the company's recent history. The make-up of the current assets was such that the firm obviously had more current assets than was really necessary for the general operation and well-being of the firm. Mr. Thomas, therefore, thought that the firm might be overcapitalized and wondered what effect this would have on the cost of capital.

Another question he considered was how the cost of capital changed over time. If the cost of capital of American Grain was at one rate today and another three years from now, then certain projects acceptable today might or might not be acceptable in the future. Thus he thought that the cost of capital might perforce have to be a constant. A third problem that he considered was the marginal nature of the cost of capital. He recognized that the weighted-average method gave an average value rather than a marginal value; and yet he realized that the more capital a firm used in its expansion, the greater the expected cost of funds. Thus, he recognized that the number of projects available in any one year would directly affect the cost of capital. He did not know, however, how he could inject this problem into his calculations for a uniform cut-off point.

Mr. Thomas decided that he would use the weighted-average method for calculating cost of capital. He recognized that certain authors had used other methods; however, he felt that in general all the pertinent literature available today depended on the weighted-average method. Thus, the two problems he faced were, first, determining the amounts that would be used in debt and equity; and, second, determining the cost of each group.

Considering the attitude of the board of directors with regard to expansion and the company's present capital structure, the company was not likely to go to the market for funds in order to expand in the near future. As a result, all expansion would be internally financed. Thus, the present structure, with long-term debt of approximately 15 per cent of total liabilities, seemed appropriate. Still he wondered about the problem of the sinking funds. As sinking-fund payments were paid each year, the amount of the long-term debt would continue to decrease. If the firm did not go to the capital market, long-term debt as a percentage of total liabilities would drop to as little as ten per cent within the next two or three years.

To determine the cost of the long-term debt, he examined the present debt structure. The costs of flotation in the past had been considerably lower than they would be at the present time. He believed that if the company were to attempt to float a bond issue in the present market, the new issue would carry a rate of between 4 3/4 and 5 per cent and would have a sinking fund. He believed that such a bond rate was consistent with a Ba rating by Moody's or Standard and Poor's. He wondered, however, how appropriate such a rate would be considering the company never planned to go to the bond market, at least in the immediate future.

While calculating the cost of common stock and retained earnings, however, Mr. Thomas found himself faced with numerous possibilities. Exhibit I shows his solution to the cost of common stock. From the graph he found a relationship between the price of stock and the earnings. He found that if he were to take out the years of low earnings, that the earnings tended to vary closely with price and that the investors seemed to be willing to maintain a ten-to-one price earnings ratio. When earnings dropped, this price earnings ratio rose considerably. But in normal times, it remained at about ten-to-one. Thus he thought that the cost of common stock could be considered as ten per cent.

He realized, however, that the price of the stock was influenced by a very narrow market. There were only 4,000 stockholders, and on a typical day only 1,000 shares were traded. An examination of the stockholders indicated that the majority of stock was held by a single family, the Nelson family. Since this stock was not traded, it acted to reduce the number of shares available in the market as well as the number of stockholders. Mr. Thomas wondered if the stock was selling at a depressed price because of the narrowness of this market.

Further, he had noted that the price of the stock dropped precipitously as a result of the reduction in dividends, strongly indicating that the type of investor who purchased American Grain stock was interested primarily in dividends. He realized that the company could raise the dividend rate. Perhaps such a raise might more than make up for the additional cost of cash used to pay the dividend in the form of higher stock values for subsequent issues of common stock. Mr. Thomas thought that one way he could analyze the narrowness of the market of his company was to use a comparable company and find the cost of capital and the price earnings ratio of their stock. He realized, of course, that such a method was open to serious questioning; still, it might be of some value. Two companies had the same general product distribution—Archer-Daniels-Midland Corp. and Ralston Purina Corp. Archer-Daniels-Midland could be considered American Grain's closest competitor. Exhibit II shows some financial data for these corporations. Exhibit III gives the balance sheets and income statements for American Grain.

On the basis, then, of his calculations, Mr. Thomas decided to use the earnings-price ratio for the cost of common. He had realized that many writers preferred to use the yield plus a factor which would take into account the growth of dividends; however, this would result in a negative value. While earnings tended to fluctuate fairly widely, he did not know why this should influence in the long run the cost of capital since the fluctuations all tended to center around a zero rate of growth. He had also considered the expected earning approach about which he had read in an article by Ezra Solomon on calculating the cost of capital. Expected earnings and actual earnings, however, seemed over the long run also to be a constant. Thus, everywhere he looked, the only acceptable method of calculating the cost of equity appeared to be the earnings-price ratio.

Of course, if the company were to earn more as a result of their present retrenchment, a new cost of capital might emerge. The likelihood of this occurring had increased by a recent adjustment in the method of keeping books for the company. The decision was made to calculate all assets and earnings in United States dollars, that is, they would be calculated only when they were converted to dollars. This would be important especially in countries such as Egypt where inflation had tended to deteriorate the value of their earnings and assets.

As a result of his calculations, then, Mr. Thomas put together the following chart showing his calculations of the weighted cost of capital:

| Type of Capital | Percentage Amount | Cost After Tax | Weighted Average |
|---|---|---|---|
| Debt | 23 | .025 | .00575 |
| Equity | 77 | .10 | .07700 |
| Cost of Capital | | | .08275 |

**EXHIBIT I**
### American Grain Company
### Relationship of Book Value, Market Price, Earnings, and Dividends

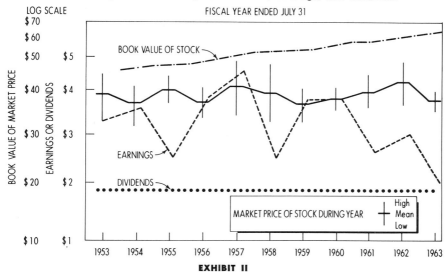

**EXHIBIT II**
### Selected Data For
### American Grain, Archer-Daniels-Midland, and Ralston Purina

|  | Am. Grain | ADM | R-P |
|---|---|---|---|
| Debt-equity ratio 1962–63 | 36.9 | 19.1 | 29.9 |
| 10-yr. compound rate of growth of earnings per share | —.03 | —.04 | —.20 |
| 10-yr. compound rate of growth of dividends per share | —.02 | — | —.17 |

**Am. Grain**

| Year | Market Price | | Yield | | Price/Earnings | |
|---|---|---|---|---|---|---|
|  | High | Low | High | Low | High | Low |
| 1963 | 38 | 23 | 3.5% | 6.5% | 18 | 11 |
| 1962 | 52 | 35 | 4.1 | 5.9 | 18 | 12 |
| 1961 | 48 | 37 | 4.2 | 5.4 | 18 | 14 |
| 1960 | 44 | 36 | 4.5 | 5.6 | 12 | 9 |
| 1959 | 41 | 34 | 4.9 | 5.9 | 11 | 9 |

**ADM**

| 1963 | 44 | 39 | 4.5 | 5.1 | 18 | 16 |
|---|---|---|---|---|---|---|
| 1962 | 42 | 33 | 4.8 | 6.1 | 15 | 12 |
| 1961 | 43 | 33 | 4.6 | 6.1 | 18 | 14 |
| 1960 | 40 | 30 | 5.0 | 6.7 | 17 | 13 |
| 1959 | 49 | 38 | 4.1 | 5.3 | 14 | 11 |

**R-P**

| 1963 | 40 | 31 | 2.1 | 2.7 | 26 | 20 |
|---|---|---|---|---|---|---|
| 1962 | 47 | 28 | 1.7 | 2.9 | 28 | 17 |
| 1961 | 45 | 39 | 3.0 | 3.5 | 15 | 13 |
| 1960 | 45 | 38 | 2.7 | 3.2 | 16 | 14 |
| 1959 | 52 | 42 | 2.3 | 2.9 | 19 | 15 |

**EXHIBIT III**

**American Grain Company**
**Income Statement**
(**In Thousands**)

| | For Period Ending | | |
|---|---|---|---|
| | 1/1/64* | 7/31/63 | 7/31/62 |
| Net revenue | $226,185 | $531,760 | $633,548 |
| Cost of revenues | 221,332 | 513,290 | 613,914 |
| Operating Income | $ 4,853 | $ 18,470 | $ 19,634 |
| Other Income, Net | 2,985 | (4,608) | (4,086) |
| Income before taxes | $ 7,838 | $ 13,862 | $ 15,548 |
| Taxes | 3,698 | 8,176 | 7,493 |
| Net income | $ 4,140 | $ 5,686 | $ 8,055 |
| Depreciation | 3,515 | 7,650 | 7,820 |
| Dividends | 1,388 | 4,218 | 5,536 |
| E/S | $ 1.53 | $ 2.11 | $ 2.91 |
| D/S | $ .50 | $ 1.50 | $ 2.00 |
| Shares Outstanding | 2,705,882 | 2,694,786 | 2,768,041 |

*6 months; compare to $204 million revenues and $4.63 million net income for like period in 1963.

**EXHIBIT IV**

**American Grain Company**
**Balance Sheet**
(**In Thousands**)

| Assets | 1/1/64 | 7/31/63* | 7/31/62 |
|---|---|---|---|
| Cash and marketable securities | $ 6,721 | $ 19,429 | $ 12,240 |
| Accounts receivable | 97,325 | 100,242 | 117,909 |
| Inventories | 89,369 | 81,949 | 82,810 |
| Total Current Assets | $193,415 | $201,620 | $212,959 |
| Plant and equipment, net | 56,598 | 90,058 | 89,143 |
| Other assets | 41,013 | 33,606 | 34,997 |
| Total assets | $291,026 | $325,284 | $337,099 |
| *Liabilities* | | | |
| Notes payable | $ 51,450 | $ 47,549 | $ 54,771 |
| Accounts payable | 33,583 | 31,468 | 34,683 |
| Accrued liabilities | 16,008 | 15,088 | 15,759 |
| Total current liabilities | $101,041 | $ 94,105 | $105,213 |
| Long-term debt† | 47,071 | 49,897 | 52,814 |
| Deferred liabilities | 3,608 | 7,234 | 7,144 |
| Minority interest | 30 | 4,000 | 3,655 |
| Capital (2,705,882 shs. out. | 63,273 | 63,013 | 64,726 |
| Retained earnings | 76,003 | 107,035 | 103,547 |
| Total net worth and liabilities | $291,026 | $325,284 | $337,099 |

*Contingent liabilities on 7/31/63 were guarantees of $7,450,000.
†Long-term debt on 7/31/63:

|  | Amt. |
|---|---|
| 3 4/5's S.F. debentures due 6/1/71 .................... | $28,700,000 |
| 5 3/8's S.F. debentures due 6/1/79 .................... | 13,600,000 |
| 4's debentures due 4/1/88 ........................... | 4,318,000 |
| 4 1/4's debentures due 4/1/98 ....................... | 3,279,000 |

## Part IV

# SHORT-
# AND IMMEDIATE-
# TERM FINANCING

# Obtaining
# Funds

# 20

CHEMCO CORPORATION

Chemco Corporation manufactured home chemicals, and for several years prior to 1962 the company lost money under aging management. New management took control in 1962 and immediately began a program to cut nonessential costs. Not until 1963, however, did the company again make a profit (the 1962 loss was $400,000). The new management also increased sales efforts and instituted a research program to develop new products. As a result, sales increased substantially, and several additions to the company's plant were made.

Early in 1965, Chemco realized that additional expansion would be necessary to take care of increased sales demand. In June, 1965, the company was offered the opportunity of purchasing the fixed assets and patents of the Ajax Chemical Company for $4,000,000, payable in cash. The patents were considered only a sweetener with the purchase price representing the plant's value. Chemco's management thought Ajax would fit very well into their manufacturing plans and give them the needed facilities to expand sales. With the new plant Chemco's management estimated that they could generate $6 million in additional sales in 1966.

In October, 1965, the board of directors of Chemco voted to buy Ajax Chemical at the asking price. An option was signed, and the board requested that Chemco's treasurer make a report on alternative methods of financing the required amount of money.

In making his report, the treasurer made the following assumptions for 1966:

1. Year-end inventory will be 20 per cent of cost of goods sold, and accounts payable will be 4 per cent of cost of goods sold.

2. A minimum cash balance of $500,000 will be necessary.

3. Accounts receivable will be one-sixth of sales.

4. Depreciation on all assets will average 10 per cent per year.

5. Selling expenses will be $500,000 plus 10 per cent of sales, and administrative expenses will be $1,000,000 plus 10 per cent of sales.

6. Research expenditures will continue at the present rate of $500,000.

7. Income taxes payable for 1966 are estimated at $700,000, and the tax rate will be 50 per cent.

8. Cost of goods sold will continue at 60 per cent of sales.

9. Industry averages for companies in similar manufacturing lines are: current ratio, 2.5–1; debt/equity ratio, .20; price earnings ratio, 18–1.

10. The company did not expect to pay dividends in 1966 and had not paid a dividend over the last eight years.

## QUESTIONS

1. Assume Chemco acquires Ajax on January 2, 1966. Present a financing plan for 1966. Show one alternative financing plan and demonstrate why it is inferior to the plan you present.

2. Suggest a dividend policy in the light of the new financing. Substantiate your choice.

**EXHIBIT I**

**Chemco Corporation**
**Income Statement**
**(end. Dec 31)**
**(In Thousands)**

|                              | 1963     | 1964     | 1965     |
|------------------------------|----------|----------|----------|
| Sales                        | $15,000  | $17,000  | $20,000  |
| Cost of goods sold           | 9,000    | 10,200   | 12,000   |
| Gross Profit                 | $6,000   | $6,800   | $8,000   |
| Admin. expense               | $2,500   | $2,700   | $3,000   |
| Selling expense              | 2,000    | 2,200    | 2,500    |
| Research expense             | 500      | 500      | 500      |
| Operating Profit             | $1,000   | $1,400   | $2,000   |
| Debt interest                | 260      | 290      | 320      |
| Net Profit before Taxes      | $740     | $1,110   | $1,680   |
| Income tax                   | 0*       | 260*     | 840      |
| Net Profit after Income Tax  | $740     | $850     | $840     |

*Losses carried forward from prior years reduce taxable income.

**EXHIBIT II**

**Chemco Corporation**
**Balance Sheet (Dec. 31)**
**(In Thousands)**

|  | 1963 | 1964 | 1965 |
|---|---|---|---|
| *Assets :* | | | |
| Cash | $  300 | $  485 | $  245 |
| Accounts rec. (net) | 2,500 | 2,800 | 3,130 |
| Inventory | 1,800 | 2,040 | 2,400 |
| Plant and equipment (net) | 6,500 | 7,350 | 8,650 |
| Total assets | $11,100 | $12,675 | $14,425 |
| | | | |
| *Liabilities and net worth :* | | | |
| Accounts payable | $  400 | $  400 | $  500 |
| Income tax payable | 0 | 200 | 535 |
| Bank loan (short term) 6%* | 1,100 | 1,825 | 2,500 |
| Debenture bonds (6%)† | 1,000 | 1,000 | 1,000 |
| Mortgage loan (6%) | 2,200 | 2,000 | 1,800 |
| Common stock ($5 par) | 1,000 | 1,000 | 1,000 |
| Capital surplus | 1,600 | 1,600 | 1,600 |
| Retained earned surplus | 3,800 | 4,650 | 5,490 |
| Total liabilities and net worth | $11,100 | $12,675 | $14,425 |
| | | | |
| (Amer. Stock Exch. Prices) | Hi-Lo | Hi-Lo | Hi-Lo Dec. 31 |
| Common Stock | 35–19 | 37–22 | 45–30–40 |

*Maximum line of credit from bank is $2,500,000. The bank requires that the company maintain a current ratio of 1.6–1.
†Due December 31, 1970. Callable at 103. Covenant restricts total long-term debt to 25 per cent of assets.

# Bank Borrowing

## 21

**KIMCO INSTRUMENT CORPORATION**

On December 10, 1962, Mr. Doug Kimbell, president of the Kimco Instrument Corporation, applied for a bank–Small-Business-Administration–participation loan in the amount of $350,000. Mr. Sam Barton, loan officer for the First National Bank, had the responsibility for making a study of the company to see whether the bank was interested in such a participation. Only three months earlier, the loan officer had turned down a term-loan request of the company's president because of the high risk involved and the poor earning record of the company. The SBA had recently simplified its bank-participation loan program, however, and Mr. Barton felt that he should reevaluate the situation in light of these changes.

The instrument company had been operating on a small scale since 1950. In 1960, the assets and rights to produce and sell the scientific instruments were acquired by thirty-six stockholders, and the Kimco Instrument Corporation was formed. Many of the initial stockholders were specialists in physics, engineering, and chemistry and became officers in the newly formed corporation. The company began to expand its operation almost immediately. Owing primarily to the efforts of Mr. Doug Kimbell, who was successful in acquiring technicians, the firm was able to carry on a vigorous research, production, and sales campaign, and approximately doubled its sales each year from 1960 through 1962, as is shown in Exhibit I.

A majority of the company's products were sold to petroleum refining and chemical companies. The company had begun, however, to produce pharmaceutical testing equipment, agricultural research instruments, and aerospace analytical instruments. It hoped to be able to gain some government contracts for aerospace equipment within the near future. The company was one of a few such companies located in the Southern part of the United States. It had selling agents in most states east of the Mississippi River and in a few of the South-western states. Its products appeared to be well accepted and were designed to meet the needs of a wide range of industries.

The growth of Kimco produced some financing problems. In order to conserve the company's resources, Mr. Kimbell located additional plant and office space in its original home office area. The new facilities were leased for a period of ten years at a monthly rental cost of $1,550. The company president felt that these facilities would be adequate for the ten-year period, 1961–1970. Large amounts of the firm's liquid assets were applied toward research and development of new allied products so that the company had to look to outside financing in order to continue with its expansion.

In early 1961, Mr. Kimbell had applied to the Small Business Administration and had received tentative approval for a $75,000, six-year, term loan. The interest rate on the loan was to be 4 per cent, as the city where the company was located was considered a distressed area because of high unemployment. In May, 1961, Mr. Kimbell approached the bank loan officer, Mr. Sam Barton, to see whether the bank would be interested in participating in the loan. Although the bank was able to charge a higher rate of interest on the share of funds which it advanced than the rate charged by the SBA, the bank was not interested in advancing funds to such a high-risk company for a six-year period of time. The loan was therefore rejected. Instead of going ahead with the SBA direct loan, Mr. Kimbell decided that the "red tape" involved in a loan made directly with the SBA would be too cumbersome, and he decided to pursue some other method of raising outside funds.

In mid-1961 the company arranged to issue additional common stock. The stock was first offered to the old shareholders on a one for one basis at $3.60 per share. In the event that the present shareholders (the number was about 210 at that time) did not exercise their subscription warrants, the company planned to market the stock itself at a public offering price of $4.00 per share. Necessary arrangements were made with the SEC for the sale of the 90,900 shares of nonvoting, Class "B" common stock. All the warrants were exercised by the existing stockholders so that the company did not have the problem of making the public sale.

The proceeds from the sale of stock were used to purchase additional equipment, to increase working capital, to continue with research and development, and to acquire a 30 per cent interest in a newly formed instrument company which was located in a large Southern city.

By May of 1962, the company was again in need of funds to carry on with its expansion program. Mr. Kimbell visited the First National Bank and asked if the bank might make a $35,000, ninty-day note. The loan was granted by the bank, upon Mr. Barton's recommendation. The note carried interest at 5 1/2 per cent and was indorsed by three officers of the company.

On August 1, 1962, Mr. Kimbell again visited the bank to ask for an extension of terms on the present note and for an additional short-term loan of $70,000. Mr. Kimbell stated that the company planned a $700,000 convertible debenture issue within the next few months and that the bank loan would be repaid out of the proceeds. The remaining funds would be used for expansion purposes and to make new investments in other developing instrument companies. The loan was granted.

On August 16, 1962, Mr. Kimbell visited the bank with a copy of the prospectus for the $700,000 convertible debenture issue and asked for an increase in his short-term loan to $140,000. The note was rewritten for $140,000, indorsements were required by three of the company's officers, and the interest rate was the same, 5 1/2 per cent.

Before the convertible debenture issue could be made, Mr. Kimbell learned that the SBA had simplified its bank-participation program in September, 1962. The new plan had been developed jointly by the SBA and the American Bankers Association. Under this plan, qualified small business firms were able to borrow up to $350,000, repayable monthly with up to ten years to pay. The interest rate charged by the SBA on their portion was

**EXHIBIT I**

**Kimco Instrument Corporation**
**Comparative Operating Statements**

| | Fiscal Year Ending August 31, | | | |
| --- | --- | --- | --- | --- |
| | 1959 | 1960 | 1961 | 1962 |
| Sales | $101,080 | $159,180 | $421,400 | $917,840 |
| Cost of goods sold | 51,660 | 87,360 | 252,000 | 491,960 |
| Gross profits | 49,420 | 71,820 | 169,400 | 425,880 |
| Operating expenses | | | | |
| Selling | 3,080 | 4,480 | 26,040 | 193,900 |
| Research and engineering | 5,880 | 10,360 | 50,120 | 106,820 |
| General and administrative | 22,820 | 54,460 | 82,740 | 106,400 |
| Total operating expenses | 31,780 | 69,300 | 158,900 | 407,120 |
| Operating profits | 17,640 | 2,520 | 10,500 | 18,760 |
| Other income | — | — | 2,240 | 1,820 |
| Other expense | 1,120 | — | — | 6,860 |
| Profit before income taxes | $16,520 | $2,520 | $12,740 | $13,720 |

**EXHIBIT II**

**Kimco Instrument Corporation**
**Shares Covered by Incentive Option Plan**

| | |
| --- | --- |
| Available for Options as of August 31, 1962 | |
| Class A Common : | 21,000 shares |
| Class B Common : | 49,000 shares |
| Options Outstanding as of August 31, 1962 | |
| Class A Common : | 7,000 shares at $2.40 per share |
| | 14,000 shares at $5.00 per share |
| Class B Common : | 2,100 shares at $5.00 per share |
| | 28,000 shares at $2.40 per share |

5 1/2 per cent (with interest payable monthly), but the bank was permitted to charge a higher interest rate. The loan application was to be made through the participating bank, which must agree to advance at least 50 per cent of the funds and handle the collections from the borrower. As an added compensation to the bank, it was to receive a $\frac{1}{2}$ per cent servicing fee and remit the remaining 5 per cent interest and the principal repayments collected on the SBA's portion to the Small Business Administration. One added attraction of this plan was that the bank's portion of the loan was to be paid

**EXHIBIT III**

**Kimco Instrument Corporation**
**Balance Sheet as of August 31, 1962**

| | | |
|---|---:|---:|
| *Assets* | | |
| Current assets | | |
| Cash | $38,628 | |
| Accounts receivable (net of $ 9,178 allowance) | 275,853 | |
| Inventories (lower of cost or market) | 308,449 | |
| Prepaid expenses | 16,433 | $639,363 |
| Investments | | |
| 42,000 shares of common in Tremont Instrument Corporation (cost) | | 42,000 |
| Fixed assets | | |
| Equipment and leasehold improvement (cost) | 210,521 | |
| Less accumulated depreciation | 52,738 | 157,783 |
| Other assets | | |
| Deferred research and development cost | 26,922 | |
| Other | 6,607 | 33,529 |
| Intangibles | | |
| Patent (legal cost) | 539 | |
| Scientific product designs (cost basis) | 247,408 | 247,947 |
| Total Assets | | $1,120,622 |
| | | |
| *Liabilities and net worth* | | |
| Current liabilities | | |
| Bank note payable | $140,000 | |
| Other notes payable | 2,835 | |
| Accounts payable | 158,550 | |
| Accrued expenses | 32,158 | $333,543 |
| Net Worth | | |
| Class A common, no par value, voting Authorized : 350,000 shares | | |
| Issued and outstanding : 284,200 shares | 284,200 | |
| Class B common, $ 1.00 par value, non-voting Authorized : 420,000 shares | | |
| Issued and outstanding : 224,840 shares | 224,840 | |
| Paid-in surplus | 251,684 | |
| Retained earnings | 26,355 | 787,079 |
| Total liabilities and net worth | | $1,120,622 |

off first with the SBA's portion postponed to the latter years. Thus, if a fifty-fifty loan for a period of ten years were made, the bank would receive its repayment during the first five years and the SBA would defer its repayment until the last five years. For SBA approval of such a loan, SBA must have satisfied itself that the loan is adequately secured and that the cash flow of the customer is sufficient to service the loan.

Mr. Kimbell determined that the SBA would require a pledge of substantially all the company's equipment, a pledge of the company's accounts receivable, a personal indorsement by the borrowers' officers, and a life insurance policy on the company's president, payable to the lenders, in the amount of the loan. All of the paper work, including the loan origination, financial statements, and supporting documents, and a two-year forecast of sales and expenses (Exhibit IV), would be filed with the bank. Since the SBA-bank loan request exceeded $150,000, approval of the SBA regional office and approval of the Washington office would have to be obtained. Should the loan be approved, $140,000 of the funds would be repaid to the First National Bank, $56,000 of the funds would be used to increase the borrower's working capital, and the remainder would be used for the acquisition of equipment.

In the event that the bank-SBA loan was not approved, Mr. Kimbell planned to proceed with the convertible debenture issue or market another issue of common stock. The debentures would probably be convertible into

**EXHIBIT IV**

**Kimco Instrument Corporation**
**Projected Statement of Income**

|  | Year Ended | |
|  | 8/31/63 | 8/31/64 |
|---|---|---|
| Sales | $1,722,000 | $3,360,000 |
| Cost of goods sold | 980,000 | 1,918,000 |
| Gross Profit | 742,000 | 1,442,000 |
| Expenses | | |
| Selling | 275,800 | 537,600 |
| Research | 147,000 | 235,200 |
| General and administrative | 130,200 | 238,000 |
| Total Expenses | 553,000 | 1,010,800 |
| Net Operating Income | 189,000 | 431,200 |
| Other income | 2,800 | 5,600 |
| Interest expenses | 16,100 | 19,180 |
| Net Income Before Taxes | $175,700 | $417,620 |
| Income taxes | 84,000 | 203,000 |
| Net income to retained earnings | 91,700 | 214,620 |
| Depreciation | 58,800 | 70,000 |
| Cash flow | 150,500 | 284,620 |
| Loan reduction | $15,840 | $35,000 |

Class "B" common stock at a price slightly in excess of the prevailing market price of the stock at the time the debentures were issued. In December, 1962, the market price range per share of Kimco was between $5.50 and $6.00. Sale of the large debenture issue would dilute the ownership and the prospective earnings of the company, owing to its large size in relation to the outstanding number of shares. The interest rate on the debenture issue would be about 6 per cent.

As an alternative, Mr. Kimbell considered making a public sale of stock. By the end of 1962, the company had approximately 280 shareholders in about twenty states. The Kimco management felt that the company could market another issue of common stock, selling the stock to the general public itself, rather than using the services of an underwriter.

Mr. Barton knew that Mr. Kimbell would want the bank's decision very soon in regard to the SBA-bank participation loan. He, therefore, began to assemble the necessary information about the company and to study the financial data so that he could make a wise decision about the loan application. In reviewing the personal fortune of the company's officers, he determined that their major assets were some 100,000 shares of the company's stock. Other assets were limited to equities in mortgaged homes, some household furnishings, and moderate amounts of liquid assets.

Mr. Barton learned that the company's sales were on net sixty-day terms and that the bad debts amounted to about $\frac{1}{2}$ per cent of sales. He was also informed by Mr. Kimbell that the work-in-process cycle was from two days to four months on the job orders. The average was about thirty days.

At the time of the loan request, the bank was fairly well loaned up. It was meeting the loan demand of its repeat borrowers, but it did not possess excess liquidity. Since Kimco already owed the bank $140,000 and the bank's share of the SBA-bank term loan was only $175,000, however, the bank would need to put up only an additional $35,000. In addition, the term loan would be adequately secured, whereas the working capital loan was unsecured. As Mr. Barton began to consider the pros and cons for granting or refusing the loan, he realized that he would have to come up with a recommendation for the loan committee by the next afternoon.

## QUESTIONS

1. After a careful review of the case, evaluate Mr. Barton's past decision to grant the short-term loans to the company. Is repayment possible? When?
2. Evaluate the forecast of sales and profits made by Mr. Kimbell, and comment on its reasonableness.
3. As Mr. Barton, would you recommend to the loan committee that the term loan be granted? If so, under what terms?

# Short-term Bank Borrowing

## 22

On September 15, 1964, Mr. Lawrence Sinca, president of the Centerville Finance Company, approached Mr. Robert Cole of the First National Bank of Centerville, Kansas, about a ninety-day line of credit in the amount of $200,000. The funds were to provide working capital for one of the company's sixteen offices. Mr. Cole made a note of the credit interview and asked that Mr. Sinca bring a copy of his most recently audited financial statements to the bank within a few days.

Mr. Cole had met Mr. Sinca upon numerous occasions during the past four or five years and had been impressed with the aggressiveness of the credit applicant. The company had sought a line of credit from the First National Bank in 1959 and again in 1960, but at that time the company was very small, operating only four and five offices, respectively. The somewhat limited operating experience of the company's officers at that time, the small net worth of the corporation, and the limited capital of the company's officers had resulted in the refusal of the loan requests. As a result of the refusals, Mr. Sinca had not again approached First National until August, 1964, when he stopped in to speak to one of the loan officers and to obtain a general impression as to the bank's willingness to consider a line of credit. He was referred to Mr. Cole who stated that the bank was interested in discussing the matter further.

The Centerville Finance Company had been formed in 1955 by three individuals: Mr. Sinca, Mr. Harold, and Mr. Boudet. Mr. Sinca had been active for a number of years in the finance company business. Mr. Harold had been a practicing certified public accountant. The third stockholder and officer, Mr. Boudet, was a local attorney. Both Mr. Sinca and Mr. Harold devoted their entire efforts toward the operation of the business, and Mr. Boudet took care of the legal work on a part-time basis. On the last balance sheet date, June 30, 1964, the three officers of the company owned about 40 per cent of the outstanding common stock, with some 18 per cent held by Mr. Sinca.

During the past two years, the company opened four and five offices, respectively, bringing to 16 the total number of offices at mid-September, 1964. Although the creation of additional offices in other cities within the state was expected to result in the creation of more notes receivable, a substantial reduction had occurred in the working capital of the company as a result of organizational and start-up costs.

Mr. Cole had had a great deal of loan experience with other consumer loan companies as he specialized in this type of customer. Although some bankers did not actively solicit the accounts of sales finance and consumer finance companies, the First National Bank had some fifty or sixty of these accounts. Mr. Cole estimated that throughout the country there were about 20 of these firms with assets in excess of $100 million, some 4,000 with assets of less than $1 million, and about 4,000 with assets between $1 and $100 million.

Even though sales finance companies and consumer loan companies compete directly with banks for consumer loans, these organizations will frequently grant higher-risk loans (at higher rates of interest) than commercial banks are willing to make. Mr. Cole realized that the sales finance companies and consumer loan companies often operated with about 70–80 per cent of their assets being provided by short-term debt; therefore, he was somewhat selective in recommending this type of customer to his loan committee. He believed that the customer should possess capable management, maintain a healthy balance between capital and debt, be able to keep delinquent accounts to a controllable level, and follow an annual clean-up for at least sixty days.

It was the policy of the First National Bank to require its consumer loan company borrowers to maintain an average demand deposit balance of about 15 per cent of the line of credit. Although the rate of interest varied somewhat with the prime rate and with the size of the line of credit, the supervision of the account required a great deal of time so that the rates usually charged on this type loan varied from 5 1/2 to 7 per cent. This type of customer was required to pledge notes receivable equal to at least 150 per cent of its loan balance, and the officers were frequently required to endorse the notes personally.

On the following day Mr. Sinca brought audited financial statements to the bank which covered the past four years of operations (Exhibits I and II). As Mr. Cole glanced over the financial statements he noted that the company's total assets had approximately doubled during the past three years. This increase, however, was predominantly caused by increasing the number of offices rather than the size of each outlet. Over this period, liabilities as percentages of assets had varied between 61 and 66 per cent. If the subordinated debt were considered liabilities rather than equity, however, the ratio of debt to assets was above 70 per cent.

When Mr. Cole questioned the wisdom of increasing the subordinated debt at an 8 per cent rate, Mr. Sinca stated that he considered the subordinated debt to be about the same as preferred stock except that the corporation had the tax benefit of deducting the interest expenses, whereas preferred dividends were paid from after-tax dollars. The subordinated debentures had maturities ranging from 1966–1972 in the following amounts:

| | |
|---|---|
| 1966 | $ 71,100 |
| 1967 | 100,000 |
| 1968 | 56,800 |
| 1969 | 52,600 |
| 1970 | 6,000 |
| 1972 | 11,600 |

The small amount of 8 per cent debentures was secured by the pledge of notes receivable, whereas the subordinated debentures were unsecured.

Mr. Sinca explained that the 8 per cent income certificates (shown on the balance sheet as current liabilities—unsubordinated) were payable fifteen days after demand and were subordinated in right of payment to all indebtedness of the company with the exception of subordinated debentures. Various real estate mortgages and equipment mortgages were also outstanding.

When Mr. Cole commented on the relative stability of officer and employee salaries, Mr. Sinca stated that the salaries of the officers of the company had remained virtually unchanged during the past four years so that total salaries had not increased as rapidly as had revenues. Mr. Sinca also explained that company policy was to hire two or three employees for each office. The office manager handled most of the loan requests, made loan decisions on applications for consumer credit in amounts up to $400, and attempted to collect delinquent payments. A home office loan committee had to pass on larger loans. Although a part of the notes were signature loans, the branch managers attempted to obtain chattel mortgages on the furniture of the credit applicant. Interest rates varied with the loan size, decreasing as the loan increased in amount. The other employee(s) handled reception, collections, typing, and bookkeeping work. Receipts were deposited intact daily except for petty cash.

The finance company had followed the practice of rebuying any treasury stock offered for sale. The current market price of the stock, although traded infrequently, was about 1 1/2 times the book value per share. The stock was then resold to new branch managers so that they would feel that their efforts would be rewarded through profit sharing of dividends declared as well as through their salaries. The company did not make any profits on trading in its treasury stock, but it was the objective of the company not to lose any money on such tradings.

Mr. Cole was informed by Mr. Sinca that a large bank in Kansas City had granted the finance company an $800,000 line of credit at 6 1/4 per cent

## EXHIBIT I

### Centerville Finance Company
### Comparative Balance Sheets

|  | Statement Date | | | |
|---|---|---|---|---|
|  | 6/30/61 | 6/30/62 | 6/30/63 | 6/30/64 |
| *Assets* | | | | |
| Cash | $144,957 | $148,497 | $279,483 | $408,587 |
| Marketable securities—muni. bonds | 84,033 | 84,342 | 84,598 | 84,909 |
| Notes receivable—total | 2,025,675 | 2,278,698 | 3,111,498 | 4,048,158 |
| Less, reserve for losses | (74,327) | (82,538) | (112,925) | (143,558) |
| Unearned finance charges | (218,723) | (269,633) | (354,627) | (465,456) |
| Notes receivable—net | 1,732,625 | 1,926,527 | 2,643,946 | 3,439,144 |
| Accounts receivable—net | — | 22,173 | 3,625 | 6,274 |
| Inventory of repossessions | 13,466 | 11,890 | 18,408 | 16,629 |
| Prepaid expenses | 9,267 | 9,497 | 5,343 | 10,792 |
| Marketable securities—stock | | | 2,720 | 2,720 |
| Total current assets | 1,984,348 | 2,202,926 | 3,038,123 | 3,969,055 |
| Fixed assets—net | 67,371 | 64,154 | 80,074 | 91,798 |
| Real estate | — | — | 40,204 | 52,956 |
| Noncurrent recs.—officers and employees | 29,227 | 6,366 | — | — |
| Deferred charges—dev. and organ. exp. new loan of. | — | — | 5,447 | 84,982 |
| Miscellaneous | — | — | 19,738 | 13,470 |
| Total noncurr. assets | 96,598 | 70,520 | 145,463 | 243,206 |
| Total Assets | $2,080,946 | $2,273,446 | $3,183,586 | $4,212,261 |
| *Liabilities* | | | | |
| Notes pay.—finance cos. | $980,000 | $928,000 | $1,188,800 | $1,250,400 |
| Notes pay.—banks | 82,059 | 154,342 | 284,000 | 1,061,000 |
| Curr. maturities—long-term debt | — | 3,600 | 16,185 | 4,526 |
| Income tax liability | 7,281 | 9,770 | 18,234 | 20,427 |
| Accrued expenses and accounts payable | 43,789 | 48,410 | 85,760 | 87,990 |
| Income certificates | 97,880 | 218,408 | 248,834 | 229,804 |
| Certificates of indebt. | 2,376 | — | — | — |
| Dealer reserves | 11,504 | 12,279 | 20,256 | 25,155 |
| Policy res. and res. for insurance losses | 16,849 | 19,067 | 33,675 | 44,705 |
| Notes pay.—misc. and other | 89,765 | 8,825 | — | — |
| Total Curr. Liabilities | $1,331,503 | $1,402,701 | $1,895,744 | $2,724,007 |
| Long-term sr. debt | | | | |
| Debentures—8%—less current portion | — | — | 22,960 | 4,841 |
| Real estate mortgages—less current portion | — | — | 29,825 | 38,810 |
| Chattel mort. and misc. | — | — | 4,861 | — |
| Total noncurr. liabilities | — | — | 57,646 | 43,651 |
| Total liabilities | $1,331,503 | $1,402,701 | $1,953,390 | $2,767,658 |
| Subordinated debt—8% deben. | 108,000 | 165,312 | 203,512 | 285,112 |
| Common stock | 176,221 | 176,221 | 187,480 | 189,176 |
| Capital surplus | 418,607 | 418,607 | 559,260 | 574,075 |
| Retained earnings | 100,741 | 164,192 | 290,294 | 406,308 |
| Less: treasury stock | (54,126) | (53,587) | (10,350) | (10,068) |
| Total net worth | 641,443 | 705,433 | 1,026,684 | 1,159,491 |
| Total cap. funds | 749,443 | 870,745 | 1,230,196 | 1,444,603 |
| Total liab. and cap. funds | $2,080,946 | $2,273,446 | $3,183,586 | $4,212,261 |

during January, 1964, and that the company had credit lines with twelve banks ranging from $8,000 to $800,000. The Giant Finance Company also provided the company with a secured line of credit in the amount of $1,250,-000 (Exhibit III) at a rate of 8 1/2 per cent. A majority of the banks required that their loans be cleaned up for at least sixty days out of each year, but the company was never completely out of debt to all the banks at one time.

A schedule showing the aging of past due notes receivable from the seven offices which had been in operation for more than two years is shown in Exhibit IV for April 30, 1964, and for August 31, 1964. When Mr. Cole appeared to be concerned about the build-up of delinquencies in Offices 4 and 5, Mr. Sinca stated that the office managers for the two branches had been a bit lax in the type of risks they assumed when granting consumer loans and that the officers had been replaced approximately a year ago. Although the collection on some of the accounts had been slow, the bad debt losses had not been excessively high.

Mr. Sinca was informed that in the event the loan were granted, notes receivable equal to 1 1/2 times the loan outstanding would be required, and that in order for a note to be pledgeable, at least one payment must have been made within the past ninety days. Since the credit applicant did not maintain a deposit account with First National, Mr. Cole explained that a compensatory balance of at least 15 per cent of the line of credit was standard policy for his bank. Although he was not sure just what the bank's loanable fund situation was at the present, he did not believe that the loan committee would approve the loan at an interest rate of less than 6 1/2 per cent. Mr. Sinca appeared to be somewhat disappointed with the interest

**EXHIBIT II**

**Centerville Finance Company**
**Comparative Income Statements**
**For the Years Ended**

|  | 6/30/61 | | 6/30/62 | | 6/30/63 | | 6/30/64 | |
|---|---|---|---|---|---|---|---|---|
|  | Amount | % | Amount | % | Amount | % | Amount | % |
| Gross income | $576,266 | 100.0 | $732,040 | 100.0 | $896,742 | 100.0 | $1,137,234 | 100.0 |
| Operating expense | 386,426 | 67.1 | 491,021 | 67.1 | 570,149 | 63.6 | 830,615 | 73.0 |
| Net profit from oper. | 189,840 | 32.9 | 241,019 | 32.9 | 326,593 | 36.4 | 306,619 | 27.0 |
| Other income* | — | — | — | — | — | — | 80,949 | 7.1 |
| Other exp.—cost of borrowing | 116,616 | 20.2 | 136,759 | 18.7 | 148,055 | 16.5 | 194,214 | 17.1 |
| Net profit before taxes | 73,224 | 12.7 | 104,260 | 18.2 | 178,538 | 19.9 | 193,354 | 17.0 |
| Fed. and st. income taxes | 6,773 | 1.2 | 9,770 | 1.3 | 18,240 | 2.0 | 21,942 | 1.9 |
| Net profit after taxes | 66,451 | 11.5 | 94,490 | 16.9 | 160,298 | 17.9 | 171,412 | 15.1 |
| Dividends | 29,550 | 5.1 | 31,566 | 4.3 | 34,197 | 3.8 | 55,398 | 4.9 |
| Inc. in retd. earnings | 36,901 | 6.4 | 62,924 | 12.6 | 126,101 | 14.1 | 116,014 | 10.2 |

*Development expenses deferred are included in operating expense and include excess of new loan office expense over income.

## EXHIBIT III

### Centerville Finance Company
### Supporting Financial Data

| | 6/30/61 | | 6/30/62 | | 6/30/63 | | 6/30/64 | |
|---|---|---|---|---|---|---|---|---|
| | Amount | % | Amount | % | Amount | % | Amount | % |
| *Breakdown of Notes Rec.* | | | | | | | | |
| Discount basis loans—direct | $1,531,346 | 75.6 | $1,374,550 | 60.3 | $1,927,204 | 61.9 | $2,334,424 | 57.7 |
| Interest bearing loans—direct | 494,329 | 24.4 | 602,349 | 26.4 | 779,728 | 25.1 | 1,117,870 | 27.6 |
| Retail installment loans | | | 302,019 | 13.3 | 404,566 | 13.0 | 595,864 | 14.7 |
| Total notes receivable | 2,025,675 | 100.0 | 2,278,918 | 100.0 | 3,111,498 | 100.0 | 4,048,158 | 100.0 |
| Average size of loans | | | 324 | | 321 | | 308 | |
| Volume of direct loans | | | | | 3,068,754 | | 4,000,764 | |
| *Past Due Notes Rec.* | | | | | | | | |
| 61–90 days | 34,146 | 1.7 | 40,434 | 1.8 | 47,765 | 1.5 | 59,551 | 1.5 |
| Over 90 days | 66,384 | 3.3 | 58,125 | 2.6 | 65,471 | 2.0 | 108,155 | 2.7 |
| Over 60 days—inst. only | 15,623 | .8 | 10,794 | .4 | 16,674 | .6 | 31,886 | .7 |
| Per cent of total receivables | 116,153 | 5.8 | 109,353 | 4.8 | 129,910 | 4.2 | 199,592 | 4.9 |
| Avg. size of past due loans | 412 | | 365 | | 318 | | 308 | |
| *Losses on Notes Rec.* | | | | | | | | |
| Charge-off and reposs. losses | 69,320 | 3.4 | 103,895 | 4.6 | 86,345 | 2.8 | 111,076 | 2.7 |
| Less recoveries | 9,353 | .5 | 20,094 | .8 | 24,760 | .8 | 25,172 | .6 |
| Net losses (% of total notes rec.) | 59,967 | 2.9 | 83,801 | 3.8 | 61,585 | 2.0 | 85,904 | 2.1 |
| Recoveries (prior year charge-offs) | | 29.0 | | 29.0 | | 23.8 | | 29.2 |
| Net losses/tot. notes rec. | | 2.9 | | 3.8 | | 2.0 | | 2.1 |
| Res. for losses/tot. notes rec. | | 3.7 | | 3.6 | | 3.6 | | 3.6 |
| *Other Data* | | | | | | | | |
| Depreciation expense and amort. | | | $11,720 | | $12,906 | | $19,062 | |
| Salaries—total | $185,660 | | 197,926 | | 245,798 | | 328,810 | |
| *Profitability Analysis :* | | | | | | | | |
| Increase in retained earnings | | | 63,451 | | 126,102 | | 116,014 | |
| Dividends | | | 31,566 | | 34,197 | | 55,398 | |
| Depreciation and amortization | | | 11,720 | | 12,906 | | 19,046 | |
| Profitability or cash flow | | | 106,212 | | 173,204 | | 190,458 | |
| Notes receivable pledged to fin. co. | | | 1,976,000 | | 2,313,600 | | 2,274,920 | |
| Notes receivable pledged to banks | | | — | | 455,200 | | 1,670,798 | |
| Total notes receivable pledged | | | $1,976,000 | | $2,768,800 | | $3,945,718 | |

**EXHIBIT IV**

**Centerville Finance Company**
**Aging of Notes Receivable**

| Office | Past Due | No. | 8/31/64 | No. | 6/30/64 |
|--------|----------|-----|---------|-----|---------|
| 1 | 30 days | 65 | $20,367.98 | 21 | $8,320.18 |
|   | 60 days | 24 | 7,616.20 | 7 | 3,336.71 |
|   | 90 days | 33 | 13,019.01 | 32 | 14,894.41 |
| 2 | 30 days | 79 | 27,734.92 | 80 | 24,002.89 |
|   | 60 days | 18 | 3,588.50 | 17 | 6,858.01 |
|   | 90 days | 35 | 13,947.09 | 40 | 16,724.43 |
| 3 | 30 days | 28 | 5,844.85 | 18 | 4,605.71 |
|   | 60 days | 5 | 918.97 | 5 | 1,743.62 |
|   | 90 days | 10 | 1,226.96 | 6 | 898.47 |
| 4 | 30 days | 80 | 17,910.51 | 47 | 14,444.33 |
|   | 60 days | 28 | 5,351.50 | 14 | 4,752.63 |
|   | 90 days | 46 | 16,689.64 | 29 | 7,671.03 |
| 5 | 30 days | 53 | 20,158.51 | 37 | 11,342.90 |
|   | 60 days | 22 | 7,095.84 | 3 | 589.46 |
|   | 90 days | 49 | 15,858.50 | 25 | 8,038.95 |
| 6 | 30 days | 26 | 5,323.73 | 9 | 1,476.31 |
|   | 60 days | 2 | 433.13 | 1 | 112.98 |
|   | 90 days | 6 | 1,361.42 | 6 | 1,229.59 |
| 7 | 30 days | 27 | 7,995.75 | 10 | 1,425.15 |
|   | 60 days | 9 | 1,828.60 | 3 | 572.64 |
|   | 90 days | 10 | 1,325.64 | 6 | 2,135.06 |

**EXHIBIT V**

**Centerville Finance Company**
**Institutions Extending Credit and Basis as of August 1, 1964**

| Institution | Line of Credit | Collateral |
|-------------|----------------|------------|
| Bank A | $800,000 | Customer notes at $6^{1}/_{4}\%$ |
| Bank B | $200,000 | Customer notes at 6% |
| Bank C | $ 60,000 | Participation with Bank B at 6% |
| Bank D | $200,000 | Customer notes at 6% |
| Giant Finance Company | $1,350,000 | Customer notes at $8^{1}/_{2}\%$ |
| Bank E | $30,000 | Unsecured*—6% |
| Bank F | $30,000 | Unsecured*—6%—$ 10,000 quarterly reduction |
| Bank G | $25,000 | Unsecured—$ 2,000 monthly reduction—5% |
| Bank H | $20,000 | Unsecured*—6% |
| Bank I | $12,000 | Unsecured*—6% |
| Bank J | $8,000 | Unsecured*—6% |
| Bank K | $8,000 | Unsecured—$ 1,000 monthly reduction—6% |
| Bank L | $8,000 | Unsecured*—6% |

*Personally endorsed by principal officers of the company.

rate, but stated that he would check with Mr. Cole by telephone in a week to learn the bank's decision.

Mr. Cole turned the file over to the credit department with instructions to obtain a credit report on the Centerville Finance Company and its officers; to run a complete ratio analysis on the company and on the industry; to study the financial statements and supporting schedules for any possible weaknesses; and to obtain letters of character reference and debt-servicing history on the officers of the firm.

The credit report indicated only two or three additional pertinent facts about the company and its stockholders. The officers were generally considered to be capable managers, and the profit margin of the finance company was slightly higher than average. Its delinquencies had recently risen, but its losses on bad debts were lower than average. The net worth of the principal stockholders were as follows, consisting primarily of stock in the Centerville Finance Company:

| Stockholder | Assets | Market Value of Centerville Stock | Net Worth | Life Insurance |
|---|---|---|---|---|
| Sinca | $116,000 | $84,000 | $80,000 | $60,000 |
| Harold | 28,000 | 10,000 | 20,000 | 30,000 |
| Boudet | 111,000 | 56,000 | 93,000 | 50,000 |

Virtually all the assets of the three officers of the Centerville Finance Company were pledged for mortgages and bank loans with the exception of their investments in the shares of the company.

Letters were written to the other lending banks and to the Giant Finance

**EXHIBIT VI**

**Centerville Finance Company**
**Median Industry Ratios**

| | Ratio | 4/30/63 | 4/30/64 |
|---|---|---|---|
| 1. | % Cash to total nonsubordinated debt | 13.24 | 13.47 |
| 2. | Ratio—total nonsubordinated debt to working capital | 2.01 to 1 | 2.11 to 1 |
| 3. | % Average monthly cash principal collections to average net monthly outstandings | 5.52 | 5.86 |
| 4. | No. of months' collections required to pay total nonsubordinated debt (net of cash) applying % in Ratio #3 to fiscal date net outstandings | 10.30 | N. A. |
| 5. | % Reserve for losses to total Installment receivables | 3.42 | 3.32 |
| 6. | % Net charge-offs to average net outstandings | 1.88 | 2.73 |
| 7. | % Loans renewed with no additional cash advanced | .52 | N. A. |
| 8. | % 60–89 day accounts—no collections received for 60 to 89 days | 1.37 | N. A. |
| 9. | % 90-day accounts—no collections received for 90 days or more. | 2.32 | N. A. |
| 10. | % of net profit (including taxes) to gross income | 12.52 | N. A. |

Company to determine the debt-servicing history of the credit applicant. Incomplete returns at the end of the week appeared to indicate that the customer was handling the annual clean-up as required, and was maintaining the required compensatory balances, except in the banks where the latter were waived. The Giant Finance Company did not require an annual clean-up, but did require that notes receivable equal to 150 per cent of the loan balance be pledged as collateral.

Mr. Cole began to study the data provided to him by Mr. Sinca, the other lenders, and the bank credit department so that he would be in a position to answer any queries which might come from the loan committee on the following morning about the advisability of making the loan. He expected Mr. Sinca to call the bank on the following afternoon to find out the bank's decision.

# Term Loans

# 23

**HERNANDEZ SAWMILLS, INC.**

On August 25, 1966, Mr. R. A. Hernandez, president of the Hernandez Sawmills, Inc., approached his loan officer, Mr. John Mills, at the First City Bank of Springville, Oregon, to discuss the possibility of renegotiating a term loan and a line of credit with the bank. Owing to substantial losses suffered in the fiscal years of 1964 and 1965 and the need of additional working capital, the monthly payments of the company's present indebtedness had become burdensome. The First City Bank was currently participating with a large correspondent bank in a $600,000 term loan to Mr. Hernandez. Some 60 per cent of the outstanding loan required balloon repayment or refinancing during the next twelve months. Mr. Hernandez believed that his company could justify increasing its total indebtedness to its bank lenders to $1,000,000 under a 15-year term-loan arrangement.

Mr. Hernandez started the sawmill as a partnership in the middle thirties. It was incorporated in 1949 when Mr. Hernandez's two sons came into the company. The other original partner in the firm, Mr. Rodriques, remained with the company until 1961, when he retired from the business. Mr. Rodriques then sold his interest in the firm to the corporation for a price of $250,000, most of which was shown as treasury stock on July 31, 1965 (Exhibit I).

The stock in Hernandez Sawmill, Inc. was closely held by Mr. Hernandez and members of his family. The president of the company personally owned about 60 per cent of the stock, each son held 10 per cent, and other members owned the remaining 20 per cent. The company had not elected Subchapter S tax treatment as the owners' personal incomes were relatively high, and it did not appear that such a tax election would result in a tax savings to the shareholders.

**149**

Although Mr. R. A. Hernandez had some $400,000 invested in the business in the form of common stock and note advances, he also owned listed securities in Container Corporation of America and Western Airline which had a market value of approximately $300,000. Other asset holdings increased his total personal equity to slightly over $1,000,000. In addition to the assets owned by Mr. Hernandez, his wife owned separate property valued at about $1,250,000. Her sole heirs were her two sons, both junior officers in the sawmill. Each of the sons had capital valued at approximately $75,000, including the book value of their stock in the Hernandez Sawmill.

Mr. Hernandez had operated the business for the past thirty years and was well known and well respected in the industry. Although he was approaching 60 years of age, both his sons had engineering degrees from reputable universities and were capable, according to their father, of running the business without his help. The ages of the sons were thirty-seven and thirty-five respectively.

The fixed assets of the sawmill company consisted of two separate sawmills located within a few miles of Springville, Oregon, a wholesale lumber company, and an office building. The latter two were located within the city. The two sawmills had an original cost of about $1.8 million and had recently been appraised at approximately 1 1/2 times their book value. The office building was valued at its original cost, $60,000, and the appraised value of the land and buildings of the wholesale lumber outlet had been set at $100,000. In addition to the above, the company owned approximately five million board feet of standing timber, which had an insured value of $200,000 and a cost of $55,000. The fixed assets were insured for at least 80 per cent of their appraised values.

The two sons, David and Robert, managed the two sawmills while the president of the company was active in operating the wholesale lumber establishment. Although the mill operation had been somewhat slower than usual during 1963 and 1964, the company was receiving at mid-1966 about as much business as it could take care of. Mr. Hernandez believed that the sales volume would increase by as much as 10 per cent and that some cost controls and improved operations in logging would reduce operating expenses by 25 per cent during the next fiscal year.

After chatting with Mr. Hernandez for a few minutes about the operation of his business, the performance of his sons, and the outlook in the industry, Mr. Mills began to review the company's financial statements. He noted that the total assets of the firm had increased by about $700,000 from 1962 to 1966, primarily because of substantial increases in inventory, fixed assets, and accounts receivable. The asset increase had been financed by liabilities which had also risen by more than $700,000. The primary sources of funds over the four-year period had been bank-participation loans, accounts payable, notes payable—equipment, and notes payable—stockholders. Mr. Hernandez expected a further increase in receivables and inventories as the volume of sales expanded.

The current ratio of the company was only slightly above 1 to 1, compared to 2.08 to 1 for the industry; the receivables turnover was 19.1 to 1 compared to the industry figure of 17 to 1; and the ratio of net worth to debt was only .14 compared to 1.85 for the industry.

Although the company reported substantial amounts of profits for 1962 and 1963, the firm showed losses of $150,000 in 1964 and $122,000 in 1965. Loss carryback, however, resulted in a lower after-tax loss than the preceding figures. These losses resulted from increases in both cost of goods sold and operating expenses as percentages of sales. Progress was indicated during the 1966 fiscal year, however, and net profit after taxes amounted to about $50,000. The actual profitability of the company had been somewhat distorted over the past few years because the company was using the most rapid depreciation writeoff permitted by the Internal Revenue Service, thus reducing its taxable income and its tax liability.

As a result of recent losses, increased need for working capital, and the heavy loan repayment schedule, Mr. Hernandez had made personal loans to the company totaling about $350,000 over the past four years. His personal supply of liquid funds was about exhausted, however, and he preferred not to have to resort to the sale of his marketable securities as this would result in substantial amounts of capital gains tax. He also felt that the market performance of both issues would improve over the next few years.

Hernandez had been a borrower from the bank for about ten years and had handled his banking relations satisfactorily. Until 1961, the firm had borrowed from the bank only on a working capital basis with 90-day renewable loans secured by a pledge of accounts receivable and inventory, other than miscellaneous equipment, and real estate notes secured with pledges of personal and real property. In 1961, however, the company had requested and received an 18-month, $150,000 term loan at an annual rate of 5 per cent. The firm was also a heavy borrower on a ninety-day renewable loan basis, pledging accounts receivable and inventory as collateral. Although the term loan was cleaned up, repayments were made primarily from funds borrowed on a short-term basis.

In November, 1965, Mr. Hernandez again sought term credit from the bank. He requested a term loan in the amount of $600,000, repayable $100,000 per quarter, plus interest. The bank and a correspondent participated equally in the 5 1/2 per cent loan. The banks required that listed and unlisted securities in the amount of $350,000 and standing timber be pledged as collateral for the loan. Although the loan was being serviced satisfactorily, the rapid repayment schedule had placed a severe strain on the working capital position of the firm. The balances in the accounts receivable and the inventories accounts had been squeezed, funds provided through depreciation had been used, and additional notes were issued to Mr. Hernandez, who brought additional funds into the business. The situation was aggravated by losses which were incurred during 1964 and 1965.

In early 1964, Hernandez Sawmills obtained a sixty-day revolving credit account with the First City Bank and its correspondents in the amount of $650,000. No annual clean-up of this loan had occurred, nor did the banker realistically expect the loan to be completely repaid within the current year. The notes carried interest at the rate of 5 1/2 per cent, and term-insurance policies in the amounts of $300,000 on Mr. Hernandez and $75,000 and $50,000, respectively, on the two sons were endorsed to the bank.

During the course of the loan interview, Mr. Hernandez stated that he planned to use the $1,000,000 to retire the present bank indebtedness, to retire some equipment notes, to reduce accounts payable by about $50,000, to make plant improvements in the amount of $120,000, and to repay $150,000 to himself. The balance of the funds would be used for increasing the working capital of the firm. He believed that his company could adequately handle monthly payments in the amount of $20,000.

When Mr. Mills appeared reluctant to discuss the possibility of rewriting the term loan and the short-term credit agreement into a long-term loan of $1,000,000, Mr. Hernandez suggested that a portion of the loan might be a 10-year amortization loan secured by plant and equipment and listed securities and by a personal endorsement by the company's president. The balance of the loan could be a revolving working capital loan based on a certain percentage of accounts receivable and inventories which could be pledged as collateral. Mr. Mills stated that the loan request would be reviewed thoroughly and presented to the loan committee. Since interest rates had increased somewhat since 1964 and the borrower was asking for longer maturities, a higher interest rate charge was probable.

The policy of the bank was to attempt to work out a financial plan which was to the best interest of its customer so long as the arrangement did not result in making an unsafe loan. The bank's lending policies typically limited real estate loans to 50 per cent of the appraised value of the property; the accounts receivable loans to 85–90 per cent of the net accounts receivable; the inventory loans to 60–80 per cent of the wholesale values of the inventories; and listed security loans to 75 per cent of their market values (other than for buying or carrying securities).

Before making a decision on the loan request submitted by Mr. Hernandez or arriving at a counterloan proposal, the loan committee, Mr. Mills knew, would consider not only the historical credit record of the borrower but also the importance of the account in terms of total average deposits maintained with the bank. Present balances of the lumber company, other businesses operated by Mr. Hernandez, and the accounts of other members of the family appear in Exhibit III and indicate that average balances for all the accounts have been $85,000 for the past eighteen months.

The First City Bank could not legally make a loan to one customer in the amount of $1,000,000 even though the loan were fully secured. Therefore, even though the loan committee might approve the loan, the bank must find two or three other banks which would be willing to participate in the loan. The liquidity position for the First City Bank was fairly tight, and although some two-thirds of the amount requested would be applied toward the retirement of other bank loans, the loan would require some additional $300,000 in funds.

**EXHIBIT I**

**Hernandez Sawmills, Inc.**
**Comparative Balance Sheets**

|  | 7/31/62 | 7/31/63 | 7/31/64 | 7/31/65 | 7/31/66 |
|---|---|---|---|---|---|
| *Assets* | | | | | |
| Current assets | | | | | |
| Cash | $65,962 | $33,118 | $136,096 | 11,476 | 53,418 |
| Marketable securities | | | | | |
| Accts. receivable (net) | 156,682 | 104,852 | 148,027 | 125,151 | 169,290 |
| Inventory | 287,435 | 371,973 | 396,436 | 362,735 | 503,071 |
| Prepaid expenses | 6,743 | 26,327 | 2,129 | 1,598 | 841 |
| Prepaid insurance | 17,993 | — | 37,220 | 38,004 | 33,595 |
| Logging advances | — | — | 3,866 | 2,349 | — |
| Income tax refund due | — | — | 65,462 | 53,053 | — |
| Total current assets | 534,815 | 536,270 | 789,236 | 594,366 | 760,215 |
| Fixed assets* | 794,242 | 848,282 | 1,542,542 | 1,708,795 | 1,955,451 |
| Less allow. for depre. | (404,152) | (533,923) | (871,259) | (997,221) | (1,120,430) |
| Fixed assets net | 390,090 | 314,359 | 671,283 | 711,574 | 835,021 |
| Other assets | | | 1,725 | 2,807 | 14,414 |
| Due from affiliates | | 87,700 | | | |
| Total assets | $924,905 | $938,329 | $1,462,244 | $1,308,747 | $1,609,650 |
| | | | | | |
| *Liabilities and Capital* | | | | | |
| Current liabilities | | | | | |
| Notes payable—bank | $285,000 | $210,000 | $200,000 | $240,000 | $320,000 |
| Notes payable—trade | — | — | — | 27,027 | 71,995 |
| Accounts pay.—trade | 84,021 | 121,888 | 170,384 | 256,380 | 173,656 |
| Income taxes payable | 81,131 | 111,259 | 9,768 | — | 1,809 |
| Accrued expenses | 52,423 | 61,391 | 75,620 | 67,737 | 84,551 |
| Notes pay.—equipment | 20,028 | 20,143 | 5,636 | 52,485 | 66,829 |
| Notes Payable—family | — | — | 70,000 | 30,000 | 24,000 |
| Other taxes payable | 18,067 | 11,820 | 13,503 | 15,444 | 17,867 |
| Total current liabilities | 540,670 | 536,501 | 544,911 | 689,073 | 760,707 |
| Long-term liabilities | | | | | |
| Notes payable—bank | 120,000 | — | 400,000 | 126,667 | 280,000 |
| Notes payable—equip. | 19,718 | 49,003 | — | 24,783 | 55,578 |
| Notes pay.—stockholders | 31,000 | 31,000 | 306,000 | 325,300 | 314,586 |
| Total liabilities | 711,388 | 616,504 | 1,250,911 | 1,165,823 | 1,410,871 |
| Capital stock | | | | | |
| Common | 66,667 | 66,667 | 70,000 | 70,000 | 70,000 |
| Capital surplus | — | — | 30,000 | 30,000 | 30,000 |
| Retained earnings | 380,183 | 488,491 | 344,666 | 276,257 | 332,112 |
| Treasury stock | (233,333) | (233,333) | (233,333) | (233,333) | (233,333) |
| Total capital | 213,517 | 321,825 | 211,333 | 142,924 | 198,779 |
| Total liabilities and capital | $924,905 | $938,329 | $1,462,244 | $1,308,747 | $1,609,650 |

*Original cost and reserve for depreciation recorded with purchase of used assets.

**EXHIBIT II**

**Hernandez Sawmills, Inc.**
**Comparative Income Statements**
**For Years Ended**

|  | 7/31/62 | 7/31/63 | 7/31/64 | 7/31/65 | 7/31/66 |
|---|---|---|---|---|---|
| Net sales | $2,630,521 | $2,683,151 | $2,375,771 | $3,333,737 | $3,209,075 |
| Cost of goods sold* | 2,130,725 | 2,115,560 | 2,225,652 | 2,986,999 | 2,691,193 |
| Gross profits | 499,796 | 567,591 | 150,119 | 346,738 | 517,882 |
| Operating expenses | 319,875 | 348,772 | 370,643 | 530,365 | 492,564 |
| Net profits from oper. | 179,921 | 218,819 | (220,524) | (183,627) | 25,318 |
| Other income | 31,059 | 57,976 | 69,806 | 62,163 | 26,196 |
| Net profit before taxes | 210,980 | 276,795 | (150,718) | (121,464) | 51,514 |
| Income taxes | 80,644 | 116,625 | (65,461) | 53,053 | 1,809 |
| Net profit after taxes | 130,336 | 160,170 | (85,257) | (68,411) | 49,705 |
| Dividends |  |  |  |  |  |
| Increase in net earnings | $130,336 | $160,170 | $(85,257) | $(68,411) | $49,705 |
| *Depreciation · · · · · · · · · · · · · · · · · · · · · · · · | N/A | 136,219 | 142,972 | 188,897 | 143,782 |

**EXHIBIT III**

**Hernandez Sawmills, Inc.**
**Deposit Balances**

|  | Aug., 1966 | |
|---|---|---|
|  | Present Balance | Average Balance |
| R. A. Hernandez | $5,460 | $55,500 |
| Hernandez Sawmills | 20 | 20,000 |
| Richard Hernandez | 12,000 | 2,080 |
| Mrs. R. A. Hernandez | 11,280 | 14,200 |
| David Hernandez | 2,100 | 2,200 |
| Mrs. R. A. Hernandez (Savings) | 10,000 |  |
| Other Accounts | 3,625 | 4,400 |

Term
Loans
(cont.)

24

FIRST CITY BANK
OF SPRINGVILLE

On October 1, 1966, Mr. John Mills, loan officer at the First City Bank of Springville, Oregon, called Mr. R. A. Hernandez, president of Hernandez Sawmills, Inc., and asked that Mr. Hernandez come to the bank at his earliest convenience to discuss his loan proposal.[1] Mr. Hernandez had applied during the previous week for an increase in his term loan, with a lengthening in payout. He had suggested that the current outstanding portions of the term loan and ninety-day working capital loan be combined and rewritten with a ten-year maturity. Some two-thirds of the $1,000,-000 loan requested would be applied to the repayment of current bank indebtedness and the remainder would be used to reduce accounts payable, to repay one of the personal notes to Mr. Hernandez, to expand fixed assets, and to increase the working capital.

On the following morning Mr. Hernandez called on the First City Bank to discuss the loan proposal. He was greeted by Mr. Mills, who explained that his loan committee had met to discuss the possibility of working out some other financial arrangement which would not be so burdensome on the borrower. When the bank had contacted its other correspondent bank about participating in a larger, longer maturity loan, the bank president considered the situation but declined to make such a participation.

"You can appreciate our problem, Mr. Hernandez. We wanted to be a help to you, but we are unable to extend the full amount of the credit. Our state lending laws will not permit us to make a loan of that size, you understand. We contacted two or three of our correspondent banks in an attempt to find one or two which would participate in

---

*For background material on the case, see the preceding case Hernandez Sawmills, Inc.

the entire package. An insurance company with which we have previously syndicated loans appeared interested in a term loan at 6 1/2 per cent for $400,000 if secured with a real mortgage on the sawmills. The insurance company would require equal monthly payments on principal and interest over an eight-year period. Our bank is prepared to grant you a 3 1/2 year, 6 per cent, term loan in the amount of $420,000. We would expect monthly repayments of $10,000 plus interest. The computation of the amounts of loans are as follows:

| | |
|---|---:|
| Inventories less accounts payable ($ 500,000 − $ 175,000 × .60) | $195,000 |
| Listed securities ($ 300,000 × .75) | 225,000 |
| Plant (appraised value of $ 1,250,000) | 400,000 |
| Total | $820,000 |

On the bank's portion of the loan, we would expect you to pledge your inventories and common stocks and to endorse your insurance policy over to

**EXHIBIT I**

**Hernandez Sawmills, Inc.**
**Pro Forma Balance Sheet**

| Account | Actual (7/31/66) | New Loan Source | New Loan Application | Pro Forma |
|---|---:|---:|---:|---:|
| Current assets | $760,215 | | $57,593 | $817,808 |
| Fixed assets (net) | 835,021 | | 120,000 | 955,021 |
| Other | 14,414 | | | 14,414 |
| | 1,609,650 | | | 1,787,243 |
| Current liabilities | | | | |
| Accounts payable | 173,656 | | 50,000 | 123,656 |
| Notes payable—trade | 71,995 | | | 71,995 |
| Notes payable—bank | 320,000 | | 320,000 | |
| Notes payable—equipment | 66,829 | | 66,829 | |
| Notes payable—family | 24,000 | | | 24,000 |
| Income taxes | 1,809 | | | 1,809 |
| Accrued expenses | 84,551 | | | 84,551 |
| Other Taxes payable | 17,867 | | | 17,867 |
| Long-term liabilities | | | | |
| Notes payable—bank | 280,000 | | 280,000 | |
| Notes payable—equipment | 55,578 | | 55,578 | |
| Notes payable—stockholders | 314,586 | | | 314,586 |
| Equity | 198,779 | | | 198,779 |
| | $1,609,650 | | | |
| Secured loan (new) | | $420,000 | | 420,000 |
| First mortgage (new) | | 400,000 | | 400,000 |
| Accounts receivable loan (existing) | | 130,000 | | 130,000 |
| | | $950,000 | $950,000 | $1,787,243 |

the bank. The bank is also willing to grant you a 5 1/2 per cent line of credit up to 80 per cent of the net accounts receivable. This package is not precisely what you asked for, but we believe that it will satisfactorily meet the needs of your company. What are your thoughts about the financial proposal?"

"Well, I've done business with your bank for a number of years, and my relatives and I keep large deposits in your business. It seems like every time I need more money, it cost me a higher interest rate. I had wanted to pull some money out of the business for other purposes, but it looks like I might not be able to do that."

"You are certainly right about the cost of money going up, Mr. Hernandez. When you make your last term-loan commitment two or three years ago, we were paying 3 per cent per annum on time deposits. Now we have to pay 4 per cent. That's an increase of one-third, and labor costs have continued to rise, so that the rate we have to charge our customers has been edging upward also; otherwise, we wouldn't be in business very long if we could not cover our costs. We certainly do appreciate the business that you and your family have been giving us, and we will do everything possible to serve you. By the way, here is a schedule of the pro forma sources and applications of funds from the proposed financial arrangement. Why not study it for a few minutes and let me know what you decide about our refinancing proposal?"

# Leasing

## 25

### THE INSTANT FOOD MANUFACTURING COMPANY

In December, 1963, Mr. Joseph Fontaine, the controller of The Instant Food Manufacturing Company of Atlanta, Georgia was evaluating various proposals for financing the installation of an IBM 1401 data processing system. At that time, certain records and reports were maintained by a computer center on a fee basis. The acquisition of a data processing unit would involve the hiring of some additional staff to operate the center, but more detailed data and earlier reporting could be achieved through the company's operation of its own center.

Mr. Fontaine did not anticipate any reduction in the number of employees in the accounting department as a result of the IBM installation. The sales had increased by some 10 per cent per year for the past three years, and if this growth rate continued in the future, as was expected by the company management, no layoff of employees in the accounting department would be necessary. Certain of the employees, however, would be retrained from desk calculator operators to assistants in the computer installation.

The controller of the firm and a sales representative of IBM had made a careful study of the company's present and probable future needs for the next five years, and had determined that an IBM 1401 data processing system would be adequate. The equipment which was to comprise the data processing system, including the purchase or leasing price, are shown in Exhibit I.

International Business Machines Corporation offered its equipment under the following three plans: monthly rental plan; installment purchase payment plan; and cash sale. Since the company wished to conserve its cash, use of the latter method would require financing with a leasing company. The monthly rental rate for the unit, including sales tax and maintenance, was $6,569 for a 176-hour monthly shift. Additional machine time was computed at 40 per cent of the hourly rate, or 1/176 ($6,569)(.40) per hour. The leasee was expected to rent the equipment for at least one year from the data of installation, but could cancel the leasing contract thereafter without penalty. The rental of IBM equipment offered somewhat more flexibility to the leasee than the outright purchase as the leasee could replace the data processing system with a more up-to-date or larger unit.

The IBM installment payment plan required a 10 per cent down payment (plus taxes) with the balance amortized in equal monthly payments over sixty months or less. The effective interest rate charged by IBM to the purchasers of its equipment was 1.0 per cent above the New York prime loan rate (total of $5\frac{1}{2}$ per cent in 1963). A 60-month amortization schedule for a $5\frac{1}{2}$ per cent loan is shown in Exhibit II.

The purchase price of the data processing system (including sales tax) was quoted as $334,000. Although the company's cash account appeared large in relation to its total assets, the company maintained checking accounts with more than a hundred banks throughout the United States, and the finance officer of the firm did not wish to reduce the cash reserves for the purchase of the equipment.

Bids were invited from large leasing companies, and offers were tendered by the National Leasing Company and the ABC Equipment Leasing Cor-

**EXHIBIT I**

**The Instant Food Manufacturing Company**
**Cost of a 1401 Data Processing System**

|  | Monthly Rental* | Purchase Price | Monthly Maintenance Charge |
|---|---|---|---|
| 1401 E-4, Proceeding unit | $2,130 | $128,550 | $68.50 |
| 3835 Expanded print edit | 20 | 750 | .50 |
| 5540 Print control additional | 60 | 2,450 | .75 |
| 7600 Sense swiches | 15 | 550 | .50 |
| 1060 Advanced programming | 105 | 3,935 | 1.00 |
| 4575 High-low equal compare | 75 | 2,800 | 1.75 |
| 5275 Multiple-divide | 325 | 11,700 | 9.00 |
| 1402 Model 1, card read punch | 550 | 30,000 | 42.00 |
| 3550 Early card read | 10 | 215 | — |
| 1403 Printer, model 2 | 775 | 34,000 | 131.00 |
| 1406 Additional core storage, Model 1 | 575 | 24,500 | 12.50 |
| 7330 Tape units (4) | 1,800 | 88,000 | 195.00 |
|  | 6,440 | 327,450 | 462.50 |
| 2% sales tax | 129 | 6,549 | 9.25 |
| Total | $6,569 | $333,999 | $471.75 |

*Monthly rental rate is quoted for a 176-hour monthly shift. Additional machine time is computed at 40 per cent of the basic hourly rate.

poration. The plans submitted by National Leasing Company called for a complete pay-back of the initial cost, including an effective interest rate of $5\frac{1}{2}$ per cent, in three, five, or eight years. Although the Internal Revenue Service ruling required that the purchase price of the equipment upon expiration of the lease be an arms-length transaction, many leasing companies were transferring title to the leasee for a nominal fee. Mr. Fontaine estimated that $5,000 would be adequate to buy the rights to the installation at the end of the leasing period. Scrap values were assumed to be similar to

**EXHIBIT II**

**Allocation of $191.02 Monthly Payment
toward Principal and Interest of a
5.5 percent loan for sixty months with
an Initial Balance of $10,000**

| Period | Principal Beginning of Period | Interest During Period | Period | Principal Beginning of Period | Interest During Period |
|---|---|---|---|---|---|
| 1 | $10,000.00 | $45.83 | 31 | $5,342.12 | $24.48 |
| 2 | 9,854.81 | 45.17 | 32 | 5,175.58 | 23.72 |
| 3 | 9,708.96 | 44.50 | 33 | 5,008.28 | 22.95 |
| 4 | 9,562.44 | 43.83 | 34 | 4,840.21 | 22.18 |
| 5 | 9,415.25 | 43.15 | 35 | 4,671.37 | 21.41 |
| 6 | 9,267.38 | 42.48 | 36 | 4,501.76 | 20.63 |
| 7 | 9,118.84 | 41.79 | 37 | 4,331.37 | 19.85 |
| 8 | 8,969.61 | 41.11 | 38 | 4,160.20 | 19.07 |
| 9 | 8,819.70 | 40.42 | 39 | 3,988.25 | 18.28 |
| 10 | 8,669.10 | 39.73 | 40 | 3,815.51 | 17.49 |
| 11 | 8,517.81 | 39.04 | 41 | 3,641.98 | 16.67 |
| 12 | 8,365.83 | 38.34 | 42 | 3,467.65 | 15.89 |
| 13 | 8,213.15 | 37.64 | 43 | 3,292.52 | 15.09 |
| 14 | 8,059.77 | 36.94 | 44 | 3,116.59 | 14.28 |
| 15 | 7,905.69 | 36.23 | 45 | 2,939.85 | 13.47 |
| 16 | 7,750.90 | 35.52 | 46 | 2,762.30 | 12.66 |
| 17 | 7,595.40 | 34.81 | 47 | 2,583.94 | 11.84 |
| 18 | 7,439.19 | 34.10 | 48 | 2,404.76 | 11.02 |
| 19 | 7,282.27 | 33.38 | 49 | 2,224.76 | 10.20 |
| 20 | 7,124.63 | 32.65 | 50 | 2,043.94 | 9.37 |
| 21 | 6,966.26 | 31.93 | 51 | 1,862.29 | 8.54 |
| 22 | 6,807.17 | 31.20 | 52 | 1,679.81 | 7.70 |
| 23 | 6,647.35 | 30.47 | 53 | 1,496.49 | 6.86 |
| 24 | 6,486.80 | 29.73 | 54 | 1,312.33 | 6.01 |
| 25 | 6,325.51 | 28.99 | 55 | 1,127.32 | 5.17 |
| 26 | 6,163.48 | 28.25 | 56 | 941.47 | 4.32 |
| 27 | 6,000.71 | 27.50 | 57 | 754.77 | 3.46 |
| 28 | 5,837.19 | 26.75 | 58 | 567.21 | 2.60 |
| 29 | 5,672.92 | 26.00 | 59 | 378.79 | 1.74 |
| 30 | 5,507.90 | 25.24 | 60* | 189.51 | .87 |

*Final payment slightly smaller because of upward rounding.

the trade-in factors in Exhibit III. The following repayment schedule was offered by National Leasing Company:

| Leasing Period | Monthly Leasing Payment Per $ 1,000 of Equipment Cost |
|---|---|
| 3 years | 30.20 |
| 5 years | 19.10 |
| 8 years | 12.90 |

After the expiration of the initial lease, the equipment could be rented under a renewal contract for 3 per cent of the original cost per year. Under this plan, the leasee was required to provide maintenance and insurance and to pay ad valorem taxes.

The leasee was granted the privilege of buying out the lease prior to the expiration of the primary term. The cost of this privilege was the payment of the balance of the principle due plus 2 per cent of the original cost of the equipment. The effective interest rate used in setting the rental fee was $5\frac{1}{2}$ per cent, or one percentage point above the prime loan rate, whichever was greater. The prime interest rate had been $4\frac{1}{2}$ per cent from 1960 through 1963.

The ABC Equipment Leasing Corporation offered to buy the IBM equipment and lease it to The Instant Food Manufacturing Company under a three-year or five-year contract. The equipment could be leased by the month after the expiration of the primary contract. Monthly rental percentages are shown in Exhibit III.

The leasing agreement permitted the equipment to be traded in to the manufacturer during the initial term. ABC agreed to pay the difference and

**EXHIBIT III**

**The Instant Food Manufacturing Company
Computer Rental Plans Submitted by
ABC Equipment Leasing Corporation
(Percentages of Initial Cost)**

| Year | Monthly Rental Percentages Contract Period 3 years | 5 years | Year-End Trade-in Factor Contract Period 3 years | 5 years |
|---|---|---|---|---|
| 1 | 2.5% | 1.9% | 77.0% | 85.0% |
| 2 | 2.5 | 1.9 | 55.0 | 68.0 |
| 3 | 2.5 | 1.9 | 25.0 | 50.0 |
| 4 | 1.5 | 1.9 | 20.0 | 32.0 |
| 5 | 1.25 | 1.9 | 12.0 | 10.0 |
| 6 | 1.00 | 1.0 | 10.0 | 8.0 |
| 7 | 0.75 | .5 | 8.0 | 5.0 |
| 8 | .50 | .5 | 5.0 | 5.0 |
| 9 | .50 | .5 | 5.0 | 5.0 |
| 10 | .50 | .5 | 5.0 | 5.0 |

determine the new cost basis by adding the out-of-pocket cost to the applicable trade-in balance. Monthly rental percentages would begin anew.

The leasee was permitted to terminate a lease contract during the initial period. Rentals, however, were to continue until the leasor found a new leasee. In the event that the used equipment were sold as a result of a broken lease, the difference between the trade-in factor and the selling price of the used equipment would be a debt to the original leasee. As an alternative, the leasee was permitted to pay the balance of the monthly

### EXHIBIT IV

**The Instant Food Manufacturing Company**
**Comparative Balance Sheets**
**As of September 30**
**(In Thousands)**

|  | 1963 | | 1962 | |
|---|---|---|---|---|
|  | Dollars | Per cent | Dollars | Per cent |
| *Assets* | | | | |
| Current assets | | | | |
| Cash and U. S. gov. sec. | $10,841 | 16.4% | $8,982 | 15.2% |
| Accounts rec. net | 9,195 | 13.9 | 8,202 | 13.9 |
| Inventory, lower of cost or market | | | | |
| Finished goods | 5,139 | 7.8 | 4,966 | 8.4 |
| Raw materials and other | 4,621 | 7.0 | 4,117 | 7.0 |
| Prepaid expenses | 936 | 1.4 | 483 | .8 |
| Total currents assets | 30,732 | 46.5 | 26,750 | 45.4 |
| Fixed Assets | | | | |
| Property, plant, and equipment | 52,366 | 79.4 | 47,365 | 80.4 |
| Less : accum. depreciation | −20,521 | 31.1 | 18,131 | 30.8 |
| Total fixed assets | 31,845 | 48.3 | 29,234 | 49.6 |
| Other assets | 3,400 | 5.2 | 2,953 | 5.0 |
| Total assets | $65,977 | 100.0% | $58,937 | 100.0% |
| *Liabilities and stockholders' equity* | | | | |
| Current liabilities | | | | |
| Accounts payable and accruals | $7,974 | 12.1% | $7,467 | 12.7% |
| Federal income tax | 5,302 | 8.0 | 4,383 | 7.0 |
| Current portion of long-term debt | 85 | .1 | 176 | .3 |
| Total current liabilities | 13,361 | 20.2 | 12,026 | 20.4 |
| Long-term debt | 8,292 | 12.6 | 8,994 | 15.3 |
| Deferred federal income tax | 2,627 | 4.0 | 1,812 | 3.1 |
| Common stock, $ 3.00 par, 5,000 shares authorized | 12,762 | 19.3 | 12,594 | 21.4 |
| Capital in excess of par volue | 587 | .9 | 92 | .1 |
| Retained earnings | 28,348 | 43.0 | 23,419 | 39.7 |
| Total capital | 41,697 | 63.2 | 36,105 | 61.2 |
| Total liabilities | 65,977 | 100.0% | $58,937 | 100.0% |

rentals due under the initial term, discounted by 5 per cent. The latter would eliminate further obligation.

The long-term debt of The Instant Food Manufacturing Company constituted about 20 per cent of the total capital on September 30, 1963. The long-term notes carried an interest rate of $5\frac{1}{2}$ per cent. The treasurer of the corporation was confident that additional debt funds were available at a similar rate. The price earnings ratio of the company's common stock was about 11, and the board of directors was not favorably inclined toward the sale of equity securities at that time. Mr. Fontaine considered the weighted-average cost of capital of the firm to have averaged about eight per cent after taxes during recent years.

**EXHIBIT V**

**The Instant Food Manufacturing Company**
**Comparative Income Statements**
**For the Year Ended September 30**
**(In Thousands)**

|  | 1963 | | 1962 | |
|---|---|---|---|---|
|  | Dollar | Per cent | Dollar | Per cent |
| Net sales | $198,271 | 100.0 | $175,958 | 100.0 |
| Cost of goods sold, selling and administrative expenses | 176,659 | 89.1 | 158,096 | 89.8 |
| Depreciation | 4,062 | 2.0 | 3,647 | 2.1 |
| Interest expenses | 507 | .3 | 572 | .3 |
| Total expenses | 181,228 | 91.4 | 162,315 | 92.2 |
| Income before federal income tax | 17,043 | 8.6 | 13,643 | 7.8 |
| Provision for federal income tax* | 9,070 | 4.6 | 7,157 | 4.1 |
| Net income | $7,973 | 4.0 | $6,486 | 3.7 |

*Deferred federal income taxes: $815 in 1963, $790 in 1962.

**EXHIBIT VI**

**The Instant Food Manufacturing Company**
**Present Value of $1 Tables**
**Compounded Annually**

| Period | $5^{1}/_{2}$ Per Cent | 8 Per Cent |
|---|---|---|
| 1 | .947867 | .925926 |
| 2 | .898452 | .857339 |
| 3 | .851614 | .793832 |
| 4 | .807217 | .735030 |
| 5 | .765134 | .680583 |
| 6 | .725246 | .630170 |
| 7 | .687437 | .583490 |
| 8 | .651599 | .540269 |
| 9 | .617629 | .500249 |
| 10 | .585431 | .463193 |

Mr. Fontaine was assigned the task of determining which of the four alternatives appeared most favorable. Leasing offered some advantage over ownership in that the entire rental fee was a deductible expense. On the other hand, depreciation equal to 20 per cent of the declining balance could be taken during the first half of the equipment's life. A depreciation switch to straight-line during the latter half was anticipated. The 7 per cent tax credit could be obtained under any of the plans as the leasors were willing to pass their tax credit through to the leasee.

As a starting point Mr. Fontaine decided to determine the present value of total cash outflows for the estimated usefulness of the data processing system. He assumed that a realistic estimate of the market value of the equipment would be similar to the estimates appearing in Exhibit III. He was not sure whether to use the $5\frac{1}{2}$ per cent interest rate or to use the weighted average cost of capital of 8 per cent, but he chose the latter.

Mr. Fontaine's calculations of the present value of total cash outflows for the ABC Leasing plan computed with the above assumptions are presented in Exhibit VII. Since depreciation would not require a cash outflow, it would not be used in the schedule on the leasing plan. Where the assets were acquired, however, the tax advantage of depreciation (rather than the leasing payment) would be considered. After studying Exhibit VII carefully to ascertain that all elements of expected cash outlays and inflows were considered, Mr. Fontaine informed his assistant that he should complete similar schedules on the other three alternatives making the necessary substitutions of costs.

**EXHIBIT VII**

**Instant Food Manufacturing Company**
**Plan 4 :   ABC Leasing Plan**

| Item | Year | | | | | Totals |
|---|---|---|---|---|---|---|
| | 1 | 2 | 3 | 4 | 5 | |
| Rental | $76,152 | $76,152 | $76,152 | $76,152 | $76,152 | |
| Maintenance | 5,661 | 5,661 | 5,661 | 5,661 | 5,661 | |
| Total | $81,813 | $81,813 | $81,813 | $81,813 | $81,813 | |
| Less:   taxes @ 50%* | 40,906 | 40,906 | 40,906 | 40,906 | 40,906 | |
| Less :   7% investment credit | 23,380 | | | | | |
| Cash outlays | 17,527 | 40,907 | 40,907 | 40,907 | 40,907 | $181.155 |
| P. V. factors | .925926 | .857339 | .793832 | .735030 | .680583 | |
| P. V. of cash outlays (discounted @ 8%) | 16,229 | 35,071 | 32,473 | 30,068 | 27,841 | 141,682 |
| Less:   scrap value after taxes (33,400–5,000) (.68058) 1/2 | | | | | | 9,660 |
| P. V. of net cash outflows (8%) | | | | | | $132,022 |

*Assuming an average tax rate of 50 per cent. Computation disregards the effect of insurance and property taxes as these would be constant under most of these financial arrangements.

# Factoring Accounts Receivable

## 26

ABC FACTORING, INC.

On June 8, 1964, Mr. John Nolan, president of the Globe Instrument Company of Chicago, Illinois, was comparing the differences between two financial proposals extended by Mr. George Sloan, representative of ABC Factoring, Inc. The first proposal was to sell outright accounts receivable to ABC and the other was to borrow from ABC by a pledge of accounts receivable.

Globe Instrument Company had been formed in 1959 with an initial capital of $100,000, and sales of medical equipment and components by the company had grown from $225,000 in 1960 to $1,355,000 in 1963. The fifteen stockholders of the firm were opposed to the issuance of more stock for the financing of working capital needs but wished to rely as heavily as possible on the use of credit.

Although the company operated at a $12,000 loss in 1960, it was able to earn after-tax profits aggregating over $68,000 from 1961–1963. The company had never declared any cash dividends, and so long as sales and the need for

| Year | Sales | After-Tax Profits |
|------|-------|-------------------|
| 1960 | $225,000 | $(12,000) |
| 1961 | 395,000 | 11,500 |
| 1962 | 745,000 | 21,550 |
| 1963 | 1,355,000 | 35,370 |

working capital continued to increase, the directors did not intend to pay any dividends.

The growth in sales had been welcomed by Mr. Nolan, but as sales increased, Mr. Nolan found that a larger investment in inventory and accounts receivable was required. Mr. Nolan had prided himself in being an efficient production control manager. He had been able to keep the inventory of raw materials, supplies, component parts, and work-in-process to approximately a three-month supply. Since goods were sold only on a job-order basis, finished goods were shipped to the customers as soon as they came off the final inspection line. The growth in sales had increased the need for more funds to be committed to inventory. Inventories had been increased from 42,000 at the end of 1960 to 215,000 at the end of 1963. Mr. Nolan believed that additional increases were desirable, but trade credit was being stretched to the maximum.

Mr. Nolan was receiving various credit terms from his suppliers, but about 60 per cent of the accounts were for terms of 1/10, n/30. Other terms were evenly distributed between 2/10, n/30 and net 30. Although Mr. Nolan realized that discounting would be to his advantage, he had been unable to do so for the past three years. During the past 18 months, his cash position had been so tight that Mr. Nolan had been as much as three to five months slow in paying the trade credit. This had resulted in some nasty collection notices, and two of his suppliers of critical parts had threatened to place the company on a C.O.D. basis if credit relations had not improved by the end of the month.

The problem had grown worse during the past year as many of Globe's customers were becoming more lax in paying for their purchases. The company was granting terms compatible with its industry, $\frac{1}{2}$/10, n/30, but few of the customers were discounting. A few of the accounts were two to three months slow in paying; therefore, Globe was unable to be prompt in its trade credit payments.

When the company was first formed, Mr. Nolan served as president and carried out the functions of production manager, sales manager, and credit manager. The growth of the size of the company, and the slowness in payment of accounts receivable had impressed upon Mr. Nolan the need for a full-time credit manager. Although such an individual would cost the company at least $7,200 per year, more vigorous collection policies could possibly reduce the bad debt losses from its current 1 1/2 per cent of sales.

Mr. Nolan had repeatedly attempted to establish a line of credit with his bank. In 1961 he was advised that the bank would be unable to accomodate the customer until it was operating at a profit. In subsequent years, Mr. Nolan was informed that the current ratio of the company and the balance between debt and equity were so poor that prudent banking policies did not permit granting the loan; therefore, the credit was refused.

While attending a business luncheon, Mr. Nolan was introduced to Mr. George Sloan of ABC Factoring, Inc., who encouraged Mr. Nolan to discuss his business outlook. Mr. Nolan was very encouraged about the acceptance of his products by hospitals and practicing physicians, but he was discouraged about the financial pressures being brought to bear on his company.

"Why don't you drop around to my office tomorrow with your financial statements and we will see what type of a deal we can make you. We have been able to help hundreds of fast-growing businesses such as yours, and I feel sure that we can work out a financial plan which will be profitable to both our companies."

On the following afternoon, Mr. Nolan visited the Chicago office of ABC Factoring equipped with financial statements and plans for the future. Mr. Nolan stated that he did not have any particular plans other than to continue to increase his sales and profits and to try to place his accounts payable on a more current basis.

After reviewing the financial statements, Mr. Sloan outlined two financing plans which were designed for small growth companies such as Globe. The first plan was factoring, or the direct sale without recourse of accounts receivable. The second plan was the pledge of accounts receivable. Since Mr. Nolan had not utilized either of the above financing plans, he asked that Mr. Sloan outline some of the main points for the two plans and to indicate the advantages of each.

"Until some twenty years ago, 90 per cent of the factoring business was confined to the textile and apparel industries. Since then, however, factoring has spread to electronics, plastics, furniture, machinery, and other industries. About one-fourth to one-third of the factoring business is now in industries outside the textile field. When we factor accounts receivable, we buy them outright without recourse, assuming the credit risks and the tasks of credit checking and collecting. Your customers are notified to make their payments directly to us. Although we reserve the right to refuse to buy any accounts, we are often willing to grant credit that you would not feel safe in granting. This is possible because of our large base of receivables, access to credit information, national scope of operation, and effective collection policies. Some four to five million accounts are factored annually.

"Your cost would be 2.5 per cent of the accounts sold and an interest charge of 7 per cent per annum for your period of trade credit plus 10 days. A reserve equal to 5 per cent of the accounts pledged would be maintained by ABC to take care of possible returns and allowances. No discounts would be passed on to Globe even though some of the customers paid within the discount period.

"Even though the expenses at first appear fairly high, we suffer all loss on bad debts on the accounts we accept, and you can devote your time to production and sales management and let us take care of your credit management.

"For our customers who are reluctant to factor their accounts, we will loan up to 80 per cent of the pledged accounts receivable which are of acceptable credit risk. Since we do not purchase your accounts, you will make all credit investigations, collect all the accounts, and remit the checks to us. We will then remit the 20 per cent credit to Globe. You will suffer the loss on bad debts, and you are expected to segregate the pledged accounts. Under this arrangement we require our customer to cover the expense of a surprise quarterly audit. The annual cost of these audits for your firm is guaranteed not to exceed $600. The only other direct cost of this plan is a daily interest charge of 1/25 of 1 per cent of the funds borrowed."

Mr. Nolan expressed his gratitude to Mr. Sloan and stated that he would consider the plans, ask his accountant to prepare some cost comparisons for the two plans, and report his decision to Mr. Sloan. Although he preferred to finance with bank credit rather than to deal with a factor or a commercial finance company, his financial situation would have to be improved before the banker would consider a loan. Temporarily, at least, he believed that he might have to accept one of the proposals.

**EXHIBIT I**

**Globe Instrument Company**
**Balance Sheets**

|  | 12/31/60 | 12/31/61 | 12/31/62 | 12/31/63 |
|---|---|---|---|---|
| *Assets* | | | | |
| Cash | $4,012 | $3,793 | $4,925 | $1,914 |
| Accounts receivables | 39,814 | 62,416 | 128,413 | 159,414 |
| Inventories | 42,015 | 51,819 | 85,401 | 165,412 |
| Other current assets | 215 | 329 | 413 | 914 |
| Total Current Assets | 86,056 | 118,357 | 219,152 | 327,654 |
| Fixed assets | 20,515 | 22,405 | 30,968 | 45,314 |
| Less depreciation | 4,103 | 8,901 | 15,215 | 22.817 |
| Net fixed assets | 16,412 | 13,504 | 15,753 | 22,497 |
| Patents | 10,500 | 30,415 | 45,306 | 56,908 |
| Other assets | 804 | 1,201 | 1,103 | 1,792 |
| Total assets | $113,772 | $163,477 | $281,314 | $408,851 |
| | | | | |
| *Liabilities and capital* | | | | |
| Accounts payable | $14,336 | $44,731 | 124,265 | 194,855 |
| Income taxes payable | — | — | 8,549 | 18,524 |
| Accruals | 11,419 | 19,213 | 27,415 | 39,018 |
| Total liabilities | 25,755 | 63,944 | 160,229 | 252,397 |
| Capital stock | 100,000 | 100,000 | 100,000 | 100,000 |
| Retained earnings | (11,983) | (467) | 21,085 | 56,454 |
| Total equity | 88,017 | 99,533 | 121,085 | 156,454 |
| Total liab. and equity | $113,772 | $163,477 | $281,314 | $408,851 |

**EXHIBIT II**

**Globe Instrument Company**
**Income Statement**

|  | 1960 | 1961 | 1962 | 1963 |
|---|---|---|---|---|
| Sales | $215,416 | $395,014 | $745,307 | $1,355,102 |
| Cost of goods sold* | 112,231 | 204,617 | 374,144 | 673,486 |
| Gross Profits | 103,185 | 190,397 | 371,163 | 681,616 |
| Expenses | 115,168 | 178,881 | 341,042 | 627,723 |
| Before-Tax Profits | (11,983) | 11,516 | 30,121 | 53,893 |
| Federal income taxes | — | — | 8,549 | 18,524 |
| Net Income | $(11,983) | $11,516 | $21,572 | $35,369 |

*Materials = 50 per cent.

*Part V*

# LONG-TERM
# FINANCING

# Debt vs. Equity

## 27

### DEAD WOOD UTILITIES COMPANY

In 1967 the Dead Wood Utilities Company was contemplating possible methods of financing an expansion of their electrical generating facilities. The community in which the company operated had shown a deterioration in its population following the closing of a nearby army post. Recent reactivation of the camp, however, had resulted in a demand for electricity almost greater than the company could provide. The company was located a few hundred miles from a government-owned dam and power plant, and it could purchase electricity from the government power plant at a wholesale price more economically then it could install its own hydroelectric generators. Funds were needed to erect a high-voltage power line from the government-owned power plant to Dead Wood.

In order to obtain funds for the expansion, the company had the choice of selling $10 million in 5 per cent, thirty-year, first mortgage bonds or selling common stock through an investment banker. The management of the company was also under pressure to expand its facilities for distributing natural gas, and if it were to maintain its franchise to operate in the area, it would have to provide the required services at reasonable rates. The company contemplated additional expansion in and around its area of operation, and management estimated that an additional $18 million in funds would have to be raised during the next three or four years. Any financing decision made at the current time should take into consideration future plans for raising capital.

In keeping with the dividend policy of most public utility companies, Dead Wood had followed a dividend payout of approximately 70 per cent in the past. Because of the pressing need for funds, however, the company reduced its dividends from an annual rate of $1.50 in

1965 to only $1.00 in 1966. The reduction had been met with a substantial amount of criticism on the part of the stockholders, many of whom owned the stock for its stability of income. The market price of the stock had declined somewhat after the dividend reduction, and the board of directors was considering the merits of restoring the old dividend rate. A few of the directors believed that such a restoration would stimulate the market value of the shares to their old 1965 high market value of $30 per share.

A conference with one of the partners of the investment banking firm disclosed that the underwriter was willing to acquire the entire issue of bonds at 97 per cent of par and to offer them at par to the general public. An additional $50,000 in expenses for such things as legal fees, the preparation of a prospectus, SEC registration fees, bond certificate engraving fees, and the like would also have to be paid by the issuing company. The company was expected to net about 96 per cent of the par value of the issue. In order to make the bonds attractive to the investors, the investment banker insisted that an annual sinking fund equal to 2 per cent of the original outstanding balance be established. The sinking-fund cash could be invested in U.S. government securities or the company's own bonds would be repurchased in the open market and retired. The bond issue was to be callable at 105 for the first five years, at 104 from the sixth to the tenth year, and callable at par during the last five years of the maturity period.

As an alternative to issuing the bonds, the company could market an issue of common stock. The current market value of the common shares was $27, and the investment banker would consider selling the issue with a 5 per cent commission rate. Other marketing costs born by the issuing company were estimated at $55,000.

Approximately a year would be required from the time that the company made a decision on the financing until the funds could be raised and the facilities be constructed. If the company were to go ahead with its other expansion projects, a definite decision would be required within the next six months. Because of the time delay in constructing the facilities and in increasing the sales of the company to a point adequate to cover the fixed and variable expenses, the company did not contemplate any favorable change in the profit picture during 1967. An overall return of 7 per cent on the company's total capital (before bond interest, but after income taxes) could be anticipated for 1968 and for subsequent years.

Financial data for Dead Wood Utilities Company are shown below. Although net profits for the company increased slightly from 1961 through 1966, the growth rate had been very slow compared to that of other nearby cities. The company had little problem in raising working capital as the current assets for a utility company are almost identical to the current liabilities. Cycle billing, customer deposits, and accrued expenses maintain a current ratio of about one to one. In addition, the company's accounts receivable, materials and supplies, and other current assets are small when compared to an industrial company. From 90 to 93 per cent of the assets of an electrical utility company are usually invested in the net utility plant. For Dead Wood Utilities Company the annual revenues normally amount to about 22 per cent of the total assets, while the figure for net income before bond interest but after federal income taxes is usually between 30 and 34 per cent of revenues.

## QUESTIONS

1. Assume a corporate income tax rate of 50 per cent. Compute the net earnings per share if the expansion is finance by (a) bonds, or (b) common stock.
2. Evaluate the underwriting costs associated with the issue. Do you believe that they are reasonable or excessive? Defend.
3. Assume a depreciation rate which averages 2.5 per cent of the net property account and prepare pro forma statements of sources and application of funds for the 1967 calendar year.
4. Which of the two methods of financing are preferable in early 1967? Defend your choice.

**EXHIBIT I**

**Deadwood Utilities Company**
**Net Profits**
**(In Thousands)**

| Year | Amount |
|------|--------|
| 1966 | $1,120 |
| 1965 | 1,040 |
| 1964 | 1,095 |
| 1963 | 1,125 |
| 1962 | 1,228 |
| 1961 | 1,193 |

**EXHIBIT II**

**Deadwood Utilities Company**
**Balance Sheet**
**(In Thousands)**

| Assets | 1965 | 1966 |
|--------|------|------|
| Currents assets | $ 2,161 | 2,225 |
| Utility plant (net) | 25,141 | 25,716 |
| Other assets | 403 | 389 |
| Total assets | $27,705 | $28,330 |
| *Liabilities and capital* | | |
| Current liabilities | $ 1,796 | $ 1,951 |
| First mortgage bonds, | | |
| 3 1/2's of 1986 | 10,000 | 10,000 |
| 4's of 1988 | 5,000 | 5,000 |
| Preferred stock, 5% | 3,000 | 3,000 |
| Common stock, $ 10 par | 5,000 | 5,000 |
| Retained earnings | 2,909 | 3,379 |
| Total liabilities and capital | $27,705 | $28,330 |

# Equity
# Issues

# 28

In April, 1964, the two officers and shareholders of a convenience grocery store chain, Wheel and Sack, Inc., were considering the methods for raising additional funds for expanding the number of their retail outlets. Mr. Joseph Osborne and Mr. Claude DeBloc had organized the corporation in 1961 and began operation with two retail outlets located in Lake Charles, Louisiana. By early 1964, the number of outlets had increased to eight. All the stores were located in and around Lake Charles, the most distant store being thirty miles from the home office.

Although the officers had erected three buildings at a low cost, they found that capital could be conserved by renting additional outlets. Since their sales were on a cash-and-carry basis to individuals, their receivables remained small. Thirty-day terms were extended to business firms and nonprofit organizations. Their inventories were financed almost entirely with trade credit.

Mr. Osborne was president of the firm, and Mr. DeBloc was secretary-treasurer. Mr. Osborner's previous business experience consisted of having been clerk and manager in a supermarket for four years. He held a degree in advertising from Louisiana State University. Mr. DeBloc had been a salesman for a national office equipment manufacturer for about ten years prior to the time the business was formed. Each of the outlets was staffed with a manager and one or two other employees. Mr. Osborne's principal duties consisted of inventory control, purchasing, advertising, and employee training. Mr. DeBloc was responsible for frequent inspections of the retail outlets, daily deposits of cash receipts, payments of wages and bills, and the maintenance of funds adequate to meet the company's needs. Mr. Osborne handled the hiring and firing of the store managers and reserved the right to require a store manager to discharge other employees when they were not "doing their job."

Since 1961 the firm had rented the facilities of five independent grocery stores, and through careful buying and expense control had managed to operate at a nice profit after paying each of the officers $9,000 annually. The officers, however, wished to open twenty new outlets within a radius of 50 miles of their city. To do so would require a substantial amount of capital. Since the officers wished to retain managerial control of the firm, they desired the use of debt or nonvoting preferred stock.

The amount of funds needed for each new outlet, in addition to normal trade credit available for inventory stocking, was about $20,000 for leased quarters or $40,000 for owned quarters. The larger amount would provide enough funds to pay 50 per cent down on a building; equip the outlet with refrigation equipment, shelves, check-out equipment, and the like; and leave about $3,000 for working capital. Virtually all the inventory could be financed with trade credit.

The mortgagors of the buildings retained a first mortgage on the real property; the trade creditors insisted upon a pro rata lien against the inventory because of the long terms of payment; and Mr. DeBloc wished to retain permission to use bank borrowing to meet working capital needs. Therefore, the funds raised for long-term expansion would have to be subordinate to the above types of creditors. Both Mr. Osborne and Mr. DeBloc were willing to pledge any other assets as collateral for a loan or bond issue and to freeze their salaries and dividends at the present level.

An officer of one of the equipment supply corporations suggested that Mr. DeBloc consider an $800,000, 8 per cent, ten-year, callable subordinated debenture bond issue. The bonds would be sold by the issuing company rather than through an investment banking firm. Mr. DeBloc discovered that the Louisiana Securities Act permitted the sale of securities to residents of the state only after proper registration. Registration could be made by notification filed with the Commissioner of Securities or by qualification. The following are extracts from Section 707 and 708 of the Louisiana Securities Act:

A. The following securities shall be entitled to registration by notification in the manner provided in this Section.

    (1) Securities issued by a person, corporation, partnership, association, company, syndicate, or trust owning a property, business, or industry which has been in continuous operation for not less than three years and which has shown during a period of not less than two years prior to the close of its last fiscal year preceding the offering of such securities, average annual net earnings, after deducting all prior charges, not including the charges upon securities to be retired out of the proceeds of sale, as follows:

        (a) In the case of interest-bearing securities, not less than one and one-half times the annual interest charge thereon and upon all other outstanding interest-bearing obligations of equal rank.

        (b) In the case of preferred stock, not less than one and one-half times the annual dividend requirement of such preferred stock and on all other outstanding stock of equal rank.

(c) In the case of common stock not less than five per centum upon all outstanding common stock of equal rank, together with the amount of common stock then offered for sale reckoned upon the price at which such stock is then offered for sale or sold.

(2) Securities entitled to registration by notification shall be registered by the filing by the issuer if a resident of this state, or by any registered dealer interested in the sale thereof, in the Office of the Commissioner, the following:

(a) Form A, Uniform Application, to be obtained from the Commissioner.

(b) Statement showing average annual net earnings for at least two years immediately preceding the year in which application for registration of and authority to offer and sell such securities is filed.

(c) Balance sheet of its assets and liabilities not more than ninety days prior to the date of filing such balance sheet.

(d) Certified copy of articles of incorporation and all amendments, if applicant is a corporation, and certificate of Secretary of State attesting to recordation of said articles in his office.

(e) The amount of commission and any other remuneration to be paid in connection with the offering and sale of the securities sought to be registered.

(f) Any other information or documents required by the Commissioner.

B. All securities required by this Part to be registered before being sold in the state, and not entitled to registration by notification, shall be registered only by qualification in the manner provided by this Section.

(1) The Commissioner shall receive and act upon applications to have securities registered by qualification, and may prescribe forms on which he may require such applications to be submitted. Applications shall be in writing and shall be duly signed by the applicant and sworn to by any person having knowledge of the facts, and filed in the Office of the Commissioner and may be made either by the issuer of the securities for which registration is applied, if such issuer be a resident of this state, or by any registered dealer desiring to sell the same within this state.

(2) The Commissioner may require the applicant to submit to the Commissioner the following information respecting the issuer and other relevant information as the Commissioner in his judgment deems necessary to enable him to ascertain whether such securities shall be registered pursuant to the provisions of this Section:

(a) The names and addresses of the directors, trustees, and officers, if the issuer be a corporation or association or trust; of all partners, if the issuer be a partnership; and of the issuer, if the issuer be an individual.

(b) The location of the issuer's principal business office and of its principal office in this state, if any.

(c) The purposes of incorporation, if incorporated, and the general character of the business actually to be transacted by the issuer, and the purposes of the proposed issue.

(d) A statement of the capitalization of the issuer; a balance sheet showing the amount and general character of its assets and liabilities on a day not more than ninety days prior to the date of filing such balance sheet; a detailed statement of the plan upon which the issuer proposes to transact business; a copy of the security for the registration of which application is made and a copy of any circular, prospectus, advertisement, or other description of such securities then prepared by or for such issuer or by or for such applicant, if the applicant shall not be the issuer, to be used for distribution or publication in this state.

(e) A statement of the issuer's income expenses and fixed charges during the last fiscal year, or if in actual business less than one year, then for such time as the issuer has been in actual business.

(f) A statement showing the price at which said security is proposed to be sold, together with the maximum amount of commissions or other form of remuneration to be paid in cash or otherwise, directly or indirectly for or in connection with the sale or offering for sale of such securities.

(g) A detailed statement showing the items of cash, property, service, patents, good will and any other consideration for which such securities have been or are to be issued in payment.

(h) The amount of capital stock which is to be set aside and disposed of as promotion stock, and a statement of all stock issued from time to time as promotion stock.

(i) Any other information or documents required by the Commissioner.

(j) If the issuer is a corporation, there shall be filed with the application a certified copy of its articles of incorporation with all amendments and of its existing by-laws, if not already on file in the Office of the Commissioner or of the Secretary of State of this state. If the issuer is a trustee, there shall be filed with the application a copy of all instruments by which the trust is created or declared and in which it is accepted and acknowledged. If the issuer is a partnership or an unincorporated association, or joint stock company, or any other form of organization whatsoever, there shall be filed with the application a copy of its articles of partnership or association and all other papers pertaining to its organization, if not already on file in the Office of the Commissioner.

(3) At the time of filing the information, as prescribed in this Section, the applicant shall pay to the Commissioner a fee of one-tenth of one per centum of the aggregate price of the securities to be registered and offered to be sold in this state, but in no case shall the fee be less than fifty dollars or more than one thousand dollars.

(4) If upon examination of any application the Commissioner shall find that the sale of the security referred to therein would not be fraudulent and would not work or tend to work a fraud upon the purchaser,

**EXHIBIT I**

**Wheel and Sack, Inc.**
**Balance Sheet**
**February 28, 1964**

| | | |
|---|---:|---:|
| *Assets* | | |
| Current assets | | |
| Cash in bank | $ 11,169 | |
| Cash on hand | 3,556 | |
| Inventories | 138,798 | |
| Employee loans | 484 | |
| Accounts receivable | 8,459 | |
| Total | | $163,466 |
| Fixed assets | | |
| Machinery, equipment, and trucks | 101,004 | |
| Building improvements | 5,760 | |
| Warehouse and office bldg. | 24,500 | |
| Buildings (3 at various locations) | 54,969 | |
| Total | 186,233 | |
| Less : reserve for depreciation | 16,900 | |
| Total | | 169,333 |
| Real estate—land | | 36,740 |
| Other assets | | |
| Prepaid Insurance | 3,544 | |
| Prepaid supplies | 2,758 | |
| Prepaid licenses | 3,670 | |
| Total other assets | | 9,972 |
| Total | | $378,511 |
| | | |
| *Liabilities and Capital* | | |
| Current liabilities | | |
| Accounts payable | $130,261 | |
| Payroll taxes payable | 3,036 | |
| Federal excess tax payable | 109 | |
| Corporation income tax payable | 1,757 | |
| Sales tax payable | 3,476 | |
| Total current liabilities | | $138,639 |
| Notes and mortgages—equipment | 56,714 | |
| Notes and mortgages—real estate and other | 146,247 | 202,961 |
| Total liabilities | | 341,600 |
| Capital and retained earnings | | |
| Common stock | 10,000 | |
| Retained earnings | 26,911 | |
| Total Capital | | 36,911 |
| Total liabilities and capital | | $378,511 |

and that the enterprise or business of the issuer is not based upon unsound business principles, he shall record the registration of such securities in the register of securities, and thereupon such securities may be sold by any registered issuer or by any registered dealer,

**EXHIBIT II**

**Wheel and Sack, Inc.**
**Comparative Income Statement**

| | Year Ended 1961 | Year Ended 1962 | Year Ended 1963 | Two Months Ended Feb. 28, 1964 |
|---|---|---|---|---|
| Gross sales | $   83,177 | $1,226,473 | $1,640,838 | $   301,705 |
| Cost of goods sold | | | | |
| Beginning inventory | | 4,246 | 110,326 | 142,515 |
| Purchases | | 1,160,574 | 1,399,262 | 243,350 |
| Less : discounts | | (2,425) | (13,256) | (2,461) |
| Total | | 1,162,395 | 1,496,332 | 383,404 |
| Ending inventory | | 110,326 | 142,515 | 138,798 |
| Cost of goods sold | 66,617 | 1,052,069 | 1,353,817 | 244,606 |
| Gross profit | 16,560 | 174,404 | 287,021 | 57,099 |
| Operating expenses | | | | |
| Advertising | | 26,784 | 35,591 | 4,408 |
| Legal and auditing | | 597 | 1,887 | 172 |
| Truck and auto. | | 1,264 | 3,746 | 570 |
| Bank charges | | 267 | 316 | 68 |
| Miscellaneous labor | | 430 | 3,128 | 210 |
| Depreciation | | 5,875 | 8,970 | 4,932 |
| Dues and donations | | 369 | 323 | 43 |
| Entertainment and travel | | 1,047 | 1,522 | 166 |
| Insurance | | 2,084 | 4,273 | 709 |
| Interest | | 4,369 | 11,234 | 1,830 |
| Laundry and uniforms | | 597 | 1,489 | 281 |
| Lease rental—equip. | | — | 5,839 | 1,637 |
| Licenses and taxes | | 5,886 | 7,789 | 589 |
| Miscellaneous | | 3,951 | 2,828 | 192 |
| Maintenance and repairs | | 4,733 | 6,636 | 514 |
| Postage | | 237 | 382 | 65 |
| Rent | | 27,765 | 32,605 | 5,708 |
| Salaries and wages | | 63,762 | 101,803 | 19,194 |
| Store supplies | | 8,166 | 7,488 | 919 |
| Utilities | | 9,179 | 21,527 | 5,074 |
| Payroll taxes | | 3,769 | 6,233 | 1,214 |
| Cash Shortages | | — | 1,489 | 413 |
| Total expenses | 23,310 | 171,129 | 267,100 | 48,907 |
| Net operating profit (loss) | (6,750) | 3,275 | 19,921 | 8,192 |
| Add. Miscellaneous Income | — | — | 2,275 | — |
| Net profit (loss) | $   (6,750) | $   3,275 | $   22,196 | $   8,192 |

subject, however, to the further order of the commissioner as herein-
after provided.

C. Revocation of registration of securities

(1) The Commissioner may revoke the registration of any security by
entering an order to that effect, with his findings in respect thereto,
if upon examination into the affairs of the issuer of such security it
shall appear that the issuer:

(a) is insolvent; or

(b) has violated any of the provisions of this Act or any order of the
Commissioner of which such issuer has notice; or

(c) has been or is engaged or is about to engage in a fraudulent
transaction; or

(d) is in any other way dishonest or has made any fraudulent repre-
sentations in any prospectus or in any circular or other literature
that has been distributed concerning the issuer or its securities; or

(e) is of bad business repute; or

(f) does not conduct its business in accordance with law; or

(g) that the affairs of the issuer are in any unsound condition; or

(h) that the enterprise or business of the issuer or the security is not
based upon sound business principles.

Mr. DeBloc was instructed that before the company could proceed with
the issue, a prospectus must be prepared to accompany the securities offered
for sale. Descriptions of the following topics were required for inclusion with
the prospectus:

1. The Company.
2. Business.
3. Use of Proceeds.
4. Capitalization (before and after issue).
5. Dividends.
6. Management.
7. Description of Common Stock.
8. Terms of Underwriting.
9. Legal Opinions (legal council and the like).
10. Financial Statements.
11. Report of Certified Public Accountants.

Mr. DeBloc also received a letter from the Commissioner of Securities
stating that an issue no greater than $400,000 would be approved and then
only if a sinking fund with annual contributions equal to one-tenth the
amount of securities issued be made with a local bank as trustee. The trustee
could invest the sinking-fund cash in U.S. government securities or in the
company's own bonds acquired at par or less. The bonds would have to be
registered as to principal, and interest could be paid by the presentation of
matured, dated, interest coupons which were to be attached to the bonds.

Mr. Osborne and Mr. DeBloc began to consider the desirability of
following through with the issue and wondered if they should not also
consider a SBA or a bank-SBA participation loan or perhaps some other
method for raising the funds for expansion.

**EXHIBIT III**

**Retail Trade Food Industry**
**Composite Balance Sheets for All Tax-Reporting Corporations**
**July, 1961-June, 1962**

|  |  |  |  |
|---|---|---|---|
| *Assets* | | | |
| Current assets | | | |
| Cash | | $ 765,175 | |
| Receivables | $ 405,570 | | |
| Less : reserves | 3,127 | 402,443 | |
| Inventories | | 1,686,047 | |
| Investments | | 55,274 | |
| Other | | 85,267 | |
| Total | | | $2,994,206 |
| Investments | | | |
| Loans to stockholders | | 5,106 | |
| Mortgages | | 14,417 | |
| Other | | 402,639 | |
| Total | | | 422,162 |
| Fixed assets | | | |
| Depreciable assets | 2,946,602 | | |
| Less : accum. depr. | 1,291,777 | 1,654,825 | |
| Depletable asset | 4,651 | | |
| Less : accum. depr. | 790 | 3,861 | |
| Land | | 154,151 | |
| Intangible assets | 9,486 | | |
| Less : Accum. amortization | 2,545 | 6,941 | |
| Other assets | | 207,144 | $2,026,922 |
| Total | | | $5,443,290 |
| *Liabilities and Capital* | | | |
| Currents liabilities | | | |
| Accounts payable | | $1,022,289 | |
| Withdrawable shares | | 1,318 | |
| Short-term notes | | 124,334 | |
| Other | | 404,323 | |
| Total | | | $1,552,264 |
| Long-term liabilities | | | |
| Loans from shareholders | | 18,936 | |
| Long-term notes, mortgages | | 607,504 | |
| Other | | 150,687 | |
| Total long-term | | | 840,127 |
| Total liabilities | | | 2,392,391 |
| Capital | | | |
| Preferred stock | | 105,265 | |
| Common stock | | 665,650 | |
| Paid-in surplus | | 788,136 | |
| Reserved | | 33,418 | |
| Retained earnings | | 1,458,430 | |
| Total capital | | | $3,051,899 |
| Total capital and liabilities | | | $5,443,290 |

**EXHIBIT IV**

**Retail Trade Food Industry**
**Composite Income Statement for All Tax-Reporting Corporations**
**July, 1961-June, 1962**

| | | |
|---|---:|---:|
| Revenue | | |
| Business receipts | | $29,780,486 |
| Other revenue | | |
| Total | | 29,958,733 |
| Expenses | | |
| Cost of sales and operations | 23,818,860 | |
| Compensation of officers | 151,132 | |
| Rent | 395,967 | |
| Repairs | 112,168 | |
| Bad debts | 8,898 | |
| Interest | 37,520 | |
| Taxes | 293,166 | |
| Contributions | 7,734 | |
| Amortization | 2,982 | |
| Depreciation | 275,878 | |
| Depletion | 371 | |
| Advertising | 326,923 | |
| Pension plan contributions | 68,659 | |
| Other employee benefit plans | 63,563 | |
| Net loss, sales other than capital assets | 1,762 | |
| Other expenses | 3,778,299 | |
| Total | | 29,343,882 |
| Net profits before taxes | | $    614,851 |

## Timing an Issue

29

GULF STATES
UTILITIES COMPANY "A"

The financial vice-president of the Gulf States Utilities Company, Mr. W. H. Gieseke, was reviewing the financial position of his company in April, 1962. The company's assets had approximately doubled during the past ten years, and a large construction program was planned for the next five years. The company planned gross additions to plant of approximately $40,000,000 during 1962, $32,000,000 during 1963, and $110,000,-000 from 1964 through 1966. This expansion program would require the need for various types of external financing in addition to the use of funds provided from internally generated sources.

Gulf States Utilities Company was incorporated in 1925 under the laws of Texas and by 1962 was conducting its principal business of generating, transmitting, distributing, and selling, at retail, electric energy in 288 communities in east central Texas and in southern Louisiana. Its areas of operation included Beaumont, Port Arthur, and Orange, Texas and Lake Charles and Baton Rouge, Louisiana. The company was selling electric energy for resale to ten municipally owned systems, to ten electric co-ops sponsored by the Rural Electrification Administration, and to two other utility companies. The company was also conducting a steam-products business and selling natural gas in the Baton Rouge, Louisiana area. Slightly more than half the company's total operating revenues were obtained in Louisiana and the remainder from Texas.

The company's electric business was substantially free from direct competition with other public utilities or municipalities except in one small Texas city of about 6,100 population. The company was, however, subject to rate regulation within its states of operation and to the provisions of the Federal

Power Act. The rates of the company in Texas were subject to the jurisdiction of municipal authorities, and the District Court had the authority to declare unlawful an extortionate or unreasonable rate. In Louisiana the Public Service Commission had jurisdiction over the rates and service of local public utility companies. In addition, the Federal Power Commission had jurisdiction over the business of and facilities for the transmission of electric energy in interstate commerce; the issuance and acquisition of securities; and other matters.

At the end of 1961, Gulf States Utilities Company had five generating stations with a peak load capacity of 1,501,000 kilowatts. A new unit with 220,000 kilowatts capacity was completed in March, 1962, another of similar size in December, 1962, and an additional unit with 220,000 kilowatts capacity was scheduled for completeion in 1963. Peak load demand for electricity increased by 155 per cent from 1952 to 1961.

Gulf States Utilities Company, and other electric-generating companies were maintaining a substantial amount of stand-by generating capacity to meet peak load demand. As a result of heavy usage of air conditioning equipment, the peak load demand for Gulf States was expected to be about 1,400,000 kilowatts during the summer of 1962. Gulf States and ten other investor-owned electric utilities, identified as the South Central Electric Companies, had a four-year program which would provide transmission facilities for the exchange of off-peak power with the Tennessee Valley Authority. The TVA had a peak load demand during the winter months which was about 2,900,000 kilowatts higher than its summer demand. This resulted from heavy usage of electricity for heating. The South Central Electric Companies combined had a summer peak load demand of about 3,000,000 kilowatts above their winter demand. The exchange of seasonal surplus generating capacity had been accepted by the Federal Power Commission. The cost to build the extra-high voltage lines to the point of interchange with the TVA was less than the cost of the installation of new generating equipment to produce the same kilowatts. Gulf States Utilities Company expected to postpone a 1966 generating unit as a result of this exchange.

At the end of 1961 the capitalization of Gulf States Utilities Company consisted of 13.2 per cent preferred stock, 33.5 per cent common equity, 6.2 per cent debenture, and 47.1 per cent mortgage debt.

As a guide in financing new investments, the company established the following goals: (1) The mortgage debt was not to exceed 50 per cent of total capitalization, (2) total long-term debt was not to exceed 55 per cent, (3) common stock and retained earnings were not to be less than 30 per cent, and (4) the balance was to be made up of preferred stock. Although the above ratios were permitted to vary slightly, the aim of the company was to maintain a fairly stable balance of these percentages so that the fixed charges were adequately covered at all times. For interim financing, the company had agreements with two commercial banks whereby it could borrow up to an aggregate of $20,000,000, one-half from each bank, through the issuance of short-term notes. The notes carried the prime interest rate at the time of issuance and were repayable at any time without penalty. No standby cost or compensatory balance was required for this interim financing. The rate was $4\frac{1}{2}$ per cent in 1962.

Thirteen issues of 30-year, first-mortgage bonds were sold by the company from 1946 through 1961 at varying coupon rates, as shown in Exhibit III. Provisions made for sinking-fund payments and for the call feature are described in Appendix A. Two issues of 20-year debentures and seven issues of cumulative, $100 per value preferred stock were made from 1944 through 1961. The issues were callable at various prices (Appendix A), and the preferred stocks were cumulative as to dividends which were payable March 15, June 15, September 15, and December 15. During the same period, the company made eleven issues of common stock either to the old shareholders on a rights basis or to the general public. In 1962 approximately 75 per cent of the common stock was held by business firms and financial institutions. Proceeds from the sale of these securities were used for funding short-term debt, for financing general construction, for meeting the working capital needs of the firm, and for refunding. Moody's Investors Service rated the mortgage bonds as Aa grade, the debentures as A grade, and the preferred as high grade.

The thirteen issues of first-mortgage bonds made by the company during the past fifteen years were sold to the general public through the use of a group of investment banking firms. Two of the issues of preferred stock were privately placed while the other five were offered to the general public. Although the company was not required by its state of incorporation to offer its common stock on a preemptive-rights basis, it used this method for marketing some of its common stock issues. The Federal Power Commission required that all securities marketed by a public utility company coming

**EXHIBIT I**

**Gulf States Utilities Company**
**Comparative Income Statements**
**Years Ended December 31**

|  | 1961 | 1960 | 1959 | 1958 |
|---|---|---|---|---|
| Operating revenues | $91,468,723 | $86,178,072 | $77,941,332 | $68,559,306 |
| Operation and maintenance | 36,773,088 | 33,828,797 | 30,932,474 | 27,590,851 |
| Depreciation | 11,835,106 | 10,122,571 | 9,232,248 | 7,897,074 |
| Amortization of plant acquisition adjustments |  |  |  |  |
| Taxes—federal income and other | 18,074,421 | 17,749,977 | 14,971,436 | 13,100,361 |
| Taxes—deferred federal income—net | 2,294,177 | 2,120,022 | 2,764,521 | 2,405,146 |
| Other deductions—net | 78,951 | 56,365 | 76,709 | 104,551 |
| Balance for interest—before special charges | 22,412,980 | 22,300,340 | 19,963,944 | 17,461,323 |
| Interest and amortization—net | 6,366,326 | 6,021,327 | 3,941,252 | 3,384,919 |
| Net income | $16,046,654 | $16,279,013 | $16,022,692 | $14,076,404 |
| Applicable to common stock | $13,630,654 | $13,863,013 | $13,657,492 | $12,241,321 |
| Earnings per share of common stock* | 1.31 | 1.38 | 1.36 | 1.29 |
| Dividends per share of common stock* | 1.00 | 1.00 | .95 | .88 |
| Common shares outstanding—end of year* | 10,373,664 | 10,023,664 | 10,023,664 | 9,523,664 |

*Restated to give effect to a two for one split in 1959.

under its jurisdiction (with the exception of rights issues of common) be made on a competitive bid basis.

Gulf States Utilities Company had had an average dividend payout over the last few years of 70 per cent. Certain limitations on the payment of cash dividends on common stock were included in the company's articles of incorporation and bond indentures. The former provided that cash dividends be limited to earnings accumulated after May 31, 1958, plus $28 million and restricted such dividends to 75 per cent of "income available to

**EXHIBIT II**

**Gulf States Utilities Company**
**Balance Sheet**

|  | Dec. 31, 1961 | Dec. 31, 1958 |
|---|---|---|
| *Assets* | | |
| Plant and Other Investments | | |
| Utility and other plant : | | |
| Electric utility and steam products plant, at original cost | $483,926,541 | $348,891,525 |
| Gas utility plant, at cost | 12,948,017 | 9,995,609 |
| Total plant | 496,874,558 | 358,887,134 |
| Less : accumulated provision for depreciation | 76,591,675 | 51,812,768 |
| Total plant less accumulated provision for depreciation | 420,282,883 | 307,074,366 |
| Nonutility property, at cost | 1,626,262 | 785,241 |
| Other investments, at cost | 39,600 | 30,600 |
| Total plant and other investments | 421,948,745 | 307,890,207 |
| Current Assets | | |
| Cash | 5,204,678 | 4,703,652 |
| Special deposits | 331,560 | 167,226 |
| Accounts receivable from customers and others less accumulated provision for uncollectibles | 7,982,471 | 6,033,211 |
| Materials and supplies (including constructon meterials), at average cost or less | 3,031,459 | 2,893,157 |
| Prepayments | 765,804 | 516,956 |
| Total current assets | 17,315,972 | 14,314,202 |
| Deferred Debits | | |
| Unamortized expense, less premium, on bonds and debentures | 223,343 | 127,127 |
| Others | 185,386 | 1,442,805 |
| Total deferred debits | 408,729 | 1,569,932 |
| Total Assets | $439,673,446 | $323,774,341 |
| *Liabilities and Stockholders' equity* | | |
| Capital stock and retained earnings* | | |
| Preferred stock, cumulative, $ 100 par value | $ 52,500,000 | $ 42,500,000 |
| Common stock, without par value, 10,373,664 shares in 1961 | 88,828,725 | 60,752,375 |
| Premium on preferred stocks | 514,651 | 443,750 |
| Retained earnings | 43,636,044 | 33,246,383 |
| Total capital stock and retained earnings | 185,479,420 | 136,942,508 |
| Long-term debt* | | |
| First mortgage bonds | 187,000,000 | 144,000,000 |
| Debentures | 24,675,000 | 11,400,000 |
| Total long-term debt | 211,675,000 | 155,400,000 |

|  | Dec. 31, 1961 | Dec. 31, 1958 |
|---|---|---|
| Current liabilities | | |
| Debentures, due within one year, less amount acquired | | |
| for sinking fund purposes | 774,000 | 265,000 |
| Notes payable to banks | 8,900,000 | 9,500,000 |
| Accouts payables | 2,734,733 | 2,168,689 |
| Customers' deposits | 873,973 | 598,794 |
| Taxes accrued | 8,340,222 | 6,127,023 |
| Interest accrued | 1,289,339 | 1,049,094 |
| Other | 1,683,642 | 1,241,859 |
| Total current liabilities | 24,595,909 | 20,950,459 |
| Deferred Credits | | |
| Unamortized premium, less expense, on bonds | 842,926 | 620,467 |
| Customers' advances for construction | 91,374 | 161,553 |
| Other | 6,852 | 124,652 |
| Total deferred credits | 941,152 | 906,672 |
| Operating Reserves | 229,447 | 222,391 |
| Contributions in aid of construction | 221,487 | — |
| Accumulated deferred federal income taxes | 16,531,031 | 9,352,311 |
| Total liabilities and stockholders' equity | $439,673,446 | $323,774,341 |

*For details see Exhibit III.

common" if the common stock equity (exclusive of premium on preferred stock) fell below 25 per cent of total capitalization. Under this provision, retained earnings unrestricted as to cash dividends on common stock amounted to $40,500,000 at the end of February, 1962. The indenture restrictions were less burdensome.

The expansion program of the company had created a need for the firm to go to the market for funds about twice each year. The timing of an issue of a particular security depends on the need for additional funds by the company and the probable acceptability of that security in the investment market. With this in mind, Gulf States worked exact offering dates into a financial calendar so that the financing would not compete with excess numbers of new issues being made by other companies. A close study of the money market and capital market was maintained, and an attempt was made to issue the type of security which resulted in the lowest cost of money to the company while keeping within the prescribed capitalization limitations.

The company was considering the offering of $17,000,000, 30-year, 4 3/8 per cent, first mortgage bonds during May or June of 1962. They felt that the bonds could be sold to the general public at 101.50 per cent of par, that the underwriting discounts would be about .72 per cent of par, and that the proceeds to the company would be $17,132,600. Some $16,000,000 of the funds were needed to repay short-term notes to the two commercial bank lenders, and the remainder would be available for general expansion purposes. The bonds, if issued, were to be secured ratably with other outstanding first mortgage bonds, would require similar sinking-fund repayments, and were to be callable at 105.90 per cent of par during the first year. Call premiums were to be reduced by .20 per cent each year during subsequent years from 1963 to 1991.

## EXHIBIT III

### Gulf States Utilities Company
### Capitalization
### as of December 31, 1961

#### Long-term Debt

First mortgage bonds—(Mature 30 years from issue date)*

Authorized, $ 1,000,000,000 principal amount :

| | |
|---|---:|
| 2 5/8% Series due 1976 (excluding $ 1,000,000 in treasury) | $ 27,000,000 |
| 3 % Series due 1978 | 12,000,000 |
| 2 3/4% Series due 1979 | 10,000,000 |
| 2 3/4% Series due 1980 | 13,000,000 |
| 3 3/8% Series due 1981 | 10,000,000 |
| 3 1/8% Series due 1982 | 10,000,000 |
| 3 3/8% Series due 1983 | 10,000,000 |
| 4 1/4% Series due 1986 | 15,000,000 |
| 4 7/8% Series due 1987 | 17,000,000 |
| 4 % Series due 1988 | 20,000,000 |
| 4 3/4% Series due 1989 | 10,000,000 |
| 5 1/4% Series A due 1989 | 16,000,000 |
| 4 7/8% Series due 1990 | 17,000,000 |
| Total first mortgage bonds | $187,000,000 |

Debentures—(Mature 20 years from issue date)

Authorized, $ 30,000,000 principal amount :

| | |
|---|---:|
| 3 % due 1969* | $ 10,050,000 |
| 4 5/8% due 1981 | 14,625,000 |
| Total debentures | $ 24,675,000 |
| Total Long-term Debt (Excluding amount of debentures due within one year) | $211,675,000 |

#### Capital Stock

| | Shares Outstanding | Amount |
|---|---:|---:|
| Preferred—cumulative—$ 100 par value— | | |
| Anthorized, 1,000,000 shares : | | |
| $4.40 Dividend | 120,000 | $ 12,000,000 |
| $4.50 Dividend | 50,000 | 5,000,000 |
| $4.40 Dividend, 1949 Series | 60,000 | 6,000,000 |
| $4.20 Dividend* | 70,000 | 7,000,000 |
| $4.44 Dividend* | 50,000 | 5,000,000 |
| $5.00 Dividend* | 75,000 | 7,500,000 |
| $5.08 Dividend* | 100,000 | 10,000,000 |
| Total preferred stock | 525,000 | $ 52,500,000 |
| Common—without par value— | | |
| Authorized, 20,000,000 shares (outstanding : | | |
| 10,373,664 shares)+ | | $ 88,828,725 |
| Total capital stock | | $141,328,725 |

*Listed on the New York Stock Exchange.
†Listed on the N.Y.S.E. and Midwest Stock Exchange.

As alternatives to the bond issue, Mr. Gieseke did not wish to overlook the feasibility of making a preferred stock or common stock issue. The company's preferred issues were trading at yields of about 4.9 per cent, which was about $\frac{1}{4}$ per cent above that for the average preferred stock. During 1961, the common stock had increased in price from \$35 per share to \$47 per share. The market value per share had declined somewhat in December, 1961 and in April, 1962, was between $41\frac{1}{2}$ and $43\frac{1}{2}$. Underwriting discounts on preferred issues had averaged about .75 per cent in the past and about 3 per cent on common issues (exhibit VI). Other flotation costs which were born by the issues amounted to about \$80,000 for each security offering.

Since the company's line of credit was almost used up and because the company was again in need of funds, Mr. Gieseke knew that the board of directors of the company should proceed with a security issue. He also realized that additional outside funds would be needed in November or December of 1962, and he began to make tentative plans for another security issue.

### EXHIBIT IV

**Bond Yields, Preferred Stock Yields, and
Common Stock Yields for Utility Company
1946-1962**

| Year | Average Yield on Aa Utility Bonds | Average Yield on Utility Perferred (High Grade) | Utility Dividend Yield on Common | Utility Earning Yield on Common |
|------|------|------|------|------|
| 1946 | 2.58 | 3.48 | 4.23 | 6.43 |
| 1947 | 2.67 | 3.64 | 5.32 | 7.33 |
| 1948 | 2.92 | 4.03 | 5.85 | 8.12 |
| 1949 | 2.76 | 3.88 | 5.86 | 8.32 |
| 1950 | 2.68 | 3.75 | 5.66 | 8.39 |
| 1951 | 2.95 | 4.02 | 5.77 | 7.50 |
| 1952 | 3.05 | 4.03 | 5.39 | 7.39 |
| 1953 | 3.32 | 4.22 | 5.33 | 7.35 |
| 1954 | 3.00 | 3.94 | 4.81 | 6.63 |
| 1955 | 3.13 | 3.94 | 4.50 | 6.52 |
| 1956 | 3.43 | 4.18 | 4.68 | 6.75 |
| 1957 | 4.03 | 4.72 | 4.92 | 6.90 |
| 1958 | 3.92 | 4.51 | 4.33 | 6.26 |
| 1959 | 4.56 | 4.79 | 3.94 | 5.76 |
| 1960 | 4.53 | 4.85 | 3.84 | 5.90 |
| 1961 | 4.46 | 4.71 | 3.10 | 4.80 |
| 1962 |  |  |  |  |
| Jan. | 4.50 | 4.58 | 3.01 | N. A. |
| Feb. | 4.52 | 4.52 | 2.93 | N. A. |
| Mar. | 4.50 | 4.48 | 2.94 | N. A. |
| Apr. | 4.47 | 4.49 | 3.02 | N. A. |

*Source: Moody's Public Utility Manual, 1962* (New York: Moody's Investors Service, 1962), pp. a4–a6.

**EXHIBIT V**

**Gulf States Utilities Company**
**High-Low Market Price of Securities**

| | 1961 | 1960 | 1959 |
|---|---|---|---|
| First Mortgage bonds | | | |
| First 2 5/8s, due 1976 | 80 1/2— 76 1/2 | 79 — 73 1/4 | 79 — 72 1/2 |
| First 3 s, due 1978 | 80 — 80 | No Sales | No Sales |
| First 2 3/4s, due 1979 | No Sales | No Sales | 80 — 71 1/2 |
| First 2 3/4s, due 1980 | 78 — 76 | 80 — 80 | 74 — 74 |
| First 3 3/8s, due 1981 | 85 5/8— 82 1/2 | 87 1/2— 80 | 85 — 85 |
| First 3 1/8s, due 1982 | 77 — 76 7/8 | 78 1/2— 77 1/2 | No Sales |
| First 3 3/8s, due 1983 | No Sales | 77 — 77 | No Sales |
| First 4 1/4s, due 1986 | 99 1/2— 94 | — | — |
| First 4 7/8s, due 1987 | 106 — 99 | — | — |
| First 4 s, due 1988 | 93 3/8— 88 1/2 | 89 3/8— 86 | 95 1/2— 86 |
| First 4 3/4s, due 1989 | 104 7/8— 99 3/4 | 100 — 94 | 105 — 96 |
| First 5 1/4s, due 1989 | 106 1/2—101 | 105 —101 1/8 | 102 5/8—100 1/2 |
| First 4 7/8s, due 1990 | 105 3/8—100 7/8 | 104 1/4—100 7/8 | — |
| Debentures | | | |
| 3 s, due 1969 | 93 — 92 1/2 | 87 1/4— 87 | 91— 87 |
| 4 5/8s, due 1981 | 102 1/4— 99 1/2 | — | — |
| Preferred stock (100 par) | | | |
| 4.40 Cum. Div. (1944) | 94 1/2— 86 1/2 | 91 1/2— 84 1/2 | 94 — 81 1/2 |
| 4.50 Cum. Div. (1947) | | Privately placed | |
| 4.40 Cum. Div. (1949) | | Privately placed | |
| 4.20 Cum. Div. (1950) | 88 1/2— 85 | 86 3/4—82 | 86 1/2— 80 |
| 4.44 Cum. Div. (1952) | 93 3/4— 91 | 91 — 87 1/2 | 91 — 88 |
| 5.00 Cum. Div. (1958) | 104 1/2—101 | 103 1/4— 97 | 104 1/2— 96 |
| 5.08 Cum. Div. (1959) | 106 —102 | 103 1/2— 97 1/2 | 105 1/2— 98 |
| Common shares, no par | 47 1/4— 35 | 38 3/8— 27 3/4 | 32 — 28 |

**APPENDIX A**

**Security Provisions**

FIRST MORTGAGE BONDS—Secured by Indenture of Mortgage of Company dated September 1, 1926, as supplemented and modified. Issuable in series, aggregate principal amount of Bonds to be outstanding at any one time limited by Indenture to $1,000,000,000, subject also to other restrictions contained in said Indenture.

*Callable:* As a whole or in part at any time on at least thirty days' notice at specified percentages of the principal amount applicable to each series at the time, plus accrued interest.

*Sinking and Improvement Fund Provisions:* In respect of the 1976 Series Bonds, $\frac{1}{2}$ per cent semiannually of the total principal amount of issued Bonds of said Series; and in respect of each of the other Series, 1.2 per cent annually of the total principal amount of issued Bonds of the respective Series. May be satisfied by property credits (on a 60 per cent basis) or by waiving the right to issue an equal amount of Bonds of any Series. (Satisfied in the past by property credits.)

*Maintenance and Replacement Provisions:* An amount equal to 15 per cent of operating revenues (less cost of electricity and gas purchased for resale and rentals) shall be spent by the Company for maintenance or additions to property, or to the extent not so spent the balance of such 15 per cent less certain credits for debt retirement, and the like, shall be deposited with the Trustee in cash or Bonds or prior lien debt. This provision operates cumulatively from December 31, 1945.

*Interest:* Payable semiannually at Manufacturers Hanover Trust Company, New York, N. Y., Trustee and Registrar.

DEBENTURES—*Debt, Lien, and Dividend Restrictions:* The Debentures are unsecured but have the benefit of certain restrictions under Trust Indentures relating thereto, including restrictions on the issue or assumption of funded debt and the payment of dividends on Common Stock.

*Callable:* As a whole or in part at any time on at least thirty days' notice at specified percentages of the principal amount at the time applicable to each series, plus accrued interest.

*Sinking Fund:* In respect of the 1969 Debentures, annually, on or before August 31, beginning 1952, an amount sufficient to redeem on September 1, $450,000 principal amount of Debentures; and in respect of the 1981 Debentures, annually, on or before september 30, beginning 1962, an amount sufficient to redeem, on October 1, $375,000 principal amount of Debentures. In each respective case, the Sinking-Fund requirements may be satisfied in whole or in part by delivering Debentures or by crediting redeemed Debentures.

*Interest:* With respect to the 3 per cent Debentures due 1969, semiannually, payable at the principal office of the Trustee and Registrar, Irving Trust Company, New York, N. Y.; and with respect to the 4 5/8 per cent Debentures due 1981, semiannually, payable at the principal office of the Trustee and Registrar, The American National Bank of Beaumont, Beaumont, Texas:, or, at the option of the bearer or registered holder at the principal corporate trust office of Morgan Guaranty Trust Company of New York, New York, N. Y.

*Voting Rights:* Preferred Stock is not entitled to vote except for certain protective purposes, at which time all series have one vote per share voting as a class.

The Common Stock is entitled to one vote per share for election of directors and all other corporate purposes, subject to certain volting rights of the Preferred Stock.

PREFERRED STOCK—$100 par value.

*Redemption or Voluntary Liquidation, Per Share:*

$4.40 Dividend—$108; $4.50 Dividend—$105; $4.40 Dividend, 1949 Series—$103; $4.20 Dividend—$102.818; $4.44 Dividend—$103.75.

$5.00 Dividend—$106.25 through January 31, 1968; reduced to $104.25 thereafter.

$5.08 Dividend—$108.63 through December 31, 1963; $106.63 through Dec. 31,1968. reduced to $104.63 thereafter.

*Dividends:* cumulative, payable March 15 and Quarterly.

# Pricing a Preemptive Issue

## 30

**MERCURY AIRLINES, INC.**

On March 17, 1964, Mr. David H. Knutson, financial vice-president of Mercury Airlines, was meeting with the underwriters of the investment banking firm of Vickers and Brown in order to set the subscription price and determine the underwriting costs for the company's preemptive stock issue which was going to be marketed the following day. This meeting marked the end of a series of events which had begun more than a year before when the company first had determined it needed additional equity capital.

Mercury Airlines was incorporated in Illinois in 1934 and since that time had operated exclusively as a commercial airline. Its principal revenues came from passengers, mail, and property that were carried along scheduled airline routes certified by the Civil Aeronautics Board. The company operated over both domestic and foreign routes. Domestically, the principal east-west routes were between New York, Chicago, Kansas City, Denver, and San Francisco. The principal north-south route was Chicago to Miami. Overseas, the company flew from San Francisco to Honolulu and over the southern route to Japan. Flights went from New York, Chicago, and San Francisco to Tokyo, Manila, Taipei, Seoul, and Okinawa. As a result of the long-distance flights overseas, the company's average length of flight was one of the highest in the industry, thereby making it one of the most profitable airlines.

The management of Mercury Airlines had consistently remained abreast of current management practices in the industry. Over the past few years, the company's earnings had risen continually. The profitability of operations was a result of a very favorable load factor and several cost-saving innovations involving equipment and its maintenance.

The present breakeven load factor

for Mercury averaged 37 per cent, which was the lowest in the industry in 1964. Once the planes had paid passengers for 37 per cent of a flight's capacity, costs for any additional passengers were small and included only food, reservation expenses, and insurance. Approximately 65 per cent of passenger revenues above the breakeven load factor went to net income before taxes. During 1963, average loads had been over 50 per cent of capacity.

Mercury's management had gradually eliminated its propeller aircraft and replaced these with jet and jet-prop equipment. More recently the company had standardized the types of jet aircraft and jet engines to be used. By the end of 1964, the company expected to be operating with only three types of aircraft, all of which came with only fan-jet engines that provided an 18 per cent fuel savings. This standardization was expected to result in considerable cost savings owing to a reduced need for varied spare parts and fewer dual pilot qualifications.

The continual need for new and more modern aircraft made the financing of new equipment purchases a major problem. Typically airlines are financed heavily with debt which is periodically replaced with new equity capital. Almost every firm in the industry had a debt/equity ratio in excess of one, and some were over two. With new jets costing approximately $5,000,000 each, adding four or five a year made the use of debt mandatory. Normally an airline would purchase new flight equipment and parts through the use of conditional sales contracts, bank loans, and long-term notes. When the

**EXHIBIT I**

**Statement of Earnings**
**Mercury Airlines, Inc. and Subsidiary**

|  | Year Ended December 31, | | |
|---|---|---|---|
|  | 1963 | 1962 | 1961 |
| Operating revenues | $168,788,040 | $150,453,420 | $111,052,512 |
| Operating expenses |  |  |  |
| Flying operations | 42,906,211 | 38,947,732 | 29,268,829 |
| Maintenance | 26,203,309 | 23,243,505 | 17,252,807 |
| Passenger service | 11,412,619 | 9,586,053 | 7,178,262 |
| Aircraft and traffic servicing | 19,690,557 | 17,658,487 | 12,445,830 |
| Reservations, sales and advertising | 16,985,125 | 15,687,673 | 11,973,343 |
| Administrative and general | 6,515,803 | 7,678,729 | 6,093,596 |
| Depreciation and amortization | 19,158,899 | 18,445,190 | 17,117,959 |
|  | $142,872,523 | $131,247,369 | $101,330,626 |
|  | $ 25,915,517 | $ 19,206,051 | $ 9,721,886 |
| Other income (deductions) | 4,165,260 | 4,577,359 | 2,827,947 |
| Earnings before taxes | $ 21,750,257 | $ 14,628,692 | $ 6,893,939 |
| Taxes on earnings | 11,297,300 | 7,398,300 | 3,232,800 |
| Net earnings for the year | $ 10,452,957 | $ 7,230,392 | $ 3,661,139 |
| Dividends on preferred | — | 592,187 | 592,245 |
| Dividends on common | 1,822,668 | 1,109,556 | 1,108,521 |

EXHIBIT II

## Statement of Financial Position
### Mercury Airlines, Inc. and Subsidiary

|  | December 31, | | |
| --- | --- | --- | --- |
| *Assets* | 1963 | 1962 | 1961 |
| Currents assets |  |  |  |
| Cash | $ 12,866,565 | $ 16,371,029 | $ 15,991,175 |
| Notes receivable from sale of aircraft | 6,911,619 | — | — |
| Trade receivables, less allowance of $ 105,000 | 15,248,025 | 14,037,703 | 12,532,949 |
| Flight equipment parts, at average cost, less allowance for depreciation (1963-$ 2,765,206 ; 1962-$ 2,529,171) | 6,100,076 | 6,475,526 | 5,880,199 |
| Maintenance and operating supplies at average cost | 2,176,335 | 2,181,111 | 2,377,424 |
| Prepaid expenses | 2,706,816 | 2,414,788 | 2,064,721 |
| Total Current assets | $ 46,009,436 | $ 41,480,157 | $ 38,846,468 |
| Investments and other assets at cost | 638,615 | 320,332 | 154,890 |
| Property and equipment, net | 145,266,100 | 139,659,738 | 143,996,164 |
| Deferred charged | 4,850,542 | 5,426,375 | 6,105,694 |
|  | $196,764,693 | $186,886,602 | $189,103,216 |

|  | 1963 | 1962 | 1961 |
| --- | --- | --- | --- |
| *Liabilities and stockholders' equity* |  |  |  |
| Current liabilities |  |  |  |
| Trade accounts payable | $ 10,662,050 | $ 8,428,916 | $ 12,021,592 |
| Collections as agent (taxes, payroll deductions) | 2,488,578 | 2,642,246 | — |
| Accrued taxes (other than income taxes) | 1,316,345 | 2,048,746 | — |
| Salaries, wages, and vacations | 7,764,811 | 5,584,258 | 5,416,706 |
| Air travel card deposits | 1,195,100 | 1,187,875 | 1,176,400 |
| Unredeemed ticket liability | 1,865,862 | 1,038,843 | 1,012,669 |
| Income taxes—estimated | 6,750,302 | 1,464,362 | 663,338 |
| Current maturities of long-term debt | 7,739,845 | 11,053,845 | 11,521,560 |
| Total Current Liabilities | $ 39,782,893 | $ 33,431,091 | $ 31,812,265 |
| Long-term debt, less current maturities |  |  |  |
| Notes payable to insurance companies | 40,000,000 | 40,000,000 | 40,000,000 |
| Notes payable to banks | 19,000,000 | 21,000,000 | 34,000,000 |
| Subordinated note payable | 2,314,000 | 7,500,000 | 7,032,285 |
| Conditional sales contracts | 3,681,515 | 6,467,528 | 9,253,541 |
|  | $ 64,995,515 | $ 74,967,528 | $ 90,285,826 |
| Deferred credits | $ 23,550,338 | $ 18,776,100 | $ 12,828,600 |
| Stockholders' equity |  |  |  |
| Preferred stock, $5^1/_4\%$ Cum. Conv. $25 par | — | 11,240,375 | 11,280,850 |
| Common stock, $10 par value: authorized 4,500,000 shares ; issued and outstanding 1963—1,824,452 shares ; 1962—1,388,459 shares | 18,244,520 | 13,884,590 | 13,864,030 |
| Capital surplus | 13,587,113 | 6,612,905 | 6,586,281 |
| Retained earnings | 36,604,314 | 27,974,013 | 22,445,364 |
|  | $68,435,947 | $59,711,883 | $54,176,525 |
|  | $196,764,693 | $186,886,602 | $189,103,216 |

debt/equity ratio neared the limit selected by management, much of the debt would be funded through equity financing.

Mercury Airlines' management preferred to keep its debt/equity ratio within the lowest quartile of the industry. Thus, in December, 1962, when the ratio reached 1.24, Mr. Knutson began making plans for some equity financing. Because of an unfavorable market at the time, he put off the prospective issue and made the necessary purchases for the year by using conditional sales contracts, revolving credit, retained earnings, and proceeds from the sale of used flight equipment.

On February 2, 1964, the company placed its order with Boeing Co. for thirteen new jet aircraft at an approximate cost of $67,000,000. Although this order probably could have been handled without new equity funds, the company needed to begin balancing their financial position. By 1970 the new Supersonic Transports (SST) were to be delivered, and clearly those

**EXHIBIT III**

**Mercury Airlines
Stock Growth Record Comparison**

firms in the best financial shape would be in the most advantageous position to exploit the market. In addition to preparing for the SST planes, the company expected to continue its present rate of expansion, which would require the purchase of several new jets each year. For the future the company needed financial flexibility, and an equity issue would provide that.

By early 1964 a favorable time was at hand for the floating of a new stock issue. The stock market was approaching record highs, and the present strength of the economy was projected to continue at least through the third quarter of the year. In examining his long-range financial plans, Mr. Knutson believed that he would need to raise approximately $30,000,000. An issue of this size could have a drastic effect on the market price of the stock, since it would result in a substantial amount of dilution in current earnings per share. Such an issue would increase the number of shares outstanding by about 25 per cent and would double the size of the capital plus the capital surplus accounts. The issue would be used to make deposits on the newly ordered planes, to retire subordinated paper and conditional sales contracts, and to reduce the outstanding revolving-credit balance.

Mercury Airlines' common stockholders had preemptive rights, which meant that each present stockholder must be offered the opportunity of purchasing his pro rata share of any new stock issue. Since the company would have to first offer a new issue to its own stockholders, it would have to price the issue so as to insure maximum participation. A poorly priced issue could cause the company considerable financial difficulty. Although Mr. Knutson knew that the issue could be underwritten and that a failure would

**EXHIBIT IV**

**Mercury Airlines**
**Annual Stock Price Fluctuations**

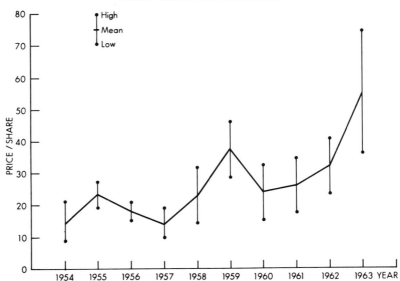

## EXHIBIT V
### Mercury Airlines
### Selected Data on Preemptive-right Issues

| No. Shs. | Company | Date of Issue | Mkt. Price on Issue | Subscript Price | Rts. Needed to Buy 1 Sh. | Size of Issue (Mill. $) | Type Underwr. | Underwr. Commiss. | | Co.'s Net Proceeds | Sales (Mill. $) | Total Assets (Mill. $) |
|---|---|---|---|---|---|---|---|---|---|---|---|---|
| 146,735 | C, Brewer & Co., Ltd. | 10/28/63 | 71.4 | $60.00 | 5 | 8,804 | (1) | 2.0% | 1.20 | $58.80 | $99.8 | 98.7 |
| 742,144 | Burroughs Corp. | 7/19/63 | 27.5 | 23.75 | 9 | 17,626 | (1) | 3.7% | .875 | 22.875 | 387.4 | 390.3 |
| 76,773 | Federal Services Fin. Corp. | 9/25/63 | 22.4 | 18.00 | 5 | 1,381 | (1) | 3.0% | .54 | 17.46 | 3.4 | 45.6 |
| 467,265 | Florida Power Corp. | 10/10/63 | 71.4 | 40.00 | 20 | 18,291 | (1) | 0.7% | .28 | 39.72 | 86.8 | 373.4 |
| 718,354 | Pacific Power & Light | 10/30/63 | 26.6 | 23.75 | 20 | 17,061 | (1) | 0.8% | .189 | 23.561 | 106.5 | 650.5 |
| 139,940 | Piedmont Nat'r'l Gas | 9/ 9/63 | 17.5 | 16.00 | 10 | 2,239 | (1) | 1.2% | .20 | 15.80 | 21.2 | 50.8 |
| 115,692 | Central Mutual Tel. | 1/ 2/64 | 38.4 | 23.50 | 3 | 906 | (1) | 1.5% | .35 | 23.15 | 1.6 | 5.3 |
| 119,350 | Central Nat'l Bk.-Clev, | 1/28/64 | 58.5 | 52.00 | 10 | 6,200 | (1) | 1.5% | .80 | 51.20 | 34.7 | 858.6 |
| 206,410 | Florida Tel. Corp. ● | 3/12/64 | 29.1 | 20.00 | 5 | 4,128 | (1) | 1.7% | .35 | 19.65 | 7.8 | 34.5 |
| 306,450 | Mid-America Pipeline | 3/16/64 | 17.5 | 9.00 | 6 | 2,758 | (1) | 3.9% | .35 | 8.65 | 14.6 | 83.3 |
| 1,143,939 | Potomac Elec. Pwr. | 1/ 8/64 | 20.6 | 19.00 | 15 | 21,735 | (1) | 1.0% | .20 | 18.80 | 108.0 | 677.9 |
| 36,000 | Reliance Universal Inc. | 3/18/64 | 39.0 | 34.00 | 10 | 1,224 | (1) | 1.2% | .40 | 33.60 | 21.0 | 13.6 |
| 97,431 | San Jose Wtr. Wks. | 1/ 3/64 | 35.2 | 32.00 | 5 | 3,115 | (1) | 1.3% | .40 | 31.60 | 6.9 | 53.8 |
| 32,492 | Security Trust of Rochester | 1/17/64 | 45.6 | 41.00 | 15 | 1,332 | (1) | 1.3% | .55 | 40.45 | 12.6 | 246.1 |
| 4,200 | Somerset Trust Co. | 1/14/64 | 120.0 | 100.00 | 10 | 420 | (1) | 3.5% | 3.50 | 96.50 | 2.2 | 29.6 |
| 527,571 | United Util., Inc. | 3/10/64 | 43.0 | 39.50 | 10 | 20,839 | (1) | 1.5% | .60 | 38.90 | 60.6 | 210.0 |

(1) Underwriter buys any unsubscribed shares Underwriting Commission variable, Depending on number of shares accepted by public.

mean that investment bankers would have to absorb the loss, the effect of such a situation could result in a very depressed market for months or years. Thus, proper pricing and timing would be most important in planning this issue.

Mr. Knutson had been watching the market very closely, and by the first of February he thought that the time was right to prepare for the issue. By the 25th of February, he had prepared most of the necessary material which would be in the registration statement. Since the rules of the New York Stock Exchange required that once the board of directors had approved a new stock issue, the public must be notified within forty-eight hours, Mr. Knutson knew that he must work around the clock in order to be prepared to file with the Securities and Exchange Commission (SEC) after the board's approval. A special meeting of the board was called on February 27 at which time an issue of approximately $30,000,000 was approved. The next day Mr. Knutson filed his prepared registration statement with the SEC. A nineteen-day waiting period was then required before the price could be set and the stock offered.

During the required waiting period, Mr. Knutson knew that he must consolidate all of his information in such a manner that the final terms and pricing of the issue would minimize any drastic effect on the market price of the stock. The important variables to be considered in insuring a successful issue were:

### EXHIBIT VI

**Mercury Airlines**
**Closing Quotations—**
**New York Stock Exchange**

| Date | Closing Quote |
|---|---|
| Feb.   17 | $89 1/2 |
| 18 | 89 |
| 19 | 88 1/8 |
| 20 | 89 1/2 |
| 24 | 84 1/2 |
| 25 | 83 |
| 26 | 85 1/8 |
| 27 | 84 1/2 |
| Mar.   4 | 83 1/4 |
| 5 | 81 1/2 |
| 6 | 83 |
| 9 | 84 1/2 |
| 10 | 85 7/8 |
| 11 | 88 1/8 |
| 12 | 87 3/4 |
| 13 | 88 1/8 |
| 16 | 87 1/2 |
| 17 | 87 |
| 18 | 89 1/4 |

1. *Rights given to the stockholders.* The decision was made that each stockholder would get one right for each share of stock presently held.
2. *Rights required to purchase one new share.* In order to keep the market value of each right relatively high, four rights would be necessary to subscribe to one new share.
3. *Subscription price.* This would be determined on the final day and would be a most important decision.
4. *Underwriting commission.* This also would be determined on the final day through negotiation.

A meeting was set for March 17 for the company officers, the board of directors, and the underwriters to determine the subscription price and the underwriting commissions.

Mr. Knutson had certain goals in setting the subscription price. He thought that the issue should "buy good will." In other words, he wanted to make sure that those stockholders who did not have sufficient cash available or who did not wish to increase their investment in the company at this time, could sell their rights in the market and receive sufficient money to compensate them for their inability to take part in the financing. He knew that Mercury Airlines had many small stockholders and that these stockholders were primarily interested in growth. Approximately 34 per cent of the common stock outstanding was held by institutional investors, while 13 per cent was owned by management. The average stockholding was 250 shares, and the average noninstitutional stockholder owned only 100 shares. Thus, many would probably not wish to purchase the additional shares.

In preparing for the final selection of price Mr. Knutson collected information on other past preemptive-right issues as well as details about the company's and industry's stock prices (see exhibits). He thought that this information would give him ranges within which he could set his subscription price. He believed that the issue should be slightly underpriced so that the market value of the rights would have a slight appreciation upon issuance. He realized, however, that if he were to do this, in an attempt to satisfy the smaller stockholders and guarantee a successful sale, a basic conflict would arise. A lower subscription price would result in a greater number of shares being issued, and therefore greater dilution and more chance for unfavorable movements in the market price of the stock.

Underwriting commissions were also a problem that must be resolved. Two methods could be used. Either the whole issue could be underwritten at one specific cost, or the shares sold to the stockholders could bear one rate and any unsold shares would bear another higher rate. Mr. Knutson was not sure which of the two alternatives would give him the lower total cost.

Mr. Knutson realized that all of the above-cited information must be ready for the forthcoming meeting and presented in such a manner that the board could see the reasoning behind his recommendations; furthermore, he must be sufficiently briefed to be able to answer effectively any questions that might come up in the course of the negotiations.

# Expansion Financing

# 31

COLLINS RADIO COMPANY

In November, 1962, the board of directors of Collins Radio Company was considering ways of raising additional funds for continued expansion. The sales of the company had increased from about $12,000,000 in 1950 to more than $200,000,000 during the fiscal year ended July 31, 1962. This sales growth had created a continuous problem of raising new funds for asset expansion. In the past the major sources of funds for expansion had been internally generated funds from depreciation, amortization, and retained earnings; long-term debt of various types; increases in short-term debt; and the leasing of a portion of the real property and equipment.

The company was incorporated under the laws of the State of Iowa in 1937 as successor to a Delaware corporation of the same name formed in 1933 to supersede the sole proprietorship of the company's founder, Arthur A. Collins. At the end of World War II, Collins Radio Company was engaged in aviation and military electronics. By 1962, however, it was designing and manufacturing telecommunication, space communication, electronic computer, and navigation equipment.

A major part of the company's activities had been centered on highly specialized military equipment and systems. During the past few years, the company had been receiving about 1,000 prime contracts and subcontracts annually from the U. S. government.

Although the profits' margin derived from this work was rather slim, technical competence and efficient production produced consistent earnings.

By 1962 Collins Radio Company had become a world leader in aviation electronics. Large research expenditures had been involved in meeting the demanding technical requirements for the production of aviation electronic equipment. Although this was a large market, it was not considered to be an expanding one.

In 1953 Collins began the development of microwave relays and multiple-channel telecommunication equipment. The largest purchasers of these types of equipment were United States telephone companies, the U. S. government, and large industrial concerns. A vast overseas market existed for this type equipment, and since the basic research has already been done, foreign sales were expected to be profitable. Although the telecommunication area was unprofitable during its developmental stages, it became profitable to Collins Radio Company in 1961.

In 1961 the Company began to develop digital computers for science, data processing, and telecommunication message switching. Initial installations were made in the telecommunication message switching field because of the company's extensive experience in this area. The management of Collins planned to develop large processing centers having integral data communication systems. One of Collins' contracts called for the building of a $2 million data processing system for Delta Airlines. Although this area of the business had not been in operation a sufficient period of time to become profitable, the management of the company believed that market acceptance had been gratifying. Potential purchasers include United States and foreign airlines, railroads, and governmental agencies.

The company's space communication and navigation programs were initiated in 1947. Collins Radio Company and the National Bureau of Standards established the first lunar communication relay in 1952. The company provided the complete electronic communication system for Project Mercury and received contracts for building the communication system for Project Gemini and the telecommunication system for the Apollo program. Although the design of these systems would require large research and developmental expenses, these costs would be principally covered by payments from the U. S. government. The company also built stations for tracking orbital flights and deep sea probes.

Other small, though profitable, areas of operation included the manufacture of amateur radios, broadcast transmitters and antennas, and super-power transmitters for the U. S. Information Agency.

**Sales**

Sales of the Company increased from about $12 million in 1947 to $90 million in 1954. From 1955 through 1959, annual sales fluctuated between $107 and $127 million but jumped to $190 million in 1960. Net sales for the fiscal year ended July 31, 1962 amounted to $208 million, which included $61 million of commercial and foreign government sales. The balance was sold to the U. S. government. The company's backlog of orders on July 31, 1962, was $230,000,000 and consisted of many moderate-size contracts for a wide variety of equipment on a relatively short delivery cycle. This wide range of orders requires a large investment in inventories, but the diversification insures against significant cancellation of orders. During recent years, the company has been attempting to expand its sales to commercial and foreign governments so that it will not be so dependent on U. S. defense contracts.

### Net Income

The net earnings as a percentage of sales ranged from 3.43 per cent in 1960 to a low of 1.01 per cent in 1958 for the ten-year period, 1953–1962. Exhibit III indicates that earnings per share and market price per share varied widely from 1957 to 1962. Although the company paid cash dividends of $.32 per share in 1955, 1956, and 1957, cash dividends were discontinued in 1957. From 1958 through 1962, the board of directors of Collins Radio Company followed the policy of retaining the earnings for expansion, and accordingly, did not declare cash dividends. A 4 per cent stock dividend, however, was declared in 1959 and 1960. In November, 1962, the board of directors did not foresee a return to a cash dividend policy within the near future. The most restrictive of the company's debt contracts (Regulation V-loan agreement) limited cash dividends to 25 per cent of net income subsequent to July 31, 1961.

### Employee Benefits

In August, 1962, Collins Radio was employing a labor force of about 15,000 in its Cedar Rapids, Dallas, Newport Beach, Santa Ana, and Toronto plants. The company established a retirement plan in 1947 to supplement Social Security benefits, and the shareholders of the company approved a stock option plan in 1956.

The retirement plan was noncontributory, and the amount of monthly retirement benefits depended on the length of service and the highest five-year average salary during the ten-year period prior to retirement. The formula for determining monthly benefits was: 2 per cent $\times$ years of service $\times$ average gross pay, less $110.50. For a person with twenty years service and $1,000 average monthly income, the monthly retirement benefit at age sixty-five was $289.50. The plan provided somewhat reduced benefits for earlier retirement and for joint survivor benefits. The retirement plan provided for retirement for an employee of age forty-five or above with ten or more years service, although benefits did not begin until a person was fifty-five. The plan also provided permanent disability benefits equal to retirement benefits to a person forty-five or older who had fifteen years service with the Company.

In 1962, the First National Pension Trust of Chicago was administering the Collins Radio Retirement Trust. The trustee had the discretionery power to hold, invest, and reinvest the assets of the fund.

The employers intended to make future contributions in such amounts as in the aggregate over a period of time would be sufficient to meet the cost of the specified benefits. The company, however, was under no obligation (labor contracts) to make future contributions. After the contributions were made to the trust, the assets were irrevocably available for the payment of benefits under the plan. Company payments to the fund amounted to $2,055,000 in 1960 and $2,175,000 in 1961. Payments in the 1962 calendar year were expected to be approximately $2,000,000.

On November 13, 1956, the stockholders of Collins Radio Company approved a restricted stock option plan which granted key officers and employees the right to receive stock options at the discretion of a committee appointed by the board of directors. The purchase price was 95 per cent of the market price of the common on the date the options were granted, was not exercisable within twelve months of the issue date, expired ten years from date of issue, and expired with termination of employment. On October 31, 1962, options to purchase 52,767 common shares by twenty-seven employees at $24.15 per share were outstanding. Some 60 per cent of the options were held by the officers and directors; however, the company president and executive vice-president were not eligible to receive options under the plan. Some 60,152 shares had been acquired through the use of options by July 31, 1962, and 47,862 shares were available for the granting of new options on that date.

### Financing Past Expansion

The management of Collins Radio Company had used numerous methods for financing the expansion of the company. On July 31, 1962, Regulation V-loans totaled $56,000,000. The 90-day, renewable notes were used for the purpose of financing inventory and accounts receivable under U.S. government contracts. Proceeds from the sale of the inventories and collection of the receivables were assignable upon the request of the lender. Some $3,000,000 of other short-term notes, primarily bank loans, were outstanding, while long-term mortgage debt exceeded $12,800,000.

In March, 1960, a syndicate headed by Kidder, Peabody, and Company underwrote a $12,000,000 issue of 20-year, 4 3/4 per cent convertible subordinated debentures. The debentures were convertible to common stock at $61.54, and were sold to the public at par. Underwriting commissions were $42,000, and other expenses associated with the issue and paid by the company totaled $80,000. A. H. Gordon, chairman of the board of Kidder, Peabody, and Company, Inc., had been a member of the board of directors of Collins Radio Company since 1955.

In several transactions in 1962, Collins had acquired through purchase and manufacture some $2,700,000 in equipment, sold the equipment to Bankers Leasing Company of Boston, and leased the equipment for ten-year periods. During the fiscal years 1961 and 1962, some $7,300,000 in equipment was sold and leased back. The monthly rent was sufficient to pay for the equipment in ten years and to give the leasor a return of $5\frac{1}{2}$ to $6\frac{1}{4}$ per cent. Collins Radio Company had renewal privileges at reduced rental rates upon the expiration of the lease contracts. Approximately 1,000,000 square feet of the company's floor space, or about 40 per cent, were being leased on July 31, 1962. On that date, annual leasing payments on real property totaled about $527,000, while the cost of leasing equipment was about $445,000.

## Planned Expansion During 1962-63

The company planned to erect a $1.2 million building, containing 103,000 square feet of space, on a 32-acre tract at the Richardson (Dallas) site. The value of the land had been appraised at $175,000. The building was to be used for warehouse, office, and engineering space. For tax purposes, the building had an estimated life of thirty years. The company used the sum-of-the-years-digits method of computing depreciation.

The management of Collins Radio Company expected that the cost of new equipment needs during the year would be about $13,000,000 and that inventories would build up by some $20,000,000. These were indicated by the backlog of orders on hand on July 31, 1962. Other asset totals would remain relatively unchanged.

## Financing Alternatives

Three alternatives were available to the company for financing the Richardson building. Cash on hand or funds generated internally could have been used to finance the building. As an alternative, the trustee for the Collins Radio Retirement Trust expressed a willingness to buy the building for $1.4 million, and to lease the building and land to Collins under a twenty-year contract. The monthly leasing rent would be sufficient to repay the $1.4 million investment in addition to an annual return of 5 1/2 per cent. Monthly rent would be $9,630.43 for twenty years, but the company would have six 5-year renewal options at an annual rental cost of $42,000. Similar leasing terms as those outlined above were available from other commercial leasing companies.

The company had numerous alternatives for the raising of funds

**EXHIBIT I**

**Collins Radio Company and Subsidiaries**
**Consolidated Balance Sheets**
**as of July 31**
**(In Thousands)**

|  | 1962 | 1961 | 1959 |
|---|---|---|---|
| *Assets* |  |  |  |
| Current assets |  |  |  |
| Cash | $6,412 | $6,966 | $5,858 |
| Accounts and notes receivable |  |  |  |
| U. S. government | 32,871 | 27,821 | 21,017 |
| Other (net of bad debts) | 15,325 | 14,365 | 7,502 |
| Inventories (lower of cost or market) | 70,441 | 54,901 | 44,214 |
| Prepaid expenses | 1,013 | 1,822 | 626 |
| Total current assets | $126,062 | $105,875 | $79,217 |
| Property, plant, and equipment (cost) |  |  |  |
| Land and improvements | 1,348 | 1,338 | — |
| Buildings, machinery, and equipment | 49,299 | 44,899 | — |
| Total | $50,647 | $46,237 | 22,250 |
| Less accumulated depreciation | 21,051 | 15,968 | 9,356 |
| Net Fixed Assets | $29,596 | $30,269 | $12,894 |
| Other assets and deferred charges | 1,960 | 1,548 | 1,263 |
| Total assets | $157,618 | $137,692 | $93,374 |
| *Liabilities* |  |  |  |
| Current liabilities |  |  |  |
| Regulation V-Loans (90-day renewable) | $56,000 | $40,400 | $31,000 |
| Other notes payable | 2,840 | 10,226 | 2,762 |
| Accounts payable—trade | 11,586 | 7,884 | 6,526 |
| Accounts payable—other | 2,751 | 3,076 | 1,335 |
| Accrued liabilities | 6,766 | 6,156 | 3,568 |
| Federal and foreign income taxes price revision refund | 2,758 | 4,165 | 4,939 |
| Total current liabilities | 82,701 | 71,907 | 50,130 |
| Deferred income taxes | 390 | — | — |
| Long-term liabilities |  |  |  |
| 4 3/4% conv. subord. deb. of 1980 | 12,000 | 12,000 | — |
| 5 1/2% first mortgage notes | 4,550 | — | 2,880 |
| First mortgage sinking fund |  |  |  |
| bonds, 5 1/2 to 6% rates | 8,266 | 7,116 | — |
| Other | 428 | 478 | 10,868 |
| Total long-term liabilities | $25,634 | $19,594 | $13,748 |
| Stockholders' equity |  |  |  |
| Preferred stock |  |  |  |
| Common stock, $1 par, |  |  | 1,135 |
| 6,500,000 shares authorized | 2,230 | 2,213 | 1,813 |
| Capital in excess of par value | 27,125 | 26,727 | 13,595 |
| Retained earnings | 19,928 | 17,251 | 12,953 |
| Total stockholders' equity | 49,283 | 46,190 | 29,496 |
| Total liabilities | $157,618 | $137,692 | $93,374 |

sufficient to finance the build-up of inventories and the acquisition of new machinery. Internally generated funds would meet a portion of the needs. Since the company was financing heavily with debt, the U. S. government was reluctant to increase the Regulation V-loan limit unless additional equity funds were provided. The restrictive provision under the Regulation V-loans limited the cash dividend payout to 25 per cent of net income unless

### EXHIBIT II

**Collins Radio Company and Subsidiaries**
**Consolidated Statements of Income and Retained Earnings**
**for the Years Ending July 31**
**(In Thousands)**

|  | 1962 | 1961 | 1959 |
|---|---|---|---|
| Net sales | $207,776 | $215,769 | $117,864 |
| Cost of sales | 167,509 | 176,062 | 92,613 |
| Gross profits | 40,267 | 39,707 | 25,251 |
| Selling, research, development, and administrative expense | 30,413 | 30,905 | 15,370 |
| Interest expense | 3,984 | 3,583 | 2,197 |
| Other expenses—net* | 392 | (84) | 20 |
| Total Expenses | 34,789 | 34,404 | 17,587 |
| Net income before Income Taxes | 5,478 | 5,303 | 7,664 |
| Provision for federal and foreign income taxes | 2,800 | 2,758 | 3,945 |
| Net Income | 2,678 | 2,545 | 3,719 |
| Special credits (liq. of subsidiaries) | — | 539 | — |
| Retained earnings, beginning of year | 17,251 | 14,171 | 11,723 |
|  | 19,929 | 17,255 | 15,442 |
| Dividends (1959 includes $ 2,302 in stock) | — | 4 | 2,489 |
| Retained earnings, end of year | $19,929 | $17,251 | $12,953 |

*Note:* Costs and expenses include depreciation and amortization charges of: $5,605 for 1962 (declining balance method): $4,248 for 1961; and $2,063 for 1959.

### EXHIBIT III

**Collins Radio Company**
**Selected Data on Common Stock**

| Fiscal Year Ended July 31 | | | Calendar Year Basis | | |
|---|---|---|---|---|---|
| Period | E/S | Div./Sh. | High M. V. | Low M. V. | Market |
| 1957 | 1.20 | .32 | 26 3/8 | 8 1/2 | OTC |
| 1958 | .51 | Nil | 23 | 10 1/4 | OTC |
| 1959 | 1.87 | 4% Stock | 72 1/8 | 21 1/4 | NYSE |
| 1960 | 3.02 | 4% Stock | 76 | 42 1/2 | NYSE |
| 1961 | 1.39 | Nil | 49 1/4 | 29 1/8 | NYSE |
| 1962 | 1.20 | Nil | 41 1/2 | 18 1/2 | NYSE |
| 1963 |  |  |  |  |  |
| Aug.-Oct. | .32 | — | 29 1/4 | 19 3/4 | NYSE |
| Oct. | — | — | 22 | 19 3/4 | NYSE |

additional equity were obtained. Should the company raise $12 or $15 million in junior securities, the restrictive provision would be waived. In addition, the Regulation V-loan limit would be increased by an amount equal to about 60 per cent of the new equity funds acquired.

The board of directors of the company was not in favor of a preferred issue, but it did consider a preemptive-rights issue of common stock. In November the stock had traded between $21–26 per share and would probably have to be discounted to $15 or $16 a share to insure the success of the issue. Some 800,000 new shares of stock would have to be sold to raise $12,000,000 in funds. The size of the issue would be relatively large in comparison to the 2,230,000 shares outstanding in October, 1962. At that time Arthur A. Collins and his family owned 24.4 per cent of the common stock, other directors and officers of the company owned 1.7 per cent, and the balance was in the hands of the general public.

One of the directors, Mr. A. H. Gordon, believed that his investment banking firm would head up a syndicate to market an issue of 20-year, convertible subordinated debentures. The current yield on similar securities was about 4 3/4 per cent. Mr. Gordon believed that the underwriting syndicate would discount the issue by 2 per cent. Other expenses were expected to be about $80,000. In order to make the issue attractive to prospective purchasers, the conversion price would have to be very close to the prevailing market price on the issue date. A call feature would provide Collins Radio Company with some flexibility for future financing.

# Refunding

## 32

GULF STATES
UTILITIES COMPANY " B "[1]

In July, 1963, the financial vice-president of Gulf States Utilities was considering the current yields on Aa grade utility bonds and high-grade utility preferred stock to determine whether a refunding of any of the outstanding issues of the company would prove profitable. The company had considered a refunding in December, 1962, but had not made any definite decision by the following July. The current yields were considerably below the coupon rates on three of the bond series and on two of the preferred stock series. In determining whether to refund an issue, the company in the past had considered the call premium, duplicate interest or dividends, estimated expenses of issuance of replacement securities, federal income tax reduction, and the direction of movement of security yields. Another method for determining the feasibility of refunding a bond issue had recently appeared in an article in *Public Utilities Fortnightly* entitled "A Guide to Bond Refunding," and the financial vice-president wished to apply the reasoning and suggestions of the article to his own situation. He would then be in a better position to make a recommendation to the board of directors of the company about the refunding consideration.

Exhibit I indicates the call premiums, 1963–1966, for the First 4 7/8s of 1987, First 5 1/4s of 1989, First 4 7/8s of 1990, and the $5.00 and $5.08 cumulative preferred stock. Call premiums on the series range from 5.30 per cent to 8.63 per cent during 1963, but decline over time. Both the bond issues and preferred issues are callable in whole or in part at any time with at least 30 days' notice at specified call prices, plus accrued interest or dividends.

---

[1] For a history of the case, refer to Case 29, Gulf States Utilities Company (A).

When an issue is replaced by a refunding series, both issues are outstanding for a period of approximately thirty days. The duplicate interest or dividends are considered a reduction of the interest (or dividend) savings from the refunding.

Gulf States made seven issues of bonds between 1956 and 1962 with a total par value of $112,000,000. The underwriting cost as a percentage of the proceeds to the company varied from a low of .677 per cent to a high of .876 per cent. The weighted-average underwriting cost for the series was .752 per cent. Underwriting costs on the $5.00 and $5.08 cumulative preferred stock issues averaged 1.825 per cent of the proceeds to the company. Other expenses of issuance for the $17 million bond issue made in 1962 were approximately $80,000. A similar figure could be used in determining the feasibility of a refunding issue.

For federal income tax purposes, the call premium on a bond issue, less any unamortized premium, is deductible in total in the year of refunding. This tax deduction does not apply to the call premium on preferred issues. In 1963, the company was in the 52 per cent federal income tax bracket.

Another minor consideration in a decision on refunding is the possible effect that the refunding has on the future ability of the company to market new issues of securities. Since the Federal Power Commission requires that regulated utility companies include the call feature in its debt and preferred issues, and since investors may logically expect a call when it is advantageous to the company, the management of the Gulf States Utilities Company did not feel that a refunding issue would adversely affect its ability to finance future expansion.

When the board of directors of Gulf States determines that the time is advantageous to refund an issue, the company must study the movement of bond yields (or preferred stock yields) in order to market the new series at the lowest possible cost to the company. To refund the issue too soon, before yields bottom out, results in less than maximum savings on the refunding. Conversely, if the company fails to market the refunding issue before yields turn up, it misses its best opportunity for refunding.

Long-term Aa grade public utility bonds traded at average yields of from 4.26 per cent to 4.32 per cent to maturity during the first half of 1963, as is shown by Exhibit III. Bond yields firmed up somewhat during the middle of July, 1963, however. This was influenced by the increase in the Treasury bill yield rate and prospects for an increase in the rediscount rate. Yields on high-grade utility preferred stocks had been falling from January through June 28, 1963, but the trend was reversed in the early part of July (see Exhibit IV). Yields on Gulf States' preferred issues, except for those kept artificially high by the call prices, were between 4.3 and 4.4 per cent during June, 1963.

The financial vice-president felt that many other corporations would be marketing bond issues while the yields were relatively low. This demand for funds might stimulate the rise in bond and preferred yields for a time, but he felt that the company should investigate the feasibility of making a funding or refunding issue within the near future.

Many methods have been suggested for evaluating the feasibility of a bond refunding proposal. Some financial consultants suggest that a bond refunding proposal should be contrasted to other alternate investment opportunities. That is, if the after-tax, discounted present value of the interest savings is adequate to return a higher discounted rate of return on the initial cash outflow than the weighted-average cost of capital, the refunding would be economically feasible. Some economists, statisticians, and financial consultants believe that the current rate of bond interest should be used as a discount rate while others defend the return on common equity.

An illustration of the refunding feasibility of the First 5 1/4s of 1989, computed by the discounted present value rate of return method, is illustrated in Exhibit VII. The illustration is based upon the assumptions that a refunding bond issue in the amount of $16,000,000 can be sold with a coupon rate of 4 1/2 per cent at a 4 3/8 per cent yield to maturity. The present value tables which appear in Exhibit VI were used to determine the approximate market value of the proposed bond issue. In order to determine the current market value of a bond from present value tables, one must know the coupon rate of the bond in question, the current yield to maturity, and the years to maturity.

The market value of a bond at any point in time is the aggregate value of: (1) the face of the instrument (assume $1,000), discounted by the current yield for the appropriate number of semiannual periods (since interest on bonds is usually paid twice annually), plus (2) the present value of the expected future flow of interest income per period discounted by the appropriate yield to maturity for the desired number of periods. The present value of $1.00 table is used for the former, while the present value of $1.00 per period is used in the later calculation.

Applying the after-tax costs associated with the refunding issue, a present value rate of return on the initial cash outlay of 9.0 per cent is achieved from the interest savings obtained throughout the balance of the maturity of the old bond issue. This 9.0 per cent return was substantially above the current cost of interest, and it was significantly higher than the after-tax weighted average cost of capital to the firm, which was about 4 per cent at mid-1963.

Other financial advisors, however, do not approve of this method because the decision to refund or not to refund is influenced by the arbitrary spread between the coupon rate and yield on the new bond proposal. If a 4 3/4 interest rate were set on the new bond issue, rather than the 4 1/2 per cent rate, the smaller initial cash outflows and reduced interest savings would produce a significantly higher discounted rate of return. By manipulating the relative sizes of cash inflows and outflows, an almost infinite range of discount factors can be obtained.

Another approach to determining the economic feasibility of a bond refunding proposal has been suggested by a financial consultant, Eugene Merrill, in an article in *Public Utilities Fortnightly*.[2] Mr. Merrill stated that:

---

[2]Eugene S. Merrill, "A Guide to Bond Refunding," *Public Utilities Fortnightly*, September 27, 1962, pp. 385–393.

The proper guide for a utility company considering a bond refunding is the return it expects to earn on the common equity. If the expected return is 12 per cent, then, for the refunding to be desirable, the rate of the new issue must afford interest savings which will provide a 12 per cent return on the dollar cost of call and amortize this investment over the life of the old bond.

The dollar cost of calling a bond issue before maturity represents an investment by the common stockholders. Whether the cost of call is immediately debited to surplus or whether it is deferred and debited to surplus over a period of years, the cost is always the responsibility of the common stockholders.

An examination of this statement by the financial vice-president of GSU immediately raised the question: How does a utility company arrive at the return it expects to earn on the common equity? The vice-president knew that the rate of return on the investment of a utility company is restricted by regulatory authority. Regardless of whether this restriction takes the form of a specified percentage on the net plant investment, or a specified percentage on some other basis, this restriction will be equivalent to some percentage on the individual company's total capitalization. A company, in establishing its capitalization ratios, immediately determines the potentiality of the return that it can expect to earn on the common equity.

A company seeking an Aa rating on its highest form of debt, might establish as its goal capitalization ratios as follows:

Common stock equity (including surplus)    30–34%

Secured debt                               46–50%

The balance of capitalization is to be made up of preferred stock and unsecured long-term debt, with total secured and unsecured long-term debt not to exceed 55% of total capitalization.

These ratios set the maximum and minimum limits of the return on the common equity. Assuming that the regulatory authority having jurisdiction over the company allows that company to earn 6 per cent on its net plant investment, which return might be equivalent to a 6 1/2 per cent rate of return on the company's total capitalization, the return on the common equity will be determined as follows:

The rate of return on total capitalization is equal to (a) the percentage of the total capitalization represented by the outstanding senior securities, multiplied by the average rate of interest on such senior securities, plus (b) the percentage of the total capitalization represented by the common equity, multiplied by the rate of return on the common equity.

In order to convert this statement to a mathematical equation, let us assume that:

$R$ = Return on Total Capitalization Allowed by Regulatory Authority.
$S$ = Per Cent of Total Capitalization Represented by Outstanding Senior Securities.
$r$ = Average Rate of Interest on Senior Securities.

$C$ = Per Cent of Total Capitalization Represented by Common Stock Equity.

$I$ = Rate of Return on the Common Stock Equity.

The formula for determining the rate of return on the common stock equity would be:

$$R = (S \times r) + (C \times I)$$

From the capitalization ratios set forth previously, the equation for the minimum common equity of 30 per cent (assuming an average rate of interest on senior securities at the time of the adoption of capitalization ratios was 3.25 per cent) would be as follows:

$$0.065 = (0.70 \times 0.0325) + (0.30 \times I)$$

Solving alegebraically for $I$, it is determined that $I = 14.08$ per cent. In like manner, the equation for the maximum common equity of 34 per cent would be:

$$0.065 = (0.66 \times 0.0325) + (0.34 \times I)$$

Solving algebraically for $I$, it is determined that $I = 12.81$ per cent. The potential return on the common equity that such a company may expect is between 12.81 per cent and 14.08 per cent.

Let us now assume that after fifteen years of rapid growth the utility company has managed to stay within its capitalization ratios so that even though the current interest rate is substantially higher, the average interest rate on the senior securities has only increased to 4.02 per cent. Applying the same equation, we find that:

$$0.065 = (0.70 \times 4.02) + (0.30 \times I)$$
$$I = 12.29 \text{ per cent.}$$

and

$$0.065 = (0.66 \times 4.02) + (0.30 \times I)$$
$$I = 11.31 \text{ per cent.}$$

The return that the company may now expect on the common equity is between 11.31 per cent and 12.29 per cent.

By reducing the average interest rate 1/100 of 1 per cent, or from 4.02 per cent to 4.01 per cent, the potential return on the common equity would be increased to between 11.33 per cent to 12.31 per cent. This is equivalent to approximately a $.003 increase on the earnings per share of common stock of Gulf States.

On the surface it appears that the lower the common equity ratio, the higher the potential of the return on the common equity. But the point of diminishing returns is rapidly reached as the common equity ratio is reduced because when the ratio is reduced to a certain point, the company is immediately faced with paying higher interest rates. This effect would tend to lower the potential of the return on the common equity and offset the apparent advantage gained by reducing the common equity ratio.

Thus, with the rate of return on the total capitalization fixed, in effect, by regulatory authority and the capitalization ratios fixed by company financial policy, the equation leaves only one element that the company may change, namely, the average rate of interest on its senior securities. For this reason it is very important to the long-range earning per share growth that refunding be undertaken when it is clearly advantageous to the company.

Since the current return on the common equity of GSU was about 12 per cent, it was a simple matter to apply the suggestions of Mr. Merrill to the

**EXHIBIT I**

**Gulf States Utilities Company**
**Call Prices for Refunding Purposes**
**Selected Mortgage Bond and Preferred Stock Series**

| | Call Prices | | | |
|---|---|---|---|---|
| Issue | 1963 | 1964 | 1965 | 1966 |
| First 4 7/8s, 1987 | 105.30 | 105.10 | 104.90 | 104.65 |
| First 5 1/4s, A, 1989 | 107.10 | 106.85 | 106.55 | 106.30 |
| First 4 7/8s, 1990 | 105.40 | 105.20 | 105.00 | 104.80 |
| $5 cumulative preferred | 106.25 | 106.25 | 106.25 | 106.25 |
| $5.08 cumulative preferred | 108.63 | 106.63 | 106.63 | 106.63 |

**EXHIBIT II**
**Gulf States Utilities Company**
**Underwriting Costs of Selected Issues**

| Series | Issue Date | Issue Size (millions) | Offering Price | Proceeds to Comp. | Underwriting Cost (% of proceeds) |
|---|---|---|---|---|---|
| 4 1/4s of 1986 | (1956) | $15 | 100.848 | 100.08* | .767 |
| 4 7/8s of 1987 | (1957) | $17 | 101.50 | 100.619 | .876 |
| 4s of 1988 | (1958) | $20 | 102.655 | 101.965 | .677 |
| 4 3/4s of 1989 | (1959) | $10 | 102.427 | 101.689 | .726 |
| 5 1/4s A of 1989 | (1959) | $16 | 102.603 | 101.830 | .759 |
| 4 7/8s of 1990 | (1960) | $17 | 100.867 | 100.1099 | .756 |
| 4 3/8s of 1992 | (1962) | $17 | 101.500 | 100.78 | .714 |
| Weighted average | | | | | .752 |
| $5 cum. preferred | (1958) | $7.5 | 102.25 | 100.5199 | 1.7301 |
| $5.08 cum. pref. | (1959) | $10.0 | 102.625 | 100.709 | 1.916 |
| Weighted average | | | | | 1.825 |

*Bond premiums amortized ratably over the life of the issue.

facts surrounding GSU's proposal. Exhibit VIII presents the expenses for tax purposes, the cost to call the issue, and the net cost to call as a percentage of the principal amount. These figures will be applied in an example for determining the decline in the bond interest rate to make refunding profitable.

Mr. Merrill also stated:[3]

> The interest reduction required to give the desired equity return may be computed by reference to standard annuity tables. The steps are as follows: [GSU figures have been supplied by the casewriter.]

**EXHIBIT III**

**Average Yields on Aa Grade Public Utility Bonds**
**From January 1 to July 11, 1963\***

| Day | January | February | March | April | May | June | July |
|---|---|---|---|---|---|---|---|
| 1 | — | 4.28 | 4.27 | 4.27 | 4.31 | — | 4.29 |
| 2 | 4.29 | — | — | 4.28 | 4.31 | — | 4.29 |
| 3 | 4.29 | — | — | 4.28 | 4.31 | 4.28 | 4.29 |
| 4 | 4.29 | 4.28 | 4.27 | 4.29 | — | 4.29 | 4.29 |
| 5 | — | 4.28 | 4.27 | 4.29 | — | 4.29 | 4.29 |
| 6 | — | 4.28 | 4.26 | — | 4.31 | 4.29 | — |
| 7 | 4.29 | 4.28 | 4.26 | — | 4.31 | 4.29 | — |
| 8 | 4.28 | 4.28 | 4.26 | 4.29 | 4.28 | — | 4.29 |
| 9 | 4.28 | — | — | 4.28 | 4.28 | — | 4.31 |
| 10 | 4.28 | — | — | 4.29 | 4.28 | 4.29 | 4.32 |
| 11 | 4.27 | 4.28 | 4.26 | 4.29 | — | 4.29 | 4.32 |
| 12 | — | 4.28 | 4.27 | — | — | 4.29 | |
| 13 | — | 4.28 | 4.27 | — | 4.28 | 4.29 | |
| 14 | 4.27 | 4.28 | 4.27 | — | 4.28 | 4.29 | |
| 15 | 4.27 | 4.28 | 4.27 | 4.29 | 4.28 | — | |
| 16 | 4.27 | — | — | 4.29 | 4.28 | — | |
| 17 | 4.27 | — | — | 4.29 | 4.28 | 4.29 | |
| 18 | 4.27 | 4.28 | 4.27 | 4.29 | — | 4.29 | |
| 19 | — | 4.28 | 4.27 | 4.30 | — | 4.29 | |
| 20 | — | 4.28 | 4.27 | — | 4.28 | 4.29 | |
| 21 | 4.27 | 4.28 | 4.27 | — | 4.28 | 4.29 | |
| 22 | 4.27 | — | 4.26 | 4.30 | 4.28 | — | |
| 23 | 4.27 | — | — | 4.30 | 4.28 | — | |
| 24 | 4.27 | — | — | 4.30 | 4.29 | 4.29 | |
| 25 | 4.27 | 4.28 | 4.26 | 4.30 | — | 4.29 | |
| 26 | — | 4.28 | 4.26 | 4.30 | — | 4.29 | |
| 27 | — | 4.28 | 4.26 | — | 4.28 | 4.29 | |
| 28 | 4.27 | 4.27 | 4.26 | — | 4.28 | 4.29 | |
| 29 | 4.27 | | 4.27 | 4.31 | 4.28 | — | |
| 30 | 4.28 | | — | 4.31 | 4.28 | — | |
| 31 | 4.28 | | — | | 4.28 | | |

\**Source:* Moody's Investors Service, *Moody's Bond Survey*, Selected January—July, 1963.

---

[3]*Ibid.*, p. 391.

1. Determine the total dollar cost for calling the old issue. These costs include the redemption premium and duplicate interest. Other costs, such as publication of the call notice, are usually minimal and have not been included in the example. The cost of financing attaches to the new issue and should be considered in determining the cost of the new issue.

2. Express the dollar cost of call in terms of principal amount. [For the GSU refunding proposal, the net cost to call (Exhibit VIII) was estimated to be $677,000 or 4.231 per cent of the principal amount involved.]

3. From an annuity table, find the annual payment necessary to pay off $1 over the remaining years of the old bond at the desired equity return. [For the twenty-seven-year GSU issue, with a rate of 12 per cent, this would be 0.1259.]

4. Determine the annual interest reduction required to provide the desired equity return and to amortize the investment in calling the bonds by multiplying the cost of call as determined in Step 2 by the annuity factor as determined in Step 3. [For the GSU First 5 1/4s of 1987, this would amount to 4.231 × 0.1259 equals 0.533, or fifty-three basic points.]

5. Subtract the interest reduction required as determined in Step 4 from the coupon rate on the old bond to give the required interest cost on the new bond.

**EXHIBIT IV**

**Gulf States Utilities Company**
**Yields on High-Grade Public Utility Preferred Stock***

| Date | Yield |
|---|---|
| 1961 | 4.82—4.60 |
| 1962 | 4.67—4.43 |
| 1963 | |
| January-June | 4.40—4.32 |
| June 14 | 4.34 |
| 21 | 4.34 |
| 28 | 4.33 |
| July 5 | 4.35 |
| 11 | 4.35 |

*Source:* Moody's Investors Service, *Moody's Bond Survey*, Selected Issues.

**EXHIBIT V**

**Gulf States Utilities Company**
**Price Range and Yields on Selected Issues**
**For June, 1963**

| Series | Hi | Lo | Yield | 1963 Call Price |
|---|---|---|---|---|
| $5.08 cumulative preferred | 110 1/2 | 109 | 4.6% | 108.63 |
| $5.00 cumulative preferred | 107 3/4 | 106 1/4 | 4.7% | 106.25 |
| $4.44 cumulative preferred | 100 1/2 | 100 1/2 | 4.4% | 103.75 |
| $4.20 cumulative preferred | 97 3/4 | 96 1/2 | 4.3% | 102.818 |

In our illustration, 5.25 per cent less .53 per cent yields a difference of 4.72. A refunding of the issue at a yield to maturity of less than 4.72 per cent would be economically feasible under this approach.

A refunding guide indicating the reduction in the interest rate required to amortize the cost of a call and to provide a return of 12 per cent on the funds committed is shown in Exhibit IX. The feasibility of calling a bond issue for refunding could easily be determined by: (1) computing the net cost to call

**EXHIBIT VI**

**Gulf States Utilities Company**
**Present Value Tables**

| | Number of Periods | Semi-Annual Rates of Interest | | | | |
|---|---|---|---|---|---|---|
| | | 2 | 2 1/16 | 2 1/8 | 2 3/16 | 2 1/4 |
| Present Value of 1.00 | 42 | .435304 | .424248 | .413479 | .402989 | .392772 |
| | 43 | .426769 | .415674 | .404875 | .394363 | .384129 |
| | 44 | .418401 | .407274 | .396450 | .385921 | .375677 |
| | 45 | .410197 | .399044 | .388201 | .377659 | .367410 |
| | 46 | .402154 | .390980 | .380124 | .369575 | .359325 |
| | 47 | .394268 | .383079 | .372214 | .361663 | .351418 |
| | 48 | .386538 | .375338 | .364469 | .353921 | .343685 |
| | 49 | .378958 | .367753 | .356885 | .346345 | .336122 |
| | 50 | .371528 | .360321 | .349459 | .338931 | .328726 |
| | 51 | .364243 | .353040 | .342188 | .331676 | .321493 |
| | 52 | .357101 | .345906 | .335068 | .324575 | .314418 |
| | 53 | .350099 | .338915 | .328096 | .317627 | .307499 |
| | 54 | .343234 | .332067 | .321269 | .310828 | .300733 |
| | 55 | .336504 | .325356 | .314584 | .304174 | .294115 |
| | 56 | .329906 | .318781 | .308038 | .297663 | .287643 |
| | 60 | .304782 | .293784 | .283189 | .272981 | .263149 |
| Present Value of 1.00 per Period | 42 | 28.2348 | 27.9153 | 27.6010 | 27.2919 | 26.9879 |
| | 43 | 28.6616 | 28.3309 | 28.0059 | 27.6863 | 27.3720 |
| | 44 | 29.0800 | 28.7382 | 28.4023 | 28.0722 | 27.7477 |
| | 45 | 29.4902 | 29.1373 | 28.7905 | 28.4499 | 28.1151 |
| | 46 | 29.8923 | 29.5282 | 29.1707 | 28.8194 | 28.4744 |
| | 47 | 30.2866 | 29.9113 | 29.5429 | 29.1811 | 28.8259 |
| | 48 | 30.6731 | 30.2867 | 29.9073 | 29.5350 | 29.1695 |
| | 49 | 31.0521 | 30.6544 | 30.2642 | 29.8814 | 29.5057 |
| | 50 | 31.4236 | 31.0147 | 30.6137 | 30.2203 | 29.8344 |
| | 51 | 31.7878 | 31.3678 | 30.9559 | 30.5520 | 30.1559 |
| | 52 | 32.1449 | 31.7137 | 31.2909 | 30.8765 | 30.4703 |
| | 53 | 32.4950 | 32.0526 | 31.6190 | 31.1942 | 30.7778 |
| | 54 | 32.8383 | 32.3847 | 31.9403 | 31.5050 | 31.0785 |
| | 55 | 33.1748 | 32.7100 | 32.2549 | 31.8092 | 31.3727 |
| | 56 | 33.5047 | 33.0288 | 32.5629 | 32.1068 | 31.6603 |
| | 60 | 34.7609 | 34.2408 | 33.7323 | 33.2351 | 32.7490 |

a bond issue expressed as a percentage of the principal amount, and (2) entering the table under the corresponding column and reading down to the appropriate years to maturity. If the redemption cost obtained by the above procedure plus the yield to maturity on the refunding issue was lower than the coupon rate of the old issue, then to refund the issue would produce a return of more than 12 per cent on the new funds required for the proposal.

**EXHIBIT VII**

**Gulf States Utilities Company**
**Bond Refunding Feasibility**
**of $16,000,000 5 1/4s**
**of 1989 at Mid-1963**

|  | 5 1/4s of 1989<br>$ 16,000,000 |
|---|---:|
| Refunding issue : 4 1/2% to yield 4 3/8% | |
| | |
| Computation of cash outlay | |
| Value of bonds—new | |
| Size of issue ×.272981 | $4,367,696 |
| Value of interest | |
| Size of issue ×.0225 × 33.2351 | 11,964,636 |
| Total issue price | $16,332,332 |
| | |
| Less : refunding costs | |
| Principal plus premium | |
| 16,000,000 × 107.10 | $17,136,000 |
| Underwriting cost : (.75% of total above) | 122,492 |
| Other costs to issuer | 80,000 |
| Interest (.0525 × 1/12 × issue size) | 70,000 |
| Total cash outlay | $17,408,492 |
| Initial cash investment | 1,076,160 |
| Less : tax advantage | |
| (.52) (call pre.-um.prem + extra int.) | |
| .52 (1,136,000 − 184,000 + 70,000) | 531,440 |
| Net cash outlay | $544,720 |
| | |
| Potential interest savings | |
| Interest on old | $840,000 |
| Interest on new | 720,000 |
| Difference | $120,000 |
| Less : bond prem-underwriting costs ÷ life of old issue 1/26 (332,332-202,492) | $4,994 |
| Annual savings before taxes | 115,006 |
| Less : tax shield of 52% | 59,803 |
| Savings after taxes | $55,203 |
| Payback (cash outlay ÷ saving after tax) | 9.87 yrs. |
| Time adjusted rate of return* | 9% |

*Will increase as tax rate declines.

One final approach to the decision was to use the *marginal cost of capital concept*. The above procedure outlined by Mr. Merrill could be applied, but it would be necessary to substitute 12 per cent with the cost of the "cheapest" source of credit. In our case, Aa grade utility bonds were yielding about 4.375 per cent to maturity. In applying the above method to our example and using the data from Exhibits VI and VIII, we determine the following:

| | |
|---|---|
| Coupon rate on old issue | 5.25% |
| Less: $4.231 \times \dfrac{1}{31.5050 \times 1/2}$ | 0.27 |
| Yield level to produce a 4 3/8% return on funds committed | 4.98% |

Each of the above three methods appeared to support a decision to refund the 5 1/4s of 1987; however, the financial vice-president of the firm was still faced with the decision as to the timing of the refunding operation. He believed that the preparation of a schedule showing the levels of profitable refunding from 1963 to 1966 for the two 4 7/8 per cent bond issues and the $5.00 and $5.08 preferred issue would also prove helpful.

**EXHIBIT VIII**

**Gulf States Utilities Company**
**Computation showing the breakeven point**
**for calling $16,000,000 principal amount**
**of First Mortgage Bonds, 5 1/4% Series A**
**due 1989, on or about December 20, 1962**

| | |
|---|---|
| *Expenses for Tax Purposes* | |
| Call premium (effective 12/20/62 107.10) | $1,136,000 |
| Duplicate interest | 70,000 |
| Unamortized premium on debt (as of November 30, 1962) | (188,622) |
| Total | $1,017,378 |
| Federal income taxes @ 52% | $529,037 |
| | |
| *Cost of Call* | |
| Principal amount | $16,000,000 |
| Call premium | 1,136,000 |
| Duplicate interest | 70,000 |
| Federal income tax reduction | (529,037) |
| Net cost to call | $16,676,963 |
| Net cost to call as per cent of principal amount | 104.231% |
| Years to maturity | 27 |

## EXHIBIT IX

### Refunding Guide†
### Reduction in Interest Rate Required to Amortize Cost of Call and to Provide a Return of 12 Per Cent
### (In Basis Points)*

| Years to Maturity | Redemption Cost as Per Cent of Principal Amount | | | | | | | | | | | | | | |
|---|---|---|---|---|---|---|---|---|---|---|---|---|---|---|---|
| | 110 | 109-1/2 | 109 | 108-1/2 | 108 | 107-1/2 | 107 | 106-1/2 | 106 | 105-1/2 | 105 | 104-1/2 | 104 | 103-1/2 | 103 |
| 30 | 124 | 118 | 112 | 106 | 99 | 93 | 87 | 81 | 75 | 68 | 62 | 56 | 50 | 44 | 37 |
| 29 | 125 | 118 | 112 | 106 | 100 | 94 | 87 | 81 | 75 | 69 | 62 | 56 | 50 | 44 | 37 |
| 28 | 125 | 119 | 113 | 106 | 100 | 94 | 88 | 81 | 75 | 69 | 63 | 56 | 50 | 44 | 37 |
| 27 | 126 | 120 | 114 | 107 | 101 | 94 | 88 | 82 | 76 | 69 | 63 | 57 | 51 | 44 | 38 |
| 26 | 127 | 120 | 114 | 108 | 101 | 95 | 89 | 82 | 76 | 70 | 63 | 57 | 51 | 44 | 38 |
| 25 | 128 | 121 | 115 | 108 | 102 | 96 | 89 | 83 | 77 | 70 | 64 | 57 | 51 | 45 | 38 |
| 24 | 129 | 122 | 116 | 109 | 103 | 96 | 90 | 84 | 77 | 71 | 64 | 58 | 52 | 45 | 38 |
| 23 | 130 | 123 | 117 | 110 | 104 | 97 | 91 | 84 | 78 | 71 | 65 | 58 | 52 | 45 | 39 |
| 22 | 131 | 124 | 118 | 111 | 105 | 98 | 92 | 85 | 79 | 72 | 65 | 59 | 52 | 46 | 39 |
| 21 | 132 | 126 | 119 | 112 | 106 | 99 | 93 | 86 | 79 | 73 | 66 | 60 | 53 | 46 | 39 |
| 20 | 134 | 127 | 121 | 114 | 107 | 100 | 94 | 87 | 80 | 74 | 67 | 60 | 53 | 47 | 40 |
| 19 | 136 | 129 | 122 | 115 | 109 | 102 | 95 | 88 | 81 | 75 | 68 | 61 | 54 | 47 | 40 |
| 18 | 138 | 131 | 124 | 117 | 110 | 104 | 97 | 90 | 83 | 76 | 69 | 62 | 55 | 48 | 41 |
| 17 | 141 | 133 | 126 | 119 | 112 | 106 | 98 | 91 | 84 | 77 | 70 | 63 | 56 | 49 | 41 |
| 16 | 143 | 136 | 129 | 122 | 115 | 108 | 100 | 93 | 86 | 79 | 72 | 65 | 57 | 50 | 42 |
| 15 | 147 | 140 | 132 | 125 | 118 | 110 | 103 | 95 | 88 | 81 | 73 | 66 | 59 | 51 | 44 |

*Note: Each figure represents the cost of call times the annual payment necessary to amortize $1.00 at 12 per cent over the indicated number of years; for example, 107 for 20 years: 7 per cent times 0.13388 equals 0.937 per cent or 94 basis points.

†Source: Eugene S. Merrill, "A Guide to Bond Refunding," Public Utilities Fortnightly, September 27, 1962, pp. 393.

# Determining
# a Financial
# Structure

## 33

**NORTHERN FOODS, INC.**

On July 10, 1964, Mr. F.N. Dove, president of Northern Foods, Inc., was trying to decide what steps he should take to improve the company's financial position. The company's avowed purpose was rapid external growth, and although the company had several excellent opportunities for acquisitions, the depressed price of its stock in the market made the consummation of these potential acquisitions difficult. Mr. Dove believed that if he could make the company's financial structure more acceptable to lenders and investors, he could launch the company into the type of expansion program for which it was originally formed.

Northern Foods, Inc. (NFI) was incorporated in the state of Ohio on May 12, 1961, for the purpose of acquiring businesses engaged in food processing and distribution. The original group of incorporators was composed of Cleveland businessmen who learned about a Chicago meat processing company that was for sale on a cash basis. In order to make the purchase, the businessmen formed Northern Foods, Inc. and a subsidiary, Quality Meat Company (Delaware). NFI was to act as the corpus holding the stock of various operating companies, and Quality Meat Company (Delaware) was to acquire the assets of a Chicago meat processor, Quality Meat Company (Illinois). Exhibit I shows selected financial data on the Illinois company.

Quality Meat Company (Illinois) had been in the meat processing and provision business for over thirty years. Its principal product was pork, which it processed into hams, bacon, sausage, wieners, boloney, liverwurst, pepperoni, and various cold luncheon meats. The company's products were sold under the "quality" brand or under private labels, and its two plants were located in the Calumet City. Sixty-six per cent of the company's sales were in the Chicago area. Although the meat processing industry was highly competitive, Quality Meat Co. maintained a strong competitive position.

On June 2, 1961 Quality Meat Co. (Illinois) had net sales of $27,174,456 and assets totaling $5,346,958, of which $4,137,681 were financed by capital stock and retained earnings. On July 7, 1961, NFI through its subsidiary Quality Meat Co. (Delaware) purchased the assets of Quality Meat Co. (Illinois) for $5,799,177, of which $799,177 represented liabilities that were assumed by the acquiring company. The net book value of the assets acquired was $4,049,565.

In order to finance the acquisition, NFI used the following financial arrangements:

| | |
|---|---:|
| 5% promissory notes due 2/1/62 | $1,500,000 |
| 6% convertible debentures due 6/1/71 | 800,000 |
| 7% chattel mortgage notes due 7/12/66 | 600,000 |
| Sale and leaseback of land and bldgs. | 1,250,000 |
| Short term loan | 1,050,000 |
| Total | $5,200,000 |

The 5 per cent notes were sold to approximately 105 institutions and individuals by one of the founders of NFI. The notes provided that the holder could convert his notes on the due date to common stock at a conversion price of $2.00 a share. If the noteholder preferred cash for his notes, he would also receive warrants for 1,250 shares of common stock for each $5,000 of notes held. The warrants were convertible at a price of $2.00 a share through May 15, 1963. The promoters of the company held notes aggregating $280,000 (including $125,000 held by a founder who was also an investment banker); in addition the promoters controlled corporations holding notes amounting to $235,000. All of those notes were to be converted to common stock on the due date.

The 6 per cent registered convertible debentures were sold to various individuals and firms. They were noncallable and convertible at the option of the holder at any time until maturity at a conversion price of $2.50 per share of common. The indenture called for a sinking fund in the amount of $133,000 to be started June 1, 1965, and also required the firm to maintain net working capital of $800,000.

The 7 per cent chattel mortgage notes were placed with two institutions and were payable in quarterly installments of $35,815. The notes were secured by a first mortgage on all machinery and equipment of the company and its subsidiaries.

The sale and leaseback was made with Acme Leasing, Inc. Under the agreement, Quality Meat (Delaware) sold its land and buildings to Acme Leasing for $1,250,000 and leased it back for twenty-five years at annual payments of $125,000. Two additional five-year renewal options were available at the option of the leasee. All payments were to be made by Quality Meat (Delaware) and were guaranteed by NFI. In order to raise the necessary funds for the sale and leaseback, Acme Leasing sold 7 1/8 per cent notes maturing in twenty-five years. Payments on the notes were $26,863 quarterly, which included principal and interest. The notes of Acme Leasing were unconditionally guaranteed by NFI, although the leasing company was not directly affiliated with NFI.

The short-term loan was made with American Factors Inc. of Chicago. Under the arrangements, Quality Meat pledged all of its accounts receivables and inventories under a factor's lien. The financing was to be on a continuing basis so that generated accounts receivable would be continuously factored. Terms of the loan called for interest of 1/28 of 1 per cent per day (13 per cent per year) with a minimum interest of $71,500. By December 1, 1961, the amount of the loan outstanding had been reduced to $611,588; and as the amount of the loan decreased further, the effective interest rate would begin to exceed 13 per cent. In order to hedge against this, the company purchased a $500,000, 5 1/2 per cent subordinated promissory note from the Ohio Corporation due in March, 1963.[1]

On the 24th of January, 1962, Northern Foods, Inc. issued 800,000 shares of common stock, of which 642,500 of the total shares issued went to holders of the 5 per cent promissory notes in payment of the notes and the balance or 157,500 shares were sold to the general public. The price to the public was $2.50 per share, and $.25 of that went to the investment banker, who was also one of NFI's founders, as commission. Those note holders who did not convert were paid cash and issued warrants to purchase 53,750 shares at $2.00 a share, exercisable through May 15, 1963. The stock issue was oversubscribed and received a very popular reception by the general public. Shortly after the issue, it was being traded at $2.75.

At the conclusion of its first year's operations, NFI and its principal subsidiary, Quality Meat, had sales of $26 million and net profits of $246,375, both of which were down from the previous levels of the acquired company. During the year, a second product line was added, O'Brien Stew, which was sold in the Cleveland market. Operating results in the next two years showed improvement so that by June, 1964, the company's financial position had brightened considerably. By 1964, the financing secured by accounts receivables and inventories had been eliminated, and the chattel mortgage had been reduced to $170,000. In addition, the firm had paid off all short-term bank borrowing.

Because of the circumstances in the financing of the sale and leaseback, NFI management decided to repurchase the land and buildings through the assumption of the 7 1/8 per cent promissory notes of Acme Leasing Inc. On June 30, 1964, the unpaid principal on the notes was $1,194,675. Acme Leasing received $205,480, plus $52,500 in earnings over the three years they held the buildings, for a total profit of about $260,000 for the three years.

---

[1]After the market break on May 30, 1962, and the subsequent loss of $1,500,000 by Ohio, this note appeared to be headed for default. Because of a change in fortunes at the Ohio Corp., the note was paid when due, much to the relief of NFI management.

NFI made the repurchase in order to obtain flexibility in the use of its property and because the repurchase provided NFI with a substantial increase in its cash flow. Thus, by June, 1964, the company was coming out from under the liabilities assumed through its original financing. Three financial problems still needed correction before the firm could consider itself on solid ground. The first was the high interest presently being paid on its long-term debt. The second was the convertible debentures. The third was the market price of the common stock. Actually, all three problems were related.

In the present market, the firm could probably obtain long-term funds from an insurance company for $1,000,000 at 5 1/2 to 6 per cent. The present chattel mortgage had only one more year to run, and NFI would have to pay 1 per cent extra in order to prepay. On the mortgage notes the repayment penalty was also 1 per cent. The restrictions in the notes, however, were minor, whereas if these notes were to be refinanced, the restrictions might be considerably increased. The present long-term market was quite favorable, but Mr. Dove thought it might be best to wait for at least six more months. He thought the problem of the debentures and the common stock was much more critical.

After the original issue, there was a brief flurry of interest in the common stock, but three months later, on May 30, 1962, the stock market broke. All stocks, both national and local, dropped drastically in price. The tremendous activity of the preceding three years and the unprecedented interest in the market by small stockholders had held the market up even though profits had not kept pace. Many electronics stocks were selling for price earnings ratios in excess of 100, and these stocks led the market down. In the local market, including Cleveland, the investor, previously held in thrall by the prospect of getting rich quick, stopped buying and started selling. The local stocks, even where the company's value was based on solid earnings, tumbled, and no one was interested in buying. Not until 1964 did the market show any recovery, and even then the small potential stockholder had not returned.

NFI had approximately 700 stockholders with management holding approximately 20 per cent of the stock outstanding. The market was narrow and not much trading occurred, for no stock dealer was making a market for the issue in early 1964. Since the market price of the stock had never returned to its original issue price, stockholders who held their shares had paper losses, which had the effect of keeping the stock price depressed. (See Exhibit IV for market prices.) Mr. Dove, noted that if NFI stock were selling at the same price earnings ratio as comparable competitors, the stock would be double its current price. He wondered if he should encourage a stock dealer to take a position on NFI stock. In talking with potential dealers, he was told that to make the stock acceptable, he would have to get rid of the convertible debentures. As long as they were outstanding, they would tend to depress the market price in the amount of their potential dilution effect.

Mr. Dove realized that originally issuing the debenture without a call feature had been a mistake. Under the present circumstances, only two conditions might be favorable for converting the convertibles: when the yield on the stock after conversion was greater than the yield on the bonds; or when the market price of the stock was higher than the conversion price and a downturn in price was expected. Both these possibilities seemed remote. Obviously, the debenture holders would not convert without some possibility of immediate profit.

There were eighteen debenture holders, three of whom held $405,000 of debentures, and nine of whom held $68,000. Thus, the average holder of debentures had large holdings and probably did not need immediate cash.

## EXHIBIT I

### Quality Meat Co. (Illinois)
### Selected Data

|  | 1961 | 1960 | 1959 | 1958 |
|---|---|---|---|---|
| Sales | $27,170,456 | $23,444,964 | $22,926,820 | $19,745,814 |
| Net profits | 440,348 | 550,622 | 367,527 | 297,159 |
| Depreciation | 171,432 | 187,067 | 146,704 | 112,828 |

### Balance Sheet 6/2/61

| | |
|---|---|
| Cash | $1,268,101 |
| Accounts receivable, net | 1,329,129 |
| Loans receivable | 1,510 |
| Inventories | 891,399 |
| Prepaid expense | 45,845 |
| Current assets | 3,535,984 |
| Investments | 14,000 |
| Land | 140,266 |
| Buildings | 1,511,464 |
| Machinery | 1,125,902 |
| Automobiles and trucks | 46,262 |
| Less : depreciation | (1,178,147) |
| Net property | 1,659,747 |
| Cash surrender value of life ins. | 151,227 |
| Total assets | $5,346,958 |
| Accounts payable | $342,834 |
| Accrued liabilities | 234,244 |
| Federal taxes | 132,199 |
| Deposit from NFI | 500,000 |
| | 1,209,277 |
| Common stock | 200,000 |
| Retained earnings | 3,937,681 |
| Total liabilities and net worth | $5,346,958 |

EXHIBIT II

**Northern Foods, Inc.**
**Consolidated Balance Sheet for the Years Ending June 30**

| Assets | 1964 | 1963 | 1962 |
|---|---|---|---|
| Current assets | | | |
| Cash | $227,694 | $394,700 | $46,770 |
| Notes receivable | — | — | 600,000 |
| Accounts receivable | 1,487,068 | 1,383,674 | 1,257,093 |
| Inventories of raw meats, meat products, ingredients and supplies, at lower of first-in, first-out cost or market | 1,090,056 | 1,002,168 | 828,702 |
| Prepaid expenses | 56,508 | 64,367 | 82,343 |
| Total current assets | $2,861,326 | $2,844,909 | $2,814,908 |
| Cash surrender of life insurance | 185,847 | 149,505 | 126,536 |
| Plant and equipment, at cost, less reserves of $ 422,605 in 1964, $ 278,719 in 1963, and $ 120,916 in 1962 | 3,007,047 | 1,662,021 | 1,616,434 |
| Total assets | $6,054,220 | $4,656,435 | $4,557,878 |
| | | | |
| Liabilities | | | |
| Current Liabilities | | | |
| Current installments on long-term debt | $148,739 | $117,370 | $109,501 |
| Loans payable | — | 220,000 | 633,288 |
| Accounts payable | 766,374 | 613,225 | 272,098 |
| Accrued liabilities | 359,351 | 325,913 | 310,052 |
| Accrued federal and state income taxes | 263,045 | 217,574 | 75,997 |
| Total current liabilities | $1,537,509 | $1,494,082 | $1,400,936 |
| Long-term debt, less current installments above | | | |
| 7-1/8% mortgage notes | 1,072,242 | — | — |
| 7% chattel mortgage | 170,043 | 295,848 | 413,218 |
| 6% convertible debentures, subordinated to all bank borrowing and lease payments | 800,000 | 800,000 | 800,000 |
| Total long-term debt | $2,042,285 | $1,095,848 | $1,213,218 |
| Reserves | | | |
| Deferred income taxes | $173,348 | $125,104 | $63,485 |
| Deferred officer's compensation | 5,564 | 1,100 | — |
| Total reserves | $178,912 | $126,204 | $63,485 |
| Stockholders' Investment | | | |
| Common stock, 10¢ par, 805,000 shares issued | $80,500 | $80,500 | $80,500 |
| Paid-in surplus | 1,553,175 | 1,553,175 | 1,555,676 |
| Reinvested earnings | 886,839 | 531,626 | 244,063 |
| Less : treasury stock, 150,000 shares at cost | (225,000) | (225,000) | — |
| Total stockholders' investment | $2,295,514 | $1,940,301 | $1,880,239 |
| | $6,054,220 | $4,656,435 | $4,557,878 |

Mr. Dove talked to one of the largest debenture holders, an insurance company, about conversion. He was told by the investment manager that there was no possibility of the insurance company converting in the next two years regardless of the stock price. They were very pleased with the progress of the company and pleased with their investment, and they felt that anything that came now would only serve to substantiate their faith.

Mr. Dove thought that he should get an idea from one or two other of the convertible holders as to what they would take for their bonds above par. He inquired about paying 8 per cent over par to a holder of $30,000 debentures. The bondholder indicated that he might be interested if a firm offer were made. Mr. Dove believed that a premium of 15 per cent over par would induce most to accept cash, but he wondered if a plan to force conversion might not be better. He was unsure, however, as to how this could be done. If the company's stock could be expected to sell at a 10–1 price earnings

**EXHIBIT III**

**Northern Foods, Inc.**
**Consolidated Income Statement**
**for the Year Ended**

|  | 1964 | 1963 | 1962 |
|---|---|---|---|
| Net sales | $30,125,332 | $27,760,722 | $25,966,612 |
| Cost of sales | 27,397,508 | 25,288,540 | 23,688,906 |
| Gross profit | $2,727,824 | $2,472,182 | $2,277,706 |
| Expenses |  |  |  |
| Selling, administrative and general | $1,901,226 | $1,782,138 | $1,544,414 |
| Interest expense, net | 86,750 | 105,399 | 196,414 |
| Other (income) expense, net | (28,865) | (34,918) | (31,497) |
| Total expenses | $1,959,111 | $1,852,619 | $1,709,331 |
| Profit before provision for federal income taxes | $768,713 | $619,563 | $568,375 |
| Provision for federal and state income taxes | 413,500 | 332,000 | 322,000 |
| Net profit | $355,213 | $287,563 | $246,375 |

**EXHIBIT IV**

**Northern Foods, Inc.**
**Selected Quotations on Stock in Cleveland**
**Over-the-Counter Market**

| | |
|---|---|
| March, 1962 | 2.50 |
| June, 1962 | 1.75 |
| December, 1962 | 1.50 |
| June, 1963 | 1.62 |
| October, 1963 | 1.75 |
| December, 1963 | 2.00 |
| June, 1964 | 2.13 |

## EXHIBIT V
### Financial Data—Selected Companies

| Companies | Date | Stock Price on Date | Latest 12-mo. Earn/Sh | P/E | Net Sales (mil) | Total Assets (mil) | Net Profit (mil) | Net Worth (mil) | Net Profit to Net Worth (%) | Div/Sh |
|---|---|---|---|---|---|---|---|---|---|---|
| Armour | 11/ 2/63 | 41.0 | 2.97 | 13.8 | 1810 | 455 | 16.3 | 215 | 7.5 | 1.4 |
| Cudahy | 11/ 2/63 | 7.3 | — | — | 323 | 59 | 1.9 | 30 | — | — |
| Morrell | 10/26/63 | 25.1 | 2.05 | 12.2 | 613 | 87 | 2.5 | 50 | 5.0 | .8 |
| Swift | 10/26/63 | 40.4 | 2.85 | 14.2 | 2473 | 610 | 17.1 | 395 | 4.3 | 1.6 |
| Wilson | 10/26/63 | 38.3 | 2.84 | 13.5 | 700 | 149 | 7.3 | 101 | 7.3 | 1.6 |
| Corn Products | 12/31/63 | 59.6 | 2.26 | 26.4 | 856 | 544 | 50.3 | 324 | 15.5 | 1.4 |
| Cons. Foods | 12/31/63 | 47.5 | 2.50 | 19.1 | 600 | 195 | 11.5 | 93 | 12.8 | — |
| Gen'l. Foods | 3/31/64 | 90.2 | 3.33 | 27.1 | 1338 | 726 | 83.5 | 498 | 17.1 | 1.8 |

| Companies | Date | Price on Date | Latest 12-mo. Earn/Sh | P/E | Mean '63 Price | Mean '63 Earn/Sh | P/E |
|---|---|---|---|---|---|---|---|
| Armour | 5/ 2/64 | 50.6 | 3.39 | 14.9 | 59 | 2.86 | — |
| Cudahy | 4/18/64 | 8.1 | .4 | 20.3 | 8 | .71 | — |
| Morrell | 4/25/64 | 25.4 | 2.58 | 9.9 | 27 | 2.01 | 13.4 |
| Swift | 4/25/64 | 45.6 | 3.19 | 14.3 | 42 | 2.78 | 15.0 |
| Wilson | 4/25/64 | 41.0 | 3.66 | 11.2 | 39 | 2.91 | 13.4 |
| Corn Products | 6/30/64 | 61.0 | 2.28 | 26.8 | 54 | 2.17 | 24.9 |
| Cons. Foods | 6/30/64 | 58.0 | 2.61 | 22.2 | 41 | 2.41 | 17.0 |
| Gen'l Foods | 6/30/64 | 87.6 | 3.37 | 25.9 | 84 | 3.23 | 26.0 |

ratio in a year or two, substantial savings would accrue to present stockholders by redeeming the bonds now. Mr. Dove decided to pursue this line of reasoning.

With the likelihood of new acquisitions within six months, Mr. Dove decided he must make whatever changes he could make in the financial structure now. He wanted to be as flexible as possible when the time came for buying new companies.

## Part VI

# VALUATION
# OF
# EXPANSION

Macrae
Bales
Brooks


Acid Test Ratio

$$\frac{CA}{CL}$$

Receivables Turnover $\qquad \dfrac{\text{Annual Sales}}{\text{Acc Rec}}$

Inventory Turnover $\qquad \dfrac{\text{Cost of Goods Sold}}{\text{Average Inventory}}$

Debt to net Worth $\qquad \dfrac{\text{Total Debt}}{\text{Tangible Net worth}}$

Operating Ratio $\qquad \dfrac{\text{Total Oper Ex} + \text{Cost of Goods sold}}{\text{Net Sales}}$


1. Should we accept Prop?
2. How to finance   Ins Co Loan, Sbic Loan

# Acquiring a Company

## 34

A-TEX CORPORATION

In April, 1965, the president of A-Tex Corporation of Austin, Texas, met with five businessmen from Houston to discuss the creation of a new company. The purpose of the new company would be to purchase the production and distribution facilities for a line of industrial equipment which A-Tex had been handling for the past few years. The reason A-Tex wanted to divest themselves of the industrial equipment portion of their business was that their present major effort was being placed in the electronics area and a tremendous demand for their projects had severely taxed their capacities. The management of A-Tex believed they should concentrate solely on electronics.

A detailed market analysis of the industrial equipment sales had been made during the early months of 1965, and it indicated that sales for 1966 could reach $3,000,000 provided the present facilities were expanded. The cost of expansion was estimated to be $1,000,000 in plant and $500,000 in net working capital. The analysis also indicated that a continuous increase in sales over the next decade should be anticipated, and that companies in this field had experienced an average return of 6 per cent after taxes on their assets.

The president of A-Tex told the five businessmen that A-Tex would transfer all assets and liabilities to them for $1,500,000. (The $300,000 in long-term debt shown in the balance sheet should not be considered since it is part of A-Tex's capital structure and cannot be isolated.) In addition, he distributed to them the financial statements for the industrial equipment portion of A-Tex's operations. The data had been accounted for separately and independently. (See Exhibits I and II.)

**QUESTIONS**

1. Would you as one of the businessmen accept this proposition? Why?
2. Assuming you accepted the proposal, how would you finance it? (Include in your plan the additional $1,500,000 for expansion.)
3. What outside facilities would you recommend to assist you in securing the necessary capital? Why?

**EXHIBIT I**

**Balance Sheet Data**

|  | 12/31/63 | 12/31/64 |
|---|---|---|
| Assets |  |  |
| Cash | $120,000 | $90,000 |
| Receivables | 283,620 | 396,000 |
| Inventory | 273,522 | 360,924 |
| Net plant | 660,858 | 626,076 |
| Total assets | $1,338,000 | $1,473,000 |
| Liabilities and net worth |  |  |
| Accounts payable | $233,025 | $290,850 |
| Accruals | 24,975 | 27,150 |
| Notes payable | 30,000 | 105,000 |
| Long-term debt* | 300,000 | 300,000 |
| Equity capital* | 750,000 | 750,000 |
| Total liabilities and net worth | $1,338,000 | $1,473,000 |

**EXHIBIT II**

**Profit and Loss Data**

|  | 12/31/63 | 12/31/64 |
|---|---|---|
| Operating revenue (Net credit sales) | $2,190,000 | $2,805,000 |
| Operating expenses (Net cost of sales and exp.) | 1,815,600 | 2,293,650 |
| Net before interest | 374,400 | 511,350 |
| Interest on long-term debt | 15,000 | 15,000 |
| Net before taxes | 359,400 | 496,350 |
| Taxes (50%) | 179,700 | 248,175 |
| Net after taxes | 179,700 | 248,175 |

*The $300,000 in long-term debt and $750,000 in equity capital represent the amount of long-term capital which A-Tex has allocated to this particular phase of the operation; therefore, the $300,000 in long-term debt remains the obligation of A-Tex Corporation.

On March 12, 1964, Mr. F. H. Knapp, financial vice-president of Featherstone's, Inc., received a request from John Phillips, executive vice-president of the firm, to make an immediate investigation of Knitwear, Inc., in order to determine a potential price and terms for a possible acquisition by Featherstone's. In his request, Phillips stated that he had been contacted one week earlier by a New York business agent who had informed him that Knitwear was for sale, and wondered whether he would like to buy it. At the time, Phillips, whose primary interest was marketing, had been very interested in expanding Featherstone's sales, and a check of Featherstone's regional sales managers indicated unanimous interest in acquiring Knitwear.

Phillips indicated that there were only three days left in which to decide whether to acquire the firm. Knitwear's financial situation was critical with $1,800,000 in short-term notes in default. One bank who held the majority of the short-term defaulted notes had given Knitwear until March 15th to "do something" or else the bank would file involuntary bankruptcy against Knitwear. Knitwear was also in default on its long-term note because its working capital was below the specified minimum; however, this did not appear to be an important consideration at the present time. Although Featherstone's had considered acquiring Knitwear in prior years, price considerations had made any arrangement unsatisfactory; under the present financial situation, Featherstone's appeared to be able to name its own price and terms.

### History of Featherstone's

Featherstone's, Inc. came into ex-

233

istence in 1925 when Mr. F. C. Featherstone purchased a small men's shirt manufacturing company. Featherstone's manufactured men's shirts exclusively until World War II when they shifted to army uniforms and GI underwear. By the end of the war, Featherstone's had net sales of $7,000,000. During the post-war period Mr. Featherstone retired from active operations in the business and a new president took over, continuing the policies of the old management—a policy of internal growth coupled with an occasional acquisition of a small firm. By 1954, Featherstone's had sales in excess of $30,000,000, and the product line by this time had grown substantially. They still manufactured men's shirts under the now famous name of "Featherstone's"; in fact, the brand name was sufficiently well known in the industry to account for approximately 10 per cent of all men's dress shirts sold. In addition to men's shirts they manufactured a complete line of men's underwear, pajamas, neckties, and selected sports apparel including sport shirts and bermuda shorts. In 1959, Featherstone's entered the women's field and began manufacturing blouses. Featherstone's venture into the area of women's clothing came about through a purchase of a company known as, Fashions, Inc. From the period 1954 to 1963 sales doubled and net earnings tripled.

The company was highly regarded in the financial community, and the stock had experienced excellent growth. The financial position of the company was considered extremely satisfactory; bank relations were excellent; and management was considered among the top in the industry. An analysis made by Standard and Poor's in January, 1964, stated:

> Featherstone's is one of the oldest brands in men's clothing, and its past record is considerably better than that of most companies in this highly competitive field. Its improved earnings experienced in recent years reflect expanding facilities in new products as well as more aggressive merchandising. The shares seem fairly priced at going levels and should be held for moderate growth over the long term.

### History of Knitwear

Knitwear, located in Greenville, North Carolina, began business in 1949 to manufacture women's sweaters. From its inception, it had put out a product well received in the market, and as a result it grew rapidly, becoming the best-known name in the field of women's sweaters. The company had grown slowly at first; however, by 1950 sales were $5,000,000, and by 1955 they exceeded $12,000,000. The major sales emphasis was on the "sweater-girl look" which Knitwear pioneered and which proved extremely popular. By 1959, however, several competitors had entered the field, and Knitwear's line had to be expanded to meet increased competition and a new demand for more variation in sweaters. During the period of growth up to 1959, the company had manufactured a line of approximately twenty different sweater styles. With the advent of more heavy competition, however, the line had been increased to seventy-five styles.

The sweater industry by 1963 had a sales volume of approximately $200,000,000 at retail, or approximately $120,000,000 at cost. Of this, Knitwear accounted for approximately 10 per cent of the sales at the retail level with the two nearest competitors having 9 per cent and 8 per cent respectively. Approximately twenty-three other firms were in the business on a national basis, and many others operated on a local basis. While Knitwear brands had been well accepted in the past and Knitwear was still a name that shoppers recognized, the more recent emphasis on style had begun to cut into the importance of a brand name. Thus, small companies without a name in the industry had been able to make considerable gains through good styling. As a result, Knitwear's sales peaked in 1960, and from that point on, sales and profits began to decline.

### Evaluation of Knitwear by Phillips

Mr Phillips placed full responsibility for Knitwear's present financial position on poor management. Prices for sweaters had not declined at the retail level and volume had increased, so that Knitwear's declining sales appeared to be the result of their inability to produce sweaters efficiently. Knitwear's primary problem was its inability to plan its production schedules properly. From 1960 on, more and more of the total sweaters sold were sold at year-end sales because the firm was unable to deliver during the early part of the season. The major sales in the sweater lines occurred during the months of August, September, October, and November. Normally, a manufacturer would deliver in May and June. Knitwear, however, delivered a larger portion of its goods in July and even into August with the result that many retail stores would cancel their orders. In 1963, the firm received a million dollars in cancellation orders because they were unable to deliver at the required time.

The inability to deliver sweaters on time was caused by a number of problems:

1. Failure of the design department to design new sweaters in sufficient time to prepare for adequate production schedules.
2. Failure to order raw materials in time to get delivery for the peak production season.
3. Failure to coordinate the various styles. The firm was producing too much of one style which was ultimately not finding sufficient consumer favor and too little of a style that was receiving consumer favor.

The firm had no cost accounting system, and it had no idea how much any given sweater cost. In addition, there was no control over the production schedule so that no one knew how much time it took to produce a given sweater.

Knitwear's management inefficiency appeared to stem from its "one-man show" president. For example, the president had sixty people reporting to him, and if someone wanted to see him it might take as long as six weeks. The president personally made each and every decision. In one of his more disastrous decisions the company's old, but reasonably efficient building in the middle of town was abandoned for a new modern building out in a rural area. After the move, management discovered that the majority of the employees were at the bottom of the economic strata and without transportation. As a result, the company had to hire buses to pick these people up for work. In time, the cost became so great that the firm switched its operations back to the plant in town and leased out the new building at far less than its cost.

The inefficiencies which plagued the company were in turn reflected in employees' attitudes. These became progressively worse as supervisors were unable to make decisions and inaction replaced decision making. Middle managers and designers felt as if the president did not trust them. This attitude carried down to the bottom-most echelon.

Mr. Phillips felt that with changes in management, Knitwear could break even by the next year. This estimate was based on the following:

1. *The organization of the company.* Mr. Phillips felt that there were some fairly competent people in the company, and that Featherstone's could supply at least two to three executives.
2. *The controls area.* Featherstone's was considered one of the foremost companies in the industry in the area of controls. Phillips believed that with the application of budget controls, profit analysis, inventory models, production schedules, and design controls a great deal of the present problems in these areas could be eliminated. In addition, proper planning could get the production schedule to the place where the company would be producing sweaters in time to deliver to the fall market.
3. *Purchasing.* Featherstone's purchasing department was well organized and could probably effect almost immediate savings in an area of purchases, first, because they had been in a highly competitive position themselves and understood the nature of inventory, and, second, because they could buy in larger quantities than Knitwear.
4. *Personnel relations.* Mr. Phillips noted that most of the employees did not make their base piece rate (most work at Knitwear was done on a piece-rate basis); however, since all workers were guaranteed a minimum rate regardless of the number they produced, many were overpaid. Obviously, the attitude of the employees was poor, supervision was lacking, and control was missing; a total reevaluation of the rate of pay would be necessary. Featherstone's felt that they had considerable experience in this field.
5. *Overhead.* Knitwear had some overhead costs which could possibly be reduced by combining with Featherstone's.

**EXHIBIT I**

**Featherstone's, Inc.**
**Comparative Balance Sheet**

|  | 1963 | 1962 | 1961 |
|---|---|---|---|
| *Assets* | | | |
| Current assets | | | |
| Cash | $1,294,196 | $1,225,709 | $3,255,866 |
| Receivables | | | |
| Trade | 10,408,578 | 10,011,140 | 9,043,871 |
| Other | 616,411 | 586,619 | 544,561 |
| Inventories | | | |
| Finished goods | 11,025,223 | 10,432,648 | 9,855,405 |
| Goods in process | 8,000,477 | 6,541,342 | |
| Raw materials | 4,709,886 | 4,751,554 | 9,714,536 |
| Prepaid expenses | 788,371 | 735,892 | 548,181 |
| Total current assets | $36,843,142 | $34,284,904 | $32,962,420 |
| Investments | | | |
| Cash value of life insurance | — | — | 430,560 |
| Investments at cost | 280,474 | 398,264 | 406,230 |
| Plant and equipment at cost | | | |
| Land | 496,748 | 453,144 | 431,257 |
| Plant | 6,229,445 | 5,005,999 | 4,556,375 |
| Machinery and equipment | 11,438,574 | 11,035,934 | 9,796,813 |
| Less depreciation | (9,779,908) | (8,940,986) | (7,827,443) |
| Total fixed assets | 8,665,333 | 7,952,355 | 7,793,792 |
| Good will | 1 | 1 | 1 |
| Unamortized debenture | 85,467 | 123,960 | 145,803 |
| Total assets | $45,593,943 | $42,361,220 | $40,902,016 |
| | | | |
| *Liabilities* | | | |
| Current Liabilities | | | |
| Notes payable | $2,200,000 | $    — | $    — |
| Current installment of long-term debt | 800,000 | 800,000 | 396,000 |
| Accounts payables | 2,878,655 | 2,908,819 | 2,462,005 |
| Accrued expenses | 2,745,115 | 2,865,407 | 2,420,465 |
| Taxes payable | 2,170,525 | 2,446,187 | 1,735,857 |
| Total Current Liabilities | $10,794,295 | $9,020,413 | $7,014,327 |
| Long-term debt | | | |
| $5^1/_2\%$ notes payable | $2,300,000 | $3,000,000 | $3,800,000 |
| 5% convertible subordinate debentures | 2,826,000 | 3,911,000 | 4,307,000 |
| Minority interest in subsidiary | 374,376 | 296,895 | 259,691 |
| Stockholders' ownership | | | |
| $5^1/_4\%$ cumulative preferred | — | — | 2,122,416 |
| Common stock, $5 par | 6,360,508 | 6,064,905 | 5,923,640 |
| Capital in excess of par | 4,114,303 | 3,313,807 | 2,977,307 |
| Retained earnings | 18,824,461 | 16,754,200 | 14,497,635 |
| Total liabilities | $45,593,943 | $42,361,220 | $40,902,016 |

**EXHIBIT II**

**Featherstone's, Inc.**
**Statement of Operations**
**(In Thousands)**

|  | 1963 | 1962 | 1961 |
|---|---|---|---|
| Net sales | $79,450 | $75,998 | $71,636 |
| Cost of sales | 55,775 | 53,137 | 50,219 |
| Gross profit | 23,675 | 22,861 | 21,417 |
| Operating expenses* | 15,993 | 15,862 | 15,184 |
| Operating profit | 7,682 | 6,999 | 6,233 |
| Other income | 431 | 704 | 405 |
| Other deductions | (1,102) | (690) | (946) |
| Net | (671) | 14 | (541) |
| Earnings before taxes | 7,011 | 7,013 | 5,692 |
| Federal and state taxes | 3,527 | 3,657 | 3,045 |
| Earnings before minority interest | 3,484 | 3,356 | 2,647 |
| Less minority interest | 57 | 60 | 41 |
| Net earnings before insurance credit | 3,427 | 3,296 | 2,606 |
| Special life insurance credit |  | 349 |  |
| Net earnings | $3,427 | $3,645 | $2,606 |
| *Includes depreciation and amortization of | $695 | $628 | $659 |

## Knapp's Evaluation of the Potential Acquisition

Mr. Knapp was skeptical of Phillips' projection of a next-year breakeven. He noted that designs for the coming year had already been started, material orders had been placed, and production was started. It seemed unlikely that Featherstone's could make any appreciable change in the present pro forma estimates. (See Exhibits V and VI) He believed, however, that very likely Knitwear could breakeven in 1965. There seemed little likelihood that the cost of goods sold and other expenses would change to any marked degree until the present shipping cycle was through. Knapp's estimated losses for the fiscal year 1964 would range between $700,000 and $2,000,000. He knew, however, that Phillips still believed that the firm could breakeven on the basis of sales and that Phillips would want to bargain on that basis.

Mr. Knapp estimated that Knitwear would need approximately $2,800,-000 in new money to survive the next two years. This money could be borrowed by Featherstone's on a short-term basis at the prime rate and lent to Knitwear in the form of a debenture, either convertible or with warrants attached. Although Phillips had suggested that as much as 90 per cent of the outstanding stock could be optioned at $4 a share, Knapp believed this was high. The new money could be used as a wedge to prevent the short-term lenders from taking any action, and it might convince them to expand the line of credit. The lenders' choice seemed small in this area. The long-term

**EXHIBIT III**

## Knitwear, Inc.
### Comparative As of August 31, Balance Sheet
### (In Thousands)

| | 1963 | 1962 | 1961 | 1960 | 1959 | 1958 |
|---|---|---|---|---|---|---|
| *Assets* | | | | | | |
| Current assets | | | | | | |
| Cash | $ 251 | $ 1,069 | $ 1,323 | $3,120 | $3,576 | $3,438 |
| Accounts and notes receivable (net) | 2,395 | 2,631 | 2,828 | 2,037 | 1,691 | 1,111 |
| Refundable federal income taxes | 983 | 931 | 138 | — | — | — |
| Receivables from insurance of note | — | — | 2,000 | — | — | |
| Inventories | 4,297 | 4,668 | 3,421 | 3,166 | 2,280 | 1,894 |
| Prepaid expenses | 96 | 350 | 335 | 232 | 257 | 171 |
| Total current assets | $8,022 | $9,649 | $10,045 | $8,555 | $7,804 | $6,614 |
| Investments | 146 | 130 | 55 | 42 | 32 | 18 |
| Plant and equipment (net) | 626 | 735 | 830 | 698 | 760 | 838 |
| Deposits and other assets | 46 | 138 | 143 | 117 | 84 | 86 |
| Total assets | $8,840 | $10,652 | $11,073 | $9,412 | $8,680 | $7,556 |
| | | | | | | |
| *Liabilities and capital* | | | | | | |
| Current liabilities | | | | | | |
| Notes payable to banks | $1,800 | $ | $ | $ | $ | $ |
| Current Installment on Long-term Debt | 42 | 42 | | | | |
| Accounts payable | 2,299 | 2,433 | 1,696 | 1,620 | 1,141 | 736 |
| Accrued expenses | 297 | 410 | 832 | 707 | 674 | 440 |
| Profit sharing contribution | — | — | — | — | 90 | 181 |
| Federal taxes on income | — | 39 | 63 | 568 | 587 | 674 |
| Total current liabilities | $4,438 | $2,924 | $2,591 | $2,895 | $2,492 | $2,031 |
| Long-term debt: | | | | | | |
| 5 3/4% unsecured note payable | 2,000 | 2,000 | 2,000 | — | — | — |
| Other contracts | 53 | 93 | — | — | — | — |
| Total long-term debt | $2,053 | $2,093 | 2,000 | — | — | — |
| Stockholders' equity | | | | | | |
| 5% cumulated convertible Preferred stock | 667 | 667 | 667 | 667 | 667 | 667 |
| Common stock ($ 1 par) | 720 | 720 | 690 | 680 | 678 | 675 |
| Capital in excess of par | 1,115 | 1,115 | 878 | 797 | 775 | 756 |
| Retained earnings | (153) | 3,133 | 4,247 | 4,373 | 4,068 | 3,427 |
| Total stockholders' equity | $2,349 | $5,635 | $6,482 | $6,517 | $6,188 | $5,525 |
| Total liabilities and capital | $8,840 | $10,652 | $11,073 | $9,412 | $8,680 | $7,556 |

debt was a 5 3/4 per cent, twelve-year unsecured note which was held by the Security Life Insurance Company. It called for annual installments of $150,000 starting in 1963, and continuing until the note was due in 1975.

**EXHIBIT IV**

**Knitwear, Inc.**
**Comparative Statement of Profit and Loss**
**(In Thousands)**

|  | 1963 | 1962 | 1961 | 1960 | 1959 | 1958 |
|---|---|---|---|---|---|---|
| Net sales | $19,432 | $20,859 | $24,291 | $24,671 | $21,647 | $18,982 |
| Cost of goods sold | 17,217 | 16,169 | 17,358 | 17,090 | 14,508 | 12,369 |
| Gross profit | $2,215 | $4,690 | $6,933 | $7,581 | $7,139 | $6,613 |
| Expenses |  |  |  |  |  |  |
| Warehousing and traffic | $513 | $540 | $535 | $537 | $536 | $438 |
| Advertising and sales promotion | 926 | 1,245 | 1,119 | 1,284 | 1,153 | 1,023 |
| Sales | 2,433 | 2,670 | 2,834 | 2,658 | 2,287 | 1,968 |
| Administration | 1,936 | 1,669 | 1,721 | 1,343 | 1,315 | 1,237 |
| Total | $5,808 | $6,124 | $6,209 | $5,822 | $5,291 | $4,711 |
| Net operating profit (loss) | (3,593) | (1,434) | 724 | 1,759 | 1,848 | 1,902 |
| Other expenses (including interest) | (606) | (213) | (109) | (140) | (32) | (51) |
| Net profit (loss) before taxes | $(4,199) | $(1,647) | $615 | $1,619 | $1,816 | $1,851 |

**EXHIBIT V**

**Knitwear, Inc.**
**1963-64 Production Units**

|  | 1962-63 | 1962 Cumulative | 1963-64 Actual | 1963-64 Pro Forma | 1963-64 Cumulative |
|---|---|---|---|---|---|
| September | 566,778 | 566,778 | 396,674 |  | 396,674 |
| October | 238,718 | 805,496 | 161,440 |  | 558,114 |
| November | 39,250 | 844,746 | 61,440 |  | 619,554 |
| December | 41,862 | 886,608 | 121,064 |  | 740,618 |
| January | 98,934 | 985,542 | 43,362 |  | 783,980 |
| February | 125,464 | 1,111,006 |  | 43,200 | 827,180 |
| March | 159,498 | 1,270,504 |  | 93,000 | 920,180 |
| April | 214,916 | 1,485,420 |  | 242,000 | 1,162,180 |
| May | 310,432 | 1,795,852 |  | 296,000 | 1,458,180 |
| June | 342,160 | 2,138,012 |  | 310,000 | 1,768,180 |
| July | 410,156 | 2,548,168 |  | 240,000 | 2,188,180 |
| August | 449,674 | 2,997,842 |  | 394,000 | 2,582,180 |

The most important parts of the indenture called for minimum working capital of $4,000,000 and no cash dividends on common stock except from net earnings after 1962. In 1963, Security Life had waived the amortization payment and had lowered the working capital requirement to $2,500,000. Mr. Knapp noted that Knitwear had a tax loss carry-forward of $1,974,000 which might be available until August 31, 1968; he would not be able to use the tax loss unless the firm earned substantial profits or the two companies were merged, and a merger seemed out of the question, for the laws of the state forbade mergers where a company had a negative surplus.

**EXHIBIT VI**

**Knitwear, Inc.**
**Summary of Net Shipments for Year Ended Aug. 31, 1963**

|  | 1963 | | 1964 Pro Forma | |
|---|---|---|---|---|
|  | Units | Dollars | Units | Dollars |
| Full price | 2,219,222 | $15,887,813 | 1,832,180 | $13,050,000 |
| Off price | 778,620 | 3,544,724 | 750,000 | 3,000,000 |
|  | 2,997,842 | $19,432,537 | 2,582,180 | $16,050,000 |

**EXHIBIT VII**

**Knitwear, Inc.**
**Common Stock Bid Prices**

|  | Hi | Lo |
|---|---|---|
| 3/1/64 | $2\frac{7}{8}$ | $2\frac{7}{8}$ |
| 1963 | $7\frac{1}{4}$ | $1\frac{5}{8}$ |
| 1962 | 15 | 4 |
| 1961 | 19 | $9\frac{7}{8}$ |
| 1960 | $13\frac{1}{4}$ | $8\frac{1}{4}$ |
| 1959 | $14\frac{3}{8}$ | $10\frac{3}{4}$ |

Knapp knew he would be expected to find a way of getting the required funds to keep the company operating, while minimizing the risk to Featherstone's. He also doubted that the financial community would look with favor on this acquisition, regardless of the terms.

# Acquisition

## 36

On September 18, 1962, the management of the Albemarle Paper Manufacturing Company announced by letter to its shareholders that it was negotiating for the acquisition of the Ethyl Corporation, a chemical company owned 50 per cent by General Motors Corporation and 50 per cent by Standard Oil Company (New Jersey). A special meeting of the shareholders was called for November 12, 1962, where a proposal to amend the company's charter, a stock option plan, and other matters would be considered. The proposed amendment of the articles of incorporation would: (1) restate the purpose of the corporation so that it could operate in the chemical industry; (2) change the company's name to Ethyl Corporation, should the acquisition be consummated; (3) increase the number of shares of authorized stock to 156,000 shares of Class "A" common stock, $5 per value, 2,000,000 shares of Class "B" common stock, $5 par value, and 100,000 shares of cumulative preferred stock, $100 par value; and (4) give the board of directors the power to proceed with the acquisition of Ethyl Corporation if in the directors' opinion a fair price for the stock and satisfactory financing details could be worked out.

The Albemarle Paper Manufacturing Company was a manufacturer of kraft paper, multi-wall paper bags, shopping bags, waxed paper, asphalt-laminated waterproof paper, printed paper, folding paper boxes, and corrugated shipping containers. The company was incorporated in Virginia in 1887 and had acquired six wholly owned subsidiaries between 1955 and 1960. These subsidiaries were: Raymond Bag Company, Middleton, Ohio; Halifax Paper Company, Roanoke Rapids, N. C.; Seaboard Manufacturing Corporation, Richmond, Virginia; Interstate Bag Company, Walden, New York; Richmond Container Corporation, Richmond, Virginia; and the Randolph Paper Box Company, Richmond, Virginia. The parent company had also acquired the operating assets of other small companies and merged with Tredegar Company in 1957. Since the net sales and after-tax profits of the consolidated company was less in the fiscal year ended April 1, 1962, than for the previous year, the board of directors was interested in further diversification into other areas of industry.

Ethyl Corporation was chartered in 1924 under the laws of Delaware by General Motors Corporation and Standard Oil Company (New Jersey) for the purpose of commercializing the use of tetraethyl lead in motor and aviation gasoline. Ethyl had manufacturing plants located in Baton Rouge, Louisiana; Houston, Texas; Pittsburg, California; Orangeburg, S. C.; and Sarnia, Ontario. Ethyl also operated a research laboratory in Detroit (as well as in the Baton Rouge plant), had executive offices in New York City, and maintained 16 regional and district offices around the country. Tetraethyl lead continued to be Ethyl's principal product, although competition in the industry increased after the company's patents expired in 1947. The company's share of the market had declined since 1947, and it was estimated that Ethyl was accounting for about one-half the total sales of tetraethyl lead compound in 1962. A bulk of the remainder was being made by E. I. duPont de Nemours and Company, although Houston Chemical Corporation of Beaumont, Texas, and Nalco Chemical Company at Freeport, Texas, had entered the field.

Consumption of tetraethyl lead in the United States reached a peak in 1956. After that date, a decline occurred in its overall usage, primarily for two reasons. First, a shift to jet aircraft which do not use gasoline reduced the market for the compound, and, second, the popularity of compact automobiles with their consumption of lower octane gasoline resulted in reduced sales of tetraethyl lead compound. It is believed, however, that the adverse factors affecting the sales of the industry have been felt and that although competition will remain keen, the industry's volume of antiknock compound will begin to rise during the next few years. Octane ratings in the United States, as well as overseas, are again on the increase. In 1962 Ethyl was selling antiknock products to about 235 United States, forty Canadian, and sixty-five overseas refineries.

For many years, Ethyl has carried on research activities and has developed other chemical compounds. The company's sales of other than antiknock compounds amounted to only 3 per cent of the total in 1957, increased to 11.5 per cent of the total by 1961, and was expected to be about 13 per cent during 1962. The research was to be continued should the facilities be acquired by Albemarle.

The management of Albemarle was interested in the acquisition of Ethyl for a number of reasons. It realized that Ethyl was several times as large as its own company and that it would be entering an entirely different field. However, competitive inroads by plastic companies have been made into the paper industry by the introduction of paper substitutes. The management wished to keep abreast of these developments in the chemical industry, and to diversify into areas other than the paper industry. Ethyl had several well-located, modern plants which had a fair market value substantially in excess of the book value, and the stockholders of Ethyl appeared willing to consider the sale of their interest. Should the acquisition be made, the key personnel of Ethyl were expected to remain with the combined company to direct future operations and expansions.

Audited financial statements for Ethyl Corporation were not available; however, audited net profits for the two companies, Ethyl and Albemarle, as well as depreciation, income taxes, and interest expenses are shown in Exhibit III. Combined pro forma net income was estimated for 1962 for the two companies. This net income was based on the retirement of all the presently outstanding indebtedness of Ethyl and Albemarle (except for about $3 million of funded debt of an unconsolidated subsidiary of Albemarle) and the inclusion of the interest on the proposed debt of the combined company should the acquisition be made.

The first mortgage bond indenture of Albemarle would not permit the company to incur funded debt in excess of the capital and surplus of the company and its subsidiaries. The bonds were, however, callable at 104 1/2 per cent of par. The convertible subordinated debentures were callable at 107 in 1962, 106 in 1963, 105 in 1964, and so forth, and were convertible into Class "B" common stock at $15.9838 a share until July 1, 1963, and at $17.419 thereafter until July 1, 1968.

The 6 per cent, cumulative, $100 preferred stock was voting only when dividends were two years in arrears (and then only one vote per share), and were callable at 102 in 1963, at 101.5 in 1964, and at 101 thereafter. The 149,039 shares of Class "A" common had one vote per share and had preemptive rights. The 880,688 outstanding shares of Class "B" common stock had no voting or preemptive rights but shared equally with the Class "A" shareholders in dividend payments and in liquidation rights.

The purchasing price of Ethyl Corporation stock was to be paid for in cash and with $20,000,000, five-year, 5 3/4 per cent subordinated notes. In order to raise the additional funds to retire the outstanding indebtedness of Albemarle and Ethyl, to meet the cash payment to General Motors and Standard Oil Company (New Jersey), and to meet working capital needs, the management of Albemarle recommended that the combined company borrow $180,000,000 (in addition to the five-year subordinated notes). Some $16,000,000, 5 1/2 per cent, two-year notes (one-half maturing at the end of each year) could be issued to a group of banks. An issue of $114,000,000, 5 3/4 per cent, senior notes, maturing in sixteen years (with $8 million retirement required annually beginning at the end of year three) were to be sold to a group of institutional investors. It was also expected that $50,000,-000 of 5 3/4 per cent, subordinated notes, maturing twenty years from date of issue and requiring an annual sinking-fund contribution of $8,000,000 per year beginning at the end of the seventeenth year (the balance to be a balloon note due at the end of the twenty years), could also be sold to institutional investors. Each $1,000 principal amount of the twenty-year subordinated notes would be accompanied by a warrent to purchase eight shares of the combined company's Class "B" common stock at a price of $27.50 per share prior to final maturity of the notes. The price was protected by an antidilution clause, and authorized, unissued stock would be reserved for meeting this commitment. The proposed capital structure of the combined company appears in Exhibit IV.

In order to hold key employees and executives of both Albemarle and Ethyl Corporation, the board of directors of Albemarle proposed a stock option plan under which a committee of three be appointed and have the power to issue stock options from time to time up to an aggregate acquisition of 150,000 shares of Class "B" common stock. No member of the committee or director who was not an officer or employee of the company or its subsidiaries would be eligible to receive stock under the plan. The committee was to be free to set the option price, which could not be less than 110 per cent of the fair market price of the stock at the time the options were granted if the recipient owned 10 per cent or more of the voting shares of the company, nor less than 95 per cent of the fair market price of the stock to other participants. The former options were to mature in five years from the date of issue, and the latter in ten years from the date of issue, except that the options had to be exercised within three months after termination of employment (or else expire). Shorter expiration dates could be set by the committee at the time the options were granted. The options were not transferrable but could be exercised by the recipients' beneficiaries within twelve months following his death.

If the acquisition of Ethyl Corporation were consummated, it was believed that the public interest in its securities would be materially increased. In October, 1962, a controlling group (P. D. Gottwald, P. D. Gottwald, Jr., and Bruce Gottwald) owned in the aggregate 53.69 per cent of the voting Class "A" common stock. The management of the corporation had worked out a plan whereby the voting distinctions between the two classes of common stock would be eliminated. The plan called for the deposit of the stock by the controlling group with trustees under a voting trust agreement. For five years, or until Mr. P. D. Gottwald ceased to be an executive officer of the combined company, the controlling group would select the three trustees who would vote the stock. At the end of the five-year period, or possibly sooner, the voting trustees were to be chosen, one by the owners of the trust certificates, one by the holders of the subordinated notes (other than any held by the selling stockholders), and a third to be selected by the two thus chosen. The controlling group would have the right to call a meeting of the stockholders of the combined company for the purpose of eliminating the voting distinction between the two classes of stock. Although the controlling group of Albemarle realized that this plan would eliminate their controlling position, they believed that the importance of acquiring Ethyl Corporation transcended their personal interest as controlling stockholders, and accordingly, agreed to the plan.

Although the board of directors of Albemarle had the power to acquire properties, it did need the consent of a majority of each class of common shareholders before it modified its charter. A charter amendment was required before the company changed its name, changed the purpose of the corporation, and adopted the stock option plan. The management wished to change the name of the combined company to Ethyl Corporation so as to preserve the valuable trade name in the petro-chemical industry. The management of the Albemarle company believed that it was to the best interest of its stockholders to vote in favor of the proposed amendments to its charter.

**EXHIBIT I**

**Albemarle Paper Manufacturing Company**
**Consolidated Income Statements**
**For the Years Ended**
**(In Thousands)**

|  | April 1, 1962 | April 2, 1961 |
|---|---|---|
| Net sales | $44,284 | $46,117 |
| Cost of sales | 33,564 | 33,980 |
| Expenses | 3,727 | 3,649 |
| Depreciation and depletion | 2,295 | 2,078 |
| Operating profit | 4,698 | 6,410 |
| Other income | 687 | 532 |
| Total income | 5,385 | 6,942 |
| Interest | 814 | 879 |
| Discounts allowed | 945 | 879 |
| Minority interest | 6 | 9 |
| Income taxes | 1,858 | 2,740 |
| Net income | 1,762 | 2,435 |
| Previous retained earnings | 11,494 | 9,809 |
| 6% preferred dividends | 250 | 262 |
| Common dividends |  |  |
| Cash | 509 | 488 |
| Stock | 1,261 | — |
| Retained earnings | $11,236 | $11,494 |
| Times interest earned | 5.45 | 6.89 |
| Earnings/Share—6% pref. (dollars) | 42.89 | 56.36 |
| Earnings/Share—" A " and " B " |  |  |
| common (dollars) | 1.47 | 2.23 |
| Number of 6% pref. shares | 41,084 | 43,195 |
| Number of " A " and " B " shares | 1,029,674 | 976,956 |

**EXHIBIT II**

## Albemarle Paper Manufacturing Company
### Consolidated Balance Sheet
### (In Thousands)

|  | April 1, 1962 | April 2, 1961 |
|---|---|---|
| *Assets* | | |
| Cash | $2,156 | $3,336 |
| Accounts receivable | 6,344 | 4,442 |
| Inventories | 5,547 | 5,508 |
| Prepaid items | 761 | 259 |
| Total current assets | 14,808 | 13,545 |
| Timber | 4,089 | 4,081 |
| Land and buildings | 43,271 | 39,877 |
| Total | 47,360 | 43,958 |
| Less depreciation and depletion | 18,413 | 16,191 |
| Net property | 28,947 | 27,767 |
| Land, office site | 275 | 569 |
| Investments and advances to subsid. | 2,155 | 1,730 |
| Other investments (cost) | 175 | 100 |
| Other assets | 565 | 382 |
| Total assets | $46,925 | $44,093 |
| | | |
| *Liabilities and capital* | | |
| Accounts payable | $1,720 | $1,757 |
| Accruals | 1,572 | 1,261 |
| Income tax reserves | 1,203 | 2,083 |
| Total currents liabilities | 4,495 | 5,101 |
| Debentures, $5^{1}/_2$s, 1978 (convertible) | 2,522 | 2,592 |
| Mortgage bonds (5.3 and 5.5%) | 13,000 | 10,500 |
| Deferred income tax reserves | 2,106 | 1,951 |
| 6% preferred stock ($ 100) | 4,326 | 4,381 |
| Class "A" common ($ 5) | 745 | 710 |
| Class "B" common ($ 5) | 4,403 | 4,175 |
| Retained earnings | 11,235 | 11,494 |
| Capital surplus | 4,315 | 3,251 |
| Total capital | 25,024 | 24,011 |
| Less reacquired stock | 222 | 62 |
| Net stock and surplus | 24,802 | 23,949 |
| Total liabilities and capital | $46,925 | $44,093 |

## EXHIBIT III

### Adjusted Earnings of Ethyl and Albemarle
### Years Ended December 31 for Ethyl and Succeeding April 1 for Albemarle
### (In Thousands)

|  | 1957 | 1958 | 1959 | 1960 | 1961 | Estimated 1962 |
|---|---|---|---|---|---|---|
| Reported net profit |  |  |  |  |  |  |
| Ethyl | $29,661 | $25,156 | $27,807 | $24,066 | $24,370 | $18,000 |
| Albemarle | 1,921 | 2,133 | 2,139 | 2,434 | 1,762 | 2,475 |
| Total | 31,582 | 27,289 | 29,946 | 26,500 | 26,132 | 20,475 |
| Add back |  |  |  |  |  |  |
| Ethyl |  |  |  |  |  |  |
| Depreciation | 11,412 | 11,236 | 11,871 | 11,615 | 11,383 | 7,900 |
| Income taxes | 31,711 | 26,098 | 28,789 | 25,769 | 25,829 | 20,400 |
| Interest paid* | 765 | 716 | 655 | 585 | 515 | 400 |
| Albemarle |  |  |  |  |  |  |
| Depreciation | 1,482 | 1,607 | 2,041 | 2,077 | 2,294 | 2,400 |
| Income taxes | 2,378 | 2,266 | 1,958 | 2,740 | 1,857 | 3,025 |
| Interest paid* | 409 | 450 | 647 | 878 | 814 | 853 |
| Total | 79,739 | 69,662 | 75,907 | 70,163 | 68,824 | 55,453 |
| Deduct : |  |  |  |  |  |  |
| Ethyl interest income† | 2,900 | 1,900 | 2,400 | 3,300 | 2,600 | 1,000 |
| Pro forma depreciation‡ | 15,400 | 15,400 | 15,400 | 15,400 | 15,400 | 15,400 |
| Pro forma interest | 11,460 | 11,460 | 11,460 | 11,460 | 11,460 | 11,460 |
| Subtotal | 29,760 | 28,760 | 29,260 | 30,160 | 29,460 | 27,860 |
| Combined income |  |  |  |  |  |  |
| Before taxes | 49,979 | 40,902 | 46,647 | 40,003 | 39,364 | 27,593 |
| Income taxes (52%) | 25,989 | 21,269 | 24,256 | 20,802 | 20,469 | 14,348 |
| Combined pro forma net income | $23,990 | $19,633 | $22,391 | $19,201 | $18,895 | $13,245 |

*Existing debt of Ethyl and Albemarle to be retired.
†Temporary investments to be liquidated prior to acquisition.
‡Depreciation for combined company adjusted to new cost basis.

## EXHIBIT IV

### Ethyl Corporation
### Pro Forma Debt and Capital Stock

| Security | Authorized | To Be Outstanding |
|---|---|---|
| *Long-term indebtedness* | | |
| Two-year term notes | | $16,000,000* |
| Senior notes due 1978 | | 114,000,000 |
| Subordinated notes due 1967 | | 20,000,000 |
| | | 50,000,000 |
| *Capital stock* | | |
| 6% Cumulative preferred stock series A, B, C, and D, par value $100 per share | 100,000 Shs. | 47,059 Shs. |
| Class "A" common stock, par value $5 | 156,000 Shs. | 149,036 Shs. |
| Class "B" common stock, par value $5 | 2,000,000 Shs. | 1,038,441 Shs. |

*$8,000,000 of this will be carried in current liabilities as it matures within one year.
†Includes shares issuable for Albemarle's outstanding convertible debentures which will be called if the transaction is consummated. Excludes the shares reserved for the exercise of warrants and the stock options.

## EXHIBIT V

### Albemarle Paper Manufacturing Company
### Selected Earnings and Market Price Data

| Year | E/S (Year ended following 3/31) | Class A Common | | Class B Common | |
|---|---|---|---|---|---|
| | | High | Low | High | Low |
| 1962 | | | | | |
| Aug. | | | | $30\frac{3}{4}$A* | $29\frac{1}{2}$B* |
| Jan.-Aug. | | | | $29\frac{7}{8}$ | 16 |
| 1961 | $1.47 | 35 | 28 | $29\frac{1}{2}$ | 20 |
| 1960 | 1.93 | 34 | $22\frac{1}{2}$ | $27\frac{1}{2}$ | 21 |
| 1959 | 2.52 | 45 | $36\frac{1}{2}$ | $43\frac{1}{2}$ | 37 |
| 1958 | 2.62 | $36\frac{1}{2}$ | $20\frac{1}{4}$ | 40 | $16\frac{1}{4}$ |
| 1957 | 3.45 | 26 | 18 | 23 | 16 |
| 1956 | 2.67 | 32 | $21\frac{1}{2}$ | $32\frac{1}{4}$ | $26\frac{1}{4}$ |
| 1955 | 1.76 | 36 | $23\frac{1}{4}$ | 36 | $23\frac{1}{4}$ |

*Unlisted. Bid and Ask quotations.

## EXHIBIT VI

### Leading Chemical Companies
### Price/Earnings Ratios

| Year | High | Low |
|---|---|---|
| 1961 | 27.52 | 23.08 |
| 1960 | 29.99 | 21.75 |
| 1959 | 28.13 | 22.18 |
| 1958 | 30.16 | 23.19 |
| 1957 | 24.59 | 19.78 |
| 1956 | 26.96 | 21.42 |
| 1955 | 23.93 | 16.92 |

## Merger

## 37

### DYNAMICS
### AEROSPACE CORPORATION

In early 1964, the chairman of the board of directors and the president of Dynamics Aerospace Corporation were considering the possible advantages to be gained from an acquisition of Electro-Bateau, Inc. by DAC. An acquisition of the assets of the latter company or a merger of the two companies would require the majority approval of each type of shareholder in each of the companies, but the combination should result in some expense reduction to the combined company.

The objective of the management of Dynamics was to increase the earnings base and earnings per share of their common stockholders. The company had been following the policy of expanding through external means during recent years and had acquired or merged with numerous other small companies in the aerospace and electronics areas.

The board of directors of Electro-Bateau, Inc. had been approached the previous year regarding a merger, acquisition plan, or consolidation of the two firms. Although the management of Dynamics believed that such a move would reduce administrative expenses, reduce research and development costs, and increase the operating efficiency of the companies, the directors of Electro-Bateau were reluctant to discuss such a proposal at that time. When Dynamics management met with the board of Electro-Bateau, Inc. One year later (March, 1964) the former company had acquired through market purchases almost 40 per cent of the voting stock in the latter company. Since this amount of stock far exceeded the number of shares of voting stock held by the management of Electro-Bateau, the management knew that they must seriously consider the offer made by Dynamics.

Dynamics Aerospace Corporation was incorporated in California in 1956. During the first eight years of its existence, it grew rapidly through mergers and acquisitions. Its shares were actively traded in the over-the-counter market until 1961 when it listed its securities for trading on the American Stock Exchange. The company was engaged in research and production in the areas of guidance controls, communications systems, air conditioning systems, missile components, and other electronic instruments. The company was operating four plants with about a million square feet of floor space in California, Florida, Massachusetts, and Texas. The formation of electronics companies in the early 1950s had been much more active in these four states than in the other ones. The home office was located in California, but research and production facilities were located in each of the four states. After an acquisition of a company had been facilitated, the company continued its operation as a division, chiefly under the direction of the old management. The board of directors of Dynamics Aerospace Corporation, however, was active in setting company policy in financial management and in reviewing the reports submitted by the operating divisions.

Exhibits I and II indicate that DAC expanded by almost 200 per cent during 1963, primarily because of external expansion. After listing its securities on the ASE in 1961, the stocks declined slightly but began a rise of almost 300 per cent from early 1961 to mid-1963. The earnings per share of the company were $.21 in 1960; $.12 in 1961; $.70 in 1962; and $.75 in 1963.

From 1962 to 1963, net income increased by 64 per cent while sales almost tripled. Current assets amounted to about one-half the total assets of the firm, and its current ratios at the end of 1962 and 1963 were, respectively, 1.51 to 1 and 1.45 to 1. From two-thirds to three-fourths of the assets of the firm were being financed with debt, roughly one-half of which was long term. On December 31, 1963, the company had outstanding a first mortgage bond issue; two callable, convertible debenture issues; and a note issue. The notes payable current account was composed of a $7,000,000 bank loan and current maturing portions of the long-term debt. The mortgage bond issue was held privately, had been issued in 1961, and matured in 1973. Interest was payable semiannually, and the bonds were callable after July 1, 1965, at 104, reduced by one-half a percentage point each year until maturity. Indenture provisions required that $108,000 of the bonds be retired at par each year with funds paid into a sinking fund. Other restrictive clauses of the bond indenture limited (1) cash dividend payments, (2) acquisition of the company's own capital stock, or (3) retirement of the subordinated debentures in excess of sinking-fund requirements, to not more than 50 per cent of the net income of the company after December 31, 1960, plus $100,000. The company was also required to maintain net current assets of at least 200 per cent of the senior funded debt or 100 per cent of total funded debt.

The 5 1/4 per cent, convertible debentures of 1974 had been issued by a subsidiary corporation, and were later assumed by Dynamics when the two were combined. Although $1,318,000 of the bonds were outstanding at the end of 1960, $90,000 of the issue (shown as a current liability under notes payable) were callable at par for sinking-fund purposes. The entire issue was callable with thirty days' notice on July 1 of each year at 104 in 1963 and reduced by one percentage point each three years until maturity. Each $1,000 debenture was convertible into Dynamics Aerospace Corporation common shares to July 31 of each year as follows:

| Year | Common Shares |
|------|---------------|
| 1964 | 49.0496 |
| 1969 | 45.1209 |
| 1973 | 41.2797 |

Cash was to be paid in lieu of fractional shares, and the conversion ratios were protected against dilution. The debentures traded from 88 to 109 in 1963 and from eighty-four to 111 in 1962.

The $406,000 of $5\frac{1}{2}$ per cent convertible debentures of 1973 were held privately and were callable at 106 to October 30, 1964, and at reduced schedules thereafter. An annual sinking fund of $60,000 to redeem the debentures at par was required starting in 1965. The bonds were convertible into common at $6 per share to October 30, 1965, at $7 per share for the next four years, and at $8 per share thereafter until maturity. The bond indenture prohibited the payment of dividends in excess of consolidated net income after June 30, 1958.

The 4 1/2 per cent, $18 par, preferred shares were cumulative as to dividends, convertible into common stock, had one vote per share, and had preference in liquidation equal to dividend arrearages and par value plus share for share participation after common received $18 per share. The shares were convertible into one share of common at the following schedule until June 30 of each year.

| Year | 1 Share of Common for |
|------|-----------------------|
| 1968 | 1 pref. share |
| 1969 | $1\frac{1}{8}$ pref. share |
| 1970 | $1\frac{1}{3}$ pref. share |
| 1973 | $1\frac{1}{2}$ pref. share |

The shares were callable in whole or in part with thirty days' notice at $20 per share after June 30, 1968. Shares outstanding on July 1, 1973 were to be called for redemption. The shares had been issued at mid-1963 in connection with a merger.

At the end of 1963, Dynamics Aerospace Corporation had 1,277,000 shares of $.30 par common stock outstanding. Some 3,000,000 shares were authorized but the following were reserved for:

| Purpose | Number of shares |
|---------|------------------|
| For conversion of preferred | 95,000 |
| For conversion of debentures | 132,000 |
| For warrants | 34,000 |
| For stock options | 150,000 |

Common had one vote per share (cumulative) for the election of directors. The company had never paid any cash dividends, but at the end of 1963 about $1,000,000 of retained earnings were available for cash dividend payments.

The long-term notes payable of the company were comprised of $1,500,000 of 6 per cent senior notes, repayable $120,000 annually from 1968 to 1976 with the balance due at the end of 1974. Another $400,000 in bank notes were outstanding with maturities from 1961 to 1967. The 6 per cent senior notes carried warrants to purchase 32,500 shares of common at $20 per share to the end of 1967 and at $23 per share thereafter until December 31, 1972, when the warrants expired.

Electro-Bateau was incorporated in Massachusetts in 1956 and had expanded from that date through 1963 by acquiring other small companies. It operated in the area of missile components, data processing, mobile homes, fishing and pleasure boats and motors, and small pleasure aircraft. It also had a fully owned subsidiary, a captive finance company. The company had operating facilities in Massachusetts, California, and Florida.

Revenues, profits, and earnings per share for Electro-Bateau for the years 1957–1961 are reported in Exhibit IV. Although sales more than doubled over the five-year period, profits did not keep pace with sales increases. There were actually sales and profit declines from 1957 to 1958 and from 1958 to 1959, but revenues and profits turned up in 1960. Although the company had followed a stable dividend policy (with dividends increasing from time to time), the market value of the shares fluctuated widely. The shares were listed on the American Stock Exchange and traded from about $15 to $25 per share in both 1962 and in 1963.

At the end of 1960, Electro-Bateau was being financed with about 43 per cent short-term debt, 9 per cent long-term debt, and 48 per cent equity. The 5 1/4s convertible debentures of 1977 were callable to July 31, 1965, at 104 and thereafter at reduced rates of one percentage point each two years. The conversion privilege was protected by an antidilution clause, and an annual sinking-fund redemption of $187,500 of the debentures was required at the end of each year, 1965–1979. The debentures were convertible into common shares until July 31, 1970, at $24 per share. The indenture required that net tangible assets be at least 175 per cent of funded debt and limited dividend payments to net income after December 31, 1959, plus $1,000,000 and proceeds from the sale of additional stock after that date. The market price of the bonds was from 89–111 1/2 in 1962 and from 91–117 in 1963.

The common stock consisted of the following: 1,500,000 shares authorized; 595,000 shares outstanding at the end of 1963; 110,000 shares reserved for debenture conversion on that date; and 41,000 shares reserved for options. Dynamics Aerospace Corporation held 228,000 of the common shares by early March, 1964.

The board of directors and the president of Dynamics Aerospace believed that the creditors of a merged or acquired company would be willing for the surviving company to assume the debts of the former. The shareholders, however, were expected to have difficulty in reaching an exchange agreement as to the ratio between the equity securities. The book value per share, market value per share, earnings per share, or a combination of the above were the usual methods for arriving at the exchange ratio. The average market value per share over the last year or two appeared to be an attractive method as it considered the tangible and intangible values of the securities to the general public.

In early 1964, the directors of Dynamics Aerospace Corporation submitted the following acquisition proposal to the board of directors of Electro-Bateau for consideration. The latter was expected to study the proposal and then present it to its stockholders at a specially called stockholders meeting where it would be voted upon by the voting stockholders of Electro-Bateau. The offer was as follows:

> An exchange of Electro-Bateau common stock for the combined company's debentures and warrants at the rate of one share of Electro-Bateau for $26.00 of 5 1/2 per cent, convertible debentures, a five-year warrant to purchase 1/5th share of Dynamics common at $18 a share, and a five-year warrant to purchase an additional 1/5th share at $24 per share. The debentures were to be convertible into new common shares at the rate of 1 1/4 shares for one debenture during a five-year period and a lower rate thereafter. The companies would have equal representation on the board of directors of the surviving company for a five-year period of time.

**EXHIBIT I**

**Dynamics Aerospace Corporation**
**Income Statements**
**for Years Ended December 31**
**(In Thousands)**

|  | 1963 | 1962 |
|---|---|---|
| Net sales | $44,534 | $14,426 |
| Cost of goods sold | 40,026 | 11,931 |
| Gross profit | 4,508 | 2,495 |
| Expenses |  |  |
| Selling and general | 2,504 | 1,559 |
| Net profit from operation | 2,004 | 936 |
| Profits on sale of assets | — | 134 |
| Other income | 101 | 38 |
| Total | 2,105 | 1,108 |
| Less : Interest | 384 | 141 |
| Other deductions | — | 25 |
| Income taxes | 806 | 382 |
| Net income | $915 | $560 |
| Preferred dividends | — | 14 |
| Other dividends | — | 10 |
| No. preferred shares (thousands) | 57 | 11 |
| No. common shares (thousands) | 1,277 | 806 |
| E/S on common | .75 | .70 |
| Market value* |  |  |
| High | $25\frac{1}{4}$ | $26\frac{3}{4}$ |
| Low | 12 | 10 |
| Unfilled orders (Sub-contracts) | $30,000 | $15,000 |

*High-Low of 11 5/8–6 7/8 in 1961.

## EXHIBIT II

### Dynamics Aerospace Corporation
### Balance Sheets
### As of December 31
### (In Thousands)

|  | 1963 | 1962 |
|---|---|---|
| *Assets* |  |  |
| Cash and U. S. securities | $2,585 | $563 |
| Receivables | 8,493 | 3,112 |
| Unbilled contract work | — | 369 |
| Inventories (ave. cost or mkt.) | 10,461 | 2,774 |
| Prepayments | 156 | 44 |
| Total current assets | 21,695 | 6,862 |
| Land, property, and equipment | 6,551 | 1,975 |
| Depreciation | (2,772) | (441) |
| Net Properties | 3,779 | 1,534 |
| Receivables | 636 | 265 |
| Investments in and advances to affiliates | 1,093 | 38 |
| Other investments (cost) | — | 57 |
| Intangibles | 664 | 928 |
| Deferred charges | 171 | 75 |
| Total assets | $28,038 | $9,759 |
|  |  |  |
| *Liabilities and capital* |  |  |
| Notes payable | $9,122 | $2,244 |
| Accounts payable | 3,884 | 1,568 |
| Accruals | 1,177 | 304 |
| Income taxes | 744 | 418 |
| Total current liab. | 14,927 | 4,534 |
| Debentures (convertible) |  |  |
| $5\frac{1}{4}$ s of 1973 | 407 | 660 |
| $5\frac{1}{2}$ s of 1974 | 1,228 | — |
| 1st $5\frac{1}{4}$ s, 1973 | 984 | — |
| Notes payable | 1,773 | 1,624 |
| Total liabilities | 19,319 | 6,818 |
| Capital |  |  |
| Reserve for fed. inc. taxes | 159 | 3 |
| 6% preferred stock ($ 1) | — | 11 |
| $4\frac{1}{2}$% convertible pref. ($ 18 par) | 1,708 | — |
| Common stock ($ .30 par) | 383 | 241 |
| Capital surplus | 672 | 1,295 |
| Retained earnings | 5,797 | 1,391 |
| Total capital | 8,719 | 2,941 |
| Total capital and liab. | $28,038 | $9,759 |

**EXHIBIT III**

**Electro-Bateau, Inc.**
**Income Statements**
**Years Ended December 31**
**(In Thousands)**

|  | 1963 | 1962 |
|---|---|---|
| Unfilled orders (primarily missile subcontracts) | $60,300 | $75,900 |
| Sales | 64,165 | 76,398 |
| Costs and expenses | 59,982 | 71,791 |
| Depreciation and amortization | 1,051 | 1,026 |
| Operating profit | 3,132 | 3,581 |
| Other income | 30 | 8 |
| Total | 3,162 | 3,589 |
| Less : Interest | 226 | 209 |
| Federal income tax | 1,850 | 1,910 |
| Minority interest | (81) | — |
| Total other deductions | 1,995 | 2,119 |
| Net income | $1,167 | $1,470 |
| No. common shares | 595 | 595 |
| E/S of common | 1.96 | 2.47 |
| Div/Sh of common | 1.20 | 1.20 |
| M/V per common share | $24\frac{7}{8}-15\frac{7}{8}$ | $25\frac{1}{2}-15\frac{3}{8}$ |

**EXHIBIT IV**

**Electro-Bateau, Inc.**
**Selected Data**
**(In Thousands)**

| Year | Per Share M/V of Common | Net Sales | Net Profits | No. of Common Shares | E/S on Common | D/S |
|---|---|---|---|---|---|---|
| 1961 | $35\frac{1}{2}-19$ | $99,958 | $2,687 | 594 | $4.53 | $1.14 |
| 1960 | $29\frac{1}{2}-12\frac{3}{8}$ | 71,188 | 1,846 | 544 | 3.39 | .96 |
| 1959 | $27\frac{1}{4}-18\frac{3}{4}$ | 35,456 | 1,241 | 542 | 2.29 | .96 |
| 1958 | * | 44,128 | 1,428 | 540 | 2.65 | .96 |
| 1957 | * | 44,886 | 1,992 | 540 | 3.69 | .48 |

*Not comparable.

EXHIBIT V

**Electro-Bateau, Inc.**
**Balance Sheets**
**As of December 31**
**(In Thousands)**

|  | 1963 | 1962 |
|---|---|---|
| *Assets* |  |  |
| Current assets |  |  |
| Cash | $6,869 | $5,342 |
| Receivables | 8,520 | 10,390 |
| Inventories | 14,275 | 20,573 |
| Progress payments | (7,327) | (12,399) |
| Repayments | 534 | 552 |
| Total current assets | 22,871 | 24,458 |
| Machinery and equipment | 8,925 | 6,679 |
| Less : Depreciation and amortization | 4,028 | 3,248 |
| Net Property | 4,897 | 3,431 |
| Other fixed assets (Mobil Homes Sub.) | — | 2,062 |
| Investments and advances to subsid. | 1,059 | 205 |
| Patents other | 1,457 | — |
| Deferred charges | 191 | 134 |
| Total assets | $30,475 | $30,290 |
|  |  |  |
| *Liabilities and capital* |  |  |
| Current liabilities |  |  |
| Notes payable | $5,506 | $3,482 |
| Accounts payable | 3,936 | 5,422 |
| Accruals | 2,103 | 3,243 |
| Federal income taxes payable | 1,446 | 1,471 |
| Total current liabilities | 12,991 | 13,618 |
| Debentures, $5\frac{1}{4}$ s of 1980 | 2,645 | 2,644 |
| Mortgage notes | 89 | 64 |
| Minority interest | 323 | — |
| Common stock ($ 1 par) | 357 | 358 |
| Capital surplus | 6,132 | 6,122 |
| Retained earnings | 7,938 | 7,484 |
| Total liabilities and capital | $30,475 | $30,290 |

# Determining Price and Method of Acquisition

## 38

HOUSTON
PETROLEUM COMPANY[1]

On January 5, 1962, Mr. E. W. Wells, vice-president of economics and finance for the Houston Petroleum Company was visiting with an officer of the Southwest National Bank of Tulsa. The bank officer was a member of the board of directors of Claremont Petroleum Corporation, and he indicated to Mr. Wells that Claremont's management was interested in selling the assets of their firm and would welcome a bid by Houston Petroleum.

The Houston Petroleum Company was a large, fully integrated company. It produced gas, oil, and petro-chemicals, and was considered one of the nation's top twenty oil companies. It marketed its gas products under the "Petro" brand in twenty-five states. The Houston company had in recent years been expanding its gas stations with the result that it was now purchasing oil from independent oil producers. The management of Houston considered this an unsatisfactory situation and, consequently, was very interested in purchasing additional producing properties as well as increasing the amount of reserves that would be available to them.

On hearing of the possibility that Claremont could be purchased, Mr. Wells notified the top management of Houston Petroleum who expressed considerable interest in the prospect. Shortly thereafter, a three-man team composed of Mr. Wells, a corporate staff specialist in reserves and evaluation, and a local land department manager contacted the management of Claremont who had already been notified by the Tulsa banker to expect a call from Houston. The Claremont top management confirmed their interest in arranging a cash sale at an early date. One of the major reasons for the sale was the need to liquidate the

---

[1]This case was originally written by Kenneth W. Olm and had been revised by Richard L. Norgaard.

holdings of the estate of a major stockholder. While the owners of Claremont were anxious to liquidate their holdings, they were concerned about obtaining a fair value for their property and not a distressed price. They were also concerned with minimizing the tax consequences from the sale. Lastly, they were interested in the fate of their employees, especially those not in top management.

Rather than conduct a negotiation in tight secrecy, the management invited employees of Claremont to listen in at negotiation sessions so that they would be informed of proceedings. The Claremont executives informed Mr. Wells that they had contacted the management of National Oil Co. who had also been invited to give them a bid. Mr. Wells knew the executives of National and realized that they could be depended on to offer a fair price to Claremont. He concluded, therefore, that he would not be in a position to offer Claremont a minimum price, nor would he be able to bargain except in broad terms.

The Houston Company had conducted a quick and necessarily cursory examination of the oil and gas production records of Claremont. Such records were available to the public, and because of stringent rules regarding their keeping, were considered to be highly reliable. The preliminary examination indicated that Claremont had production which Houston was interested in acquiring. Houston's top management then gave their approval to conduct a detailed evauation of Claremont's assets and an "evaluation team" was set up to conduct the study. An "acquisition team" was also set up to conduct the formal negotiations for the purchase.

Staff specialists of Houston examined in detail all of the assets held by Claremont in order to arrive at an evaluation of each major group of assets. Petroleum engineers, geologists, and landmen worked as a team of specialists to forecast the flow of production from each well or related group of wells for each year that the wells were expected to be productive. These production flows were translated into income flows by forecasting prices and costs of operation. The income flows were then valued by applying the discount rate considered appropriate for such properties. Nonproductive leaseholds were evaluated by the market value method. Fee land and improvements and inventories were generally accepted at book value.

Mr. Wells recognized that in respect to any proposed acquisition of petroleum-producing properties a critical relationship was the current cost of finding petroleum reserves versus the cost of acquiring reserves of any proposed seller. The Houston company was generally considered to be fairly successful in their exploration activities and their current average cost of finding liquid petroleum reserves was estimated to be approximately $1 per barrel. This was somewhat below the present current industry average. Houston was, therefore, disinclined to purchase primary reserves at a cost any greater than their own estimated cost of buying and developing equivalent reserves. Other factors involved in making a purchase decision were: (1) the possibilities of secondary reserves, (2) the possibility of unexplored lease holdings, (3) the current need for more daily production to balance refinery needs, (4) the extent the proposed production purchase and expected cash flow therefrom fit into Houston's current operations and present corporate cash flow, (5) competitive strategy and plans for expansion of operations, (6) the availability of cash or other favorable means for financing the purchase, and (7) tax minimization possibilities.

Mr. Wells realized that the desire of the Claremont stockholders for cash rather restricted the method by which the company could be financed. Over the last six years approximately four billion dollars worth of oil producing properties had been bought or sold by the oil & gas industry. The methods used to finance these changes included the following: $2.2 billion in nineteen transactions were financed by stock, $1.8 billion in twenty-five transactions were financed by the "ABC" method, $240 million in three transactions were financed by cash, and $100 million in four transactions were financed by stock and cash. In the present situation an exchange of stock could not be considered. Mr. Wells did not consider the cash position of his company sufficient to use that method nor did he want to go to the stock or bond market at the present time to finance an issue sufficiently large for the purchase. Consequently, he decided to use the ABC method.

### The ABC Transaction

In an "ABC" transaction, "A" is the seller (in this case Claremont), "B" is an operator who wants to purchase the property and produce petroleum therefrom at a profit (in this case Houston), and "C" is the buyer of the production payment, or the middleman (generally a nonprofit or charitable institution). Under present tax laws, no tax on the gain from the sale is levied against "A" if "A" plans a complete liquidation within 12 months and if it divests itself of all economic interest in the property being sold. Shareholders of "A" need only to pay a tax on their profits in the stock. If "C" is a tax-exempt institution, no tax is levied against the income accruing to "C" as a result of the transaction.[2]

The buying company, for their protection, under the ABC method, requested a ruling from the tax authorities that none of the reserved production payment would be construed as income to them. The purchaser derived the principal benefit from the ABC transaction because the reserved production payment was considered a depletable economic interest in the oil in place. The holder of the production payment was considered to own part of the oil in the ground and was taxed on the proceeds of such part of the oil as if he produced it himself. The proceeds of the oil accruing to the production payment holder were excludable from the purchaser's gross income provided a ruling had been obtained. The effect was that the pur-

---

[2]For further details on the ABC transaction, see "The ABC Transaction," *Oil and Gas Taxes* (Englewood Cliffs, N.J.: Prentice-Hall, Inc., 1960), Section 2011, par. 1–7, pp. 2211–28; and Kenneth G. Miller, ed., "The Case for ABC," *Oil and Gas Tax Quarterly* (Albany, N.Y.: Mathew Bender & Co., Inc.), Vol. xi, No. 1 (October, 1961), pp. 1–24.

chaser's taxable income from the property was much less during the period of payment than if they had purchased the whole property in the conventional manner. The purchaser's taxable income would be reduced $72\frac{1}{2}$ per cent of the amount of the production payment (100%—$27\frac{1}{2}$% depletion allowance). Assuming a 50 per cent tax rate, the purchaser would save $36\frac{1}{4}$ cents (50% of $72\frac{1}{2}$%) in taxes for every dollar of the selling price that was represented by the production interest.

Mr. Wells requested that the Southwest National Bank of Tulsa, a major oil bank, give him an estimate of the amount of funds they would advance under the ABC arrangement. He was subsequently informed that the bank would make available $47,600,000 secured by the production payments from the property of Claremont Oil. Under the terms of the loan, the bank would provide $35.6 million at $5\frac{1}{2}$ per cent interest and the remaining $12 million at 5 7/8 per cent interest. The principal and interest were to be realized solely from 80 per cent of the proceeds of the hydrocarbons produced from the reserved properties. Proceeds from the remaining 20 per cent of the production were to be retained by Houston to cover estimated costs of operations and taxes. This 20 per cent was considered sufficient by Houston to meet all their normal contingencies and leave approximately 2 per cent to 4 per cent margin for profit. Houston, however, did not consider the 2 per cent to 4 per cent as profit since any change in the allowables in the State of Texas could drastically change their cash inflow without changing their costs. As a consequence Houston looked at anything they could earn on these payments as merely insurance against a potential loss. They estimated that they would be able to pay off the Tulsa bank in approximately 12 years. During that time Houston would not get any significant return on whatever money they advanced. Thus, Mr. Wells realized that the price he finally determined for the properties would be paid in cash by Houston Petroleum Co. and would be the difference between the total purchase price given to Claremont and the $47,600,000 which they would get as a result of the bank loan.

### Property Valuation

The proved reserves of the Claremont company were estimated by an independent consulting engineering firm at twenty-four million barrels of oil and condensate and 740,000 million cubic feet of gas. Average prices received on the oil were approximately $2.85 a barrel and for gas were approximately 14¢ per thousand cubic feet. Working interest properties contained 242 net oil wells and 20.5 net gas wells plus 165 net gas wells under development contracts with a large company. A total of secondary reserves and primary net reserves held by Claremont were independently estimated by Houston before the purchase at thirty-five million barrels of oil and condensate and 660 billion cubic feet of gas. Leases on 350 thousand undeveloped acres were also included in the transaction, but these were not valued by Houston. The only substantial asset other than the production properties was a home office with an original cost of nearly $700,000. Houston did not know what value it had at the present time, but it did not appear to be worth, in a quick sale, more than $200,000.

Mr. Wells realized that Houston would not get any direct benefit from the purchase of Claremont's properties until about the thirteenth year, at which time the entire property would be owned by Houston without encumbrance. Mr. Wells estimated that the property would continue to produce until the twenty-fifth year or a total of thirteen years. He estimated that approximately 12 million barrels of oil plus 370,000 million cubic feet of gas would be available at the beginning of the thirteenth year. He believed that he would be able to extract these in equal amounts over the next thirteen years. His costs to extract the oil and gas would not be the gross $2.85 a barrel for oil and 14¢ for gas but the net of the amount necessary to pay the lease royalties. Lease royalties would average 12 1/2 per cent of the gross amount received. In addition, Mr. Wells estimated conservatively that operating costs would be 20 per cent of the gross revenues. These costs would include power, employees, supplies, and all costs necessary to bring the oil to the well head.

In evaluating how much he should pay, Mr. Wells only wanted to consider the oil. Although he realized the gas could show substantial value, he knew that the top management at Houston considered gas as a plus rather than a specific value to be considered and that what the company was primarily interested in was the oil. He further recognized that there were certain unknown quantities that made his projections of $2.85 a barrel for oil for the next twenty-five years somewhat tenuous. The principle problem was the question of foreign oil. Middle East oil could be produced and delivered in the United States for approximately $1.80 a barrel. This was considerably less than the $2.85 a barrel for domestic crude. The main reason that the domestic crude market continued to be as high was because of the import quotas established by the government and production proration in the United States. If, in the future the import quotas were to be increased substantially, the value of the domestic oil available would be definitely decreased.

Mr. Wells also realized that problems such as severely limited production allowables in the State of Texas which were averaging less than 30 per cent of possible production would also influence the value of the oil wells. Instead of being able to extract the oil in thirteen years it might be considerably longer. He did not feel, however, that he was in a position to evaluate this problem, and he decided as a consequence to ignore any possible changes from the present situation.

Mr. Wells realized that the shareholders of Claremont valued their company at more than the market value of their stock. As a general rule, the securities market tended to value the stocks of a going concern in the petroleum industry at a lower figure than its presumed liquidation value. such relationships were usually brought out when petroleum companies

**EXHIBIT I**

**Houston Petroleum Company**
**Three-Year Summary, 1959-1961**

| Operations | 1961 | 1960 | 1959 |
|---|---|---|---|
| Exploration and production | | | |
| Net exploratory wells completed | | | |
| Oil | 6 | 14 | 7 |
| Gas | 3 | 5 | 12 |
| Net development wells completed | | | |
| Oil | 72 | 115 | 78 |
| Gas | 21 | 29 | 33 |
| Net dry holes | 55 | 58 | 80 |
| Net reserves at year end | | | |
| Crude oil (thousand barrels) | 474,900 | 483,500 | 488,300 |
| Natural gas liquids (thousand barrels) | 44,100 | 48,400 | 32,600 |
| Natural gas (million cubic feet) | 4,337,100 | 4,030,000 | 3,501,100 |
| Net crude oil production (thousand barrels) | 34,498 | 34,932 | 33,535 |
| As a per cent of refinery crude oil runs | 64.7 | 63.4 | 57.9 |
| Net natural gas liquids production (thousand barrels) | 2,922 | 2,444 | 2,332 |
| Net natural gas production (million cubic feet) | 152,669 | 129,104 | 105,132 |
| Refining | | | |
| Raw material throughput (thousand barrels) | 56,684 | 58,854 | 61,799 |
| Marketing | | | |
| Petroleum products sales (thousand barrels) | 56,766 | 57,515 | 58,553 |
| Crude oil sales (thousand barrels) | 22,341 | 22,201 | 19,591 |
| Natural gas sales (million cubic feet) | 187,375 | 156,231 | 124,550 |

**EXHIBIT II**

**Houston Petroleum Company**
**Selected Financial Data, 1953-1962**

| Year | Sales | E/S | D/S | Market Price | |
|---|---|---|---|---|---|
| | | | | High | Low |
| 1962 | 458,450,695 | 4.92 | 1.910 | 65 | 41 |
| 1961 | 434,770,816 | 3.99 | 1.875 | 64 | 40 |
| 1960 | 427,369,856 | 3.73 | 1.375 | 43 | 30 |
| 1959 | 410,640,154 | 2.98 | .880 | 47 | 36 |
| 1958 | 399,165,943 | 2.72 | 1.430 | 45 | 34 |
| 1957 | 426,115,531 | 4.15 | 2.010 | 53 | 33 |
| 1956 | 389,648,691 | 3.73 | 2.010 | 54 | 43 |
| 1955 | 359,503,866 | 3.45 | 1.830 | 47 | 34 |
| 1954 | 334,252,727 | 4.00 | 1.675 | 45 | 29 |
| 1953 | | 4.88 | 1.385 | 30 | 25 |

## EXHIBIT III

### Houston Petroleum Company
### Balance Sheet, 1961-1963

|  | 1963 | 1962 | 1961 |
|---|---|---|---|
| *Assets* |  |  |  |
| Cash | $57,090,657 | $58,050,809 | $62,620,280 |
| U. S. government securities and other marketable securities | 29,895,022 | 27,680,013 | 29,409,326 |
| Accounts and notes receivable | 106,958,914 | 97,098,344 | 89,749,954 |
| Crude oil inventories | 9,404,172 | 9,743,445 | 6,995,332 |
| Petroleum and chemical products | 39,079,762 | 43,259,799 | 37,813,448 |
| Materials and supplies | 2,502,066 | 2,561,666 | 2,157,742 |
| Taxes and insurance prepaid | 12,207,942 | 11,746,547 | 12,315,232 |
| Total current assets | $257,138,535 | $250,140,623 | $241,061,314 |
| Investments and advances | 53,120,365 | 40,320,962 | 35,309,610 |
| Oil lands and development | 730,078,689 | 685,674,340 | 635,917,955 |
| Less depl. and depreciation res. | 404,713,748 | 380,343,953 | 360,370,634 |
| Net oil lands and development | $325,364,941 | $305,330,387 | $275,547,321 |
| Other properties | 459,475,546 | 432,380,587 | 428,484,339 |
| Less : depreciation reserves | 246,361,434 | 235,597,636 | 223,028,978 |
| Net other properties | $213,114,112 | $196,782,951 | $205,455,361 |
| Total properties, less reserves | $538,479,053 | $502,113,338 | $481,002,682 |
| Other deferred charges | 4,604,404 | 4,323,486 | 4,095,701 |
| Total assets | $853,342,357 | $796,898,409 | $761,469,307 |
| *Liabilities* |  |  |  |
| Accounts payable (trade) | $60,500,245 | $50,404,301 | $43,972,949 |
| Accrued payrolls | 2,689,824 | 2,491,924 | 2,527,841 |
| Motor fuel, sales and excise taxes | 9,234,315 | 10,665,020 | 13,726,334 |
| Interest accrued on funded debt | 626,899 | 638,299 | 654,919 |
| Dividends payable | 5,540,066 | 6,726,735 | 4,372,448 |
| Current portion long-term debt | 2,200,000 | 2,200,000 | 2,100,000 |
| Fed. and other taxes on income | 7,718,853 | 11,967,229 | 3,576,324 |
| Property and other taxes | 14,415,937 | 7,494,327 | 7,426,497 |
| Total Current Liabilities | $102,926,139 | $92,587,835 | $78,357,312 |
| Long-term debt | 164,376,000 | 167,969,000 | 173,200,000 |
| Reserve for insurance | 4,439,252 | 4,354,189 | 4,145,041 |
| Deferred income (prop. sold) | 3,136,352 | 1,986,000 | 1,809,998 |
| Deferred income tax | 8,200,000 | — | — |
| Deferred investment credit | 2,376,837 | — | — |
| Minority interest | 8,695,365 | 9,729,680 | 11,307,467 |
|  | 191,223,806 | 184,038,869 | 190,462,506 |
| Surplus |  |  |  |
| Common stock ($ 25 par) | 235,160,725 | 228,582,650 | 222,999,550 |
| Earned surplus | 224,711,644 | 203,708,307 | 189,411,539 |
| Premium on sale of capital stock | 99,320,043 | 87,980,748 | 80,238,400 |
| Total stockholders' equity | $559,192,412 | $520,271,705 | $492,649,489 |
| Total liabilities and Equity | $853,342,357 | $796,898,409 | $761,469,307 |

**EXHIBIT IV**

**Claremont Petroleum Company**
**Summary of Earnings**

| | Year Ended December 31, | | |
|---|---|---|---|
| | 1959 | 1960 | 1961 |
| Income | | | |
| Oil and gas sales | $2,989,153 | $5,945,917 | $6,027,094 |
| Other income | 32,530 | 95,175 | 229,223 |
| | $3,021,683 | $6,041,092 | $6,256,317 |
| Expenses | | | |
| Operating expense | $615,583 | $1,222,962 | $1,371,746 |
| Depreciation, depletion and amortization | 883,327 | 1,707,796 | 1,828,247 |
| Exploratory costs (net) | | | |
| Leases expired and abandoned | 406,092 | 476,539 | 490,663 |
| Lease rentals | 180,485 | 192,921 | 147,060 |
| Dry hole costs | 81,505 | 420,009 | 257,816 |
| Gain on sale of undeveloped leases | (83,363) | (449,890) | (114,523) |
| Interest expense | 260,177 | 1,335,409 | 1,317,887 |
| General and administrative expense | 384,218 | 575,364 | 544,025 |
| Amortization of debt discount and issuance expense | 30,230 | 89,863 | 89,863 |
| | $2,758,254 | $5,570,973 | $5,932,784 |
| Net income | $263,429 | $470,119 | $323,533 |
| Number of shares of common stock outstanding at the close of each period | 3,731,834 | 3,749,934 | 3,728,000 |
| Earnings per shares of common stock outstanding at the closs of each period (no dividends have been paid) (average number of stockholders, 6,100) | $.07 | $.13 | $.09 |

were liquidated. The market price in many instances would be as much as 60 per cent of the eventual liquidation value. For example, prior to Claremont's negotiations on the sale of the company, their common stock bid and asked prices on the over-the-counter market were bid, high 5-7/8, low $3\frac{1}{2}$ asked high 6, low 3-3/4. After negotiation had been started the bid and asked range was bid, high $6\frac{1}{4}$, low 6, asked, high $6\frac{1}{2}$ low 6-3/8. Mr. Wells knew that Houston normally demanded a return of 15 per cent on the money they invested. He did not know, however, in this case whether this percentage might be appropriate since the investment was so much larger than the customary capital budgeting expenditure. He wondered if using a calculated cost of capital might change the price considerably. In any event, he decided that he would make a bid which Houston could live with and not worry about what their competitors would bid.

**EXHIBIT V**

**Claremont Petroleum Company**
**Balance Sheet**

|  | Dec. 31, 1961 | Dec. 31, 1960 |
|---|---|---|
| *Assets* | | |
| Current assets | | |
| Cash | $309,035 | $555,187 |
| Accounts receivable | | |
| Oil and gas sales | 561,782 | 856,000 |
| Joint operators and others | 81,721 | — |
| Inventory of tubular goods and equipment, at average cost | 208,916 | 287,852 |
| Total current assets | $1,161,454 | $1,699,039 |
| Property and equipment, at cost | | |
| Oil and gas producing properties, wells, and equipment | $37,811,845 | — |
| Undeveloped leases and royalties | 1,397,694 | 38,329,687 |
| Other property and equipment | 617,930 | — |
|  | $39,827,469 | $38,329,687 |
| Less—Reserves for depreciation and depletion | 6,076,446 | 4,298,712 |
|  | $33,751,023 | $34,030,975 |
| Other assets | | |
| Unamortized portion of debt discount and issuance expense | $1,168,224 | $1,276,992 |
| Deposits, prepayments, other | 28,603 | — |
|  | $1,196,827 | $1,276,992 |
| Total assets | $36,109,304 | $37,007,006 |

| | | |
|---|---|---|
| *Liabilities* | | |
| Current liabilities | | |
| Accounts payable | $510,820 | $701,247 |
| Accrued liabilities (including $150,493 accrued | | |
| interest) | 283,473 | — |
| Amount due within one year on long-term debt | 367,600 | 1,819,000 |
| Total current liabilities | $1,161,893 | $2,520,247 |
| Long-term debt, secured by property and equipment | | |
| 6% note payable to a bank | $3,375,000 | $4,475,000 |
| 6½% notes payable to various trusts and | | |
| insurance companies | 7,500,000 | 7,500,000 |
| 6½% sinking fund subordinated debentures | | |
| due January 1, 1975 | 6,500,000 | 6,500,000 |
| 4% and 5½% loans to acquire and develop certain | | |
| properties (less $367,000 due within one year) | 1,029,346 | 1,128,200 |
| Total long-term debt | $18,404,346 | $19,603,200 |
| Proceeds from sale of future production, being | | |
| credited to income as oil and gas as produced | $1,379,633 | — |
| Stockholders' investment | | |
| Common stock $ 1.00 par value : authorized, | | |
| 10,000,000 shares ; issued and outstanding | | |
| 3,728,000 shares | $3,728,000 | $3,749,934 |
| Reacquired stock, 17,966 shares | | (69,600) |
| Capital surplus | 10,243,553 | 10,315,235 |
| Retained earnings (restricted as to payment of | | |
| cash dividends) | 1,191,879 | 887,990 |
| | $15,163,432 | $14,883,559 |
| Total liabilities and equity | $36,109,304 | $37,007,006 |

## Part VII

# SPECIAL
# PROBLEMS

# Executive Stock Option

**39**

AIR CONTROL
PRODUCTS, INC.

On June 22, 1960, the stockholders of Air Control Products, Inc., approved a restricted stock option plan for key employees. On September 21, 1960, Mr. H. A. Keller, president of the firm, requested that 75,000 shares of stock which were to be optioned be listed with the company's present outstanding stock on the New York Stock Exchange. The request was made so that the company could begin distribution of the options.

Air Control Products, Inc. was formed in 1951 in Miami, Florida, by Mr. H. A. Keller to manufacture jalousies, windows, and doors. The company was almost immediately successful, and sales and profits so indicated. Exhibit I shows the company's growth from 1955–1960. By 1960 the company had substantially diversified, and the product line included the manufacturing and selling of jalousies, windows, doors, awning-type glass windows, aluminum door thresholds, carpets, and aluminum furniture. In addition, the company also distributed glass and fibre glass, dairy and food products. Its principal offices were located in Miami with operations in 14 states and nationwide distribution of its products. Exhibits II and III show the company's current financial position.

By 1960 the company had grown so that in addition to the board of directors and company officers, there were several other key employees including managers of divisions. The board of directors believed that a stock option plan would be beneficial in creating greater bonds between the employees who would be most instrumental in the future success of the company and its stockholders.

The purpose of the stock option and important provisions of the plan approved by the board were as follows:

1. *Purpose.* This plan is intended as an incentive and to encourage stock ownership by certain key employees of Air Control

**271**

Products, Inc., and/or its various subsidiaries (the "Company") in order to provide such employees with a proprietary interest or to increase their proprietary interest in the Company's success and to encourage them to remain in the employ of the Company.

2. *Administration.* The Board of Directors of the Company (the "Board") shall administer the Plan and are authorized, subject to the provisions of the Plan, from time to time to establish such rules and regulations as it may deem appropriate for the proper administration of the Plan, and to make such determinations under, and such interpretations of, and to take such steps in connection with, the Plan or the options granted thereunder as it may deem necessary or advisable.

3. *Stock.* The stock to be optioned under the Plan shall be shares of the Company's Common Stock of the par value of fifty cents (50¢) per share (the "Stock"), and is presently unissued stock of the Company. The total amount of Stock on which options may be granted under the Plan shall not exceed 75,000 shares. The shares involved in the unexercised portions of any terminated or expired options under the Plan may again be subjected to options under the Plan, but there shall be no arrangement for cancellation of any option accompanied by a new option, to the same optionee, at a lower price.

4. *Award of Options.*The Board of Directors of the Company at any time and from time to time prior to August 1, 1965, may grant options to such key employees of the Company as it may, in its sole discretion, select and for such numbers of shares as it shall designate, but no one optionee shall receive options under the Plan covering an aggregate of more than 2,500 shares. The date on which an option shall be granted shall be the date of the Board's authorization of such grant or such later date as may be determined by the Board at the time such grant is authorized. Any individual may receive more than one option.

No member of the Board or any officer of the parent corporation, Air Control Products, Inc., shall be eligible to receive an option under the Plan.

5. *Price.* In the case of each option granted under this Plan the option price shall be the higher of:

   (a) 95% of the average of the highest price and the lowest price at which the Stock shall have been sold in the regular way on the New York Stock Exchange during the full week beginning on a Monday and ending on a Friday, inclusive, immediately preceding the date of the grant of such option;

  or

   (b) 95% of the average of the highest price and the lowest price at which the stock shall have been sold in the regular way on the New York Stock Exchange on the date of the grant of such option.

6. *Term of Options.* No option granted under this plan may be exercised prior to two years from the date of the grant.

Any provision of this Plan notwithstanding, no option shall be exercised in any amount later than ten years from the date such option shall have been granted.

7. *Stock Dividend, Reclassification, Merger, Consolidation, and so forth.* The total amount of Stock on which options may be granted under the Plan and option rights (both as to the number of shares of Stock and the option price) shall be appropriately adjusted for any increase or decrease in the number

of outstanding shares of Common Stock of the Company resulting from payment of a stock dividend on the Common Stock, provided such stock dividend, at any one time, is in excess of 20 per cent on the Common Stock outstanding. In the event such a stock dividend shall be 20 per cent or less, no adjustment shall be made on options or option rights granted under the Plan.

Anything contained herein to the contrary notwithstanding, upon the dissolution or liquidation of the Company, or upon any merger or consolidation in which the Company is not the surviving corporation, each option granted under this Plan shall terminate; but if a period of two years from the date of the grant of any such option shall have expired, the optionee shall have the right, immediately prior to such dissolution, liquidation, merger, or consolidation, to exercise his option in full to the extent not theretofore exercised.

The foregoing adjustments and the manner of the application of the foregoing provisions shall be determined by the Board in its sole discretion.

8. *Amendment, Modification, and Termination of the Plan.* The Board, at any time may terminate; and at any time and from time to time may amend or modify, the Plan; provided, however, that no such action of the Board, without approval of the stockholders, may (a) increase the total amount of stock on which options may be granted under the Plan, or the total amount of Stock which may be optioned to one optionee, (b) change the manner of determining the option price, (c) withdraw the administration of the Plan from the Board, or (d) permit any person while an officer of the parent company, Air Control Products, Inc., or a member of the Board to be eligible to receive an option under the Plan; and provided further, that no amendment, modification, or termination of the Plan shall in any manner affect any option theretofore granted under the Plan without the consent of the optionee or the transferee of the option.

9. *Indemnification and Exculpation.* Each person who is or shall have been a member of the Board shall be indemnified and held harmless by the Company against and from any and all loss, cost, liability, or expense that may be imposed upon or reasonably incurred by him in connection with or resulting from any claim, action, suit, or proceeding to which he may be or become a party or in which he may be or become involved by reason of any action taken or failure to act under this Plan and against and from any and all amounts paid by him in settlement thereof (with the Company's written approval) or paid by him in satisfaction of a judgment in any such action, suit, or proceeding, except a judgment in favor of the Company based upon a finding of his lack of good faith; subject, however, to the condition that upon the institution of any claim, action, suit, or proceeding against him, he shall in writing give the Company an opportunity, at its own expense, to handle and defend the same before he undertakes to handle and defend it on his own behalf. The foregoing right of indemnification shall not be exclusive of any other right to which such person may be entitled as a matter of law or otherwise, or any power that the Company may have to indemnify him or hold him harmless.[1]

---

[1]For the full details of the plan see "Listing Application, New York Stock Exchange," A-19081, September 21, 1960.

## QUESTIONS

1. What is the purpose of stock options?
2. Evaluate the important pros and cons of restricted stock options.
3. Of what potential cash value is a 2,500 share option given on October 1, 1960 at a price of *9.62 per share* (market price 10.8) to an optionee of Air Control Products, Inc.?
4. What are the principal provisions of a restricted stock option *today*? (See Prentice-Hall or Commerce Clearing House tax guides.)
5. Evaluate the Air Control Products, Inc., Option Plan from the viewpoint of an outside stockholder who holds 1,000 shares. Should he have voted for this plan?

### EXHIBIT I

**Air Control Products, Inc.**
**Selected Financial Data**
**1955-1960**

| | | | | | | Price Range | |
|---|---|---|---|---|---|---|---|
| Years | Sales | Net Income | Shares | E/S | D/S | Hi | Lo |
| 1960 | 31,243,000 | 977,000 | 1,326,656* | .74 | .50 | $20\frac{1}{4}$ | $9\frac{7}{8}$ |
| 1959 | 27,707,000 | 1,688,000 | 1,326,656 | 1.26 | .50 | $22\frac{3}{4}$ | 16† |
| 1958 | 18,396,000 | 1,352,000 | 663,328 | 2.04 | .65 | 28 | $11\frac{3}{8}$ |
| 1957 | 15,385,000 | 962,000 | 613,960 | 1.57 | .60+5% Stock | $12\frac{1}{4}$ | $7\frac{1}{8}$ |
| 1956 | 10,297,000 | 626,000 | 611,400 | 1.02 | $.52\frac{1}{2}$ | 9 | $6\frac{7}{8}$ |
| 1955 | 6,289,000 | 447,000 | 600,000 | .74 | .20 | — | — |

*2,545 shareholders on July 22.
†After stock split; before 39 1/2—26 1/2.

### EXHIBIT II

**Air Control Products, Inc.**
**Income Statement**
**July 31,**
**(In Thousands)**

| | 1960 | 1961 |
|---|---|---|
| Sales | $31,243 | $27,707 |
| Cost of sales | 22,311 | 18,923 |
| Selling and general expenses | 6,534 | 5,967 |
| Operating profit | 2,398 | 2,817 |
| Other income net | 101 | 82 |
| Total income | 2,499 | 2,899 |
| Interest | 385 | 156 |
| Fire loss | 78 | — |
| Loss on equipment repossessed | 119 | — |
| Income taxes | 940 | 1,056 |
| Net income | $977 | 1,687 |
| Dividends | 663 | 514 |

EXHIBIT III

**Air Control Products, Inc.**
**Balance Sheet as of July 31**
**(In Thousands)**

|  | 1960 | 1959 |
|---|---|---|
| *Assets* |  |  |
| Cash | $2,212 | $1,406 |
| Receivables, net | 5,283 | 5,436 |
| Inventories | 5,729 | 5,311 |
| Prepayments | 166 | 105 |
| Other current assets | 191 | 36 |
| Total current assets | 13,581 | 12,294 |
| Net Property | 1,240 | 1,225 |
| Misc. receivables | 219 | 97 |
| Deferred charges | 113 | — |
| Good will | 55 | 73 |
| Total assets | $15,208 | $13,689 |
| *Liabilities and capital* |  |  |
| Accounts payable | $1,836 | $2,079 |
| Notes payable | 1,671 | 2,223 |
| Accruals | 268 | 379 |
| Dividends payable | 166 | 166 |
| Income taxes payable | 669 | 757 |
| Total current liabilities | 4,610 | 5,604 |
| Notes payable* | 4,500 | 2,300 |
| Common stock ($ .50 par)† | 663 | 663 |
| Paid-in capital | 1,669 | 1,669 |
| Retained earnings | 3,766 | 3,453 |
| Total Liabilities and capital | $15,208 | $13,689 |

*6 1/4 notes payable $300,000 annually to December 1,1974.
†Includes 652,090 shares owned or controlled by H. A. Keller, Chairman of Board and President.

## Dividend Policy

**40**

AMERICAN HOIST
AND DERRICK CO.

Mr. John E. Carroll, president of the American Hoist and Derrick Co., of St. Paul, Minnesota, was contemplating his dividend recommendation at the next board of directors meeting. The board would be meeting on February 15, 1964. Because the results of the previous year had been the finest in the company's history, Mr. Carroll believed that some change in the present dividend would be needed. In addition, he wondered whether he should continue giving a stock dividend.

**History of the Company**

American Hoist and Derrick was founded as a partnership in 1882 to service freight elevators. By 1900 the partnership expanded by building derricks, locomotive cranes, hand hoists, and pile drivers. During World War II the company concentrated on winches and gantry-mounted hoisting machines. Most of these were used during the war by the U. S. Maritime Commission. By the end of the war, American Hoist and Derrick was producing 80 per cent of all the winches for ship construction in the United States. The company built approximately 50,000 winches during World War II. But by the end of the war almost all of the orders for deck equipment, winches, and shipyard cranes were cancelled; fortunately a huge civilian demand had been built up. This demand was for such equipment as locomotive cranes, hoists, derricks, and standard tools of the construction trade. By 1951 the company, under the new direction of J. E. Carroll, began intensive marketing of crawlers, crane shovels, and truck cranes. In addition to substantial orders from the civilian market, they got orders from the government which helped them get a strong foothold in this line. By 1955 the company began acquiring other companies. During the subsequent years it had added several companies, including Lebus Corporation, the McKissick Products Corporation, and the Conveyor Company, and also had organized Machinery Investment Corporation, a captive financial subsidiary used to finance dealers and purchasers of American Hoist and Derrick equipment. These acquisitions broadened considerably the product line of American Hoist and Derrick. During the year 1963 the manufacturing mix was divided as follows:

56% Heavy equipment including crawlers, truck cranes, locomotive cranes, hoists, derricks, drag line shovels.

17% Wire rope, fittings, blocks, hooks, bolts, oil field tools, and forge equipment.

15% Asphalt mixing and paving equipment, materials handling, conveyor systems, sweepers.

12% Repair parts.

Towards the end of 1963 the company obtained two contracts from the government with an approximate total value of $30,000,000. These contracts called for the construction of 890 truck-mounted cranes, with both hoist and truck to be manufactured by the company. Actual delivery of completed vehicles was expected to start in April, 1964, at the rate of two per day. This contract was expected to continue on until the summer of 1966.

American Hoist and Derrick had not ignored the overseas market. Approximately 20 per cent of all business was done overseas. The company sold both overseas and in the United States through independent distributors. The company's backlog of orders was approximately $20,000,000 as of January, 1964. Of special interest to Mr. Carroll was the company's interest in development. Fifty engineers were employed in designing, developing, and improving the present equipment. Approximately 82 per cent of the company's sales volume during the year 1963 were items which had been developed over the last ten years. Mr. Carroll planned to continue to emphasize development of new products.

At one time the industry in which American Hoist and Derrick operates was highly competitive. In 1952 approximately 27 companies were making products competitive with American Hoist and Derrick, but by January, 1964, only nine remained. Some of the companies had been bought out. American Hoist and Derrick, for instance, had bought out three. Some had quit voluntarily. This was the case in several large companies where a subsidiary was manufacturing competitive equipment and found it could not make a profit and, therefore, switched its equipment to another line. Several of the companies simply went bankrupt.

American Hoist and Derrick considered its product line to be in the commercial size area as opposed to products in the large excavating area. It did not produce any products for large excavations, such as tractors, bulldozers, or earth movers. In the commercial sizes American Hoist and Derrick was considered the largest company with approximately 23 per cent to 24 per cent of the total sales in this area. It did not, therefore, consider itself competitive with such companies as Caterpillar Tractor Company or Allis-Chalmers Manufacturing Co. American Hoist and Derrick employed approximately 3,400 people and had plants in ten states. The principal plant, located in St. Paul, had 700,000 square feet of floor area.

### Dividend Record

From 1954–1959 American Hoist and Derrick paid a stable dividend of $1.20 per share. Since the business was cyclical, this tended to vary the payout ratio from 51 per cent to 70 per cent. By 1959, however, Mr. Carroll had become very disturbed over the dividend policy. He believed that a payout of 70 per cent was adversely affecting the cash position of the company. In addition, the high payout prevented the company from continuing its growth. He did not think that the present dividend was necessary in light of the payout ratios of other companies. At the same time he noticed that the high payout ratio had not prevented the stock from dropping to $16 in 1959, with the corresponding yield of 71 per cent. As a result in the second quarter of 1960, he requested that the board lower the dividend rate to 60¢ a share. In order to prepare the stockholders for such a drastic cut, Mr. Carroll sent out a general letter to all stockholders explaining the reason for the cut. He explained it as follows:

1. The company's recent acquisition of a distressed firm whose outlook was highly uncertain meant a period of consolidation in which the company might need all possible cash. Until such time as this acquisition was fully digested, a high dividend rate was not possible.
2. The company's attitude towards growth had changed from its old policy of slow, modest internal growth to more rapid growth both internal and external.
3. A stable dividend policy was not appropriate in the capital goods market. Stable dividends in other types of industries might work well, but where a firm was faced with a cyclical demand such a dividend policy could invite unnecessary problems.

Mr. Carroll had picked 60¢ as the dividend rate on an arbitrary basis. This amounted to half of the old dividend rate and represented a payout of approximately 44 per cent of the earnings. Mr. Carroll realized when looking back that had he known the earnings would have held up so well in 1960 he would not have cut the dividend as far as he did. He did feel, however, that the 60¢ dividend would give the firm a considerable amount of cash with which to continue its growth.

Reaction by the stockholders to the president's letter and the dividend cut was generally quite favorable. Management felt that a cut in dividends had long been overdue. Several stockholders wrote and suggested that the firm could just as well cut out the dividend entirely as far as they were concerned. This attitude was further attested to in 1962 when the dividend was raised to 80¢; some stockholders wrote letters stating that the dividend raise was unnecessary. A few stockholders complained about the cut. Investment bankers as a group did not like the cut at all. However, the effect on the stock price of the cut appeared to be minor in Mr. Carroll's opinion.

## Stockholders

The stockholders were composed of three groups—large stockholders, management, and small stockholders. Three blocks of stock of 6 per cent, 5 per cent, and 4 per c .t were held by individuals. Approximately 18 per cent of the stock was held by management; the remaining shares were divided in small units among 2,200 stockholders. A large number of employees owned stock which .hey purchased through an employee-purchase plan. In the past Mr. Carroll had been impressed with the interest of his employees in the company. Many of them attended the annual stockholders' meeting and took an active interest in the progress of the company. Mr. Carroll noticed that ownership of stock by employees gave them a certain respect among their fellow employees and encouraged more employees to own stock and attend stockholder meetings.

## The Stock Dividend

When the dividend rate was reduced in 1960, the company also declared a 3 per cent stock dividend. By capitalizing this at the market rate, stockholders who needed cash could sell the additional stock received and get approximately the same dividend rate that they had received before. No stock dividends were given, however, in 1961 or 1962. A study of the stock transfer records indicated that very few stockholders sold their stock dividends.

In 1963 another 3 per cent stock dividend was issued. Although Mr. Carroll realized that few of his competitors gave stock dividends and although he appreciated the arguments against stock dividends, he thought they offered cash to those who wanted it and appreciation to those who held the additional shares. He further believed that the market made no movement in response to a modest stock dividend. For the wealthy stockholder the 3 per cent stock dividend was a source of tax avoidance since it would not be taxed until realized. This feeling was verified by many stockholders in high tax brackets who informed Mr. Carroll of their pleasure in receiving a stock dividend. He realized that a stock dividend might be of little value to the small stockholder; however, here again he was very pleased to see very few of them sold their stock dividends, which strongly indicated to him that they did not need the cash dividend and were pleased that the company would continue to hold the money and reinvest it for their benefit.

As further support for issuing a stock dividend, Mr. Carroll developed what he called the Rate of Dividend Inflation Theory.

Mr. Carroll noted that the price of labor went up approximately 3 per cent a year and that prices of the company's general products lines also advanced approximately 3 per cent a year. He noticed, with some chagrin, however, that some of his competitors were adjusting their prices upward at a rate of from 6 to 8 per cent a year. On the basis of these advances in costs and prices he thought that the stockholder also deserved a 3 per cent raise, and he believed that the stock dividend was the best method to accomplish this. In addition, he noticed that giving a 3 per cent stock dividend produced a compounding effect if the cash dividend rate was held constant. An individual receiving a 3 per cent stock dividend annually would start receiving larger dividends even though the rate itself had not changed.

### Factors Determining Cash Dividends

Mr. Carroll believed he could separate the problem of cash dividend from the problem of stock dividend, although he knew they were indirectly related. Cash dividends had always been of significance in cyclical industries, and the price of stock seemed in many ways dependent on the dividend. In reading on the subject he had been impressed with the fact that cash dividends were the most important determiner of the market price of stock, and that a high correlation existed between high dividend rates and high stock prices. He did not underestimate the importance of high stock prices, and this problem would become especially acute since the company would probably float an issue of stock around July. Mr. Carroll had also noted that some theorists felt that no correlation whatsoever existed between dividends and the market price of stock and that one dividend was as good as another. He wondered if he could determine the validity of either idea, and for that purpose he had his finance department prepare a summary comparison of his company with those of its competitors. (See Exhibit III.)

The original reduction in the company's dividend rate was made to conserve cash. The present plans for the company called for continued expansion both internally and externally. For the next year, however, there were no immediate plans for acquisitions; still the rapidly increasing sales would continue to place a strain on the cash balances. For the year ending November 30, 1964, the company estimated its sales would reach approximately $66 million with after-tax profits of $2.1 million. This increase in sales plus an equal one in the following year would place an impossible strain on the cash balance if additional funds were not obtained externally. Paying dividends then appeared to be the equivalent of asking the stockholders for money and then partially returning the money to them less taxes paid to the government. If the company simply retained more earnings and sold less stock, the stockholders would appear to be better off by the amount of the taxes saved.

While a new issue of stock was not the only avenue for acquiring new money, Mr. Carroll felt that the company's debt-equity ratio was too high and had to be lowered. Mr. Carroll planned to obtain approximately $4.5 million in new equity capital in the middle of the year, which would bring the debt-equity ratio into the 30 per cent range. He thought that the present high leverage maintained by the company might have served to depress the price of the company's stock. He did not think, however, that the investor paid any attention to Machinery Investment Corporation, the company's wholly owned unconsolidated financial subsidiary when considering the problem of leverage. (See Exhibit IV.)

The exact amount of dividends to pay each period had been a recurring problem for American Hoist's management and board of directors. Any reduction at the present time was out of the question. At the same time the general feeling among management was that a stable amount or stable payout was simply a "no-think" policy which had no place in a cyclical industry. What was correct appeared to be a dividend which would result in maximum stock prices. Although management had been working on this problem in an attempt to find a satisfactory answer, results so far had been quite discouraging.

## Factors Determining Stock Dividends

The dilemma facing Mr. Carroll with respect to the amount of cash dividends to be paid was no greater than the dilemma about stock dividends. He wanted to continue to pay a stock dividend of 3 per cent, but he believed that he would have to indicate what future plans he anticipated in this area. He knew the board of directors would want to take this into account in determining the cash dividend to be paid. Mr. Carroll based his desire for the stock dividend on two factors. First, stock dividends had been received very well by the stockholders, and the consensus seemed to indicate that they wanted more. In fact, they appeared to prefer stock dividends to cash dividends. This conclusion seemed borne out by the other companies that had tried similar experiments, the most notable one being Citizens Utility. The second factor was the problem of inflation. Mr. Carroll deeply believed that a 3 per cent stock dividend might be an excellent answer to the problem of inflation. Although the present rate of inflation did not appear to be 3 per cent, certainly the rate had been that or better in the past and might again be that in the future. Exactly what the true rate of inflation was Mr. Carroll was not sure, nor was he sure how it should be measured (see Exhibit V for one measure).

While Mr. Carroll planned to recommend the 3 per cent stock dividend for this year, he decided he would have to lay out the advantages of the dividend as well as the number of years he believed that dividends could be paid. He knew he would have to answer questions from at least one of the directors who could be expected to echo the thinking of investment bankers and investment analysts. These people consistently opposed stock dividends.

Mr. Carroll was still uncertain about his recommendation on the cash dividend. Although he was reluctant to raise the dividend, he knew the ever-increasing sales and profits made continuation of the present dividend difficult. The investment people unanimously wanted the dividend raised, for they believed it would improve the performance of the stock. No such pressure, however, had been received from the stockholders. Whether the stockholders demanded dividends or not, however, Mr. Carroll wanted to give them the best possible price on their stock; and this might well

### EXHIBIT I

#### American Hoist and Derrick Company
#### Income Statements
#### (In Thousands)

|  | Pro forma 6 mon. ending 5/23/64* | Years ending November 30 | | |
|---|---|---|---|---|
|  |  | 1963 | 1962 | 1961 |
| Revenue | $30,400 | $48,970 | $42,927 | $37,753 |
| Costs and expenses |  |  |  |  |
| Cost of products sold | — | $41,769 | $37,001 | $32,346 |
| Selling and administrative | — | 3,736 | 3,534 | 3,255 |
| Interest | — | 575 | 528 | 504 |
| Miscellaneous | — | 38 | 56 | 41 |
| Total expenses | $29,070 | $46,118 | $41,119 | $36,146 |
| Earnings before taxes on income | $1,330 | $2,852 | $1,808 | $1,607 |
| Taxes on income‡ | 675 | 1,225 | 460 | 510 |
|  | $655 | $1,627 | $1,348 | $1,097 |
| Net earnings of machinery |  |  |  |  |
| Investment corporation | 50 | 105 | 84 | 108 |
| Net earnings | $705 | $1,732 | $1,432 | $1,205 |
| Net earnings per share of capital stock[a] | $.78† | $2.08 | $1.75 | $1.51 |
| Dividends declared |  |  |  |  |
| Cash |  | .80 | .65 | .60 |
| Capital stock |  | 3% |  |  |

*6 months 12/1/63–5/23/64.
†Earnings for same period in 1963 were $0.58.
‡Includes income of American Hoist and Derrick only.
[a]Includes earnings of American Hoist and Derrick Company and Machinery Investment Corporation.

involve an increase in the cash dividend. He decided, therefore, that he would prepare a summary of his findings in this matter and from this summary make a specific recommendation.

**EXHIBIT II**

**American Hoist and Derrick Company**
**Balance Sheets**

|  | Pro Forma 5/23/64 | 11/30/63 | 11/30/62 | 11/30/61 |
|---|---|---|---|---|
| *Assets* |  |  |  |  |
| Cash | 2,000,000 | $3,530,915 | $2,267,533 | $3,117,780 |
| Accounts receivable, net | 8,215,000 | 5,219,578 | 3,676,388 | 3,575,812 |
| Inventories | 21,950,000 | 19,321,321 | 17,264,380 | 14,260,671 |
| Prepaid expenses | 275,000 | 205,644 | 222,691 | 294,963 |
| Total current assets | 32,440,000 | $28,277,458 | $23,430,992 | $21,249,226 |
| Investment | 2,200,000 | $2,151,850 | $1,845,944 | $1,761,841 |
| Cash value of life insurance | 400,000 | 395,300 | 333,900 | 325,400 |
| Patents and patterns | 65,000 | 76,549 | 106,184 | 135,802 |
| Net plant | 7,600,000 | 7,493,630 | 7,122,110 | 7,172,610 |
| Total assets | $42,705,000 | $38,394,787 | $32,839,130 | $30,644,883 |
| *Liabilities* |  |  |  |  |
| Accounts payable | $7,240,000 | $3,448,480 | $3,022,596 | $1,141,221 |
| Accruals | 3,540,000 | 3,170,761 | 2,649,058 | 2,279,312 |
| Taxes payables | 1,100,000 | 1,285,850 | 421,475 | 575,239 |
| Current install. on long-term debt | 20,000 | 20,000 | 527,000 | 527,000 |
| Total current liabilities | $11,900,000 | $7,925,091 | $6,620,129 | $4,522,772 |
| Long-term debt | 9,600,000 | $9,600,000 | $6,597,000 | $7,104,000 |
| Purchase contract | 90,000 | 100,000 | 120,000 | 140,000 |
| Total liabilities | $21,590,000 | $17,625,091 | $13,337,129 | $11,766,772 |
| Capital stock (stated value $10) | 8,413,000 | 8,331,090 | 7,960,420 | 8,185,130 |
| Paid-in capital | 850,000 | 819,837 | 595,909 | 670,551 |
| Retained earnings | 11,852,000 | 11,618,769 | 10,945,672 | 10,022,430 |
| Total net worth | $21,115,000 | $20,769,696 | $19,502,001 | $18,878,111 |
| Total liabilities and net worth | $42,705,000 | $38,394,787 | $32,839,130 | $30,644,883 |

EXHIBIT III

Financial Comparison of American Hoist and Derrick Company With Selected Competitors

| Year | Cash Flow Per Share | Earnings Per Share | Dividends Per Share | Yield | Price Earnings Ratio | Payout Ratio | Capitalized Stock Dividend | Debt/Equity Ratio |
|---|---|---|---|---|---|---|---|---|
| American Hoist & Derrick | | | | | | | | |
| 1963 | $3.07 | $2.08 | $.80 | 4.9% | 7.7× | 38% | $.48 | 46.7% |
| 1962 | 2.81 | 1.75 | .65 | 5.05 | 7.4 | 37 | — | 34.4 |
| 1961 | 2.60 | 1.51 | .60 | 4.6 | 8.7 | 39.7 | — | 38.4 |
| 1960 | 2.75 | 1.71 | .75 | 5.04 | 8.7 | 43.8 | .44 | 42.5 |
| 1959 | 2.58 | 1.70 | 1.20 | 5.8 | 12.1 | 70.6 | — | 38.8 |
| Bucyrus-Erie Company | | | | | | | | |
| 1963 | 3.21 | 1.71 | .60 | 3.47 | 10.12 | 35 | None | 32 |
| 1962 | 3.06 | 1.25 | .20 | 1.18 | 13.60 | 16 | | 29 |
| 1961 | 2.57 | 1.12 | nil | nil | 17.30 | nil | | 21 |
| 1960 | 6.80 | 5.33 | nil | nil | 3.48 | nil | | 39 |
| 1959 | 1.94 | .94 | nil | nil | 30.12 | nil | | 33 |
| Koehring | | | | | | | | |
| 1963 | 3.65 | 2.30 | .85 | 4.1 | 8.8 | 36.9 | None | 36 |
| 1962 | 2.66 | 1.71 | .40 | 3.4 | 6.8 | 23.4 | | 39.8 |
| 1961 | 1.70 | .71 | .30 | 2.7 | 15.8 | 42.3 | | 42.2 |
| 1960 | 1.11 | .04 | .60 | 4.9 | 30.6 | 150.0 | | 71.6 |
| 1959 | 2.44 | 1.37 | .50 | 3.0 | 12.1 | 36.5 | | 25.8 |
| Northwest Engineering | | | | | | | | |
| 1963 | 5.22 | 4.50 | 2.65 | 8.2 | 7.2 | 58.9 | None | None |
| 1962 | 5.37 | 4.65 | 2.20 | 7.9 | 6.0 | 47.3 | | |
| 1961 | 3.60 | 2.89 | 1.25 | 4.2 | 10.2 | 43.3 | | |
| 1960 | 4.04 | 3.34 | 1.80 | 5.3 | 10.3 | 53.9 | | |
| 1959 | 5.69 | 5.00 | 2.50 | 6.3 | 8.0 | 50.0 | | |

| Year | Cash Flow Per Share | Earnings Per Share | Dividends Per Share | Yield | Price Earnings Ratio | Payout Ratio | Capitalized Stock Dividend | Debt/Equity Ratio |
|---|---|---|---|---|---|---|---|---|
| Link Belt Company | | | | | | | | |
| 1963 | $6.51 | $4.06 | $2.40 | 4.63% | 12.78× | 59% | None | None |
| 1962 | 5.77 | 3.20 | 2.40 | 5.07 | 14.80 | 75 | | |
| 1961 | 4.98 | 2.70 | 2.40 | 4.75 | 18.70 | 89 | | |
| 1960 | 5.59 | 3.25 | 2.40 | 4.57 | 16.15 | 74 | | |
| 1959 | 5.73 | 3.65 | 2.70 | 4.15 | 17.81 | 74 | | |
| Baldwin-Lima-Hamilton | | | | | | | | |
| 1963 | 1.37 | .24 | .40 | 3.03 | 54.95 | 166 | None | None |
| 1962 | 1.78 | .45 | .40 | 2.64 | 33.61 | 89 | | |
| 1961 | 1.02 | .33 | .45 | 2.82 | 48.30 | 136 | | |
| 1960 | 1.10 | .31 | .60 | 4.19 | 46.17 | 194 | | |
| 1959 | 1.95 | 1.17 | .60 | 3.69 | 13.89 | 51 | | |
| Barber Greene | | | | | | | | |
| 1963 | 2.84 | 1.66 | .84 | 5.7 | 8.8 | 50.6 | None | 27.6 |
| 1962 | 2.62 | 1.38 | .84 | 5.4 | 11.2 | 60.9 | | 30.7 |
| 1961 | 2.30 | 1.37 | .84 | 5.9 | 10.4 | 60.9 | | 16.3 |
| 1960 | 2.01 | 1.09 | .84 | 5.9 | 12.9 | 77.1 | | 18.4 |
| 1959 | 2.05 | 1.26 | .61 | N.A. | N.A. | 48.4 | | 24.6 |

**EXHIBIT IV**

**Machinery Investment Corporation**
**Balance Sheet**

|  | 11/30/63 |
|---|---|
| *Assets* | |
| Cash | $687,367 |
| Accounts receivable | 10,324,877 |
| Accrued interest | 59,965 |
| Current Assets | $11,072,209 |
| | |
| *Liabilities and net worth* | |
| Notes payable | $8,629,824 |
| Interest | 8,649 |
| Commissions | 132,176 |
| Taxes payable | 149,710 |
| Current liabilities | $8,920,359 |
| Notes payable parent | $1,300,000 |
| Capital stock | 150,000 |
| Retained earnings | 701,850 |
| Total liabilities and net worth | $11,072,209 |

**Income Statement**

| | |
|---|---|
| Revenues | $647,178 |
| Expenses | 402,272 |
| Earnings before taxes | $244,906 |
| Taxes | 140,000 |
| Net earnings | $104,906 |

**EXHIBIT V**

**Rate of Inflation as Measured by the Commodity Price**
**Index During Post Korean Period** * †

| | |
|---|---|
| 1963 | 106.7 |
| 1962 | 105.4 |
| 1961 | 104.2 |
| 1960 | 103.1 |
| 1959 | 101.5 |
| 1958 | 100.7 |
| 1957 | 98.0 |
| 1956 | 94.7 |
| 1955 | 93.3 |
| 1954 | 93.6 |
| 1953 | 93.2 |

*The compound rate of inflation was 1.3 per cent annually with a correlation in excess of 0.90.
†*Source: Federal Reserve Bulletin.*

**EXHIBIT VI**

**American Hoist and Derrick Company**
**Price Range for Stocks**

|  | Bid Price | | Asked Price | |
|---|---|---|---|---|
|  | High | Low | High | Low |
| 1959 | $23\frac{1}{4}$ | 18 | $23\frac{3}{4}$ | $18\frac{3}{4}$ |
| 1960 | 19 | 11 | $19\frac{1}{2}$ | $11\frac{1}{2}$ |
| 1961 | $14\frac{3}{4}$ | $11\frac{1}{2}$ | $15\frac{1}{4}$ | $11\frac{3}{4}$ |
| 1962 | $15\frac{1}{2}$ | $10\frac{1}{4}$ | 16 | $10\frac{3}{4}$ |
| 1963 | $18\frac{1}{2}$ | $13\frac{3}{4}$ | $18\frac{3}{4}$ | $14\frac{1}{4}$ |

## Proxy Battle

## 41

On July 5, 1964, Mr. J. C. Wilson, a Chicago businessman, was considering what action he should take with regard to two different proxies which he had received. One proxy came from the management of the Telex Corporation and the second from a group known as the Telex Investors Policy Committee (TIPCO). Mr. Wilson had bought 500 shares of Telex at $20 per share; subsequently, the stock had risen to $45 per share but then had fallen precipitously to $4 per share. The major fall had occurred during May of 1962; prior to that time, however, Mr. Wilson had sold 200 shares at $40 per share so that in July, 1964, he owned 300 shares, which he had held in the belief that they would be a good long-run investment. He had been troubled by the fact that the company had not grown as he had hoped; consequently, he was uncertain which proxy he should sign. He had received a considerable amount of material from both sides in the proxy fight and knew that he must now make his final decision as to which group might give the company the best long-run chance of success and which should, therefore, receive his proxy.

TELEX, INCORPORATED

### History

The Telex Corporation was formed in 1940, in Minneapolis, Minnesota, to manufacture hearing aids. Sales expanded steadily until 1956 when they reached $4,500,000. By 1958, however, gross sales had dropped to $3,000,000, and the price of Telex stock had suffered accordingly. When this depressed condition continued, the controlling stockholders were readily receptive, in February, 1959, to an offer they received for the outright sale of the company. In exchange for

98 per cent of the outstanding shares, the owners received approximately $1,000,000.

The group that bought Telex was organized by a man named Arnold J. Ryden. Mr. Ryden had negotiated for Telex with an ambitious design in mind. He planned to use the company as a nucleus around which to form, through mergers, a large corporate amalgam that would produce an extensive line of electronic devices. His hope was to duplicate the success of Litton Industries, which had expanded rapidly through acquisitions and had become a leader in the manufacture of electronic and general office equipment. Mr. Ryden believed he could provide the financial acumen to build Telex into an equivalent or greater corporate giant, and many investors, impressed by his past accomplishments, were willing to ride along with him.

### Arnold J. Ryden

Mr. Ryden, born in 1921, was a graduate of the University of Minnesota where he had majored in sociology. Later he received a Master's degree in business administration from Harvard. His career started in banking, but he soon found his true field in corporate promotion where he showed considerable skill. In 1957, he raised $600,000 to help start Control Data Corporation. Other financial ventures followed, and by 1962 he was credited with having raised over $10,000,000 to provide funds for corporate beginnings. One of his most notable promotions was Midwest Technical Development Corporation, a venture capital firm that was the second to be formed in the United States under the new Small Business Investment Company Act. This company's assets grew from $200,000 to $9,000,000 in three years and provided Ryden with the funds to obtain an interest in some twenty-two other firms, including Telex. By early 1962, Mr. Ryden's personal fortune was estimated as close to $4,000,000. But in May, 1962, Arnold Ryden's meteoric rise in the world of corporate finance leveled off and then began a long downward spiral. Two factors contributed to the change in his fortunes.

The first factor was related indirectly to the cause of Ryden's upward climb: an affluent market. The period of 1957–1962 had not been particularly good for business, but investor interest increased because of a surplus of investable funds and a few spectacular stock gains which aroused a get-rich-quick feeling in the public. This feeling was manifest in local stock market booms which hit the country from 1958 through 1961. Investors, hungry for profits and wanting to put their money to work, found a vehicle in the electronics industry. Its glamor and rapid expansion provided the catalyst; the investors provided the money. In the local markets, stock prices soared and paper profits approached fantastic highs. In three years, Control Data went from $1 to $160, and Telex went from $4 to $47; a similar story was repeated in many parts of the nation. Arnold Ryden was one of the most prominent among the men who gave the public promising media for investments and provided firms with money for expansion. As must happen to all such markets, however, values became excessively inflated, and on May 30, 1962, the local markets started to break; prices dropped back to pre-1957 levels. Hardest hit were the new, small electronic companies including Telex.

The second factor affecting Ryden's fortunes was a civil suit filed by the Securities and Exchange Commission which accused Ryden and 17 other Midwest Technical Development officers of using the company as a "vehicle for locating and discovering investment opportunities for their own personal interest." The suit made Ryden "poison" in the financial community, and although it was resolved in 1963 without any substantial penalties, the damage had been done.[1]

### Expansion of Telex

During the period 1959–1962, before the twin disasters of a breaking market and a federal lawsuit struck him, Arnold Ryden carried out a plan of expansion for Telex. In rapid succession, several companies were acquired and consolidated through merging; these companies included Waters Conley, Elco Electronics, Lumen, Ballastran, and Aemco. By 1961 the sales of Telex had reached almost $21,000,000 with assets in excess of $15,000,-000. Some of the acquisitions were distress companies with loss carry-forwards and inadequate product lines, but Ryden believed he could overcome these handicaps by extensive research and development. During this period, Telex stock was extremely active, climbing rapidly after each acquisition. Toward the end of 1961, however, problems developed. The company had borrowed heavily in an attempt to wring the last dollar out of each merger, and finally the financial structure of the coporate complex began to deteriorate. Evidences of the trouble caused a wave of stock selling, and the price of Telex stock dropped considerably. Stockholders of some of the merged companies suffered serious financial losses.

In late 1961, when Telex stock was dropping but the extent of the company's difficulties was not yet generally known, Mr. Ryden was approached by M. E. Morrow, president of Midwestern Instruments, of Tulsa, Oklahoma. Mr. Morrow's company, which manufactured electronic parts and various instruments for the space industry, had been involved in a serious strike that had lasted approximately six months and had cost the company over $500,000. In addition, Midwestern had spent a great deal of money on research and development, and the results could not be realized fully until some time in the future. Although the company's prospects were excellent and its earnings good, Mr. Morrow needed to raise funds for immediate uses. He had read about Arnold Ryden in *Fortune* magazine and sought him out to propose a merger.

On March 27, 1962, Midwestern Instruments was merged with Telex. At that time, the stock of Telex was selling for $18 a share and the stock of

---

[1]For more details see "Man Under Fire," *Forbes*, August 1, 1962., pp. 30–31.

Midwestern Instruments was selling for $8. The merger was made on the basis of one share of Telex stock for two and a quarter shares of Midwestern Instruments plus $450,000 in cash. The total number of Telex shares involved was 582,772. Telex sales at the time were approximately $24,000,000 and Midwestern sales were $8,000,000. The merger gave Midwestern stockholders 44 per cent of the stock of Telex and made Mr. Morrow the single largest shareholder of the combined company.

Shortly after the merger, Morrow, who continued as president of Midwestern Instruments, Division of Telex, was elected to the Telex board of directors. On attending his first board meeting, he discovered that Telex was in far greater trouble than he had realized. A group of dissident stockholders was threatening a proxy fight at the annual meeting in July, 1962. The dissidents included owners of companies bought by Telex at the height of the market. In addition, a considerable amount of short-term debt was coming due and immediate arrangements had to be made to fund or otherwise liquidate it. In order to forestall the proxy battle and the bad publicity, Arnold Ryden agreed to resign the chairmanship of the board and to seat representatives of the dissenting group. M. E. Morrow replaced Ryden as board chairman.

Operating results for 1962 were poor, and net earnings were disastrous. Pressure increased to remove Ryden completely from management, but the corporate charter required cumulative voting which made removal impossible. The board of directors then proposed to the stockholders that Telex be changed from a Minnesota to a Delaware corporation, thus eliminating the requirement of cumulative voting. During the period of awaiting stockholder decision, M. E. Morrow became president as well as board chairman of Telex. The charter change was authorized, and the offices of the firm were moved from Minneapolis to Tulsa, Oklahoma, home office of Midwestern Instruments. All operations were subsequently directed from there.

### The Proxy Fight

The ouster of Ryden and his replacement by Morrow appeared at first to benefit the company (see financial reports for fiscal 1963 and 1964, Exhibits I and II). Operating improvement came from: (1) consolidation of markets and sales, and (2) elimination of unprofitable subsidiaries. The stock rose briefly in 1963. By 1964, however, the stock price dropped to approximately $5 per share, and in February of that year, a group of stockholders organized to oppose the new management of Telex.

The new opposition group was headed by Arnold J. Ryden. Despite the setbacks he had received, Ryden still believed he could build Telex into a great industrial complex. He had little confidence in the management of M. E. Morrow or the current board of directors, and he was not the kind of man to retreat if the means for fighting were at hand. He had started rebuilding his personal fortune through financial promotions and in addition had assumed the presidency of a small company, Minneapolis Scientific Controls Corporation. He still owned 35,000 shares of Telex, and he had associates who also owned substantial blocks of Telex stock. He reasoned that he might regain control of the company if he could add to his voting power by securing additional voting proxies before the next annual meeting. The drop in stock prices, naturally disturbing to all stockholders, offered him an advantage in waging a successful proxy battle.

Ryden put his plan into immediate action. He created the Telex Investors Policy Committee, Inc. (TIPCO), and named one of his associates as spokesman. The group then selected a slate of nominees for the Telex board of directors to replace the present board, and sent out a mailing to all Telex stockholders proposing the TIPCO nominees to "get Telex moving ahead again." Ryden's name did not appear at first on the new slate; he had hoped to avoid open involvement in the fight and to act, rather, from behind the scenes. This hope was soon dispelled, however, and his name was added to TIPCO's proposed list (see Exhibit III).

Mr. J. C. Wilson, the Chicago stockholder introduced in the first paragraph of this study, started receiving proxy material on May 1, 1964, and the deluge continued up to July 5th. Management on the one side and TIPCO on the other sent out voluminous material, each detailing the alleged incompetence of the opposition. In addition to the mail, Mr. Wilson received phone calls from both groups and was invited to attend meetings. His first intimation of the ensuing proxy fight came from a preliminary letter sent out by TIPCO, a letter that preceded the communication containing the list of proposed replacement directors. TIPCO pointed out that Telex's fourth quarter sales ending March 31 were only breaking even, which was a continuation of the past downward trend. They predicted that at this rate the next quarter sales ending June 30, 1964, would show a loss. Excerpts from the letter are as follows:

May 28, 1964

To Telex Shareholders:

We—and many shareholders in our company—have been deeply disturbed over the past several months at what has been happening to Telex.

Since present management assumed control of the company in mid-1962, the market price of the stock has declined to its present level—approximately $4 7/8 per share.

At the same time, Telex sales are dropping—more than 20 per cent in the last fiscal year alone. For the first nine months of fiscal 1964, earnings dropped more than 50 per cent from the same period in the previous year.

To many shareholders, these and other factors have led to dissatisfaction with present management and its direction of your company.

To coordinate what otherwise would be scattered and unsupported efforts, several shareholders last September organized a nonprofit corporation called TIPCO—Telex Investors Policy Committee. The members of TIPCO, together with other shareholders already contacted by the committee and who feel as we do, *represent more than 250,000 shares.*

Since its organization, TIPCO has made several attempts to obtain information from management that would assist all shareholders *in evaluating the company's* current progress and future prospects. Specifically, TIPCO:

(1) Sent a representative to Telex headquarters in Tulsa in March, to ask:
   (a) What could shareholders expect in the company's fourth quarter, and in the near future?
   (b) Does the company have any new substantial government or private contracts that would indicate increased sales opportunities?

In each case, the company declined to answer.

(2) Still in the belief that Telex management might be receptive to a direct approach, sent a letter—and a subsequent telegram—to management, asking specific questions about the M3000 program, the Magna-cord operation, the acquisition of Astrocom, and other pertinent matters.

We continue to be concerned that management refuses to provide the most basic information. We are concerned that the quarterly reports to shareholders do not show income taxes or nonrecurring gains or losses as separate items.

As concerned shareholders of Telex, we have come to the conclusion that the only way to preserve and to enhance the value of our stock is to seek out and sponsor a completely new board of directors that would get Telex moving ahead again.

Toward this end, when you receive management's proxy for the forthcoming annual meeting, we ask that you do *not* sign it. Instead, put it aside until you have had an opportunity to review qualifications of the nominees for a new board of directors. This information will be coming to you in the next few days.

In the meantime, we would be most interested in hearing your suggestions regarding this most important matter.

Sincerely,

Harold E. Farnes
Director, TIPCO, Inc.
First National Bank Building
Minneapolis, Minnesota
(owner—1,037 shares of Telex stock)

Management's reply to this letter followed twelve days later. The basic points of the letter are as follows:

TO THE SHAREHOLDERS OF THE TELEX CORPORATION:

The company's shareholders have received a letter dated May 28, 1964, from a group referring to themselves as the Telex Investors Policy Committee, Inc. ("TIPCO"). We believe that you would be interested in a report from your management group.

On March 13 of this year, Mr. A. J. "Bud" Ryden and Mr. Willis K. Drake (a long-time business associate and close friend of Ryden) called on the management, accompanied by Douglas Thornsjo, an attorney. The purpose of their visit, which was unknown to management until the meeting began, was to submit the following proposals:

(1) That their stock (some 80,000 shares, according to their statement) be purchased at a price substantially above market, or

(2) That management representatives sell to them all of their shareholdings, and

(3) To inform management of the formation of the Committee referred to as TIPCO.

Their statement was to the effect that management would have to agree either to buy them out or to sell out to them or they would proceed to attack management through the use of the Committee TIPCO.

Our position was made completely clear: that we would not pay a premium above market for their shares as it would be obviously unfair to other shareholders and that management representatives were not interested in selling their personal shareholdings because of the confidence that we had in the future of the Company. As you noted in the Proxy Statement, the Directors of the Company own beneficially 216,861 shares.

Since neither of their proposals to buy or sell was acceptable to management, they have now resorted to their alternative to use the Committee to attack the management.

We are sure you remember Mr. Ryden and his tenure with the Company. In July, 1962, when the shareholders caused the removal of Ryden as president, the Company was then on the verge of bankruptcy. The present management immediately faced the problem of repaying short-term borrowed money in the amount of $4,225,000. Two million, two hundred twenty-five thousand dollars of this was owed to the bank, and the bank was demanding payment. These conditions do not prevail today. The Company is in a strong financial condition.

We have viewed with interest the Ryden Committee's criticism of the market value of the stock of your Company. All of us have no difficulty in remembering the tremendous declines in stock values during the time that Mr. Ryden and his associates, including Mr. Drake, were managing the Company. During the two years preceding his removal as president, the market value of the stock declined approximately 90 per cent, and the shareholders who acquired their stock during these two years will remember this most vividly. At the time of Ryden's removal the market price of Telex was $4 bid.

On April 15, a certified list of shareholders of the Company was furnished to Thornsjo as attorney for the Committee. Mr. Ryden has now admitted that this list of shareholders is under his control. This conclusive evidence of Ryden's direction of the Committee dispels any doubt as to his guiding hand in their program.

Yours very truly,

M. E. Morrow

These two letters clearly established the lines for the ensuing battle. The management of Telex was going to center its attack on Ryden as the controlling force behind TIPCO, and would press home the charge that Ryden was attempting to raid Telex.

Following this, another letter from TIPCO was received by Mr. Wilson. The letter stated the following principal points:

June 10, 1964

To: Telex Shareholders

(1) With the low price of Telex stock at 4 3/4 bid (even below the book value of $5.31), our investment in Telex can only be protected and enhanced if we can get TELEX MOVING AHEAD AGAIN.

(2) Management's repeated "leaks" of proposed listing on the American Exchange, of a coming $10,000,000 new military contract, and of hastily conceived acquisitions—none of these has helped the price of the stock. Since they have already "leaked" these items and others, any future announcements of actual facts will probably not have much of any effect on the price of the stock. Even the recent ill-timed paper dividend didn't help. Here is the basic problem. Too many present shareholders, possibly up to 250,000 shares, want to sell because they have NO CONFIDENCE in Mr. M. E. Morrow, his son (nominally president of Midwestern Instruments, a Telex subsidiary), and his board. Not enough new people among the general investing public are becoming interested in Telex. So how can the price go up until NEW CONFIDENCE is obtained? Only a new Board of real stature, success and dedication can get TELEX MOVING AHEAD AGAIN.

It is with confidence and determination that we announce a slate of seven directors to be elected on next July 7th.

This Board of BUSINESS BUILDERS can get TELEX MOVING AHEAD AGAIN. Here is a group of men who have achieved great success in BUILDING their own businesses. Here is a group of men who can BUILD TELEX into an industrial giant, who can maximize its now dormant potential. Because of the outstanding personal achievements of these men, the new board will engender the CONFIDENCE of present shareholders and will attract new interest in Telex. Please study carefully the business and community achievements of these men in the enclosed proxy material.

This new Board will not be a shaky coalition of two groups, neither of whom has trust or respect for the other. Rather it will be a cohesive group of independent men ready to implement plans already formulating to get TELEX MOVING AHEAD AGAIN.

(3) When elected, the new Board will attract and rebuild the best possible management team, a team which will not include the president's son and will not include a subsidiary executive who devotes his time to local political activities. This new competent management team may well include former executives who left because they had NO CONFIDENCE in Mr. M. E. Morrow. While qualified consultants may be used, the new Board would not approve of the huge fees (possibly as high as $50,000 in one year) which Mr. M. E. Morrow has paid to his fellow director, Mr. John Stambaugh, or his accounting firm.

To get TELEX MOVING AHEAD AGAIN and to rebuild its management team will take time, effort, and dedication. While the new Telex team offers you no miracles, it does promise real action in providing careful and sound profitable growth.

We believe future growth should be largely in areas of greater technology, where new engineering and improving markets are important. While the recently announced acquisition of Astrocom may be all right (we have been denied enough facts to know), there certainly are many areas where the technological content is much greater than in the field of electric motors.

(4) Growth certainly does not come by selling off a division such as Lumen. In the May 1, 1963, *Wall Street Journal*, Mr. M. E. Morrow had these things to say about Lumen, a division which he subsequently sold, explaining that it was losing money.

"Both Operations (Lumen and one other) are in the black" and "New products expected to boost Telex volume this year include magnetic amplifiers made by the Lumen subsidiary which," Mr. Morrow said, "show promise of wide use in controlling traffic lights."

With such conflicting statements and actions, there is both NO CONFIDENCE and NO GROWTH.

Sincerely,

Harold E. Farnes

In response to TIPCO's letter, the management of Telex sent out a letter attacking Ryden. They characterized him as "behind this scheme to grab control"; in addition they produced an article from *Forbes* (see footnote 1) which described Ryden in italics as belonging "to a brash young generation of businessmen who are just now learning some rough old truths about making and keeping money." Management's letter pointed out that:

1. Ryden had been fired from or resigned from several positions.
2. Under Ryden, Telex stock had gone from $45 per share to $4 per share.
3. While president of Telex, Ryden and his associates sold $42,000 worth of shares of Telex for $1,200,000 when these shares only cost them $2.40 per share.

In conclusion management pointed out that they had taken over a sick company and slowly but surely had repaired it until now it was showing profits. The job of rebuilding Telex had been difficult and arduous. Management's opinion of Arnold J. Ryden was "nothing but a trouble maker."

On June 18, Mr. Wilson received another letter from TIPCO. This letter contained many of the past statements made by the TIPCO group but added something new: the M3000 digital tape transporter. This transport,[2] which was used for moving tape in a computer system, was patented by Midwestern Instruments and had been very costly to develop. A good share of the future profits of Midwestern Instruments could be expected to come from this transport. The 1964 annual statement stated as follows:

New product developments in the past year have been particularly noteworthy. Some of the more important are herein considered: The adoption of the M3000 digital tape transporter by major computer manufacturers gave new impetus to the development of a broader line of transporters.

[2]The cabinet and tape reels used with most electronic computers.

The price of a transport unit was approximately $15,000, and other manu-facturers made similar units. AMPAX, for instance, had a tape transport of similar design and price and had sold units to General Electric. CDC, Honeywell, and IBM all manufactured their own, and Morrow believed that these cost more than Telex's. The system used by Telex for the transport was a pressure vacuum system which Morrow considered to be far better than the other systems in use. TIPCO, in their letter, asked, "Which major computer manufacturer had adopted this transport?" The answer was "no one." Management subsequently acknowledged the point, although they pointed out that it was being tested by some of the major manufacturers. The letter from TIPCO indicated that they did not believe the machine was nearly as superior as Morrow indicated, and, in fact, it turned out to be a failure.

TIPCO also pointed out that: (1) much of the 1963 financial performance for which Morrow had taken credit was made possible by the previous management; (2) Morrow took over in the middle of the year and that with or without his management the company would have shown a good profit; (3) management's desire to list Telex on the American Stock Exchange was merely an effort to solicit votes without any real value; and (4) the company should have a full-time treasurer which they would find to replace "Mr. Morrow's crony John Stambaugh." TIPCO's five-point program to get Telex "moving ahead again" included:

1. New York Stock Exchange listing,
2. Broadening and improving investor interest and confidence,
3. Doubling sales and earnings,
4. Improving the financial condition, and
5. Building a strong management team.

TIPCO charged that management had indiscriminately eliminated divisions which were profitable. Management answered as follows:

In July, 1962, when we assumed responsibility for operations, three operating divisions—Lumen, Ballastran, and the acoustics division—were losing money. Drastic and immediate action was called for. A complete review was made of product lines, manufacturing methods, and facilities; cost ana-lysis by products was undertaken; market analysis was made; personnel were reviewed. As a result, Management determined that two of these divisions—Lumen and Ballastran—should be disposed of and major changes made in the acoustics division. Ballastran was sold in February of 1963, and Lumen in August of 1963. Both sales were made for consideration in the excess of book value.

Management continued to justify the present financial position as follows:

The Management believes that the foundation of any financial program for the Corporation is the making of profit. Sales for volume's sake alone is foolhardy; retention of loss operations so as not to acknowledge a mistake is poor business. As a result of reduction of corporate overhead, reduction in interest expense, elimination of loss operations, elimination of nonprofitable divisional sales, and a reduction in personnel, losses were turned into profits. The Company, which had for the two years ended March 31, 1963, lost $2,177,435, changed under your Management for the two years ended March 31, 1964 to a profit of $2,481,520, an improvement of $4,658,955.

Because of the improvements in the operating results and the present Management's reputation with financial institutions, we were able to secure favorable long-term financing in a total amount of $2,500,000 from the Northwestern National Bank, The Guardian Life Insurance Company of America, and Knights of Columbus, and short-term bank credit of $4,000,000 on an unsecured basis from the Northwestern National Bank and Chemical Bank New York Trust Company.

We now have established lasting relationships which will aid in good, strong growth of the Company. We have a financial ability to accommodate substantial increases in sales volume.

TIPCO's nominees for the board of directors sent a special letter out on June 25. They pointed out that they were not stooges or captives of Ryden as Morrow had portrayed them. They believed that they could put together the kind of successful program which would make Telex an important firm. They stated, "We genuinely believe that we with our seven nominees can make Telex a hundred million dollar company with the New York Stock Exchange listing within just a few years." They again emphasized their program and said, as follows:

> To go along with our proposed board of seven strongly independent and very successful business builders, we have engaged a nationally recognized executive research firm to find us the best president available in the United States. We also believe Telex is entitled to a full-time treasurer and are seeking an outstanding qualified man to replace Morrow's personal friend, John Stambaugh. Along with the basic efforts to rebuild the management team and to solidify present operations, it will be our goal to implement an aggressive merger-acquisition program.

Finally, TIPCO's nominees pointed out that they were going to considerable expense to help the stockholders in an attempt to get the company moving upward again. Their stated opinion was that much of the present problem at Telex resulted from the board's inaction, discord, and mutual suspicion, all of which were caused, in part at least, by two antagonistic groups within the board, one led by M. E. Morrow and the other by R. P. Scherer, Jr.

R. P. Scherer, Jr. was one of the officers who got caught in the exchange of his merged company with Telex when Telex stock suffered its worst drop. He had been one of the dissatisfied stockholders who had threatened Ryden with a proxy battle in 1962. In replying to the accusations of TIPCO, Scherer sent out a personal letter asking the stockholders to support management.

Finally, one of the last letters that Mr. Wilson received was from Telex management pointing out that TIPCO nominees owned a very modest $\frac{1}{2}$ per cent of the outstanding stock of the company. In addition, the letter placed the following announcement prominently in a box.

### PRESENT MANAGEMENT DEMANDED BY CREDITORS

In December 1963 the Company issued First Mortgage Bonds due in 1976 aggregating $2,500,000 which were purchased by well-recognized national institutional investors, including a large Minneapolis bank. In addition, loan agreements have been entered into with two large national banks, including the aforementioned Minneapolis bank, providing for $4,000,000 of open-line credit to be used for the Company's seasonal production needs.

These loan arrangements contain conditions providing for the immediate payment of these loans and cancellation of further credit if the management of the company shall be changed. The imposition of these conditions indicates the CONFIDENCE THESE LEADING INSTITUTIONS HAVE IN PRESENT MANAGEMENT.

**EXHIBIT I**

**Telex Corporation**
**Balance Sheet (March 31)**

| | 1964 | 1963 | 1962 | 1961 |
|---|---|---|---|---|
| *Assets* | | | | |
| Cash and government securities | $2,141,305 | $2,114,898 | $1,394,352 | $1,393,867 |
| Accounts receivable, net | 2,112,561 | 2,336,862 | 3,093,331 | 2,753,905 |
| Refundable income taxes | 39,708 | 27,977 | 37,481 | 207,170 |
| Inventories | 5,881,286 | 5,071,896 | 6,791,126 | 6,421,218 |
| Prepaid expense | 193,279 | 67,141 | 86,318 | 114,998 |
| Current assets | $10,368,157 | $9,618,774 | $11,402,658 | $10,891,158 |
| Investment in Data Products | 439,401 | 463,573 | 22,741 | |
| Notes receivable Ballestran Corp. | 166,717 | 210,000 | | |
| Cash surrender value and other inv. | 98,564 | 86,495 | 152,861 | 143,783 |
| Net property | 1,999,627 | 1,985,079 | 2,044,556 | 2,406,338 |
| Good will | 723,311 | 723,311 | 704,470 | 2,119,947 |
| Other deferred charges | 121,627 | 9,486 | 19,733 | 63,276 |
| Total assets | $13,917,404 | $13,096,718 | $14,347,019 | $15,624,502 |
| *Liabilities and net worth* | | | | |
| Notes payable | $1,066,674 | $2,262,336 | $4,291,821 | $1,861,585 |
| Accounts payable | 1,084,371 | 1,628,085 | 1,948,326 | 2,086,213 |
| Accruals | 370,619 | 398,520 | 347,982 | 584,303 |
| Taxes | 420,305 | 510,028 | 654,704 | 967,150 |
| Long-term debt due | 100,000 | 184,153 | 84,153 | 88,788 |
| Current liabilities | $3,041,969 | $4,983,122 | $7,326,996 | $5,588,039 |
| Long-term debt | 3,011,000 | 1,496,715 | 1,105,868 | 2,541,021 |
| Common stock ($ 1 par) | 1,480,397 | 1,449,743 | 1,484,214 | 1,290,898 |
| Capital surplus | 5,410,954 | 5,167,138 | 6,712,613 | 5,679,234 |
| Earned surplus | 973,084 | | (2,282,672) | 525,310 |
| Total liabilities and net worth | $13,917,404 | $13,096,718 | $14,347,019 | $15,624,502 |

After he had evaluated all of the letters and financial information, Mr. Wilson, the Chicago stockholder, still was not sure what he should do. He realized that the proxy fight, in no small part, was a clash of personalities: Arnold Ryden versus M. E. Morrow, and he knew he must separate the question of personalities from the problems of the firm. Had Morrow done a competent job of managing Telex? If he had, Mr. Wilson was inclined to support him. The most important question, however, was which group could best promote the company's welfare in the future. Mr. Wilson found this question very difficult to answer—in spite of all the "information" he had received. Did Ryden want to use Telex again mainly as a vehicle for gaining personal wealth? On the other hand, if Ryden, in taking over the firm, could manage to increase the price of the stock, then what point was there in evaluating his motives?

Mr. Wilson disliked voting against management when the company appeared to be solvent, yet he must try to protect his own interests. Perhaps a different group, a different management, might build a more profitable business. He would like to see the company embarked on a rapid expansion program as well as listed on the New York Stock Exchange. But one thing Mr. Wilson knew: He had to make up his mind that very day which side he would choose . . . which proxy he would sign.

**EXHIBIT II**

**Telex Corporation**
**Consolidated Income Statement**
**Years Ending March 31**

|  | 1964 | 1963 | 1962 | 1961 |
|---|---|---|---|---|
| Net sales | $26,032,417 | $33,927,969 | $30,390,420 | $20,864,019 |
| Gain on sale of Data Products stock | 107,567 | | | |
| Gain on sale of Lumen, Inc. | 47,750 | | | |
| Other income | 142,351 | 288,336 | 167,605 | 163,493 |
|     Total revenue | $26,330,085 | $34,216,305 | $30,558,025 | $21,027,512 |
| | | | | |
| Cost of products sold | $21,417,263 | $27,881,432 | $26,243,560 | $17,967,602 |
| Selling expense | 1,896,339 | 2,043,199 | 2,057,635 | 1,693,876 |
| General and administrative | 1,603,180 | 2,056,462 | 1,758,447 | 1,267,146 |
| Interest | 306,426 | 440,403 | 373,790 | 238,751 |
| Loss on sale of Electro-Logic Corp. | | 114,277 | | |
| Other | 93,293 | 119,619 | 115,598 | 98,868 |
|     Total costs | $25,316,501 | $32,655,392 | $30,549,030 | $21,266,243 |
| Earnings before taxes | 1,013,584 | 1,560,913 | 8,995 | (238,731) |
| Federal and state taxes | 40,500 | 52,477 | (1,800)* | 70,000 |
| Charge-off of Data Systems Div. | — | — | (1,521,185) | (358,314) |
|     Net earnings | $973,084 | $1,508,436 | $(1,510,390) | $(667,045) |

*Tax rebate.

## EXHIBIT III

### Tipco Directors

Hal N. Carr, Minneapolis, Minnesota

President and general manager, North Central Airlines, Inc.; president, Metropolitan Airport State Bank, Minneapolis; president, United Investors Corporation, Minneapolis.

Became director of North Central in 1952 and president and general manger in 1954. In the ten years from 1953–63, North Central revenues increased from $4,881,715 to $28,101,209; a net loss in 1953 of $91,573 was erased and turned into a profit of more than $500,000 in 1963; number of passengers carried annually grew from 217,663 to more than 1,214,000, and cities served increased from forty-three to ninety-one.

Telex shares owned—100

George F. Cashman, South Gate, California

President, Hallmark Financial Corporation; president, Hallmark Insurance Exchange; president, American Hallmark Life Insurance Company; president, Cashman Financial Corporation; chairman, Western Thrift and Loan, all of Los Angeles; president, Enoch Chevrolet, South Gate; president, Service Chevrolet, Pasadena.

First employment, accountant. In 1948, purchased ownership in Konawa, Okla., automobile dealership selling average of seventy-two cars per year. Today, combined dealerships owned by Mr. Cashman sell 10,000 cars per year. Formed Hallmark Financial Corporation in 1961 to handle automobile financing. Today, company controls assets in excess of $40,000,000 including a bank, a savings and loan association, and a retail operation.

Telex shares owned—100

Gordon J. McGrath, Mankato, Minnesota

Chairman and president, Minnesota Automotive, Inc., Mankato; manufacturer of hydraulic components and systems for the motor turck industry.

Purchased additional interest in 1952 and again in 1960. Sales of Minnesota Automotive have grown to $1,500,000 in last year.

Telex shares owned—100

Leonard E. Lindquist, Minneapolis, Minnesota

President, National Connector Corporation, Minneapolis, manufacturers of precision electrical connectors for the electronics industry; senior partner, law firm of Lindquist, Magnuson, and Glennon.

Became president of National Connector in 1961—at that time company had twenty employees and gross sales of $77,000. Company has grown continually to present $4,000,000 sales volume, 200 employees.

Telex shares owned—100

Arnold J. Ryden, Minneapolis, Minnesota

President, Minneapolis Scientific Controls Corp., Minneapolis; manufacturers of battery chargers, fencers, automatic energizing equipment, and automotive ignition systems.

One year ago, purchased interest in and became president of Minneapolis Scientific Controls Corp. In one year, company has gone from a large loss situation to profitable operation, and the market price of its stock has tripled.

Telex shares owned—34,935

Harold C. Lyman, Minneapolis, Minnesota
Executive vice-president, A. D. Strong Company, Minneapolis; industrial and commercialy realty firm.
Through positions of increasing responsibility, has helped build A. D. Strong Company to its present position as area's largest commercial and industrial real estate brokerage firm.
Telex shares owned—5,817

Robert E. Short, Minneapolis, Minnesota
President, Admiral Merchants Motor Freight, Inc.; president, Los Angeles Lakers professional basketball team.
Today, Admiral Merchants Motor Freight employs 800 persons, has annual gross sales of $15,000,000, and is one of 100 top trucking firms in the nation.
Telex shares owned—100

**EXHIBIT IV**

**Proxy Statement**

---

THE TELEX CORPORATION
CORPORATE OFFICES
41st STREET & SHERIDAN ROAD
TULSA, OKLAHOMA

NOTICE OF ANNUAL MEETING OF SHAREHOLDERS

TO THE SHAREHOLDERS OF THE TELEX CORPORATION:

The annual Meeting of the Shareholders of The Telex Corporation (the "Company"), a Delaware corporation, will be held at the offices of the Company, 41st Street and Sheridan Road, Tulsa, Oklahoma, on Tuesday, July 7, 1964 at 10: 00 A.M. C.S.T. for the purpose of considering and acting upon the following matters:

1. To give consideration to the listing of the Company's capital stock with the American Stock Exchange.
2. To fix the number of Directors of the Company for the ensuing year at eight (8) as recommended by the Board of Directors.
3. To vote for the election of Directors.
4. To do any and all things and transact any and all business that may properly come before the meeting.

The Board of Directors has fixed the close of business on May 22, 1964, as the record date for determination of shareholders entitled to notice of and to vote at said meeting. The stock transfer books will not be closed.

By Order of the Board of Directors,

J. B. BAILEY, Secretary

---

# Reorganization under Chapter XI

**42**

HILLSIDE
INDUSTRIES, INC.

During June, 1962, Mr. Philip Hall, an attorney retained by Freeman Trailers, Inc., had filed and received approval for a petition for an Arrangement under Chapter XI of the Bankruptcy Act for Hillside Industries.

Hillside was a small corporation primarily engaged in repairing and overhauling aircraft engines and other parts for agencies of the United States government. The company had suffered severe losses throughout its short history, and although presently solvent, it would not be able to pay its debts as they matured. Through a series of contracts as subsequently detailed, the management of Hillside was the responsibility of Freeman Trailers.

As of July 1, 1962, Mr. Hall was undecided as to the terms to be included in the proposed Arrangement. He had arranged for a meeting with Mr. Freeman, the president of Freeman Trailers, and with the president of Hillside on July 3, and he desired to present them with an Arrangement for their review.

**Background**

Henderson Field, not far from Hillside, Washington was constructed by the Army Air Corps during World War II as a training school. After the war the field became the property of the City of Hillside, which leased it to Hillside Aviation Corporation for an industrial facility.

The buildings clustered near the field consisted of four large metal hangers and a number of wooden barracks buildings. Hillside Aviation converted the buildings into an industrial facility by connecting three of the hangers to form one large building and by removing the partitions within the barracks buildings. This provided approximately 120,000 square feet of floor space in the hangers with ceiling clearance of fourteen feet and an additional 68,000 square feet in the barracks buildings with ten feet of ceiling clearance. In addition, Hillside Aviation installed gas lines, power lines, overhead air connections, electrical and air drops, and a heating system.

Shortly after the war Hillside Aviation Corporation employed over 1,300 workers and enjoyed satisfactory earnings. With the general reduction in the size of the Air Force, however, less and less work came to Hillside so that the level of employment slowly fell until finally in 1960 the company closed down the plant.

## Operations Under Hillsides Industries, Inc.

The Henderson Field facility was basic to the economy of Hillside and the surrounding area. The various activities at the field were largely responsible for building up the economy of the area, and the inactivity during the recent years was the principal reason for the area's economic distress.

Shortly after the facility was closed down, a group of Hillside business leaders realized that operations at Henderson Field were not only to their best interests, but also necessary to the livelihood of the entire community. Consequently, they contacted the president of Hillside Aviation Corporation and made an agreement whereby the businessmen would put up the capital to purchase the facility and the original plant manager would be in charge of operations. Thus, Hillside Industries, Inc. was founded on April 5, 1960. The newly formed company planned to continue to bid upon and perform contracts for the overhaul and modification of military aircraft and aircraft components.

Although Hillside Industries obtained a substantial amount of work under government contracts and built up its payroll to a high of 260 people, its various operations were not wholly successful. From the beginning the company suffered severe losses, and in December 1960, it applied for and received a $50,000 working capital loan from the Small Business Administration. This loan was granted primarily because the Hillside, Washington, area had been reclassified to the category of having a "substantial and persistent labor surplus." The loan was secured by a second lien on the plant, a factor's lien on inventory, and, in the words of one of the officers, "a chattel mortgage on everything loose." Far from providing the panacea for which the businessmen had hoped, this $50,000 only allowed the company a short breathing spell before further losses were incurred.

Many reasons existed for the financial desperation at Hillside. Mr. Freeman, the president of Freeman Trailers, later summed up the situation as follows:

It [Hillside Industries] is undercapitalized and has been plagued by lack of working capital throughout its life. It purchased the Henderson Field facility on a $145,000 eight-year note, and the monthly payments required to amortize this loan have severely taxed its limited cash resources. Furthermore, the plant itself is in many ways a liability to Hillside Industries rather than an asset. Hillside Industries' operations cannot effectively use the 188,000 square feet of available plant space, and the excess over what is needed is simply dead-weight. The existence of this excess floor space encourages inefficiencies and lost motion by permitting operations to be spread out over more space than is actually needed. To be sure, the company is losing a substantial amount of money; and, the Directors are sure that the company is going under at any time.

### Freeman Trailers, Inc.

Freeman Trailers was a small manufacturer of commercial and military trailers with its principal plant in Seattle, Washington. It was a well-managed, adequately financed company which desired to expand its operations both in the commercial and military trailer fields beyond the capabilities of its Seattle plant. It had been looking at the Hillside area for several months as a possible location for a second plant.

The Hillside area was attractive to Freeman because of its favorable labor supply, the skills available in Hillside, and its ready accessibility to Freeman's markets.

Earlier in 1961, Freeman and Hillside carried on extensive negotiations looking toward a possible lease of space in the Henderson Field facility to Freeman or toward the acquisition of the entire facility by Freeman through a merger of the two corporations. Freeman's accountants reviewed the books of Hillside Industries and found no concurrence between the actual situation and that portrayed in the accounts. Revising the balance sheets through a complete internal audit, the accountants concluded that Hillside was on the verge of bankruptcy. Therefore, no merger agreement was reached. However, an arrangement was made whereby Freeman accepted management responsibility of Hillside Industries on a contract basis in order to attempt to save the company from bankruptcy.

Freeman hoped that they could work out the existing contracts and preserve the solvency of the corporation and that a possible merger could be effected at a later date. However, it soon became apparent that this could not be done, and the petition for reorganization under Chapter XI became necessary.

### Chapter XI, Bankruptcy Act

Chapter XI provides the machinery whereby a debtor may offer an arrangement with his unsecured creditors either for an extension of time in which to pay the debt in full or in installments, an extension of time in which to pay a prescribed percentage of the debt in installments, or to make a straight cash settlement. The actual procedure is much the same as in a straight bankruptcy liquidation.

A petition is submitted voluntarily by the company to the Referee of the Bankruptcy Court requesting an Arrangement under Chapter XI. The court issues an order approving the petition and requests that a statement of affairs, the financial statements, a statement of executory contracts, and the proposed Arrangement be filed with the court. An order is also issued enjoining all persons from commencing or continuing any action at law or suit against the company's business.

After the petition has been filed and approved, the company presents its arrangement or proposal at a meeting of the creditors. At this meeting the company's statements are examined by the creditors to determine if the proposal is feasible, equitable, and in their best interests. The court also determines whether the statutes contained in the Act have been complied with and whether the debtor is guilty of some act which would be a bar to getting a discharge from the debts.

If these contingencies are satisfied, a majority, both in number and dollar amount, of the creditors of each class must accept the proposal in writing within six months for it to be presented in a hearing before the Referee of the Bankruptcy Court. If a majority do not accept, the proposal is altered by the debtor company until it is accepted. At the hearing the expression of the majority is persuasive to the Referee, but not conclusive. He hears the arguments of the dissenters and the acceptors and may either confirm or deny the Arrangement. If he confirms it, it is carried out; if he denies it, it returns to the company to be altered to begin the process again.

### Current Situation

In writing his proposed Arrangement, Mr. Hall had before him both the actual and projected balance sheets and income statements as presented in Exhibits I and II. He also had a monthly projected cash flow, Exhibit III, and a list of the unsecured creditors, Exhibit IV.

During the month of June, Mr. Freeman had succeeded in having two of the unprofitable contracts revoked by the government agencies involved and had acquired an Air Force contract with extremely high profit potential. He, therefore, considered the financial projections to be quite appropriate.

In Chapter XI proceedings the preferred practice is to divide the unsecured creditors into two classes. Class A consists of those to whom the debtor owes the sum of $100 or less, and Class B unsecured creditors are those to whom the debtor owes in excess of $100. The Class A creditors are paid either in full or a specified percentage, depending on the Arrangement, during the month in which the Arrangement is confirmed while payments to the Class B creditors are deferred until completion of the Class A payments.

From the undercurrent of feeling and emotion, Mr. Hall was certain that he could count on obtaining approval of the Arrangement by a majority in number owing to the large number of Class A creditors that would receive payment immediately. However, he was not so certain of obtaining the required majority in dollar amount.

Mr. D. A. Palmer of Helmco, Inc., to whom the company owed $15,300, was quite adamant in his opinion of the pending Arrangement. Helmco was somewhat involved in financial difficulties of its own, and Mr. Palmer wanted an immediate settlement. He realized that although an immediate settlement would not recover his credit in full, as much as a 60 per cent recovery now

**EXHIBIT I**

**Hillside Industries, Inc.**
**Balance Sheet**

|  | Actual July 1, 1962 | Projected January 1, 1963 |
|---|---|---|
| *Assets* |  |  |
| Current assets |  |  |
| Cash | $11,734 | $44,500 |
| Accounts receivable | 63,152 | 105,700 |
| Inventories | 173,978 | 155,253 |
| Prepaid Expenses | 4,738 | 3,900 |
| Total current assets | $253,602 | $309,353 |
| Fixed assets | 233,520 | 234,400 |
| Less depreciation | 24,429 | 43,000 |
| Net Fixed Assets | $209,091 | $191,400 |
| Organization expense | 690 | 700 |
| Total assets | $463,383 | $501,453 |
|  |  |  |
| *Liabilities* |  |  |
| Current liabilities |  |  |
| Accounts payable | $158,319 | — |
| Notes payable | 42,662 | — |
| Accrued expenses | 24,312 | — |
| Total current liabilities | $225,293 | $228,700 |
| Long-term debt |  |  |
| Notes payable | 1,897 | — |
| Mortgage | 127,932 | — |
| SBA loan | 47,807 | — |
| Total long-term debt | $177,636 | $171,300 |
| Capital stock and surplus |  |  |
| Common stock | 80,100 | 80,100 |
| Paid-in surplus | 55,000 | 55,000 |
| Retained earnings | (74,646) | (33,647) |
| Total liabilities and equity | $463,383 | $501,453 |

**EXHIBIT II**

**Hillside Industries, Inc.
Income Statement**

| | Actual January, 1962-June, 1962 | Projected July, 1962-December, 1962 |
|---|---|---|
| Sales | $562,032 | $936,500 |
| Cost of goods sold | 533,599 | 762,700 |
| Gross profit | $28,433 | $173,800 |
| Less operating expenses | 60,574 | 139,500 |
| Earnings from sales | ($32,141) | $34,300 |
| Other income | 9,305 | 9,700 |
| Other expenses | (1,548) | (3,000) |
| Net profit | ($24,384) | $41,000 |

**EXHIBIT III**

**Hillside Industries Inc.
Monthly Cash Flow**

| | Actual 6/30/62 | Projected 7/31/62 | 8/31/62 | 9/30/62 |
|---|---|---|---|---|
| *Cash Receipts* | | | | |
| Cash on hand | $12,452 | $11,731 | — | — |
| Cash received | 95,611 | 140,100 | 156,500 | 161,000 |
| Total | $108,063 | $151,831 | — | — |
| *Cash Disbursements* | | | | |
| Payroll | $38,327 | $32,600 | $34,100 | $34,100 |
| Payroll taxes | 6,259 | 5,000 | 5,200 | 5,200 |
| SBA loan | 815 | 800 | 800 | 800 |
| Mortgage payable on bldg. | 1,145 | 1,100 | 1,100 | 1,100 |
| Interest | 1,105 | 1,100 | 1,100 | 1,100 |
| Mortgage fee | 2,537 | 2,700 | 3,000 | 3,000 |
| Material | 40,641 | 83,400 | 65,500 | 75,500 |
| Utilities | 1,139 | 1,000 | 900 | 900 |
| Office supplies | 463 | 200 | 300 | 300 |
| Insurance | 553 | 500 | 400 | 400 |
| Travel | 193 | — | — | — |
| Production supplies | 360 | 200 | 300 | 300 |
| Maintenance | 344 | 300 | 400 | 400 |
| Property taxes | 2,451 | — | — | 2,500 |
| Court costs | — | 500 | — | — |
| Legal and accounting costs | — | 600 | 200 | 200 |
| Class A creditors | — | — | — | — |
| Class B creditors | — | — | — | — |
| Total disbursements | $96,332 | $130,000 | $113,300 | $125,800 |
| Bank balance (EOM) | 24,880 | | | |

would be far more suited to his circumstances than that derived from a long, drawn-out settlement.

Mr. Palmer was quite influential personally and had been successful in enlisting the aid of other larger creditors. Mr. Hall did not know how many of the creditors agreed with Mr. Palmer, but he hoped they constituted less than the majority in amount required to approve his Arrangement.

### EXHIBIT IV

#### Hillside Industries, Inc.
#### List of Unsecured Creditors

| Creditor Class | Number | Due |
|---|---|---|
| $1— 100 | 62 | $1,576 |
| 101— 1,000 | 38 | 33,214 |
| 1,001— 5,000 | 12 | 25,945 |
| 5,001—10,000 | 6 | 43,351 |
| 10,001—20,000 | 2 | 31,658 |
| 20,001— | 3 | 65,237 |
| | | $200,981 |

Hillside had the following creditors with individual amounts owed in excess of $ 5,000 :

| | |
|---|---|
| Modern Supply | $5,241 |
| Northwest Oil | 5,430 |
| American Chemical | 7,325 |
| Warner Aviation | 7,700 |
| Franklin Electric Supply | 8,255 |
| Western Tool | 9,400 |
| Helmco, Inc. | 15,300 |
| Industrial Wholesale | 16,358 |
| First National Bank* | 20,000 |
| Seattle Manufacturing | 22,575 |
| Northern National Bank* | 22,662 |

*Notes payable.

# Readjustment

## 43

ELECTRO-DYNAMICS,
INCORPORATED

In March, 1964, the board of directors of Dynamics Aerospace Corporation and the board of Electro-Bateau, Inc., reached an exchange agreement of securities for the acquisition of the latter corporation by Dynamics Aerospace Corporation. The plan, which was approved by the stockholders of the two corporations in July, 1964, called for the exchange of each Electro-Bateau common share for debentures and warrants of the combined company. The rate was one share of stock in Electro-Bateau for $26 in 5 1/2 per cent convertible debentures and a 5-year warrant for 1/5th share of stock at $18 and an additional 1/5th share of stock at $24 per share.

The acquisition of the new facilities left the combined company debt heavy, made the company more diversified and somewhat unwieldy, and left a substantial potential dilution in the earnings per share and market value because of the outstanding warrants and convertible debentures and preferred stock. The company had changed its name to Electro-Dynamics, Inc. During the latter part of 1964 and early 1965, the board of directors of the combined company, under the leadership of the finance officer, began a study of the profitability of the individual divisions of the company in an attempt to reach a decision as to whether to divest the company of some of the less profitable operations. During 1964 and 1965, the company sold the data processing, mobile home, and captive finance company divisions. It planned further divesting of the air conditioning system division and the boat and motors division as soon as buyers could be obtained who were willing to pay reasonable prices for the facilities. The sale of the facilities resulted in a substantial reduction in the sales volume and brought about a loss in 1965 equivalent to almost $3 per share of common stock. Although this loss would depress the market value of the common stock for a period of time, the directors believed that once the corporation returned to a profitable operation that the market price per share would recover. The directors generally believed that a recognition of the loss in a single year rather than in two or three years would have less of a depressing effect on the stock's market value.

In early 1965, the company acquired all the voting stock of another small electronics firm, but the board of directors of Electro-Dynamics planned no further acquisitions during 1965 or 1966 until some of the problems of the combined company could be ironed out. The company did, however, plan some additional divestment and relocation of widely scattered facilities near the main California plant.

After the divestment program was completed, the company would be operating with the following five divisions: communication systems, electronic instruments, guidance controls, missile components, and small pleasure aircraft. Each of the divisions maintained its own research facilities and research staff, but some thought was being given to an organization of

**EXHIBIT I**

**Electro-Dynamics, Inc.**
**Consolidated Balance Sheet**
**As of December 31**

|  | 1965 | 1964 |
|---|---|---|
| *Assets* | | |
| Current assets | | |
| Cash and U. S. government securities | $2,954 | $2,228 |
| Notes and accounts receivable | 9,042 | 11,334 |
| Less: allowance for doubtful accts. | (399) | — |
| Tax claim | — | 548 |
| Unreimbursed costs and fees | 10,110 | 6,477 |
| Inventories, less progress payments | 13,062 | 16,106 |
| Prepaid expenses | 247 | 402 |
| Total current assets | $35,016 | $37,095 |
| Investments and other assets | | |
| Investments in and adv. to affiliates | 1,047 | 980 |
| Notes and accounts receivable and other investments | 1,805 | 1,147 |
| Less: allowance for doubtful rec. | (179) | — |
| Excess of inv. in subsidiaries over net assets acquired and net intangibles | 845 | 668 |
| Unamortized debt expense | 96 | 106 |
| Total other assets | 3,614 | 2,901 |
| Property, plant, and equipment | | |
| Land, building, machinery, equip. (cost) | 15,351 | 15,786 |
| Less allowance for depreciation | (4,713) | (3,540) |
| Total properties, net | 10,638 | 12,246 |
| Total assets | $49,268 | $52,242 |

*Liabilities and equity*

| | | |
|---|---:|---:|
| Current liabilities | | |
| Notes payable to bank | $11,700 | $14,737 |
| Accounts payable | 5,205 | 7,758 |
| Accruals | 4,088 | 3,790 |
| Income taxes payable | — | — |
| Current portion of long-term debt | 142 | — |
| Total current liabilities | 21,135 | 26,285 |
| Long-term debt | | |
| Conv. sub. deb. 5½s of 1979* | 15,929 | 15,982 |
| Conv. sub. deb. 5¼s of 1974† | 1,050 | 1,082 |
| Senior notes 6¼s | 1,500 | 1,544 |
| Mtge. bonds, 5½s of 1973 | 768 | 876 |
| Mortgages payable | 13 | — |
| Total long-term debt | 19,260 | 19,484 |
| Reserves and deferred credit | | |
| Res. for def. income taxes | 158 | 159 |
| Res. for possible future losses arising from disposition of assets | 718 | 735 |
| Total receives | 876 | 894 |
| Stockholders' equity | | |
| Minority int. | — | 204 |
| Preferred stock, $ 18 par | 1,362 | 1,383 |
| Common stock, $ .30 par | 418 | 416 |
| Capital surplus | 1,772 | 1,726 |
| Retained earnings | 4,445 | 1,850 |
| Total equity | 7,997 | 5,579 |
| Totol lia. and equity | $49,268 | $52,242 |

*Convertible into common at $25.
†Convertible into common at $24.

a single research center to carry out the research for all five of the operating divisions.

As the stock and assets in the divisions which had and were being sold were liquidated, the combined company had a substantial amount of funds which it could use to retire a portion of its short-term debt, long-term debt, and the preferred stock. The officers and directors of the company believed that eliminating some of the fixed charges and, if possible, removing the threat of dilution posed by the large amount of the outstanding convertible debentures and preferred shares would be to the long-run advantage of the stockholders.

As an initial step in the simplification of the capital structure of the company, the directors made a debenture exchange offer extending from mid-April, 1966, to the end of June. The company offered $6,913,000 of 4 3/4 per cent subordinated convertible debentures due October 30, 1976, and $10,100,000 of 5 1/2 per cent subordinated debentures due October 30, 1976, in exchange for the outstanding 5 1/2s and 5 1/4s totaling the same amount. Holders of the outstanding 5 1/2s due in 1976 were invited to exchange each $100 face amount for $40 face amount of the new 4 3/4s and $60 face amount of the new 5 1/2s. The holders of the outstanding 5 1/4s of 1971, which were originally issued by an acquired corporation and assumed by Dynamics Aerospace Corporation, were permitted to exchange each $100 face amount for $50 of new 4 3/4s and $50 of the new 5 1/2s.

The new 4 3/4s were: (1) to be issued in denominations of multiples of $10 and $1,000; (2) to be callable in 1966 at 105 and, thereafter at rates reduced by 0.4 per cent per year through 1978; and (3) to be convertible into common shares until maturity at $12 per share. The conversion privilege was protected against dilution by stock splits or dividends. The issue would limit the issuance of additional funded debt unless, thereafter, the consolidated net tangible assets equaled at least 175 per cent of consolidated funded debt. For the purposes of meeting the indenture requirements, senior debt excluded indebtedness under revolving credit agreements, debt subordinated to debentures, or any debt incurred in contracts with the U. S. government. The indenture also limited cash dividend payments and stock repurchases to $750,000 plus the consolidated net income after December 31, 1963, less the excess of expenditures for stock acquired over the net proceeds of stock sold after that date.

The 5 1/2 per cent subordinated debentures of 1979 were to have the same denomination as the new 4 3/4s, were callable at the same rate schedule, and were to include the same restriction as to cash dividends and acquisition of stock. The two issues required annual sinking-fund payments of $485,000 and $639,000 from 1970 to 1978.

In May, 1966, Electro-Dynamics, Inc. advertised for tenders of its common shares. The company offered one share of $1.80 dividend, convertible preferred (with a $45 call price) plus $9 cash for three common shares. The management of the company desired to retire 750,000 shares. The company also stated its intentions of buying additional shares of the common stock in the open market. At the time the offer was made, the $18 par, 4 1/2 per cent preferred shares were trading between 11 3/4 and 12 1/4. The trading range of the common shares was from 8 3/4 to 10 5/8 for May, 1966. Each share was to be convertible to 1 1/4 share of common until 1977 and at a reduced rate thereafter.

During the history of operation, Dynamics Aerospace Corporation or its successor, Electro-Dynamics, Inc., had never paid a cash dividend on common. After the acquisition, the latter declared its first cash dividend on common in the fourth quarter of 1965 in the amount of $0.075 per share. A similar dividend was declared in the first and second quarters of 1966. The tenderer of 300 shares of common stock would be receiving twice the dividends on 100 shares of preferred as on his surrendered shares (at the prevailing dividend rate), plus a $9 cash bonus. Although the exchange would result in an immediate cost to the company, such a reduction in the number of common shares would probably result in an increase in the earnings per share on the common shares within a few years.

**EXHIBIT II**

**Electro-Dynamics, Inc.**
**Statement of Consolidated Income & Retained Earnings**
**For the Years Ended December 31**

|  | 1965 | 1964 |
|---|---|---|
| Net sales | $97,632 | $57,854 |
| Cost and expenses | 93,358 | 60,992 |
| Operating profits | 4,274 | (3,138) |
| Other costs |  |  |
| Interest | (1,746) | (1,120) |
| Other productions | (66) | (65) |
| Other income | 177 | 265 |
| Income before taxes | 2,639 | (4,058) |
| Income taxes (cr) |  | 410 |
| Prov. for losses | (44) | (300) |
| Net income | $2,595 | ($3,948) |
| # Common shares | 1,392 | 1,388 |
| E/S | 1.86 | 2.85 |

**EXHIBIT III**

**Electro-Dynamics, Inc.**
**Selected Market Value Data**

| Year | Yield on Speculative Grade Pref. | Common Stock Trading Range | $18 par Pref. Stock Trading Range | $5^1/_2$s due in 1979 |
|---|---|---|---|---|
| 1959 | 5.91% | $4\frac{5}{8}-2\frac{1}{8}$ | — | — |
| 1960 | 5.77 | $12-3$ | — | — |
| 1961 | 5.58 | $26\frac{3}{4}-10$ | — | — |
| 1962 | 5.77 | $25\frac{1}{4}-12$ | $16\frac{1}{4}-12\frac{5}{8}$ | — |
| 1963 | 5.41 | $25\frac{3}{8}-15\frac{7}{8}$ | $22\frac{3}{4}-14\frac{1}{8}$ | $94-114$ |
| 1964 | 5.34 | $15\frac{1}{2}-9$ | $15-8\frac{3}{4}$ | $72-94\frac{1}{2}$ |
| 1965 | 5.10 | $11\frac{1}{2}-8\frac{1}{8}$ | $12\frac{7}{8}-10\frac{1}{4}$ | $80\frac{1}{2}-94\frac{1}{2}$ |
| 1966 |  |  |  |  |
| Jan. | 5.07 | $11-9\frac{1}{4}$ | $13\frac{1}{4}-14\frac{3}{8}$ | — |
| Feb. | 5.07 | $12\frac{1}{8}-10\frac{1}{2}$ | $14\frac{1}{8}-15\frac{5}{8}$ | — |
| Mar. | 5.06 | $11-10$ | $12\frac{3}{8}-13\frac{5}{8}$ | — |
| Apr. | 5.07 | $10\frac{5}{8}-8\frac{3}{4}$ | $11\frac{1}{2}-12\frac{5}{8}$ | — |

## Part VIII

# COMPREHENSIVE CASES

# Cash
# and Marketable
# Security
# Management

# 44

On January 2, 1964, Mr. F. C. Johns, manager of cash control and investments for Atlantic Manufacturing Company (AMCO) made a periodic examination of the company's short-term investment portfolio. He wondered whether the portfolio's present average yield of 4.36 per cent before taxes could be increased by changes in the types of securities within the portfolio. In addition, he thought it might be time to consider the overall importance of marketable securities within the firm's working capital.

Atlantic Manufacturing Company was a large, multi-line, specialty manufacturing company. It had attained its size by heavy reliance on research and development and was considered by most financial analysts to be one of the world's leading growth companies. Over the last five years net income had grown at a compound rate of 25 per cent per year, and earnings per share had increased during the same period by 22 per cent, compounded. For the year ending December 31, 1963, sales, net profit, and assets were $762 million, $90.6 million, and $653 million respectively. Current assets totaled $351 million and were divided as follows:

| | |
|---|---|
| Cash | $45 million |
| Marketable securities | 48 |
| Accounts receivable | 100 |
| Misc. receivables | 12 |
| Inventories | 146 |
| | $351 million |

The company maintained a current ratio of 2.4—1 and used only modest amounts of long-term debt. Present long-term debt aggregated $8 million. The company had not gone to the market for new money in several years although its stock outstanding had expanded substantially as a result of mergers. For the year 1964, it was estimated that sales would reach $875 million and net profits after taxes would be in excess of $100 million.

Mr. Johns' responsibilities included the handling and controlling of cash, marketable securities, and accounts receivable. In carrying out these duties, he delegated assignments in the cash and accounts receivable areas to subordinates; however, he handled the investment portfolio himself. The short-term portfolio had become a significant factor in the company's operations, for earnings on investments during the past year were $2.5 million before taxes of approximately 30 per cent.[1] The starting point in handling the marketable securities for the company was the forecast of cash. A detailed system of forecasting had been developed in order to obtain accurate information on the amount of cash that would be available for corporate use or investment.

### Forecasting Cash

To determine the type and time to maturity of a security that can be purchased, one must know the future cash positions and the need for liquidity. The severity of both of these problems is determined by the accuracy of the forecasts of cash balances. As the accuracy of the forecast decreases, the uncertainty of the investment position increases; and this uncertainty means that care must be taken in selecting securities so that if cash is necessary at a time when an unfavorable market exists, little or no loss of principal will result. Thus, the greater the uncertainty, the shorter the maturities and the lower the overall yields; consequently, the forecasting accuracy becomes extremely important.

Over the past few years AMCO forecast its cash balance by two methods, one serving as a check against the other. The first method is known as the balance sheet method, and the second as the cash flow method. The balance sheet method is used to project cash, quarterly, for the subsequent two years. Under this method each item of the balance sheet and income statement, except cash, is projected by quarters. On each statement, cash then becomes the balancing asset. Much of the data obtained for the balance sheet method is also used in the cash flow method. While the projected statements used in the balance sheet method provide satisfactory answers and are reasonably accurate, they have one major drawback in assisting the investment portfolio manager. They do not show the crucial fluctuations of cash within each quarter.

Under the cash flow method, every known and anticipated cash disbursement and receipt is projected for the subsequent three months. Emphasis

---

[1]The tax rate reflected the tax-exempt status of municipal bonds. All non-tax-exempt securities were taxed at a rate of 50 per cent.

in this projection is placed on the first month for which every effort is made to obtain all information in order to engender maximum accuracy. This forecast is reviewed each day and revised with each pertinent change so that it is always up-to-date for one month in advance. Statistical trend analysis of the past periods is used as an additional check against the cash flow, for past experience has shown that a high correlation exists between past periods, forecasts, and actual results. The use of the balance sheet method serves as a check on the accuracy of the cash flow method, and vice versa.

A review of the past forecasts made at AMCO indicated that the balance sheet method proved remarkably accurate for the first two quarters; however, forecasts with horizons extending more than one year developed inaccuracies because of unknown factors, such as the timing alterations of capital expenditures, dividend increases, and sales variations. Cash flow forecasts for the first 30 days had proved extremely accurate and for the following 60 days workably accurate. Exhibit II shows forecast data.

### Minimum Cash Balance

The assets available for investment are the forecasted cash balances less the amount to be kept on deposit in the bank. Obviously, the more cash maintained in the bank, the less available for investment. Since banks are not allowed to pay interest on demand deposits, AMCO like any good money manager, attempted to keep its bank demand deposits at a minimum. As is typical of all demand deposit accounts, the bank charges a fee for checks either drawn or deposited. Normally, a bank makes allowances by reducing its fees if the depositor maintains certain minimum demand deposit balances. Such allowances are, in effect, equivalent to an interest payment for the use of the depositor's money.

Since most investment portfolios can earn more interest income than the bank allows by way of fee reductions for deposits, the optimal bank balance is zero. On the other hand, each day AMCO has up to 15,000 checks for deposit and might have to disburse as much as $30 million. This means that to keep operating, some bank balance must be maintained. On the average, the balance has been $5 million. When this balance is insufficient to cover the bank's fees, the bank bills AMCO for the charges.

One must remain conscious of the fact that money on the books of the bank is not money on the books of the company. Typically, the float (check payments recorded as disbursed, but not yet presented or charged to AMCO's bank account) amounts to millions of dollars and constitutes an important source of cash. Thus, the amount of cash shown on the balance sheet is not indicative of the cash in the bank. For investment purposes, the primary interest is with the cash balance shown on the books of the bank.

### Determining the Short-Term Investment Portfolio

Two paramount goals determine the securities which AMCO may buy with the company's temporary excess cash. First, the portfolio's securities should be absolutely safe from loss of principal under normal conditions. Second, the portfolio's securities should be marketable and liquid.[2] In order to guarantee protection of the principal, AMCO established certain investment limitations governing types of securities and their maturities. These limitations state that when securities are purchased from an industrial or finance company, the following financial conditions must exist:

1. 2–1 current ratio.
2. Net worth over $10,000,000.
3. Risk assets no more than 7 1/2 times net worth over a two-year period.[3]

Bonds of municipalities or other qualifying organizations are acceptable only if they are rated "A" or better by Moody's. An additional test for safety is the distribution of securities. The limitation as to percentage of a given security within the portfolio is as follows:

1. Public Housing Authority bonds      50%
2. Canadian securities                 50%
3. Municipals                          10%

No limit was established for the other types of securities except that the company never buys common or preferred stock.

The question of liquidity was divided into the safety of the security and the time over which the security will mature. Mr. Johns believed that marketability is principally a function of price and that price is a function of security. Thus, when investments are held within the scope set forth by the company management, they will be marketable. To increase their marketability and the safety of principal at the same time, the company has also established time limitations. No security is purchased that matures in more than two years except under a repurchase agreement. Bonds can be purchased with two-year maturities. All other securities have to have a one year or less maturity. In the case of Canadian obligations, a forward foreign currency exchange contract must be purchased from a bank at the time of the purchase of the security. This contract calls for U.S. dollars to be exchanged for the amount of the Canadian dollars received at the maturity of the

---

[2]Liquidity for AMCO's purposes is defined as securities that may be resold immediately to the seller at a predetermined price or yield. Although most of the portfolio could be sold in very short order at a premium or discount from carrying value that would result in a capital gain or loss owing to changes in the money market, these liquid items would be sold recording neither gain nor loss even though in some cases an adjustment of previously accrued interest income would be made.

[3]Risk assets equal assets less cash and marketable securities.

security, thus protecting the company's assets against losses resulting from fluctuations in exchange rates.

In establishing a portfolio, a list of securities which are suitable for short-term purchase was set up (see Exhibit III). A close watch was kept on interest rates available on investments in the various securities (see Exhibit IV). Using the approved securities list and available interest rates, a theorectical portfolio was established based upon the most favorable distribution of securities. This theoretical portfolio was used as the goal upon which AMCO's short-term investment portfolio success was measured. Over the last few years AMCO had consistently been able to better the theoretical portfolio through judicious selection and substitution of securities (see Exhibit V).

In addition to the continual problem of investing with which he was faced and that of reviewing the type and maturity of securities, Mr. Johns was considering another specific problem—was the present approach to cash management the best?

AMCO had two reasons for keeping large amounts of cash and marketable securities on hand. The first was to have a cushion of cash available for opportune and emergency expenditures, to keep working funds earmarked for current-year dividends and tax payments, and to have funds available for those general fluctuations always present in the normal course of business. The second reason was that management wanted to keep a conservative financial structure in order to act as a buffer against the high risks they took in their product development. The company had found that over any five-year period its product line had changed almost 100 per cent.

The company did not borrow short-term money either from banks or in the open market, although obviously AMCO could borrow at the prime rate, which currently was $4\frac{1}{2}$ per cent from banks and $3\frac{1}{2}$ per cent from the open market. Thus, the needs for temporary cash could be met through short-term borrowing if the company wished to follow a program of borrowing; then, if such were the practice, the company could take the present cash balances and either pay them to the stockholders as dividends or invest this cash in additional expansion of fixed assets or inventory.

The fact that the company had substantial unused debt capacity meant that it had a choice of maintaining its cash position by investing or by using borrowed funds. Obviously, if AMCO was earning 4.3 per cent on its liquid assets now and had to pay $3\frac{1}{2}$—$4\frac{1}{2}$ per cent for those same liquid assets from someone else, borrowing would not be advisable. On the other hand, this might not be a valid comparison. Using the cost of capital or the company's return on invested assets as a standard might show borrowing to be more advisable. The company's cost of capital ranged between 10–15 per cent, and the rate of return on invested assets was 14.4 per cent over the last three years. The whole problem of cash in a company which has a top credit rating was interesting to Mr. Johns; however, he did not believe that his corporate management would want to sacrifice the significant advantages which a large base of liquid assets provided.

## EXHIBIT I

### December 31, 1963
### AMCO Securities

| | | Amount | | | Yield For |
|---|---|---|---|---|---|
| | | In thousands | Percentages | Items | December |
| Governments | | $ — | — | — | — |
| Tax exempts* | | 20,000 | 35.7 | 180 | 4.79% |
| Bank deposits : | U. S. certificates† | 16,000 | 28.6 | 32 | 4.06 |
| | Canadian time deposits‡ | 2,300 | 4.1 | 2 | 4.55 |
| Other Marketablesᵃ | | 17,700 | 31.6 | 11 | 4.24 |
| | | $56,000 | 100.00 | 225 | 4.36% |

| Detail | Yield | Due | Par Value (In Thousands) |
|---|---|---|---|
| Bank A | 4.06% | 2–06–64 | $ 50 |
| B | 4.06 | 1–22–64 | 1,000 |
| C | 4.06 | 4–01–66 | 1,000 |
| C | 4.06 | 4–16–64 | 200 |
| D | 4.06 | 4–17–64 | 50 |
| E | 4.06 | 4–25–64 | 500 |
| F | 4.06 | 4–27–64 | 100 |
| A | 4.06 | 11–15–64 | 50 |
| G | 4.06 | 11–17–64 | 2,000 |
| F | 4.06 | 6–27–64 | 200 |
| A | 4.06 | 1–25–65 | 50 |
| H | 4.06 | 8–16–65 | 2,000 |
| I | 4.06 | 8–20–64 | 1,000 |
| A | 4.06 | 2–23–65 | 50 |
| A | 4.06 | 3–19–65 | 50 |
| A | 4.06 | 3–30–65 | 50 |
| J | 4.06 | 2–26–65 | 1,000 |
| K | 4.00 | 7–25–64 | 500 |
| A | 4.06 | 4–27–65 | 50 |
| L | 4.06 | 11–18–64 | 2,000 |
| M | 4.00 | 5–18–65 | 2,000 |
| H | 4.06 | 6–28–65 | 2,000 |
| A | 4.06 | 6–01–65 | 50 |
| A | 4.06 | 6–29–65 | 50 |
| | | | $16,000 |

*These consist of $1,100,000, due from nine months to four years, in Public Housing Authority notes, and $18,900,000 in municipals of from one month to two years.
†Each of these certificates of deposit are 4 per cent interest bearing; however, we achieve a 4.06 per cent yield since some pay interest quarterly while others pay interest at 4 per cent based on actual days over 360:
‡The time deposits owned are $300,000 at 4.06 per cent for one year, due August 6, 1964 and $2,000,000 at 4.63 per cent for eighteen months due May 13, 1965.
ᵃThis consists of $1,000,000 Farmers Home Authority Notes yielding 4 1/4 per cent August, 1964, and ten issues of Canadian discount notes issued by five Canadian finance companies with a par value of $16,700,000. Details of the discount notes are below.

| Detail | | Fully Hedged Yield | Due | Canadian Par Value (In Thousands) |
|---|---|---|---|---|
| Company | A | 4.07% | 9–15–64 | 1,000 |
| | B | 4.05 | 4–17–64 | 1,000 |
| | A | 4.05 | 4–07–64 | 2,000 |
| | C | 4.14 | 1–13–64 | 1,000 |
| | B | 4.06 | 1–14–64 | 2,000 |
| | A | 4.37 | 5–19–64 | 1,500 |
| | D | 4.43 | 5–15–64 | 3,000 |
| | D | 4.44 | 8–10–64 | 2,000 |
| | D | 4.50 | 8–14–64 | 1,500 |
| | E | 4.59 | 12–03–64 | 1,700 |
| | | | | 16,700 |

## EXHIBIT II

### AMCO Actual and Projected Cash Forecasts
### July, 1963—August, 1964

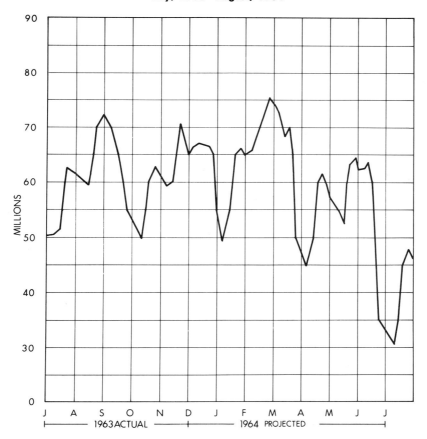

**AMCO**
**Daily Forecasts of Cash**
**(In Millions)**

| Jan. 1964 | Total Cash | Feb. 1964 | Total Cash | March 1964 | Total Cash |
|---|---|---|---|---|---|
| 2 | 51.3 | 3 | 66.7 | 2 | 74.4 |
| 3 | 51.9 | 4 | 67.4 | 3 | 74.2 |
| 6 | 52.0 | 5 | 67.4 | 4 | 73.8 |
| 7 | 49.3 | 6 | 66.3 | 5 | 73.1 |
| 8 | 49.5 | 7 | 67.1 | 6 | 73.2 |
| 9 | 49.6 | 10 | 66.7 | 9 | 73.3 |
| 10 | 49.3 | 11 | 67.1 | 10 | 72.3 |
| 13 | 57.4 | 12 | 70.3 | 11 | 72.2 |
| 14 | 57.9 | 13 | 74.7 | 12 | 71.4 |
| 15 | 63.4 | 14 | 75.6 | 13 | 71.2 |
| 16 | 63.9 | 17 | 73.8 | 16 | 70.5 |
| 17 | 63.5 | 18 | 73.9 | 17 | 68.9 |
| 20 | 66.2 | 19 | 75.1 | 18 | 60.4 |
| 21 | 65.2 | 20 | 75.4 | 19 | 48.3 |
| 22 | 64.7 | 21 | 73.6 | 20 | 47.1 |
| 23 | 66.2 | 24 | 74.3 | 23 | 48.9 |
| 24 | 67.0 | 25 | 74.1 | 24 | 47.8 |
| 27 | 67.1 | 26 | 72.0 | 25 | 47.7 |
| 28 | 66.8 | 27 | 73.3 | 26 | 48.1 |
| 29 | 65.5 | 28 | 74.3 | 27 | 48.3 |
| 30 | 64.9 | | | 30 | 47.4 |
| 31 | 65.4 | | | 31 | 45.7 |

### Explanation of Repurchase and
### Reverse Repurchase Agreements

A *repurchase agreement* involves two parties: an outside seller, and AMCO. The outside seller, usually a broker, sells to AMCO a specific security which he owns or controls and agrees to repurchase this security sometime in the future. If the broker selling the security to AMCO is of such financial stature that his credit is more important than the credit of the security, the company can purchase any security from him regardless of its rating or its maturity, and AMCO views this as merely an extension of credit. In other cases, where there is some question about the broker's financial status, the company can purchase any security from him on the basis of a repurchase agreement as long as the maturity is not in excess of four years and the Moody's rating is Baa or better. Customarily securities sold under repurchase agreements are bonds, notes, or bills. When a broker sells a security to AMCO, the interest rates that AMCO gets are generally ten to fifteen base points below the normal yield of the security.

Repurchase agreements generally last up to two years and are common devices used by brokers, banks, and many commercial firms when they have a short-term need for cash and do not want to sell a security permanently to get this cash. Instead, they sell a security on a short-term basis to a third party for cash for the period of their needs and later, when they have the necessary cash, they buy back the given security. Thus, the firm gets the advantage of the higher yields for longer-term escurities while still being able to turn them into cash on short notice. AMCO

**EXHIBIT III**

**AMCO Short-Term Types of Investments**

U. S. Governments
　Treasury bills
　Treasury notes
　Treasury bonds
　Tax anticipation securities
Instrumentalities of the U. S. (Agencies)
　Federal intermediate credit bonds
　Federal home loan banks
　Federal land banks
　Federal National Mortgage Association
　Banks for cooperatives
Finance company paper
Commercial paper
Public Housing Authority notes
Bankers acceptances
Municipal bonds
Certificates of deposit
Savings and loan associations
Corporate—preferred stocks
　　　　　—bonds
Foreign obligations
　Government
　Private companies
　Banks
Repurchase agreements
Reverse repurchase agreements

could fill up their entire portfolio with repurchase agreements. The biggest disadvantage of repurchase agreements is in their lower yields; however, some of this yield loss can be made up by having repurchase agreements on securities with longer maturities than AMCO would customarily buy on their own account.

A *reverse repurchase agreement* is similar to the repurchase agreement except that in this case AMCO sells the security and agrees to repurchase it from a broker or other company. The following is an example of an actual reverse repurchase agreement used by AMCO. In this case the security was a $2,000,000 certificate of deposit (CD) for one year and was to yield 4 per cent. The company first sold it to Company A for thirty-nine days to yield Company A 3 1/4 per cent. At the end of the thirty-nine days, it was sold to Company B to yield 3 3/8 per cent for seventy five days. At the end of seventy-five days, AMCO held the security for ninety-one days and then sold it to Company D at a yield of 3 1/2 per cent for 100 days. At the end of 100 days, it was sold to Company E, who held it the remaining seventy days of its life. At the end of the 360 days, the CD was turned in, and it earned $80,000 in interest. In the meantime, AMCO had paid out $51,345, so that for ninety-one days AMCO had received interest in the amount of $28,655, which gave the company a net yield of 5.75 per cent. Thus, by the use of reverse repurchase agreements the company was able to earn yields greater than they could by merely buying an optimal distribution of securities and holding them to maturity.

## EXHIBIT IV

### Interest Rates of Various Security Groups

|  | 30-day Treasury Bills | 90-day Treasury Bills | 9-month Hedged Canadian Paper | 1-year PHA notes | 1-1/2 yr. Municipals* |
|---|---|---|---|---|---|
| 1963 December |  |  |  |  |  |
| 6 | 3.24% | 3.58% | 4.79% | 4.16% | 4.54% |
| 13 | 3.34 | 3.58 | 4.79 | 4.16 | 4.52 |
| 20 | 3.46 | 3.59 | 4.79 | 4.16 | 4.52 |
| 27 | 3.46 | 3.58 | 4.59 | 4.16 | 4.44 |
| 1964 January |  |  |  |  |  |
| 3 | 3.49 | 3.59 | 4.54 | 4.16 | 4.60 |

*Before-tax equivalent.

## EXHIBIT V

### Theoretical Portfolio*

| % of Security in Portfolio | Type of Securities | Yields (Dec. 27) |
|---|---|---|
| 14% | 1-month Treasury bills | 3.46% |
| 10 | 3-month Treasury bills | 3.58 |
| 50 | 9-month Canadian paper | 4.59 |
| 16 | 1-year PHA notes | 4.16 |
| 10 | 1-1/2 year municipals | 4.44 |

*Theoretical portfolio weighted average yield is 4.25 per cent.

# Financial Planning

# 45

In January, 1966, Mr. J. P. World, president, and Mr. E. A. Wide, treasurer, of World Wide Discount Chain, Inc. were considering the probable needs for borrowing during the remainder of the calendar year in order to finance seasonal need for funds and to finance the operation of two or three additional retail outlets. The parent company was incorporated in Missouri in 1959 and the number of discount centers increased from two in 1960 to nine in early 1966.

The discount centers were located on the fringes of large cities in Missouri, Illinois, and Arkansas. The president and treasurer intended to expand the number of retail outlets and to increase the geographical areas of coverage to include all the major cities in the central part of the United States.

The parent company had been formed in 1959 by two major shareholders, Mr. World and Mr. Wide, and by two other minor stockholders. Mr. World and Mr. Wide each received 45 per cent of the initial stock issue, and the two other shareholders, Mr. French and Mr. Bond, each received 5 per cent. The parent company, the wholesale firm, was purchasing all the inventory for its fully owned subsidiaries, the retail outlets. The former had a fiscal year ending July 31, and the discount houses operated with fiscal years ending January 31.

Mr. World, the president of the firm, was born in 1920. He had had some eight years' experience with an advertising agency before he organized Sportscraft in 1954 to manufacture sporting goods equipment. His principal products were fishing tackle and camping equipment. His manufacturing firm met with limited success as the competition with large U. S. firms and with foreign companies grew more acute with each year.

Mr. World continued to spend a

great deal of his time in reviewing advertisement layouts and various promotional schemes. By the mid-1950s, he was convinced that the department stores were not as aggressive in their marketing techniques as were certain of the large chains and mail order houses. He believed that a more aggressive price appeal to the working class or bluecollar workers could yield tremendous profit potential.

The discount house had a tremendous appeal to Mr. World. A survey of the operating results of such discount chains as E. J. Korvette, Inc., Gem International, Inc., and others indicated that this type of merchandising could be undertaken with a nominal capital investment and with potential monetary rewards. Since Mr. World's fortune was tied up in his manufacturing business, and because he needed to devote full-time to its operations in order to operate successfully, he began to seek a buyer for the manufacturing firm.

In 1959, Mr. World sold half his interest in Sportscraft to James Bishop, who had had some manufacturing experience in sporting goods. Unfortunately, the sale freed only $30,000 in funds, and Mr. World believed that at least $100,000 in capital would be needed to organize a wholesale house and two retail discount centers. He believed that he could borrow an additional $15,000 or $20,000 from his local bank, but this would leave him far short of his initial estimated needs. Even with the building space being provided by leased quarters, a substantial investment in store fixtures and working capital would be required.

Mr. World did not wish to advertise for businessmen who were interested in forming a discount chain. He began instead by contacting some of his personal acquaintances. He preferred to set up the organization with four or five stockholders, all of whom were to be active managers in the firm. In order to round out the talents of the management group, he wished to locate specialists in the areas of accounting, finance, and retailing.

His first contact was his bank loan officer, Mr. Ed Wide. For the past four years, Sportscraft had been borrowing from a large St. Louis bank on a working capital basis. The account had been assigned to Mr. Wide. Mr. Wide was 38 years of age, had a degree in accounting, and had been with the bank for the past seven years. As Mr. Wide was a bachelor, he had been able to save about $1,500 a year since his employment with the bank. He had recently inherited $40,000 from a rich aunt and indicated some interest in going into business for himself. Mr. Wide listened with interest to the proposed plans for setting up the discount center. The more he thought about the proposal, the more convinced he became that it stood a good chance for success.

During the following few weeks, Mr. Wide and Mr. World continued to search for individuals who would make acceptable discount center managers. Mr. French had been a new car salesman for a number of years, and had a few thousand dollars to invest in the firm. Mr. Bond was a department manager at a local department store. The four individuals decided that the initial capital contribution would be prorated as follows: World, $45,000; Wide, $45,000; French, $5,000; and Bond, $5,000. Capital stock, $1 par, was distributed in the above percentages.

The four incorporators believed that having five directors who would be elected annually by cumulative voting was appropriate. The goal of the parent corporation was to expand the number of retail discount centers as quickly as possible. Although the addition of other retail centers would involve the need for other store managers, the officers of the firm were opposed to the dilution of their stock equity. They preferred to pay the store managers a basic salary and a per cent of profits in order to encourage aggressive merchandising policies.

The general officers of World Wide were to have offices in the parent organization. All purchases and borrowing for the separate retailing corporations were to be made through the wholesale firm.

The board of directors was comprised of the four stockholders plus an officer of a large textile supplier. In 1960 Mr. World was chairman of the board, president, purchasing agent, and advertising officer for the corporate group. His initial salary was $20,000 per year. Mr. Wide was secretary, treasurer, and controller, and he received an annual salary of $18,000. Each of the store managers (including French and Bond) received a salary of $600 per month plus an annual bonus of 10 per cent of their discount store's before-tax profits. In addition to their salaries and commissions, Mr. French and Mr. Bond each received $2,000 per year for serving on the board of directors of the various firms.

Numerous reasons existed for incorporating each discount house as a separate entity. The income tax laws which were in force in 1959 favored the small firm. Keeping the taxable income of each separate entity between $25,000 and $50,000 resulted in an overall tax savings over that of operating as divisions of one firm. Some states assessed a tax on chain stores which could be avoided by the separate incorporations, and the state income tax imposed on the firms was easier to compute with this type of organization.

The wholesale firm, in reality, was the parent company for each of the discount centers. The merchandise inventory was purchased by Mr. World and distributed to each of the discount centers. The salaries of the general officers, who served all the separate entities, were prorated to the separate organizations on the basis of the latters' profits. The wholesale firm billed each of its subsidiaries for cost plus five per cent. The mark-up was adequate to cover warehousing, delivery, and some administrative costs and to leave a small before-tax profit. For accounting purposes (other than income tax) Mr. Wide prepared consolidated statements (Exhibits I and II).

### Location and Layout

The directors of the firm believed that a busy intersection or thoroughfare near a large middle-income residential section was appropriate. Mr. Wide did not believe that locating within a shopping center would be particularly desirable, as the cost of leasing the space would be quite high. In 1960, Mr. Wide negotiated with a large insurance company for the construction of two discount centers, one located on the outskirts of St. Louis and the other in

East St. Louis. The one-story buildings each contained approximately 150,000 square feet and had exposed beams and direct lighting. The paved parking area surrounding each center would accommodate about 400 cars. The cost of the structure was about $12 per square foot compared to about $18 for a plush department store. Lease rental would return the entire cost of the building to the insurance company, along with a 6 per cent interest charge, over a twenty-year leasing period. The lessee had two 5-year options to renew at one-half the initial rental fee. The lessee also agreed to pay the property taxes, insurance costs, and periodic maintenance expense for the property. A combination office building and warehouse was rented on an annual renewal basis.

Each of the discount centers was designed to appeal to the working class of people. Shoppers were encouraged to dress casually and to shop on the way home from work. The centers carried low- and medium-priced lines of merchandise in men's, women's, and children's ready-to-wear and shoes; hardware and sporting goods; automobile accessories; appliances and household goods; drug items; and sundries. The intent of management was to offer a one-stop shopping center at every-day low prices. No weekend specials were offered, as the firm attempted to sell its entire stock at discounts ranging from 10 to 30 per cent below prices charged by department and specialty stores.

The display counters were plain wooden or steel frame racks. Department markers were suspended from overhead beams. The customer traffic was routed to the left of the store and was required to travel about one-fourth the distance around the perimeter of the store before it could approach the check-out counter. Mr. World believed that discount shoppers were impulse buyers, so he arranged the entrance route to parallel the drugs and sundry items. Shopping goods departments were clearly marked. Two or three floating sales ladies gave sales assistance within each center, as emphasis was placed on self-service.

In large metropolitan areas, such as St. Louis and East St. Louis, the discount centers used group store advertising. This was not possible for widely scattered discount stores, however. Each store was budgeted an estimated amount of sales with advertising appropriations of about one per cent of sales. This advertising budget was higher than the one-fourth of one per cent of sales being spent by general-line merchandising stores. World Wide typically used spot radio and TV commercials and weekend newspaper ads. The store featured daily low prices and store hours from nine to seven for six days a week. Blue laws had discouraged the management from Sunday trading.

**Purchases**

The management of World Wide had initially adopted the policy of carrying no more than three price lines in any one type of merchandise. For example, only three brands of men's white shirts were carried which retailed for $1.97, $2.49, and $3.85. Carrying large quantities of limited merchandise lines increased the size of order from the suppliers. This resulted in economies to the suppliers so that generous trade terms were granted World Wide by domestic suppliers. A large amount of the fishing tackle, toys, and transistor radios were bought directly from Japanese firms. Some lines of typewriters and office equipment were purchased directly from Italian manufacturers. The prices on the imported merchandise were substantially lower than on similar U. S. goods. Payments for the imports were handled by World Wide's St. Louis bank, the Bank of Commerce, on a sight draft basis. After the merchandise was received and accepted as to count and condition, the draft could be presented for immediate payment by the bank. The bank would then charge the amount against World Wide's account or handle it on a short-term loan basis. The medium-priced line of camping and fishing equipment was purchased from Sportscraft, one-half owned by Mr. World.

### Financing Current Assets

Mr. Wide considered himself to be a shrewd asset manager for the firm. He attempted to maintain an adequate, though not excessive, cash balance. Since all sales were for cash, no funds were tied up in accounts receivable. Annual merchandise inventory turnover had been about ten times during the 1965–66 period compared to 6 2/3 times for general-line merchandising stores. Although trade credit could be expanded by some 50 per cent, to do so would result in an average loss of about $\frac{1}{2}$ per cent of sales in purchase discounts.

### Expansion

The number of discount centers had increased to nine by the end of January, 1966. The growth in size of World Wide had necessitated the use of Mr. French and Mr. Bond in top management. Mr. French had shown his ability as an aggressive merchandiser and was promoted to sales manager. Mr. Bond was made purchasing officer of the firm. Additional discount managers and sales ladies were added to the payroll as well as receiving personnel, stock boys, and office workers. Mr. Wide's responsibilities had grown so complex that he was now directing a full-time accountant, a secretary, and a file clerk.

As the sales and profits grew in size, the level of salaries paid to the officers and directors were increased. By January, 1966, Mr. World and Mr. Wide were each receiving annual salaries of $40,000, while French and Bond were each receiving $18,000. The warehouse manager, discount center managers, and the accountant were classified as officers for payroll purposes, and were receiving compensation commensurate with their abilities.

The policy of the firm was to pay the monthly salaries of the discount managers and to accrue the commission until funds were available for distribution. The four stockholders of the firm had not drawn their full salaries in more than two years, so that total accrued salaries amounted to almost $300,000 in early 1966. Cash dividends had never been declared by the parent or its subsidiaries.

By the end of 1965, World Wide was operating discount centers in the following cities: Arkansas—Little Rock and West Memphis; Illinois—East St. Louis, Quincy, and Springfield; and Missouri—Columbia, Jefferson City, Kansas City, and St. Louis.

During the next three years, the management of the company proposed to open discount centers in Evansville and Indianapolis, Indiana; Kansas City, Topeka, and Wichita, Kansas; and Oklahoma City and Tulsa, Oklahoma.

Mr. Wide estimated that at least $275,000 in assets were needed to open a new discount center in leased quarters. His estimate called for cash, $15,000; inventory, $200,000; equipment, $40,000; and other assets $20,000. Expansion of trade credit in the past had carried about one-half the inventory, while equipment financing equal to 75 per cent of the cost of equipment and fixtures at a rate of 8 per cent was available. The balance of the fund requirements would have to be financed through the parent company.

The amount of sales almost doubled for the year ended February 28, 1966, over that of the preceding year. About 15 per cent of this increase was brought about by the addition of the Jefferson City and Columbia centers, while the remainder was attributable to sales expansion. Net profits after federal and state income taxes had risen in total amount but had declined from 2.3 to 1.8 per cent of sales for the two fiscal years. Seasonality of sales, reflected in Exhibit V, were typically low from January-April, average during the next five months, and unusually high toward the Christmas buying season. Since inventories were maintained at a level approximately equal to the next month's expected sales, some need existed for seasonal financing of inventory build-up from October to December. Mr. Wide estimated a similar increase in sales and profits for 1966–67.

### Plans for Future Growth

In March, 1966, the board of directors of World Wide were attempting to formulate some overall operating goals for their company. They desired to expand as rapidly as prudence and availability of funds permitted. Although they had just taken six-month options on tracts of land in the three Kansas cities at aggregate costs of $30,000, and had applied for charters within that state, some six to eight months additional time would be required before new outlets would be available for occupancy. If new outlets were to be opened in time for the Christmas season, plans would have·to be formulated immediately.

Mr. Wide was concerned with a number of problems. Some recent tax changes had brought about the need to reevaluate the policy for incorporating each firm separately, and some accounting changes in preparing consolidated statements were to be considered. Although the boom period had been rolling along for five years, Mr. Wide was unsure what fiscal and monetary policies would be taken and just how this might affect his availability of funds, his level of sales, and his profitability.

The independent department stores, as well as Sears Roebuck and Company and Montgomery Ward, had begun to be much more aggressive and to run more price specials than was true a few years earlier. The management of World Wide had considered the use of loss leaders, but desired to postpone this step as long as sales could be increased by other methods.

Some of the customers of World Wide had complained about the low quality of the merchandise they carried, especially the items which were imported. Mr. World had considered the broadening of his line to include high-priced merchandise, but many of these lines could not be sold at prices below the suggested retail price. The policy of marking each item with the usual price and the discount price was currently being used, but Mr. French felt that this practice could ultimately lead to shopping around and price comparisons by the customers.

A large segment of the customers were beginning to suggest that the company offer charge accounts and installment purchases. Mr. Wide was considering how the granting of credit might affect his need for funds, the increase in expenses, and the possible changes in the level of sales. He believed that one possible solution to the problem would be to organize a captive finance company which would offer up to six-month terms on the purchase of merchandise. He believed that a monthly charge equal to 1 1/2 per cent of the unpaid balance would be adequate to cover expenses and to leave a fair return on capital funds. Although some discount centers appeared to be offering more services and increasing the sales prices accordingly, this trend could possibly lead to the loss of price appeal.

To expand into other states and into other large cities appeared to be a worthwhile goal; however, as the distance from the wholesale firm increased delivery costs increased and management functions grew more complex. The directors had not opened more than one discount center in any one city, as this would perhaps reduce the sales of the existing center. This was a further possibility to consider, however, and some thought was being given to the opening of multiple centers around the fringes of some of the larger cities. Mr. World did not believe that World Wide should open a center within ten miles of one of their existing centers.

Mr. Wide had not developed any capital budgeting projections as to cost of capital and expected return on new outlet investments; however, he believed that these projections should be presented at the next board meeting along with quarterly cash receipts and disbursement schedules for the next year. He would then be in a position to request a line of credit to finance temporary working capital needs.

**EXHIBIT I**

## World Wide Discount Chain, Inc.
### Comparative Consolidated Income Statement

|  | 2/28/65 | 2/28/66 |
|---|---|---|
| Sales | $12,845,534 | $23,873,749 |
| Less cost of sales | 11,212,316 | 20,988,781 |
| Gross profit on sales | 1,633,218 | 2,884,968 |
| Operating expenses |  |  |
| Administrative | 6,540 | 12,415 |
| Advertising | 123,482 | 223,296 |
| Auto and truck | 3,142 | 5,309 |
| Bank charges | 677 | 1,174 |
| Depreciation | 37,428 | 70,650 |
| Dues and subscriptions | 863 | 1,231 |
| Franchise fee | 9,596 | 16,714 |
| Insurance | 15,054 | 26,327 |
| Legal and professional | 10,553 | 19,952 |
| Licenses and taxes | 15,325 | 35,468 |
| Payroll taxes | 32,465 | 64,222 |
| Rent | 133,332 | 245.992 |
| Repairs and maintenance | 15,322 | 21,239 |
| Salaries—employees | 474,431 | 955,448 |
| Salaries—officers | 180,416 | 269,057 |
| Supplies—office and shop | 42,110 | 83,813 |
| Telephone and telegraph | 6,937 | 12,817 |
| Traffic fees | 1,438 | 2,188 |
| Travel | 14,050 | 9,687 |
| Utilities | 31,601 | 56,145 |
| Miscellaneous | 6,022 | 28,387 |
| Total operating expenses | 1,160,784 | 2,161,531 |
| Net profit from operations | 472,434 | 723,437 |
| Other income |  |  |
| Interest income | — | 1,140 |
| Rental income | 34,769 | 74,290 |
| Vending machine | 10,625 | 42,082 |
| Total other income | 45,394 | 117,512 |
| Other Deductions |  |  |
| Amortization of organ. exp. and leasehold | 907 | 1,458 |
| Bad debts | — | 905 |
| Contributions | 1,192 | 27,228 |
| Interest | 6,140 | 13,752 |
| Life insurance premiums | — | 19,513 |
| Loss by theft | — | 329 |
| Total other deductions | 8,239 | 63,185 |
| Net profit before taxes | 509,589 | 777,764 |
| Less federal and state income taxes | 217,527 | 341,778 |
| Net profit after taxes | $292,062 | $435,986 |

**EXHIBIT II**

**World Wide Discount Chain, Inc.**
**Consolidated Balance Sheets**
**(Years Ended)**

| Assets | 2/28/64 | 2/28/65 | 2/28/66 |
|---|---|---|---|
| Current assets | | | |
| Cash | $3,720 | $6,360 | $56,566 |
| Accounts receivable—trade | — | — | 10,500 |
| Accounts receivable—officers | — | — | 2,716 |
| Loans receivable—misc. | 24,000 | 1,656 | 1,054 |
| Merchandise inventories | 1,097,314 | 1,637,569 | 2,571,571 |
| Prepaid interest | | | 3,124 |
| Total current assets | 1,125,034 | 1,645,585 | 2,645,531 |
| Fixed assets | | | |
| Air conditioning units | | 26,927 | 30,483 |
| Fixtures and Equipment | 92,126 | 146,312 | 363,948 |
| Leasehold improvements | 16,523 | 33,744 | 56,231 |
| Paving | | — | 35,866 |
| Trucks | 5,505 | 5,047 | 9,218 |
| Leasehold fee | 4,800 | 4,183 | 3,800 |
| Total fixed assets | 118,954 | 216,213 | 499,546 |
| Less depreciation | 21,059 | 63,266 | 135,978 |
| Fixed assets, net | 97,895 | 152,947 | 363,568 |
| Other assets | | | |
| Meter deposits | 370 | 532 | 591 |
| Organizational expense | 2,052 | 2,250 | 3,187 |
| Total other assets | 2,422 | 2,782 | 3,778 |
| Total assets | $1,225,351 | $1,801,314 | $3,012,877 |
| | | | |
| *Liabilities and net worth* | | | |
| Current liabilities | | | |
| Bank overdrafts | $19,754 | $32,467 | |
| Accounts payable—trade | 517,513 | 651,506 | $1,149,692 |
| Accounts payable—officers | 37,440 | 91,718 | — |
| Loans payable—bank | 90,000 | 57,224 | — |
| Notes payable—equipment | — | — | 145,358 |
| Notes payable—miscellaneous | 19,008 | 1,761 | 930 |
| Income taxes payable | — | 222,546 | 341,778 |
| Accrued salaries | — | 168,850 | 277,042 |
| Accrued sales and excise taxes | — | 18,190 | 32,020 |
| Accrued expenses | 12,969 | 354 | — |
| Accrued payroll taxes | — | 11,540 | 21,016 |
| Total current liabilities | 696,684 | 1,256,156 | 1,967,836 |
| Long-term liabilities | | | |
| Notes payable | — | — | 62,460 |
| Total liabilities | 696,684 | 1,256,156 | 2,030,296 |
| Net worth | | | |
| Capital stock | 100,000 | 100,000 | 100,000 |
| Retained earnings | 428,667 | 445,158 | 882,581 |
| Total net worth | 528,667 | 545,158 | 982,581 |
| Total liabilities and net worth | $1,225,351 | $1,801,314 | $3,012,877 |

## EXHIBIT III

### World Wide Discount Chain, Inc.
### Sales and Profits by Stores
### (Years Ended)

|  | 2/28/65 | 2/28/66 |
|---|---|---|
| **Columbia, Mo.** | | |
| Sales | — | 907,517 |
| Profit, net after-tax | — | 29,116 |
| % of sales | — | 3.2% |
| Officers' salaries | — | 5,040 |
| **East St. Louis, Ill.** | | |
| Sales | 937,213 | 1,245,305 |
| Profits, net after-tax | 33,788 | 47,279 |
| % of sales | 3.6% | 3.8% |
| Officers' salaries | 12,000 | 8,280 |
| **Jefferson City, Mo.** | | |
| Sales | — | 1,898,862 |
| Profits, net after-tax | — | 39,376 |
| % of sales | — | 2.1% |
| Officers' salaries | — | 7,200 |
| **Kansas City, Mo.** | | |
| Sales | 1,319,020 | 2,047,372 |
| Profits, net after-tax | 42,768 | 58,801 |
| % of sales | 3.2% | 2.9% |
| Officers' salaries | 37,721 | 43,920 |
| **Little Rock, Ark.** | | |
| Sales | 1,109,117 | 2,033,800 |
| Profits, net after-tax | 25,516 | 47,629 |
| % of sales | 2.3% | 2.3% |
| Officers' salaries | 28,800 | 22,320 |
| **Quincy, Ill.** | | |
| Sales | 879,978 | 950,788 |
| Profits net after-tax | 33,607 | 35,531 |
| % of sales | 3.8% | 3.7% |
| Officers' salaries | 8,400 | 5,040 |
| **St. Louis, Mo.** | | |
| Sales | 2,426,959 | 3,419,701 |
| Profits, net after-tax | 86,815 | 96,779 |
| % of sales | 3.6% | 2.8% |
| Officers' salaries | 32,400 | 75,600 |
| **Springfield, Ill.** | | |
| Sales | 811,849 | 1,086,956 |
| Profits, net after-tax | 27,964 | 30,763 |
| % of sales | 3.4% | 2.8% |
| Officers' salaries | 7,200 | 6,480 |
| **West Memphis, Ark.** | | |
| Sales | 397,224 | 876,052 |
| Profits, net after-tax | 8,794 | 26,892 |
| % of sales | 2.2% | 3.1% |
| Officers' salaries | 14,400 | 54,127 |

Totals for Retail Discount Centers

| | | |
|---|---|---|
| Sales | 7,881,360 | 14,466,353 |
| Profits, net after-tax | 259,252 | 412,166 |
| % of sales | 3.3% | 2.8% |
| Officers' salaries | 140,921 | 228,077 |

World Wide Wholesale

| | | |
|---|---|---|
| Sales (Year Ended July 31) | 4,964,174 | 9,407,396 |
| Profits, net after-tax | 32,810 | 23,820 |
| % of sales | .7% | .3% |
| Officers' salaries | 39,495 | 41,050 |

**EXHIBIT IV**

**World Wide Discount Chain, Inc.**
**Miscellaneous Financial Data**

| | Company | | |
|---|---|---|---|
| | 2/28/65 | 2/28/66 | Industry |
| *Ratios* | | | |
| Current ratios | 1.31 to 1 | 1.34 to 1 | 1.49 to 1 |
| Net worth to fixed assets | 3.56 to 1 | 2.70 to 1 | 3.48 to 1 |
| Net worth to debt | .43 to 1 | .48 to 1 | .55 to 1 |
| C. G. S. to inventory | 6.85 to 1 | 8.16 to 1 | N.A. |
| Sales to inventory | 7.84 to 1 | 9.28 to 1 | 6.50 to 1 |
| Sales to net worth | 23.56 to 1 | 24.30 to 1 | 19.94 to 1 |
| Sales to fixed assets | 83.99 to 1 | 65.67 to 1 | N.A. |
| Inventory to current debt | 1.30 to 1 | 1.31 to 1 | 1.05 to 1 |
| Net profit to net worth | 53.6% | 44.4% | 14.98% |
| *Schedule of accounts payable—officers* | | | |
| World | $16,086 | | |
| Wide | 55,844 | | |
| Bond | 20,470 | | |
| French | (682) | | |
| Total | $91,718 | | |
| *Schedule of accrued salaries* | | | |
| World | $54,000 | $65,880 | |
| Wide | 54,000 | 65,880 | |
| Other | 60,851 | 145,282 | |
| Total | $168,851 | $277,042 | |
| *Miscellaneous other data* | | | |
| Average Bank Balances | $184,870 (1964) | $206,533 (1965) | |
| Approved Credit Lines | $100,000 | $350,000 | |
| Net worth of principal stockholders | | | |
| (Including stock at book value) | | | |
| World | $410,000 | $778,000 | |
| Wide | 350,000 | 630,000 | |

EXHIBIT V

**World Wide Discount Chain, Inc.**
**Seasonality of Sales**
**By Retail Outlet**

| | Quarter of 1964–65 | | | | Quarter 1965–66 | | | |
|---|---|---|---|---|---|---|---|---|
| | 1st | 2d | 3rd | 4th | 1st | 2d | 3rd | 4th |
| Columbia, Mo. | | | | (Opened June, 1965) | | $239,695 | $296,345 | $371,477 |
| East St. Louis, Ill. | $121,182 | $117,328 | $279,194 | $419,509 | $271,718 | 258,746 | 325,764 | 389,077 |
| Jefferson City, Mo. | | | | (Opened August, 1965) | | 219,883 | 724,696 | 954,283 |
| Kansas City, Mo. | 219,642 | 256,814 | 376,807 | 465,757 | 348,400 | 405,625 | 578,125 | 715,222 |
| Little Rock, Ark. | (Opened Sept., 1964) | | 322,275 | 786,842 | 374,302 | 410,454 | 543,584 | 705,460 |
| Quincy, Ill. | 163,991 | 188,191 | 244,503 | 283,293 | 198,845 | 205,799 | 245,114 | 301,030 |
| St. Louis, Mo. | 415,735 | 490,544 | 696,000 | 824,680 | 705,173 | 769,667 | 893,608 | 1,051,253 |
| Springfield, Ill. | 116,710 | 134,447 | 241,634 | 319,058 | 200,340 | 205,733 | 318,548 | 362,335 |
| West Memphis, Ark. | 69,436 | 72,596 | 99,585 | 155,607 | 180,442 | 185,503 | 227,208 | 282,899 |
| Total | $1,106,696 | $1,259,920 | $2,259,998 | $3,254,746 | $2,279,220 | $2,901,105 | $4,152,992 | $5,133,036 |

## EXHIBIT V

### Telex
### Management's Slate of Proposed Directors

| Name of Nominee | Principal Occupation | Period Served as Director | Shares of common stock beneficially owned, directly or indirectly, by nominee or immediate family on May 22, 1964 |
|---|---|---|---|
| M. E. Morrow | Chairman of the board and president of Telex; and chairman of the board of Midwestern Instruments, Inc., a wholly owned Telex subsidiary. | March 1962 to date | 148,042* |
| R. P. Scherer, Jr. | President and general manager of R. P. Scherer Corporation, Detroit, Michigan. | July 1962 to date | 41,744† |
| S. A. Keller | Executive vice-president of Telex. | Feb. 1962 to date | 303 |
| John F. Y. Stambaugh | Certified public accountant; partner, Frazer and Torbet, Tulsa, Oklahoma. | March 1962 to date | 11,045* |
| Phillip Marco | Attorney at law; partner, Marco and Marco, Detroit, Michigan. | July 1962 to date | 415 |
| Knud I. Bruun | Owner, Turbolite Company, Houston, Texas. | July 1963 to date | 3,411 |
| J. B. Bailey | Attorney at law; partner, Farmer, Woolsey, Flippo & Bailey, Tulsa, Oklahoma; general counsel for Telex. | Feb. 1963 to date | 901 |
| Clifford V. Brokaw III | Manager; Corporate Development Department, W. E. Hutton & Co., New York City, New York. | None | 11,000 |

*Messrs. M. E. Morrow and John F. Y. Stambaugh through their controlling position of American Properties, Inc. will exercise voting rights on 32,393 shares of Telex owned by that company. Their indirect ownership of Telex shares through said corporation of approximately 19,435 shares and 6,479 shares, respectively, is included in above totals.

†R. P. Scherer Corporation is the owner of 35,729 shares. R. P. Scherer, Jr. and members of his family own 100 per cent of the outstanding capital stock of R. P. Scherer Corporation.

Cost
of
Capital

46

CONTINENTAL OIL COMPANY

On February 1, 1963, the director of the new-project division of the Coordinating and Planning Department of Continental Oil Company, Robert Gerwig, began assembling data for a report to top management on the firm's cut-off points for capital expenditures. Although the company had not made a complete appraisal of these cut-off points since 1955, Mr. Gerwig knew that, in view of Continental's continuously profitable operations, such a report could not be considered top priority. Still, he was aware that an examination of the firm's cost of capital, as well as its cut-off points, could bring some important (and possibly overlooked) facts to bear on the company's future financial decisions.

Mr. Gerwig, who had been with Continental for two years, had come to the firm directly from the University of Chicago, where he had received his Ph. D. in business economics. Since the section Mr. Gerwig headed was responsible for preparing the data for determination of the company's major investments, it was highly strategic to the company's operations.

Continental Oil Company was incorporated in 1920 and, in 1929, was merged with another oil company. Since that time, the consolidated firm had become one of the oil industry's most successful companies, with assets of over $1 billion and sales totaling nearly $900 million. The company was vertically integrated from well to station, and its principal gasoline outlets traded under the brand name of "Conoco." The company's domestic production of petroleum equaled 2.1 per cent of the total United States output, a percentage which it had been able to maintain since 1945 with only small fluctuations. Although the company had been striving for a bigger share of foreign oil, it still was producing 73.3 per cent of its total production within the continental United

States and another 12.6 per cent in Canada. The remaining 14.1 per cent was divided as follows: 8 per cent in Libya, 3.2 per cent in Venezuela, and 2.9 per cent in Iran.

Continental could be characterized as a medium-sized, fully integrated oil producer. With respect to other oil companies, it was considered a growth company, with an average increase in earnings of approximately four per cent per year. Continental's management had an excellent reputation, and it had striven to keep on top of new methods and procedures. (See Exhibits I and II for balance sheet and related financial data for the company.)

Continental had spent a substantial amount of time and money to develop its capital-budgeting program. As compared to companies of its size and smaller, Continental had developed a sophisticated approach. With respect to the firm's continuing prosperity, division managers knew and appreciated the importance of making new investments. They submitted their proposed investments through a systematic procedure, which had been laid out for them in a series of management bulletins. Through a utilization of the discounted-cash-flow method, all investments were evaluated for a rate of return; and, further, as a means of accounting for differences in risk,[1] the company had refined its procedure in order to make use of various discount rates on single projects. Unlike many other companies using the present value method, most of the management resistance to these procedures had vanished at Continental. The personnel who made investment proposals knew the cut-off point for their proposals; thus, proposals that had rates of returns which were less than the cut-off rate either were not submitted, or, if submitted, they had mitigating information attached. Authority to approve submitted proposals varied with the type, amount, and level of re-delegation. For any given proposal, one could not tell at what level it could be approved without an examination of company directives. Generally, department managers had authority to approve items with a value of $1,000 or less, provided such items were not in the budget. For budgeted items, the value approved by regional managers might be as high as $500,000. As new proposals were submitted up the scalar levels, eventually they would be placed in the following year's proposed budget, which would be approved by the firm's board of directors. Since the company was organized on a regional basis and since regional managers were generally evaluated as to fitness for advancement on the profit showing of their respective regions, Mr. Gerwig wondered whether all the complications to the question of capital-expenditure approval were really salient.

### Establishing a Cut-off Point for Capital Investments

Because the minimum acceptance point varied with risk, the company did not maintain a single cut-off point for all projects. Risk was considered

---

[1] Income and outgo cash flows would be discounted at rates which would reflect their varied expectations for recovery.

a function of departments but not necessarily of projects. Thus, in the development of wells and petro-chemical facilities, the cut-off point was 8 per cent higher than that for marketing and pipeline facilities. For example, even though a proposal might have a low-risk potential, if it were in what the company believed to be a high-risk division, it would have to take the high-risk cut-off point. The rationale for this basis of risk allocation was technological obsolescence; the petro-chemical area, for example, was subject to far greater technological obsolescence than was the marketing area (that is, new gas stations and other outlets).

Besides the element of risk, there was another reason for having different cut-off points among departments—the question of financing the investments. A proposal in the petro-chemical division which called for the development and sale of a new and untried chemical customarily would be financed with equity capital, while the extension of existing pipelines or the addition of new ones normally would be financed with a greater portion of long-term debt. Under these circumstances, the costs involved between the two proposals would be different. It could be argued that, given the company's present size, the market would not be able to differentiate adequately the internal composition of the risk and would look only at the overall financial mix. Most determinations, however, of the investment quality of stocks and bonds are made by analysts for services or for brokers, and these individuals usually are considered to be sophisticated enough to recognize certain risk variations.

If one assumed that, in any given area, the number of new investment opportunities would be approximately equal, the various minimums applied to different departments could cause misallocation among departments. Thus, the lower rate in marketing and the higher rate in petro-chemicals by themselves would tend to cause a more rapid expansion in marketing facilities, even though the company might not desire such an expansion. This was a secondary problem which was handled by top management since it was considered to be a judgment factor.

The minimums selected by the committee of management and passed on to the various departments were only suggested and did not, by themselves, constitute an absolute cut-off point. The company believed that there should not be any such thing as a fixed minimum and that, regardless of the minimum established, each proposal should be examined individually. Management considered that placing too many rules in this area would tend to result in inflexibility. Since conditions could change from month to month, such inflexibility might prove to be a serious block to a satisfactory expansion program. In other words, from management's point of view, there could be no substitute for good judgment, and the minimum cut-off points would have to be tempered with the conditions existing at a given time. The basic premise in this reasoning was that the determination of the cut-off point, as well as the calculation of the true rate of return, had so many imponderables that it could not be programmed properly or, at least, not in a satisfactory cost-to-output relationship.

The company's principal objectives in establishing the cut-off point were: (1) to raise the current dividend rate to stockholders, and (2) to expand income at a rate which would place the company among the upper 10 per cent of comparable oil companies, ranked as to income growth.

The company had established a number of different cut-off values for capital expenditures, the value depending on the particular department. The minimum for any expenditure was the cost of capital, or 7 per cent. The lowest risk departments were given a suggested minimum of 10 per cent, and the highest risk departments, 18 per cent. Other departments were ranged in between these two extremes.

### Determining the Cut-off Point

The cut-off point in each period was based on a number of criteria, including the following:[2]

1. Historical rate of return of company.
2. Historical rate of return of other companies.
3. Industry trends in rate of return.
4. Company's cost of capital.
5. Risk.

Continental's management realized that the limitation to new projects was not securing the money; the sources available to the company appeared to be unlimited. The real limit was manpower. The following two groups of criteria were used to determine the gross amount of new investment that the company would be willing to accept in any one year.

1. Will the new projects allow full utilization of the company's present manpower and existing equipment? If not, will there be a need for the hiring of additional workers who subsequently must be laid off?
2. Does the amount of new projects allow an orderly increase in sales, or will it entail pressure and long hours as well as upset normal routine? Does the new level of projects hold steady over the years so that a "feast or famine" does not occur in investment?

The company's capital expenditures over the preceding twelve years were as follows:

| Year | Capital Expenditures (Millions) | Year | Capital Expenditures (Millions) |
|------|---------------------------------|------|---------------------------------|
| 1951 | $88.7 | 1957 | $110.6 |
| 1952 | 90.7 | 1958 | 78.8 |
| 1953 | 85.0 | 1959 | 99.0 |
| 1954 | 100.0 | 1960 | 120.9 |
| 1955 | 100.6 | 1961 | 147.0 |
| 1956 | 100.3 | 1962 | 157.5 |

[2]The calculations for each of the first three rates of return have been shown in Exhibit III.

## Determining the Cost of Capital

By far the most important item in determining the cut-off point was the cost of capital. The rate that had been calculated in 1955 was 7 per cent, and, in general, this was the rate currently being used. It had been calculated on the weighted-average method, and the cost of the equity portion had been based on the required rate of return which would prevent any dilution of earnings per share (see Exhibit IV). Mr. Gerwig had realized, however, that many important factors were left out when the cost was established in this manner.

First, he did not believe the earnings per share to be the major criterion which an investor used in determining the price of stock. The one and only criterion for the price of a stock had to be based on the value of current dividends plus the expectation of future dividends—whether regular, special, extra, or liquidating. Any other assumption would have had to bring in relationships which appeared too difficult to quantify. For instance, one could assume that some investors were irrational, that management through manipulation maintained an artificial price, or that the use of stock options to pressure the market price could hold up the price of stock artificially. A second basis on which Mr. Gerwig disagreed with the calculations lay in the weights themselves. He did not believe that the distribution between debt and equity was correct. He had noted, for instance, that no mention had been made of an optimum capital structure. Further, short-term debt and rentals had not been included in the calculations. He was not sure just how these two should be handled, especially in regard to rentals and leases. This aspect was of considerable importance since oil companies depend a great deal on leases for their operations.

Continental was able to borrow short-term funds at the prime rate of 4.5 per cent, with a 10 per cent compensating balance which generally was not looked upon as an effective increase in interest rates. On long-term obligations, Continental had been given an *Aa* rating by Moody's; however, rates which applied to *Aa* bonds were not necessarily the interest rates which Continental would have to pay. For instance, if the bonds were first mortgage on a pipeline, the interest rate could be as low as 4.25 per cent, whereas, if they were debentures, the rate might run as high as 4.5 per cent. Other factors, such as a sinking fund or a call price, would also affect the yield. Further, bonds and notes of subsidiaries might have a much higher yield, depending on the indenture provisions. If a ratio were established between the average interest rates paid by Continental, as compared to the *Aa* bond yield, such a ratio could be utilized to project the rates to be used in averaging the cost of capital (see Exhibit VIII).

Mr. Gerwig believed that, in general, the determination of the cost of common stock and retained earnings was the most difficult. In order to make an adequate determination for equity, he developed the following formula:[3]

$$S = \frac{D}{(i - r)}$$

or, in terms of $i$,

$$i = \frac{D}{S} + r$$

where:

$S$ = Stock price normalized.
$D$ = Dividend payment.
$r$ = Rate of growth of dividend payments.
$i$ = Cost of equity capital.

Mr. Gerwig assumed that the stockholders' dividends would grow indefinitely at a constant rate.[4] While Mr. Gerwig considered Continental to be a growth company, he did realize that there were many points of view about what constitutes growth. Certainly, a company which expanded only at a rate equal to, or slightly greater than, the equivalent rate of the Gross National Product could not be considered a growth company. Over the preceding ten years, the GNP had increased at an average annual rate of 2.9 per cent, and most economists believed that the country would not be able to increase this rate more than 0.5 per cent over any extended period of time. It appeared that the long-run prospects for the oil industry would coincide with those for the nation, especially if action were to be taken by Congress to reduce the current depletion allowance. Even so, Mr. Gerwig, as well as all of Continental's top management, was convinced that the company would outperform the industry average.

Mr. Gerwig believed that substituting the price of stock on any given day into this formula would result in unnecessary distortions caused by day-to-day fluctuations. In order to minimize this distortion, he decided to take eighteen integrated oil companies (see Exhibit VI) and, by the use of a multiple-regression analysis, fit a curve to indicate the important determinants in the price of a stock. The equation he used was as follows:

$$P = a + bY + cD + dB + eG$$

---

[3] The formula actually developed was $S = D(1 + r)/i - r$, where $i = D(1 + r)/S + r$. The difference between the formulas was the quantity $(1 + r)$. Since $D/S = Y$ (yield), and since the problem was one dealing with future or expected yields, Mr. Gerwig believed that the next year's yield would be the most representative $[Y(1 + r)]$. He further reasoned that $Y$ should not indicate the past, since the stockholder who purchases a new stock buys on the basis of what his next year's yield may be, not what the past year's yield was. The $(1 + r)$ was dropped, however, since it did not appear to alter the final results appreciably.

[4] Although the model illustrated was a growth model, examples of stable and liquidating models may be found in Exhibit V.

where:

> $P$ = Price of the stock.
> $Y$ = Cash income per share.
> $D$ = Dividend per share.
> $B$ = Senior obligations per share.
> $G$ = Annual growth of cash income per share (last ten years).

On completing the regression equation, Mr. Gerwig obtained the following:

$$P = 13.78 + 2.157Y + 9.315D - 0.253B + 2.177G$$

The variations of actual stock prices from the calculated prices can be noted in Exhibit VI. Mr. Gerwig thought that the variation from $-27$ per cent to $+21$ per cent indicated that his curve was satisfactory, and he believed that the variation could be explained. Companies such as Ashland, Pure, Richfield, Standard of Indiana, and Standard of Ohio were net-deficit producers who had to purchase oil and, as a result, were selling at less than their normalized prices. Companies such as Continental, Phillips, and Union had a better balance of production relative to marketing. Mr. Gerwig had noted, however, that a major shortcoming of this explanation for equity prices was that a value for anticipated growth of income had not been used, except as anticipated growth and historical growth were identical. He had noted also that the equations explained 74 per cent of the variation among equity prices $(R^2)$, which, Mr. Gerwig thought, indicated a reasonably good fit. He knew that a better fit might come from a curvilinear function, such as, for instance:

$$P = a + (bY)(eG) + cD + dB$$

However, he considered that the difficulties in working out such an equation, as well as all of the other equations which possibly would fit, would not be worth the effort, especially since there was some doubt that he would be able to improve on the already determined 74 per cent $(R^2)$.

When the normalized stock price was put into the formula for equity cost of capital, the following results were obtained:

| Selected Domestic Petroleum Companies | Per Share | | Per Year | |
|---|---|---|---|---|
| | Calculated Stock Price (S) | Dividend (D) | Rate Of Growth (r) | Cost of Capital (i) |
| Conoco | $51.3* | $1.70 | 3–5%† | 6.5–8.5% |
| Conoco | 43.2 | 1.70 | 3–5† | 7.0–9.0% |
| Average of Conoco, Philips, Shell, Standard (Indiana) | 43.0 | 1.59 | 3–5† | 7.0–9.0 |

*Actual market.
†Estimated. For the period from 1952 through 1961, these companies had growth rates of cash income of 4 per cent to 6 per cent per year, as compared to an industry average of only about 2 per cent.

If perfect efficiency by the companies and zero leverage were assumed, Mr. Gerwig believed that "the 7 per cent to 9 per cent cost of capital would be the appropriate marginal project rate of return." At Continental (based on 1961 data), a 9 per cent cost of equity corresponded on the average, to a rate of return of about 11.5 per cent realized on projects. These figures indicated that major petroleum companies would have to earn between 7 per cent and 9 per cent return on investment in order to satisfy stockholder expectations.

Because the stock market tended toward long-run adjustments, Mr. Gerwig wondered whether there would be changes in the cost of equity capital over time. In order to make this determination, he applied his formula to industry figures and found that the cost of capital had changed (see Exhibit VII). He was unsure as to how he should modify his weights on the calculation of cost of capital in order to reflect this change.

As a last step before making out his report, Mr. Gerwig decided to make a first approximation of the firm's cost of capital. He was surprised by the results, which indicated that the cost of capital for the company had not changed appreciably since 1955. Considering this development and the low priority of this report, he thought perhaps it might be best to drop the whole matter.

## EXHIBIT I

### Continental Oil Company
### Capital Structure*
### (As of December 31)

|  | 1962 | 1961 |
|---|---|---|
| Current liabilities |  |  |
| Accounts payable and accrued liabilities | $120,991,467 | $95,804,603 |
| Accrued taxes, including income taxes | 18,443,590 | 15,673,918 |
| Long-term debt due within one year | 6,066,667 | 5,126,667 |
| Total Current liabilities | 145,501,724 | 116,605,188 |
| Long-term debt (at December 31, 1962) |  |  |
| Continental Oil Company |  |  |
| Debentures due 1991, 4.5 per cent (due $3,200,000† annually 1966 to 1990) | 100,000,000 | — |
| Thirty-year sinking fund 3 per cent debentures (due $4,000,000 annually to 1984) | 84,000,000 | — |

*At December 31, 1962, the company had long-term leases on certain service stations, office buildings, ocean-going tankers and other facilities, the aggregate annual rentals being approximately $12,200,000, including $3,693,000 with respect to assets sold in 1962 for $50,750,000 (the depreciated cost at date of sale) and leased back for long terms, but with options to repurchase under certain conditions.

The company and one of its subsidiaries, under agreements relating to companies in which they had substantial stock investments, had guaranteed payment of $13,650,000 of loans to such companies and, in addition, were obligated to provide specified minimum revenues from product shipments or purchases as well as (in one instance) funds, if required to maintain specified minimum working capital. No significant loss was anticipated by reason of such agreements.

†Price ranges for January 31, 1963, were as follows: Continental 4 1/2s, closed 104; Continental 3s, closed 85 3/4; Hudson Bay 4s, bid 81 1/2, asked 83 1/2. Yields were, respectively, 4.26 per cent, 4.00 per cent, and 6.10 per cent. Other issues were not traded.

| | | |
|---|---:|---:|
| Hudson's Bay Oil and Gas Company, Limited First-mortgage sinking-fund bonds (payable in Canadian currency) | | |
| Series A, 4 per cent (due annually to 1974, with $ 10,000,000 due in 1975) | 20,794,00 | — |
| Series B and C, principally 5.75 per cent (due annually to 1977) | 2,745,000 | — |
| San Jacinto Petroleum Corporation Subordinated convertible debentures, 5 per cent (due annually 1968 to 1977)‡ | 7,000,000 | — |
| Notes and debentures of other subsidiaries, 3.35 per cent to 6 per cent ($ 2,066,667 due in 1964) | 13,002,500 | — |
| Purchase and other obligations ($ 1,841,979 due in 1964) | 4,524,582 | — |
| Total long-term debt | 232,066,082 | 238,219,498 |
| Deferred credits | | |
| Sale of leasehold rights | 66,109,680 | 74,322,208 |
| Federal income taxes | 10,589,000 | 12,173,000 |
| Other | 18,174,163 | 13,916,470 |
| Total deferred credits | 94,872,843 | 100,411,678 |
| Minority interest in subsidiaries | $34,234,000 | $33,975,044 |
| Stockholders' equity | | |
| Capital stock, par value of $ 5 per share | | |
| Authorized | | |
| 24,000,000 shares | | |
| Outstanding | | |
| For 1962, there were 21,396,796 shares after deducting 112,979 shares in treasury; for 1961, there were 21,395,425 shares after deducting 98,025 shares in treasury | 106,983,980 | 106,977,125 |
| Capital surplus | 125,297,105 | 125,439,242 |
| Retained earnings | 502,134,814 | 470,491,273 |
| Total stockholders' equity | 734,415,899 | 702,907,640 |
| | $1,241,090,548 | $1,192,119,048 |

‡Convertible at the option of the holders into one share of San Jacinto Petroleum Corporation common stock and 0.34413 of a share of capital stock of the company for each $38 principal amount of debentures.

## EXHIBIT II

### Continental Oil Company
### Miscellaneous Financial Data

| Year | Gross Operating Income (Millions) | Yields Per Common Share | | | Price Range Per Share Common Stock | | | Capitalization | | | |
|---|---|---|---|---|---|---|---|---|---|---|---|
| | | Cash Earnings | Net Earnings | Dividends | High | Low | Mean | Funded Debt (Millions) | Per Cent of Total | Equity (Millions) | Per Cent of Total |
| 1953 | $476.8 | $4.81 | $2.10 | $1.30 | 32 | 24 | 28 | $53.4 | 15.6 | $289.3 | 84.4 |
| 1954 | 500.1 | 5.56 | 2.14 | 1.30 | 38 | 26 | 32 | 108.1 | 26.1 | 305.7 | 73.9 |
| 1955 | 528.9 | 6.22 | 2.38 | 1.43 | 53 | 35 | 44 | 107.5 | 24.8 | 325.2 | 75.2 |
| 1956 | 576.3 | 6.60 | 2.65 | 1.52 | 69 | 47 | 58 | 109.3 | 23.9 | 347.9 | 76.1 |
| 1957 | 608.9 | 6.80 | 6.38 | 1.60 | 70 | 42 | 56 | 151.7 | 29.4 | 364.7 | 70.6 |
| 1958 | 596.5 | 6.14 | 2.41 | 1.60 | 64 | 39 | $51\frac{1}{2}$ | 147.2 | 27.8 | 382.6 | 72.2 |
| 1959 | 685.8 | 6.60 | 2.85 | 1.70 | 70 | 45 | $57\frac{1}{2}$ | 118.8 | 18.0 | 540.4 | 82.0 |
| 1960 | 694.3 | 6.44 | 2.90 | 1.70 | 58 | 40 | 49 | 131.6 | 18.9 | 563.4 | 81.1 |
| 1961 | 805.7 | 7.53 | 3.02 | 1.70 | 61 | 46 | $53\frac{1}{2}$ | 272.2 | 26.3 | 764.2 | 73.7 |
| 1962 | 872.3 | 8.10 | 3.23 | 1.75 | 56 | 44 | 50 | 266.3 | 25.3 | 786.4 | 74.7 |

## EXHIBIT III

### Comparison of Percentage Returns for Continental Oil Company with Those of Selected Oil Companies

| Comparative grouping | Year | | | | | | | Average | | |
|---|---|---|---|---|---|---|---|---|---|---|
| | 1961 | 1960 | 1959 | 1958 | 1957 | 1956 | 1955 | For 3 Years | For 5 Years | For 7 Years |
| **Earnings on invested assets** | | | | | | | | | | |
| Group I* | | | | | | | | | | |
| High company (Ohio Oil) | 7.94 | 8.34 | 8.35 | 8.03 | 10.53 | 11.27 | 11.87 | 8.21 | 8.60 | 9.58 |
| Average of eight companies | 6.32 | 6.63 | 6.42 | 6.04 | 8.12 | 8.66 | 8.66 | 6.46 | 6.71 | 7.26 |
| Group II† | | | | | | | | | | |
| Average of five companies | 8.38 | 8.20 | 7.96 | 8.17 | 10.45 | 10.82 | 11.16 | 8.18 | 8.63 | 9.31 |
| Continental | 5.41 | 7.35 | 7.65 | 7.66 | 7.14 | 9.44 | 9.20 | 6.80 | 7.16 | 7.80 |
| **Earnings on net worth** | | | | | | | | | | |
| Group I* | | | | | | | | | | |
| High company (Shell) | 9.50 | 10.31 | 11.12 | 9.40 | 13.82 | 15.04 | 15.41 | 10.31 | 10.83 | 12.08 |
| Average of eight companies | 8.31 | 8.66 | 8.38 | 7.80 | 10.72 | 11.33 | 11.23 | 8.49 | 8.77 | 9.49 |
| Group II† | | | | | | | | | | |
| Average of five companies | 11.11 | 10.95 | 10.59 | 10.82 | 14.23 | 14.96 | 14.39 | 10.88 | 11.54 | 12.43 |
| Continental | 9.18 | 12.04 | 12.49 | 12.26 | 12.63 | 14.70 | 14.08 | 11.24 | 11.72 | 12.48 |

*The companies comprising Group I were Atlantic, Ohio, Phillips, Shell, Skelly, Sun, Sunray DX, Union. The smallest company in the group had net earnings of $23 million, and the largest, $113 million. All were considered comparable to Continental.

†The companies comprising Group II were Gulf, Socony-Mobil, Standard of California, Standard of New Jersey, Texaco. The smallest had net earnings of $211 million. These were international oil companies; however, they were not necessarily comparable to Continental.

EXHIBIT IV

### Continental Oil Company
### Excerpts From a Report to Management
### on Capital Budgeting, 1955*

1. The funds which Continental has available for investment are drawn from three principal sources: long-term debt, equity capital obtained from the sale of common stock, and retained earnings. Over the long run, it may be assumed that about 25 per cent of our funds for expansion will come from long-term debt and about 75 per cent from the sale of common stock or retained earnings.

2. Continental's credit is such that the long-term debt money can probably be secured at an average rate of somewhere around 3 1/2 per cent. Interest charges are a deductible expense for tax purposes, and hence the investment funds obtained from long-term debt may be considered to have an after-tax cost of about 1 3/4 per cent (assumes a tax rate of 50 per cent).

3. The "cost" of equity capital obtained from the sale of common stock is the rate of return which must be earned on the new money in order to avoid a dilution in our earnings per share. This required rate of return depends upon the relationship between the market price of our stock at the time the sale is made and our current earnings per share. Ordinarily, our price earnings ratio is such that the required rate of return on new equity money is about 8.5 per cent after taxes.

### Appraisal of New Capital Investments
### Illustration of Cost of Equity Capital

(The following calculations demonstrate that if Continental obtained $100 million from the sale of 1,431,000 shares of new common stock at a price of $70 per share, the money would have to be invested in such a manner as to earn $8.3 million or 8.3 per cent per annum after taxes in order to maintain our earnings per share at their present level.)

|  | At Present | After Stock Sale |
|---|---|---|
| Common shares outstanding | 9,747,000 | 11,178,000 |
| Present earnings after taxes, adjusted for intangibles (about $ 5.80 per share) | $56.5 million | $ 56.5 million |
| Earnings required on new money after taxes | — | $8.3 million |
| Net available for common stock | $56.5 million | $64.8 million |
| Earnings per share | $5.80 | $5.80 |
| Return required on new money | $\dfrac{\$8.3 \text{ million}}{\$100 \text{ million}} = 8.3\%$ per annum | |
| Ratio of per share earnings to stock price | $\dfrac{\$5.80}{\$70} = 8.3\%$ | |

As may be seen from the preceding illustration, for example, if we were to obtain $100 million from the sale of 1,431,000 shares of new common stock today at a price of $70, the new funds would have to be invested in

---

*Continental's average cost of capital was reported as 7 per cent. This cost figure was determined as described in this excerpt.

such a manner that they would earn $8.3 million or 8.3 per cent per annum after taxes in order to maintain our earnings per share at their present level.

4. Retained earnings are similar to equity capital, except that they represent an *involuntary* rather than a *voluntary* new investment by stock-holders. It may, therefore, be assumed that they also have an average "cost" of about 8.5 per cent after taxes. Alternatively, it might be said that our stockholders expect each $1 per share of earnings retained by management to be put to work in such a way that ultimately the market price of Continental's stock will increase at least $1 per share. All other things being equal, however, this will not happen unless the money is so invested that it earns a return at least equal to the present ratio of our earnings to the market price of our stock, or about 8.5 per cent.

5. If long-term debt money has an after-tax cost of 1 3/4 per cent and equity capital and retained earnings an after-tax cost of 8.5 per cent, the weighted average cost of the funds Continental has available for new investments is about 7 per cent. This average assumes, as noted above, that we will obtain about 25 per cent of our money from long-term debt and the remainder from equity stock and retained earnings.

### EXHIBIT V

#### Three Methods for Valuation of Income
#### Example Problem

Continental Oil Company's financial results are as follows:
$S$ = Stock price, $50 per share.
$D$ = Dividend, $1.70 per share.
$N$ = Net income, $3.02 per share.
$C$ = Cash income, $7.66 per share.
$A$ = Amortization of debt over 20 years, $0.56 per share per year.
$r$ = Estimated rate of growth, 4 per cent per year (reinvesting cash less dividends).

*Method I (Growth)*—Investor assumed to receive dividend income indefinitely, increasing at $r$ rate.

$$S = \frac{D}{(i - r)}$$

$$i = \frac{D}{S} + r$$

Substituting,

$$i = 7.4 \text{ per cent}$$

*Method II (Stable)*—Investor assumed to receive net income indefinitely (i.e., reinvested noncash charges would permit maintenance of income but no growth).

$$S = \frac{N}{i}$$

$$i = \frac{N}{S}$$

Substituting,

$$i = 6.0 \text{ per cent}$$

*Method III* (*Liquidating*)—Investor assumed to receive cash income, declining at 10 per cent per year, net of debt amortization.

$$S = \frac{C}{(i - r^1)}$$

$$i = \frac{C}{S} + r^1$$

$$r^1 = -10 \text{ per cent}$$

Substituting,

$$i = 5.3 \text{ per cent}$$

**EXHIBIT VI**

**Analysis of Equity Prices for Eighteen
Integrated Domestic Companies**

| | | | Market Premium | |
|---|---|---|---|---|
| Company | Equity Price* (Dollars per Share) | Observed Market Price (Dollars per Share) | Observed Price† (Dollars per Share) | Calculated Price‡ (Per cent of Observed) |
| Ashland | $30.3 | $25.1 | $(5.2) | (21) |
| Atlantic | 42.4 | 51.4 | 9.0 | 18 |
| Cities Service | 49.6 | 52.6 | 3.0 | 6 |
| Continental | 43.2 | 51.3 | 8.1 | 16 |
| Marathon | 40.6 | 40.4 | (0.2) | — |
| Phillips | 40.9 | 51.6 | 10.7 | 21 |
| Pure | 40.7 | 33.3 | (7.4) | (22) |
| Richfield | 43.3 | 39.4 | (3.9) | (10) |
| Shell | 34.3 | 35.8 | 1.5 | 4 |
| Signal | 24.5 | 25.3 | 0.8 | 3 |
| Sinclair | 43.5 | 35.3 | (8.2) | (23) |
| Skelly | 57.5 | 54.7 | (2.8) | (5) |
| Standard (Indiana) | 54.9 | 49.3 | (5.6) | (11) |
| Standard (Ohio) | 57.5 | 53.4 | (4.1) | (8) |
| Sun | 38.7 | 48.3 | 9.6 | 20 |
| Sunray DX | 32.9 | 26.0 | (6.9) | (27) |
| Tidewater | 21.7 | 19.0 | (2.7) | (14) |
| Union | 52.9 | 57.0 | 4.1 | 7 |

*Calculated from Regression equation. $P = a + 6Y + cD + dB + eG$.
†Calculated by subtracting equity price (column 1) from observed market price (column 2).
‡Calculated by dividing observed market premium price (column 3) by observed market price (column 2) multiplied by 100.

**EXHIBIT VII**

**Change in Cost of Capital among
Twenty-seven Major Companies, 1957-1962**

| Year | Stock Price Index* (S) | Dividend Index† (D) | Cost of Capital‡ |
|------|------------------------|---------------------|------------------|
| 1962 | $46.88 | $1.74 | 6.7% |
| 1961 | 45.23 | 1.69 | 6.7 |
| 1960 | 36.58 | 1.63 | 7.5 |
| 1959 | 43.33 | 1.59 | 6.7 |
| 1958 | 41.12 | 1.56 | 6.8 |
| 1957 | 44.47 | 1.62 | 6.6 |
| 1956 | 44.86 | 1.56 | 6.5 |
| 1955 | 37.73 | 1.47 | 6.9 |
| 1954 | 30.48 | 1.38 | 7.5 |
| 1953 | 25.32 | 1.36 | 8.4 |
| 1952 | 28.29 | 1.32 | 7.6 |

*For 1962, the average price per share for twenty-seven major companies (average of closing price, first eight months); for 1952 through 1961, the adjusted 1962 price was in line with Carl H. Pforzheimer and Company's "30 Oil Stock Average."

†For 1962, estimated, 3 per cent increase over 1961; for 1952 through 1961, average dividend per share for twenty-seven major companies, adjusted for stock splits and stock dividends.

‡Although the average rate of growth of dividends from 1952 to 1961 was 2.8 per cent per year, in the equation $i = D/S + r$, the value for $r$ (investor's anticipation of growth) was assumed to be constant at 3 per cent per year.

**EXHIBIT VIII**

**Aa Bond Yields**

| Period | | Composite of Corporation Bonds | Composite of Industrial Bonds |
|--------|---|-------------------------------|-------------------------------|
| 1963 | J | 4.37 | 4.23 |
| 1962 | D | 4.38 | 4.25 |
| | N | 4.40 | 4.24 |
| | O | 4.41 | 4.26 |
| | S | 4.46 | 4.29 |
| | A | 4.49 | 4.33 |
| | J | 4.49 | 4.32 |
| | J | 4.44 | 4.25 |
| | M | 4.43 | 4.25 |
| | A | 4.49 | 4.28 |
| | M | 4.53 | 4.34 |
| | F | 4.56 | 4.38 |
| | J | 4.55 | 4.38 |
| 1962 Average | | 4.47 | 4.30 |
| 1961 Average | | 4.48 | 4.33 |
| 1960 Average | | 4.56 | 4.39 |
| 1959 Average | | 4.51 | 4.36 |
| 1958 Average | | 3.94 | 3.78 |
| 1957 Average | | 4.03 | 3.89 |

*Source: *Moody's Industrial Manual, 1963* (New York: Moody's Investors Service, Inc., 1963).

# Obtaining Funds

## 47

In January, 1967, Mr. William Holoway, president and principal stockholder of the Holoway Manufacturing Company was forecasting his probable sales for the next three years and was considering methods for raising funds for expanding his business firm. A recent move of his manufacturing facilities from Montgomery, Alabama, to Birmingham, Alabama, a distance of about one hundred miles, had absorbed a considerable amount of the company's working capital so that if the company were to go ahead with its expansion plans, funds in the amount of about $300,000 would have to be raised. Mr. Holoway was considering the following possible methods for raising the funds: (1) the sale of additional common stock; (2) the sale of five-year notes to a wealthy individual which were convertible into common stock at a later date; (3) the sale of debentures to the general public; (4) an application for a bank-SBA participation term loan; or (5) funds provided by an SBIC on a convertible debenture basis.

Some ten years earlier, Mr. Holoway had organized the firm as a proprietorship. From an initial capital of about $60,000, the firm had grown to a net worth of about $350,000. In 1961, Mr. Holoway had elected to form two corporations, dividing the assets of the firm into a manufacturing corporation and a selling corporation. All the goods manufactured through the plant were sold by the selling organization, although the latter also purchased and resold numerous lines of refrigeration equipment and supplies which were not manufactured by Holoway.

The refrigeration company had operated as a seller, installer, and maintainer of commercial refrigeration products. The manufacturing company had become increasingly involved in the manufacture of component parts and assembly, although it had designed a number of new products which it expected to market. The manufacturing company's principal products were as follows: glass doors; walk-in freezers; reach-in coolers; cold storage plants; polyurethane foam building panels used for the construction of convenient grocery stores or filling stations; polyurethane foam nonrefrigerated storage boxes; and polyurethane foam weight-reducing boxes.

With the exception of one year, 1964, the combined companies earned a profit from 1957 through June, 1966. The high profit level was reached in 1961 when the company earned about $40,000 in addition to the $20,000 it paid to the company's president as a salary. Since that time the profits had been off somewhat as the company has been expensing its expenditures for research and development. Since 1962, approximately $150,000 have been applied toward research in the production of and uses for polyurethane foam materials. Profits for the combined firms for the fiscal year ended June 30, 1966, amounted to about $26,000. This was in addition to the salary paid to the company president, Mr. Holoway.

The president of the company, Mr. Holoway, was in his forties. After completing high school, he attended one of the leading trade schools which specialized in electricity, refrigeration, and radio. After completion of the school, he worked as an electrician, chief electrician's mate in the U.S. Navy during WWII, an operator of a radio repair center and appliance dealership, and owner-operator of his present firm. He was recognized by the trade as a leader in the refrigeration equipment industry.

Two other officers of the firm held engineering degrees from leading universities. The bulk of the remaining employees was made up of semi-skilled workers and experienced salesmen.

Until October, 1966, the manufacturing facilities were located in rented facilities to the rear of the refrigeration company. Inventory storage space and assembly areas were very congested and poorly organized. In July, 1966, Mr. Holoway located a large sheet metal building situated on a six-acre tract of land which would be suitable for his expanding manufacturing operations. For many weeks he considered the advantages and disadvantages of relocating the manufacturing phase of his business to the new quarters. The land and building were acquired in October, 1966, at an aggregate cost of about $162,000. The land was valued at $15,000 and the 100' by 400' building was purchased for $147,000, although Mr. Holoway believed that the replacement cost for the building would be some $200,000. The building had been vacant about twelve months, but appeared to fit the needs of the manufacturing operations without alteration other than some dividing partitions which the company could manufacture from plywood and poly-urethane foam.

In order to finance the acquisition of the new facilities, the company obtained a ten-year, 6 per cent loan equal to two-thirds of the cost price of the land and building. A second mortgage for $22,500 was given to the seller of the building. The note was due on September 30, 1967, along with 6 per cent interest. In order to obtain certain pieces of equipment, the company leased equipment which had a cash value of about $35,000. The lease rental would repay the cost plus an interest return of 8 per cent to the lessor over a five-year period. Additional lease financing at similar terms were available to the company. The life of the equipment which was leased was estimated at five years with no scrap value.

The separation of the business firms by some 100 miles created some new problems and increased the transportation costs. Labor at the new manufacturing site, however, was more abundant, and the new quarters would accommodate a level of manufacturing some six or eight times as great as was possible in the old quarters. Although no immediate plans were made to relocate the selling organization adjacent to the manufacturing plant, abundant land was available on the six-acre tract.

Sales for the six-month period ended December 31, 1966, totaled about $390,000, while the company had losses of $38,000. Mr. Holoway, however, had expected to sustain losses approximating $50,000 from the move, and he believed that the company would reach the breakeven profit point by March, 1967.

The company was ready to market a number of new products and believed that sales and profits would increase tremendously during the next three years. One of these products was an aluminum and glass door. The door was equal to or better than that manufactured by the company's competitor, and the management believed that large lots of these unbranded doors could be sold to other manufacturers of reach-in coolers and freezers. The products on which the future of the company primarily hinged were reach-in and walk-in freezers and coolers and polyurethane foam building panels. The panels consisted of a four-inch thickness of polyurethane foam sandwiched between two, one-half inch sheets of plywood. The outside was covered with a thin coat of plastic or V-crimp sheet metal. The panels were used in the construction of the walk-in and reach-in freezers and coolers, and Mr. Holoway believed that his boxes were superior to those being produced by his competitors. The only limitation to the company's ability to expand its sales was the inability to patent its products. Its plan was to keep ahead of its competitors through continuous research and development. Mr. Holoway was also hopeful that the steam reducing boxes and the nonrefrigeration storage boxes would enjoy a growing market. Foods had remained frozen in the latter for more than 24 hours during repeated tests. Mr. Holoway believed that frozen food delivery vehicles could be constructed with his product so that the need for refrigeration equipment could be eliminated. He had not pursued the possible use of the panels by railroad carriers.

Mr. Holoway and other members of his staff drew up forecasts of sales estimates for their manufactured products. These appear in Exhibit I. In order to expand the manufacturing phase of the company, however, some $300,000 in operating capital would have to be raised. The stock of the company was closely held. There were some 14 stockholders, but the president of the company (and his family) owned some 70 per cent of the shares. Some $40,000 and $15,000 blocks of stock had been sold to two other individuals, both directors, and some ten other employees held small amounts of the stock.

Mr. Holoway had been contacted by the business manager for a wealthy family, Mr. John Barrington, who indicated some interest in an investment in the firm if it appeared to offer some capital appreciation possibilities. The family had substantial amounts of funds available so that additional cash could be made available to the company should the need arise within the near future. Although no binding contract had been negotiatied, Mr. Holoway believed that five-year notes in the amount of $300,000 which carried a six per cent interest rate and which were convertible in whole or part into 150,000 shares of the stock during a five-year period would be acceptable to Mr. Barrington. In the event that conversion did not take place, the entire amount of the note would be payable at the end of the five-year period. The interest of the debt was payable quarterly.

Mr. Holoway had raised some $110,000 through sale of common shares to a few selected individuals at par value, $1 per share. He had recently been offered $2 a share for 37,500 shares by a wealthy speculator. He reasoned that if one individual were willing to pay $2 per share for the stock, a market issue of the shares could probably be made. Mr. Holoway, however, as well as the other officers and stockholders of the firm were not keen on selling large amounts of equity funds just at the time when sales and earnings could begin to rise substantially. If possible, Mr. Holoway wished to retain a controlling interest in the firm.

Mr. Holoway had spoken with three officers of chain grocery stores which had been able to market subordinated debentures. Terms of the most recent issues had been ten-year bonds which carried an 8 per cent interest rate. A sinking fund equal to the amount of the issue would probably have to be provided in order to make the issue acceptable to the general public and to the commissioner of securities.

Mr. Holoway was well acquainted with numerous individuals who had been able to obtain a bank-SBA participation loan. He realized that the SBA required a reasonable ability to repay the loan over the loan period from net profits and depreciation allowances. The maximum amount of such a loan was $350,000; the interest rate charged by the SBA on its portion of the loan was 5 1/2 per cent; the interest rate charged by most banks on their portion was 6–8 per cent; and the maximum repayment period was 10 years. Equal monthly payments of principal plus accrued interest were generally required as well as a pledge of collateral equal to the amount of the loan.

Although Mr. Holoway had not approached the management of a SBIC about a possible commitment of funds to the company, he felt relatively sure that the terms would be approximately those which were offered by Mr. Barrington.

Mr. Holoway had hoped in November, 1966, that a local bank would be willing to grant him a $200,000, five-year, 6 per cent loan. The banker, however, had been reluctant to make a term loan to the company until it was operating at a profit.

Mr. Holoway believed that each month the company delayed raising some additional working capital so that it could launch into its increased sales campaign was costing the firm thousands of dollars. He, therefore, wished to determine which of the above alternatives appeared most likely for success and which ones offered the greatest benefits to the company.

**EXHIBIT I**

**Holoway Manufacturing Corporation**
**Consolidated Projected Sales Demand**
**From January, 1967-June, 1969**

|  | Jan.-June 1967 | Fiscal 1968 | Fiscal 1969 |
|---|---|---|---|
| Aluminum-glass doors |  |  |  |
| 200 @ $70 × 6 mo. | $84,000 |  |  |
| 400 @ $70 × 12 mo. |  | $336,000 |  |
| 600 @ $70 × 12 mo. |  |  | $504,000 |
| Reach-in coolers; freezers |  |  |  |
| 135 @ $1,000 | 135,000 |  |  |
| 450 @ $1,000 |  | 450,000 |  |
| 675 @ $1,000 |  |  | 675.000 |
| Walk-in coolers and freezers |  |  |  |
| 144 @ $2,500 | 360,000 |  |  |
| 480 @ $2,500 |  | 1,200,000 |  |
| 720 @ $2,500 |  |  | 1,800,000 |
| Nonrefrigeration boxes |  |  |  |
| 600 @ $75 | 45,000 |  |  |
| 2,000 @ $75 |  | 150,000 |  |
| 3,000 @ $75 |  |  | 225,000 |
| Sale of panels |  |  |  |
| 72,000 sp. feet @ $1.00 | 72,000 |  |  |
| 240,000 sp. feet @ $1.00 |  | 240,000 |  |
| 360,000 sp. feet @ $1.00 |  |  | 360,000 |
| Pre-fab stores |  |  |  |
| 20 @ 15,000 | 300,000 |  |  |
| 40 @ 15,000 |  | 600,000 |  |
| 60 @ 15,000 |  |  | 900,000 |
| Other products | 50,000 | 100,00 | 120,000 |
| Net profits before taxes (% of revenue) | 4% | 6% | 8% |
| Cost of goods sold components |  |  |  |
| Direct materials | 75% | — | — |
| Direct labor | 10% | — | — |
| Overhead | 15% | — | — |

## EXHIBIT II

**Holoway Manufacturing Corporation**
**Comparative Income Statements**

| | Six Months Ended Dec. 31, '66 | Year Ended June 30, '66 | Year Ended June 30, '65 |
|---|---|---|---|
| Gross sales | $320,524 | $604,134 | $349,310 |
| Cost of goods sold | 318,587 | 552,893 | 325,220 |
| Gross profit | 1,937 | 51,241 | 24,090 |
| Selling expense | | | |
| Salaries | 8,287 | 11,623 | 7,829 |
| Insurance | 367 | 442 | 853 |
| Payroll taxes | 467 | 1,559 | 959 |
| Traveling expense | 1,770 | — | 13 |
| Rent | 343 | 3,600 | 3,600 |
| Advertising | 275 | 131 | 137 |
| Telephone | 3,767 | — | — |
| Miscellaneous | 313 | 429 | 828 |
| Total | 15,589 | 17,784 | 14,219 |
| Net profit (loss) on sales | (13,652) | 33,457 | 9,871 |
| General and administrative | | | |
| Salaries | 7,919 | 12,529 | 10,800 |
| Depreciation | 120 | — | — |
| Insurance | 43 | — | — |
| Payroll taxes | 545 | 1,662 | 1,440 |
| Telephone | 1,189 | — | — |
| Professional fees | 6,653 | — | — |
| Stationery and printing | 725 | 758 | 735 |
| Miscellaneous | 1,743 | 1,239 | 881 |
| Total | 18,937 | 16,188 | 13,856 |
| Net profit from operations (loss) | (32,589) | 17,269 | (3,985) |
| Other income | | | |
| Discounts earned | 3,771 | 11,532 | 3,907 |
| Interest income | — | — | 186 |
| Other deductions | | | |
| Administrative Services | 1,800 | — | — |
| Interest | 2,881 | 1,107 | — |
| Total | 4,681 | 1,107 | — |
| Net profit for the period (loss) | ($33,499) | $27,694 | $108 |

EXHIBIT III

## Holoway Manufacturing Corporation
### Comparative Balance Sheets

|  | As of Dec. 31, 1966 | As of June 30, '66* | As of June 30, '65 |
|---|---|---|---|
| *Assets* | | | |
| Current assets | | | |
| Cash | $519 | $20,937 | $12,455 |
| Accounts receivable ref. co. | 1,925 | — | — |
| Inventory | 90,637 | 100,325 | 99,208 |
| Prepaid insurance | 148 | — | — |
| Total | 93,229 | 120,262 | 111,663 |
| Other assets | | | |
| Stock—ref. co. | 240,509 | — | — |
| Utility deposits | 340 | — | — |
| Total | 240,849 | — | — |
| Land | 15,000 | | |
| Other fixed assets | | | |
| Building | 145,673 | — | — |
| Machinery and equip. | 116,985 | 58,572 | 44,385 |
| Furniture and fixtures | 2,082 | — | — |
| Total depreciable assets | 264,740 | 58,572 | 44,385 |
| Less: accumulated depr. | 29,933 | 15,749 | 14,287 |
| Total other fixed assets | 234,807 | 42,823 | 30,098 |
| Total assets | $583,885 | $164,085 | $141,761 |
| *Liabilities and capital* | | | |
| Current liabilities | | | |
| Accounts payable—ref. co. | | $6,445 | $63,972 |
| Accounts payable—trade | $86,407 | 71,286 | 28,530 |
| Mortgage payable, current | 22,500 | — | — |
| Income taxes payable | 3,283 | 7,020 | — |
| Accrued payroll taxes | 3,208 | 758 | 407 |
| Accrued payroll | 1,185 | 459 | — |
| Other accruals | 978 | 1,110 | 1,110 |
| Total | 117,561 | 87,078 | 94,019 |
| Long-term liabilities | | | |
| Mortgages payable | 103,543 | — | — |
| Notes payable | — | 9,750 | 8,250 |
| Total Liabilities | 221,104 | 96,828 | 102,269 |
| Stockholders' equity | | | |
| Capital stock | 356,700 | 37,500 | 37,500 |
| Revaluation surplus | 21,216 | — | — |
| Retained earnings (deficit) | (15,135) | 29,757 | 1,992 |
| Total equity | 362,781 | 67,257 | 39,492 |
| Total liabilities and capital | $583,885 | $164,085 | $141,761 |

*Audited.

**EXHIBIT IV**

**Holoway Refrigeration Company**
**Comparative Income Statement**

|  | Six Months Ended Dec. 31, '66 | Year Ended June 30, '66 | Year Ended June 30, '65 |
|---|---|---|---|
| Sales |  |  |  |
| Regular | $275,351 | $570,557 | $364,959 |
| Installment | 108,767 | 213,923 | 130,505 |
| Resale | 12,433 | 10,429 | 7,560 |
| Total | 396,551 | 794,909 | 503,024 |
| Less returns and allow. | 8,353 | 19,887 | 11,417 |
| Net sales | 388,198 | 775,022 | 491,607 |
| Cost of goods sold | 351,701 | 661,687 | 434,405 |
| Gross profit | 36,497 | 113,335 | 57,202 |
| Expenses |  |  |  |
| Salaries—officers | 10,313 | 15,450 | 15,315 |
| Salaries—other | 8,958 | 22,657 | 8,676 |
| Contract labor | 349 | 445 | 3,091 |
| Office expence | 741 | 2,263 | 1,943 |
| Rent | 1,800 | 4,140 | 4,140 |
| Utilities | 2,189 | 5,250 | 4,044 |
| Telephone | 3,204 | 7,242 | 6,395 |
| Repair | 519 | 2,220 | 1,743 |
| Insurance | 2,155 | 6,495 | 3,471 |
| Advertising | 2,351 | 9,306 | 9,893 |
| Payroll taxes | 967 | 1,999 | 1,350 |
| Travel and delivery | 5,627 | 13,631 | 4,965 |
| Subscriptions and dues | 498 | 2,601 | 1,871 |
| Legal and professional | 2,849 | 6,183 | 2,755 |
| Depreciation | 2,868 | 3,955 | 4,258 |
| Miscellaneous | 697 | 2,522 | 1,725 |
| Bad debt |  | 4,223 |  |
| Total | 46,085 | 110,582 | 75,635 |
| Net gain (loss) | (9,588) | 2,753 | (18,433) |
| Other income |  |  |  |
| Discounts earned | 400 | 930 | 467 |
| Administrative services | 1,800 | 10,800 | 10,800 |
| Interest and carrying charges | 3,162 | 2,013 | 3,957 |
| Miscellaneous | 333 | 2,034 | 3,408 |
| Total | 5,695 | 15,777 | 18,632 |
| Other deductions |  |  |  |
| Interest | (924) | (10,974) |  |
| Net profit (loss) for the period | ($4,817) | $7,556 | $199 |

*Audited.

363

**EXHIBIT V**

**Holoway Refrigeration Company**
**Comparative Balance Sheet**

|  | As of December 31, 1966 | As of June 30, 1965 | As of June 30, 1965 |
|---|---|---|---|
| *Assets* | | | |
| Current assets | | | |
| Cash | $2,595 | $11,005 | $19,080 |
| Accounts receivable | 74,430 | 74,479 | 47,850 |
| Notes receivable | 2,178 | 2,007 | 20,325 |
| Due from Holoway Mfg. Co. | — | 6,445 | 63,972 |
| Total receivables | 76,608 | 82,931 | 132,147 |
| Less: Bad debt reserves | (7,515) | (7,483) | (9,777) |
| Deposits on notes receivable discounted | 20,407 | 22,547 | 17,910 |
| Inventory | 35,469 | 29,559 | 5,705 |
| Prepaid insurance | 1,727 | 3,455 | 3,315 |
| Total current assets | 129,291 | 142,014 | 168,380 |
| Fixed assets | | | |
| Furniture and fixtures | 5,601 | 6,360 | 5,447 |
| Autos and trucks | 21,023 | 27,665 | 12,205 |
| Total | 26,624 | 34,025 | 17,652 |
| Less: Reserve for dspreciation | 14,891 | 11,737 | 11,889 |
| Total fixed assets | 11,733 | 22,288 | 5,763 |
| Total assets | $141,024 | $164,302 | $174,143 |
| *Liabilities and capital* | | | |
| Current liabilities | | | |
| Accounts payable—Holoway Mfg. | $1,925 | | |
| Accounts payable—trade | 7,381 | $5,430 | $31,920 |
| Floor plan notes | — | 705 | 2,795 |
| Income taxes payable | 829 | 1,971 | — |
| Accrued payroll and other taxes | 1,377 | 3,623 | 3,585 |
| Accrued salaries | 539 | 127 | — |
| Accrued insurance | 113 | — | — |
| Reserve for warranties | 12,109 | 9,299 | 6,043 |
| Total | 24,273 | 21,155 | 44,343 |
| Long-term liabilities | | | |
| Notes payable (Mr. Holoway) | — | 94,494 | 92,625 |
| Capital | | | |
| Capital | 37,500 | 37,500 | 37,500 |
| Paid-in surplus | 80,183 | | |
| Retained earnings | (932) | 11,153 | (325) |
| Total capital | 116,751 | 48,653 | 37,175 |
| Total liabilities and capital | $141,024 | $164,302 | $174,143 |

*Audited.

## APPENDIX A

### PRESENT VALUE OF $1 RECEIVED ANNUALLY FOR N YEARS

| Years (N) | 1% | 2% | 4% | 6% | 8% | 10% | 12% | 14% | 15% | 16% |
|---|---|---|---|---|---|---|---|---|---|---|
| 1 | 0.990 | 0.980 | 0.962 | 0.943 | 0.926 | 0.909 | 0.893 | 0.877 | 0.870 | 0.862 |
| 2 | 1.970 | 1.942 | 1.886 | 1.833 | 1.783 | 1.736 | 1.690 | 1.647 | 1.626 | 1.605 |
| 3 | 2.941 | 2.884 | 2.775 | 2.673 | 2.577 | 2.487 | 2.402 | 2.322 | 2.283 | 2.246 |
| 4 | 3.902 | 3.808 | 3.630 | 3.465 | 3.312 | 3.170 | 3.037 | 2.914 | 2.855 | 2.798 |
| 5 | 4.853 | 4.713 | 4.452 | 4.212 | 3.993 | 3.791 | 3.605 | 3.433 | 3.352 | 3.274 |
| 6 | 5.795 | 5.601 | 5.242 | 4.917 | 4.623 | 4.355 | 4.111 | 3.889 | 3.784 | 3.685 |
| 7 | 6.728 | 6.472 | 6.002 | 5.582 | 5.206 | 4.868 | 4.564 | 4.288 | 4.160 | 4.039 |
| 8 | 7.652 | 7.325 | 6.733 | 6.210 | 5.747 | 5.335 | 4.968 | 4.639 | 4.487 | 4.344 |
| 9 | 8.566 | 8.162 | 7.435 | 6.802 | 6.247 | 5.759 | 5.328 | 4.946 | 4.772 | 4.607 |
| 10 | 9.471 | 8.983 | 8.111 | 7.360 | 6.710 | 6.145 | 5.650 | 5.216 | 5.019 | 4.833 |
| 11 | 10.368 | 9.787 | 8.760 | 7.887 | 7.139 | 6.495 | 5.988 | 5.453 | 5.234 | 5.029 |
| 12 | 11.255 | 10.575 | 9.385 | 8.384 | 7.536 | 6.814 | 6.194 | 5.660 | 5.421 | 5.197 |
| 13 | 12.134 | 11.343 | 9.986 | 8.853 | 7.904 | 7.103 | 6.424 | 5.842 | 5.583 | 5.342 |
| 14 | 13.004 | 12.106 | 10.563 | 9.295 | 8.244 | 7.367 | 6.628 | 6.002 | 5.724 | 5.468 |
| 15 | 13.865 | 12.849 | 11.118 | 9.712 | 8.559 | 7.606 | 6.811 | 6.142 | 5.847 | 5.575 |
| 16 | 14.718 | 13.578 | 11.652 | 10.106 | 8.851 | 7.824 | 6.974 | 6.265 | 5.954 | 5.669 |
| 17 | 15.562 | 14.292 | 12.166 | 10.477 | 9.122 | 8.022 | 7.120 | 6.373 | 6.047 | 5.749 |
| 18 | 16.398 | 14.992 | 12.659 | 10.828 | 9.372 | 8.201 | 7.250 | 6.467 | 6.128 | 5.818 |
| 19 | 17.226 | 15.678 | 13.134 | 11.158 | 9.604 | 8.365 | 7.366 | 6.550 | 6.198 | 5.877 |
| 20 | 18.046 | 16.351 | 13.590 | 11.470 | 9.818 | 8.514 | 7.469 | 6.623 | 6.259 | 5.929 |
| 21 | 18.857 | 17.011 | 14.029 | 11.764 | 10.017 | 8.649 | 7.562 | 6.687 | 6.312 | 5.973 |
| 22 | 19.660 | 17.658 | 14.451 | 12.042 | 10.201 | 8.772 | 7.645 | 6.743 | 6.359 | 6.011 |
| 23 | 20.456 | 18.292 | 14.857 | 12.303 | 10.371 | 8.883 | 7.718 | 6.792 | 6.399 | 6.044 |
| 24 | 21.243 | 18.914 | 15.247 | 12.550 | 10.529 | 8.985 | 7.784 | 6.835 | 6.434 | 6.073 |
| 25 | 22.023 | 19.523 | 15.622 | 12.783 | 10.675 | 9.077 | 7.843 | 6.873 | 6.464 | 6.097 |
| 26 | 22.795 | 20.121 | 15.983 | 13.003 | 10.810 | 9.161 | 7.896 | 6.906 | 6.491 | 6.118 |
| 27 | 23.560 | 20.707 | 16.330 | 13.211 | 10.935 | 9.237 | 7.943 | 6.935 | 6.514 | 6.136 |
| 28 | 24.316 | 21.281 | 16.663 | 13.406 | 11.051 | 9.307 | 7.984 | 6.961 | 6.534 | 6.152 |
| 29 | 25.066 | 21.844 | 16.984 | 13.591 | 11.158 | 9.370 | 8.022 | 6.983 | 6.551 | 6.166 |
| 30 | 25.808 | 22.396 | 17.292 | 13.765 | 11.258 | 9.427 | 8.055 | 7.003 | 6.566 | 6.177 |
| 40 | 32.835 | 27.355 | 19.793 | 15.046 | 11.925 | 9.779 | 8.244 | 7.105 | 6.642 | 6.234 |
| 50 | 39.196 | 31.424 | 21.482 | 15.762 | 12.234 | 9.915 | 8.304 | 7.133 | 6.661 | 6.246 |

## PRESENT VALUE OF $1 RECEIVED ANNUALLY FOR N YEARS

| 18% | 20% | 22% | 24% | 25% | 26% | 28% | 30% | 35% | 40% | 45% | 50% |
|---|---|---|---|---|---|---|---|---|---|---|---|
| 0.847 | 0.833 | 0.820 | 0.806 | 0.800 | 0.794 | 0.781 | 0.769 | 0.741 | 0.714 | 0.690 | 0.667 |
| 1.566 | 1.528 | 1.492 | 1.457 | 1.440 | 1.424 | 1.392 | 1.361 | 1.289 | 1.224 | 1.165 | 1.111 |
| 2.174 | 2.106 | 2.042 | 1.981 | 1.952 | 1.923 | 1.868 | 1.816 | 1.696 | 1.589 | 1.493 | 1.407 |
| 2.690 | 2.589 | 2.494 | 2.404 | 2.362 | 2.320 | 2.241 | 2.166 | 1.997 | 1.849 | 1.720 | 1.605 |
| 3.127 | 2.991 | 2.864 | 2.745 | 2.689 | 2.635 | 2.532 | 2.436 | 2.220 | 2.035 | 1.876 | 1.737 |
| 3.498 | 3.326 | 3.167 | 3.020 | 2.951 | 2.885 | 2.759 | 2.643 | 2.385 | 2.168 | 1.983 | 1.824 |
| 3.812 | 3.605 | 3.416 | 3.242 | 3.161 | 3.083 | 2.937 | 2.802 | 2.508 | 2.263 | 2.057 | 1.883 |
| 4.078 | 3.837 | 3.619 | 3.421 | 3.329 | 3.241 | 3.076 | 2.925 | 2.598 | 2.331 | 2.108 | 1.922 |
| 4.303 | 4.031 | 3.786 | 3.566 | 3.463 | 3.366 | 3.184 | 3.019 | 2.665 | 2.379 | 2.144 | 1.948 |
| 4.494 | 4.192 | 3.923 | 3.682 | 3.571 | 3.465 | 3.269 | 3.092 | 2.715 | 2.414 | 2.168 | 1.965 |
| 4.656 | 4.327 | 4.035 | 3.776 | 3.656 | 3.544 | 3.335 | 3.147 | 2.752 | 2.438 | 2.185 | 1.977 |
| 4.793 | 4.439 | 4.127 | 3.851 | 3.725 | 3.606 | 3.387 | 3.190 | 2.779 | 2.456 | 2.196 | 1.985 |
| 4.910 | 4.533 | 4.203 | 3.912 | 3.780 | 3.656 | 3.427 | 3.223 | 2.799 | 2.468 | 2.204 | 1.990 |
| 5.008 | 4.611 | 4.265 | 3.962 | 3.824 | 3.695 | 3.459 | 3.249 | 2.814 | 2.477 | 2.210 | 1.993 |
| 5.092 | 4.675 | 4.315 | 4.001 | 3.859 | 3.726 | 3.483 | 3.268 | 2.825 | 2.484 | 2.214 | 1.995 |
| 5.162 | 4.730 | 4.357 | 4.033 | 3.887 | 3.751 | 3.503 | 3.283 | 2.834 | 2.489 | 2.216 | 1.997 |
| 5.222 | 4.775 | 4.391 | 4.059 | 3.910 | 3.771 | 3.518 | 3.295 | 2.840 | 2.492 | 2.218 | 1.998 |
| 5.273 | 4.812 | 4.419 | 4.080 | 3.928 | 3.786 | 3.529 | 3.304 | 2.844 | 2.494 | 2.219 | 1.999 |
| 5.316 | 4.844 | 4.442 | 4.097 | 3.942 | 3.799 | 3.539 | 3.311 | 2.848 | 2.496 | 2.220 | 1.999 |
| 5.353 | 4.870 | 4.460 | 4.110 | 3.954 | 3.808 | 3.546 | 3.316 | 3.850 | 2.497 | 2.221 | 1.999 |
| 5.384 | 4.891 | 4.476 | 4.121 | 3.963 | 3.816 | 3.551 | 3.320 | 2.852 | 2.498 | 2.221 | 2.000 |
| 5.410 | 4.909 | 4.488 | 4.130 | 3.970 | 3.822 | 3.556 | 3.323 | 2.853 | 2.458 | 2.222 | 2.000 |
| 5.432 | 4.925 | 4.499 | 4.137 | 3.976 | 3.827 | 3.559 | 3.325 | 2.854 | 2.499 | 2.222 | 2.000 |
| 5.451 | 4.937 | 4.507 | 4.143 | 3.981 | 3.831 | 3.562 | 3.327 | 2.855 | 2.499 | 2.222 | 2.000 |
| 5.467 | 4.948 | 4.514 | 4.147 | 3.985 | 3.834 | 3.564 | 3.329 | 2.856 | 2.499 | 2.222 | 2.000 |
| 5.480 | 4.956 | 4.520 | 4.151 | 3.988 | 3.837 | 3.566 | 3.330 | 2.856 | 2.500 | 2.222 | 2.000 |
| 5.492 | 4.964 | 4.524 | 4.154 | 3.990 | 3.839 | 3.567 | 3.331 | 2.856 | 2.500 | 2.222 | 2.000 |
| 5.502 | 4.970 | 4.528 | 4.157 | 3.992 | 3.840 | 3.568 | 3.331 | 2.857 | 2.500 | 2.222 | 2.000 |
| 5.510 | 4.975 | 4.531 | 4.159 | 3.994 | 3.841 | 3.569 | 3.332 | 2.857 | 2.500 | 2·222 | 2.000 |
| 5.517 | 4.979 | 4.534 | 4.160 | 3.995 | 3.842 | 3.569 | 3.332 | 2.857 | 2.500 | 2.222 | 2.000 |
| 5.548 | 4.997 | 4.544 | 4.166 | 3.999 | 3.846 | 3.571 | 3.333 | 2.857 | 2.500 | 2.222 | 2.000 |
| 5.554 | 4.999 | 4.545 | 4.167 | 4.000 | 3.846 | 3.571 | 3.333 | 2.857 | 2.500 | 2.222 | 2.000 |

**PRESENT VALUE OF $1**

| Years Hence | 1% | 2% | 4% | 6% | 8% | 10% | 12% | 14% | 15% | 16% |
|---|---|---|---|---|---|---|---|---|---|---|
| 1 | 0.990 | 0.980 | 0.962 | 0.943 | 0.926 | 0.909 | 0.893 | 0.877 | 0.870 | 0.862 |
| 2 | 0.980 | 0.961 | 0.925 | 0.890 | 0.857 | 0.826 | 0.797 | 0.769 | 0.756 | 0.743 |
| 3 | 0.971 | 0.942 | 0.889 | 0.840 | 0.794 | 0.751 | 0.712 | 0.675 | 0.658 | 0.641 |
| 4 | 0.961 | 0.924 | 0.855 | 0.792 | 0.735 | 0.683 | 0.636 | 0.592 | 0.572 | 0.552 |
| 5 | 0.951 | 0.906 | 0.822 | 0.747 | 0.681 | 0.621 | 0.567 | 0.519 | 0.497 | 0.476 |
| 6 | 0.942 | 0.888 | 0.790 | 0.705 | 0.630 | 0.564 | 0.507 | 0.456 | 0.432 | 0.410 |
| 7 | 0.933 | 0.871 | 0.760 | 0.665 | 0.583 | 0.513 | 0.452 | 0.400 | 0.376 | 0.354 |
| 8 | 0.923 | 0.853 | 0.731 | 0.627 | 0.540 | 0.467 | 0.404 | 0.351 | 0.327 | 0.305 |
| 9 | 0.914 | 0.837 | 0.703 | 0.592 | 0.500 | 0.424 | 0.361 | 0.308 | 0.284 | 0.263 |
| 10 | 0.905 | 0.820 | 0.676 | 0.558 | 0.463 | 0.386 | 0.322 | 0.270 | 0.247 | 0.227 |
| 11 | 0.896 | 0.804 | 0.650 | 0.527 | 0.429 | 0.350 | 0.287 | 0.237 | 0.215 | 0.195 |
| 12 | 0.887 | 0.788 | 0.625 | 0.497 | 0.397 | 0.319 | 0.257 | 0.208 | 0.187 | 0.168 |
| 13 | 0.879 | 0.773 | 0.601 | 0.469 | 0.368 | 0.290 | 0.229 | 0.182 | 0.163 | 0.145 |
| 14 | 0.870 | 0.758 | 0.577 | 0.442 | 0.340 | 0.263 | 0.205 | 0.160 | 0.141 | 0.125 |
| 15 | 0.861 | 0.743 | 0.555 | 0.417 | 0.315 | 0.239 | 0.183 | 0.140 | 0.123 | 0.108 |
| 16 | 0.853 | 0.728 | 0.534 | 0.394 | 0.292 | 0.218 | 0.163 | 0.123 | 0.107 | 0.093 |
| 17 | 0.844 | 0.714 | 0.513 | 0.371 | 0.270 | 0.198 | 0.146 | 0.108 | 0.093 | 0.080 |
| 18 | 0.836 | 0.700 | 0.494 | 0.350 | 0.250 | 0.180 | 0.130 | 0.095 | 0.081 | 0.069 |
| 19 | 0.828 | 0.686 | 0.475 | 0.331 | 0.232 | 0.164 | 0.116 | 0.083 | 0.070 | 0.060 |
| 20 | 0.820 | 0.673 | 0.456 | 0.312 | 0.215 | 0.149 | 0.104 | 0.073 | 0.061 | 0.051 |
| 21 | 0.811 | 0.660 | 0.439 | 0.294 | 0.199 | 0.135 | 0.093 | 0.064 | 0.053 | 0.044 |
| 22 | 0.803 | 0.647 | 0.422 | 0.278 | 0.184 | 0.123 | 0.083 | 0.056 | 0.046 | 0.038 |
| 23 | 0.795 | 0.634 | 0.406 | 0.262 | 0.170 | 0.112 | 0.074 | 0.049 | 0.040 | 0.033 |
| 24 | 0.788 | 0.622 | 0.390 | 0.247 | 0.158 | 0.102 | 0.066 | 0.043 | 0.035 | 0.028 |
| 25 | 0.780 | 0.610 | 0.375 | 0.233 | 0.146 | 0.092 | 0.059 | 0.038 | 0.030 | 0.024 |
| 26 | 0.772 | 0.598 | 0.361 | 0.220 | 0.135 | 0.084 | 0.053 | 0.033 | 0.026 | 0.021 |
| 27 | 0.764 | 0.586 | 0.347 | 0.207 | 0.125 | 0.076 | 0.047 | 0.029 | 0.023 | 0.018 |
| 28 | 0.757 | 0.574 | 0.333 | 0.196 | 0.116 | 0.069 | 0.042 | 0.026 | 0.020 | 0.016 |
| 29 | 0.749 | 0.563 | 0.321 | 0.185 | 0.107 | 0.063 | 0.037 | 0.022 | 0.017 | 0.014 |
| 30 | 0.742 | 0.552 | 0.308 | 0.174 | 0.099 | 0.057 | 0.033 | 0.020 | 0.015 | 0.012 |
| 40 | 0.672 | 0.453 | 0.208 | 0.097 | 0.046 | 0.022 | 0.011 | 0.005 | 0.004 | 0.003 |
| 50 | 0.608 | 0.372 | 0.141 | 0.054 | 0.021 | 0.009 | 0.003 | 0.001 | 0.001 | 0.001 |

## PRESENT VALUE OF $1

| 18% | 20% | 22% | 24% | 25% | 26% | 28% | 30% | 35% | 40% | 45% | 50% |
|-----|-----|-----|-----|-----|-----|-----|-----|-----|-----|-----|-----|
| 0.847 | 0.833 | 0.820 | 0.806 | 0.800 | 0.794 | 0.781 | 0.769 | 0.741 | 0.714 | 0.690 | 0.667 |
| 0.718 | 0.694 | 0.672 | 0.650 | 0.640 | 0.630 | 0.610 | 0.592 | 0.549 | 0.510 | 0.476 | 0.444 |
| 0.609 | 0.579 | 0.551 | 0.524 | 0.512 | 0.500 | 0.477 | 0.455 | 0.406 | 0.364 | 0.328 | 0.296 |
| 0.516 | 0.482 | 0.451 | 0.423 | 0.410 | 0.397 | 0.373 | 0.350 | 0.301 | 0.260 | 0.226 | 0.198 |
| 0.437 | 0.402 | 0.370 | 0.341 | 0.328 | 0.315 | 0.291 | 0.269 | 0.223 | 0.186 | 0.156 | 0.132 |
| 0.370 | 0.335 | 0.303 | 0.275 | 0.262 | 0.250 | 0.227 | 0.207 | 0.165 | 0.133 | 0.108 | 0.088 |
| 0.314 | 0.279 | 0.249 | 0.222 | 0.210 | 0.198 | 0.178 | 0.159 | 0.122 | 0.095 | 0.074 | 0.059 |
| 0.266 | 0.233 | 0.204 | 0.179 | 0.168 | 0.157 | 0.139 | 0.123 | 0.091 | 0.068 | 0.051 | 0.039 |
| 0.225 | 0.194 | 0.167 | 0.144 | 0.134 | 0.125 | 0.108 | 0.094 | 0.067 | 0.048 | 0.035 | 0.026 |
| 0.191 | 0.162 | 0.137 | 0.116 | 0.107 | 0.099 | 0.085 | 0.073 | 0.050 | 0.035 | 0.024 | 0.017 |
| 0.162 | 0.135 | 0.112 | 0.094 | 0.086 | 0.079 | 0.066 | 0.056 | 0.037 | 0.025 | 0.017 | 0.012 |
| 0.137 | 0.112 | 0.092 | 0.076 | 0.069 | 0.062 | 0.052 | 0.043 | 0.027 | 0.018 | 0.012 | 0.008 |
| 0.116 | 0.093 | 0.075 | 0.061 | 0.055 | 0.050 | 0.040 | 0.033 | 0.020 | 0.013 | 0.008 | 0.005 |
| 0.099 | 0.078 | 0.062 | 0.049 | 0.044 | 0.039 | 0.032 | 0.025 | 0.015 | 0.009 | 0.006 | 0.008 |
| 0.084 | 0.065 | 0.051 | 0.040 | 0.035 | 0.031 | 0.025 | 0.020 | 0.011 | 0.006 | 0.004 | 0.002 |
| 0.071 | 0.054 | 0.042 | 0.032 | 0.028 | 0.025 | 0.019 | 0.015 | 0.008 | 0.005 | 0.003 | 0.002 |
| 0.060 | 0.045 | 0.034 | 0.026 | 0.023 | 0.020 | 0'015 | 0.012 | 0.006 | 0.003 | 0.002 | 0.001 |
| 0.051 | 0.038 | 0.028 | 0.021 | 0.018 | 0.016 | 0.012 | 0.009 | 0.005 | 0.002 | 0.001 | 0.001 |
| 0.043 | 0.031 | 0.023 | 0.017 | 0.014 | 0.012 | 0.009 | 0.007 | 0.003 | 0.002 | 0.001 | |
| 0.037 | 0.026 | 0.019 | 0.014 | 0.012 | 0.010 | 0.007 | 0.005 | 0.002 | 0.001 | 0.001 | |
| 0.031 | 0.022 | 0.015 | 0.011 | 0.009 | 0.008 | 0.006 | 0.004 | 0.002 | 0.001 | | |
| 0.026 | 0.018 | 0.013 | 0.009 | 0.007 | 0.006 | 0.004 | 0.003 | 0.001 | 0.001 | | |
| 0.022 | 0.015 | 0.010 | 0.007 | 0.006 | 0.005 | 0.003 | 0.002 | 0.001 | | | |
| 0.019 | 0.013 | 0.008 | 0.006 | 0.005 | 0.004 | 0.003 | 0.002 | 0.001 | | | |
| 0.016 | 0.010 | 0.007 | 0.005 | 0.004 | 0.003 | 0.002 | 0.001 | 0.001 | | | |
| 0.014 | 0.009 | 0.006 | 0.004 | 0.003 | 0.002 | 0.002 | 0.001 | | | | |
| 0.011 | 0.007 | 0.005 | 0.003 | 0.002 | 0.002 | 0.001 | 0.001 | | | | |
| 0.010 | 0.006 | 0.004 | 0.002 | 0.002 | 0.002 | 0.001 | 0.001 | | | | |
| 0.008 | 0.005 | 0.003 | 0.002 | 0.002 | 0.001 | 0.001 | 0.001 | | | | |
| 0.007 | 0.004 | 0.003 | 0.002 | 0.001 | 0.001 | 0.001 | | | | | |
| 0.001 | 0.001 | | | | | | | | | | |

# COMPOUND RATE OF GROWTH TABLE*

| Compound Rate of Growth % per Year | Years | | | | | | | | | | | |
|---|---|---|---|---|---|---|---|---|---|---|---|---|
| | 1 | 2 | 3 | 4 | 5 | 6 | 7 | 8 | 9 | 10 | 15 | 20 |
| 1% | 1.01 | 1.020 | 1.030 | 1.041 | 1.051 | 1.062 | 1.072 | 1.083 | 1.094 | 1.105 | 1.161 | 1.220 |
| 2 | 1.020 | 1.040 | 1.061 | 1.082 | 1.104 | 1.126 | 1.140 | 1.172 | 1.195 | 1.219 | 1.346 | 1.373 |
| 3 | 1.030 | 1.061 | 1.093 | 1.126 | 1.159 | 1.194 | 1.230 | 1.267 | 1.305 | 1.344 | 1.558 | 1.806 |
| 4 | 1.040 | 1.082 | 1.125 | 1.170 | 1.217 | 1.265 | 1.316 | 1.369 | 1.423 | 1.480 | 1.801 | 2.191 |
| 5 | 1.050 | 1.103 | 1.158 | 1.216 | 1.276 | 1.340 | 1.407 | 1.477 | 1.551 | 1.629 | 2.079 | 2.653 |
| 6 | 1.060 | 1.124 | 1.191 | 1.262 | 1.338 | 1.419 | 1.504 | 1.594 | 1.689 | 1.791 | 2.340 | 3.207 |
| 7 | 1.070 | 1.145 | 1.225 | 1.311 | 1.403 | 1.501 | 1.606 | 1.718 | 1.838 | 1.967 | 2.759 | 3.870 |
| 8 | 1.080 | 1.166 | 1.260 | 1.360 | 1.469 | 1.587 | 1.714 | 1.851 | 1.999 | 2.159 | 3.172 | 4.661 |
| 9 | 1.090 | 1.188 | 1.295 | 1.412 | 1.539 | 1.677 | 1.828 | 1.993 | 2.172 | 2.367 | 3.642 | 5.604 |
| 10 | 1.100 | 1.210 | 1.331 | 1.464 | 1.611 | 1.772 | 1.949 | 2.144 | 2.358 | 2.594 | 4.177 | 6.727 |
| 11 | 1.110 | 1.232 | 1.368 | 1.518 | 1.685 | 1.870 | 2.076 | 2.305 | 2.558 | 2.839 | 4.785 | 8.062 |
| 12 | 1.120 | 1.254 | 1.408 | 1.574 | 1.762 | 1.974 | 2.211 | 2.476 | 2.773 | 3.106 | 5.474 | 9.646 |
| 13 | 1.130 | 1.277 | 1.443 | 1.630 | 1.842 | 2.082 | 2.352 | 2.658 | 3.004 | 3.395 | 6.134 | 11.523 |
| 14 | 1.140 | 1.300 | 1.482 | 1.659 | 1.925 | 2.195 | 2.502 | 2.853 | 3.252 | 3.707 | 7.138 | 15.743 |
| 15 | 1.150 | 1.323 | 1.521 | 1.749 | 2.011 | 2.313 | 2.660 | 3.059 | 3.518 | 4.046 | 8.137 | 16.366 |
| 20 | 1.200 | 1.440 | 1.728 | 2.074 | 2.488 | 2.986 | 3.583 | 4.300 | 5.160 | 6.192 | 15.407 | 38.334 |
| 25 | 1.250 | 1.563 | 1.953 | 2.441 | 3.052 | 3.815 | 4.768 | 5.960 | 7.651 | 9.313 | 29.422 | 86.736 |
| 30 | 1.300 | 1.690 | 2.197 | 2.856 | 3.713 | 4.827 | 6.275 | 8.157 | 10.604 | 13.786 | 51.186 | 190.049 |
| 40 | 1.400 | 1.960 | 2.744 | 3.842 | 5.378 | 7.530 | 10.541 | 14.758 | 20.661 | 28.925 | 155.568 | 836.681 |
| 50 | 1.500 | 2.250 | 3.375 | 5.063 | 7.594 | 11.191 | 17.086 | 25.629 | 38.443 | 57.665 | 437.893 | 332.524 |

Based on formula $S = (1 + r)^n$

## APPENDIX B
### TAX RATE SCHEDULE—INDIVIDUAL*†
### 1960-1963

| Taxable Income | Tax (before credits) |
|---|---|
| $0 to $ 2,000 | 20% |
| 2,000 to 4,000 | $ 400 plus 22% of amount over $ 2,000 |
| 4,000 to 6,000 | 840 plus 26% of amount over 4,000 |
| 6,000 to 8,000 | 1,360 plus 30% of amount over 6,000 |
| 8,000 to 10,000 | 1,960 plus 34% of amount over 8,000 |
| 10,000 to 12,000 | 2,640 plus 38% of amount over 10,000 |
| 12,000 to 14,000 | 3,400 plus 43% of amount over 12,000 |
| 14,000 to 16,000 | 4,260 plus 47% of amount over 14,000 |
| 16,000 to 18,000 | 5,200 plus 50% of amount over 16,000 |
| 18,000 to 20,000 | 6,200 plus 53% of amount over 18,000 |
| 20,000 to 22,000 | 7,260 plus 56% of amount over 20,000 |
| 22,000 to 26,000 | 8,380 plus 59% of amount over 22,000 |
| 26,000 to 32,000 | 10,740 plus 62% of amount over 26,000 |
| 32,000 to 38,000 | 14,460 plus 65% of amount over 32,000 |
| 38,000 to 44,000 | 18,360 plus 69% of amount over 38,000 |
| 44,000 to 50,000 | 22,500 plus 72% of amount over 44,000 |
| 50,000 to 60,000 | 26,820 plus 75% of amount over 50,000 |
| 60,000 to 70,000 | 34,320 plus 78% of amount over 60,000 |
| 70,000 to 80,000 | 42,120 plus 81% of amount over 70,000 |
| 80,000 to 90,000 | 50,220 plus 84% of amount over 80,000 |
| 90,000 to 100,000 | 58,620 plus 87% of omount over 90,000 |
| 100,000 to 150,000 | 67,320 plus 89% of amount over 100,000 |
| 150,000 to 200,000 | 111,820 plus 90% of amount over 150,000 |
| 200,000 and over | 156,820 plus 91% of amount over 200,000 |

### 1964

| Taxable Income | Tax (before credits) |
|---|---|
| $0 to $ 500 | 16% |
| 500 to 1,000 | $80 plus 16.5% of amount over $500 |
| 1,000 to 1,500 | 162.50 plus 17.5% of amount over 1,000 |
| 1,500 to 2,000 | 250 plus 18% of amount over 1,500 |
| 2,000 to 4,000 | 340 plus 20% of amount over 2,000 |
| 4,000 to 6,000 | 740 plus 23.5% of amount over 4,000 |
| 6,000 to 8,000 | 1,210 plus 27% of amount over 6,000 |
| 8,000 to 10,000 | 1,750 plus 30.5% of amount over 8,000 |
| 10,000 to 12,000 | 2,360 plus 34% of amount over 10,000 |
| 12,000 to 14,000 | 3,040 plus 37.5% of amount over 12,000 |
| 14,000 to 16,000 | 3,790 plus 41% of amount over 14,000 |
| 16,000 to 18,000 | 4,610 plus 44.5% of amount over 16,000 |
| 18,000 to 20,000 | 5,500 plus 47.5% of amount over 18,000 |
| 20,000 to 22,000 | 6,450 plus 50.5% of amount over 20,000 |
| 22,000 to 26,000 | 7,460 plus 53.5% of amount over 22,000 |
| 26,000 to 32,000 | 9,600 plus 56% of amount over 26,000 |
| 32,000 to 38,000 | 12,960 plus 58.5% of amount over 32,000 |
| 38,000 to 44,000 | 16,470 plus 61% of amount over 38,000 |
| 44,000 to 50,000 | 20,130 plus 63.5% of amount over 44,000 |
| 50,000 to 60,000 · | 23,940 plus 66% of amount over 50,000 |
| 60,000 to 70,000 | 30,540 plus 68.5% of amount over 60,000 |
| 70,000 to 80,000 | 37,390 plus 71% of amount over 70,000 |
| 80,000 to 90,000 | 44,490 plus 73.5% of amount over 80,000 |
| 90,000 to 100,000 | 51,840 plus 75% of amount over 90,000 |
| 100,000 to 200,000 | 59,340 plus 76.5% of amount over 100,000 |
| 200,000 and over | 135,840 plus 77% of amount over 200,000 |

**Taxable Years Beginning after 1964**

| | | | | |
|---|---|---|---|---|
| $0 to $ 500 | | 14% | | |
| 500 to 1,000 | $70 plus | 15% of amount over | $500 |
| 1,000 to 1,500 | 145 plus | 16% of amount over | 1,000 |
| 1,500 to 2,000 | 225 plus | 17% of amount over | 1,500 |
| 2,000 to 4,000 | 310 plus | 19% of amount over | 2,000 |
| 4,000 to 6,000 | 690 plus | 22% of amount over | 4,000 |
| 6,000 to 8,000 | 1,130 plus | 25% of amount over | 6,000 |
| 8,000 to 10,000 | 1,630 plus | 28% of amount over | 8,000 |
| 10,000 to 12,000 | 2,190 plus | 32% of amount over | 10,000 |
| 12,000 to 14,000 | 2,830 plus | 36% of amount over | 12,000 |
| 14,000 ot 16,000 | 3,550 plus | 39% of amount over | 14,000 |
| 16,000 to 18,000 | 4,330 plus | 42% of amount over | 16,000 |
| 18,000 to 20,000 | 5,170 plus | 45% of amount over | 18,000 |
| 20,000 to 22,000 | 6,070 plus | 48% of amount over | 20,000 |
| 22,000 to 24,000 | 7,030 plus | 50% of amount over | 22,000 |
| 24,000 to 26,000 | 8,030 plus | 50% of amount over | 24,000 |
| 26,000 to 28,000 | 9,030 plus | 53% of amount over | 26,000 |
| 28,000 to 32,000 | 10,090 plus | 53% of amount over | 28,000 |
| 32,000 to 38,000 | 12,210 plus | 55% of amount over | 32,000 |
| 38,000 to 44,000 | 15,510 plus | 58% of amount over | 38,000 |
| 44,000 to 50,000 | 18,990 plus | 60% of amount over | 44,000 |
| 50,000 to 60,000 | 22,590 plus | 62% of amount over | 50,000 |
| 60,000 to 70,000 | 28,790 plus | 64% of amount over | 60,000 |
| 70,000 to 80,000 | 35,190 plus | 66% of amount over | 70,000 |
| 80,000 to 90,000 | 41,790 plus | 68% of amount over | 80,000 |
| 90,000 to 100,000 | 48,590 plus | 69% of amount over | 90,000 |
| 100,000 and over | 55,490 plus | 70% of amount over | 100,000 |

*The same rate schedule may be used for a single return, a joint return, or a head of the household return. For a joint return, divide the taxable income by two, enter the table and compute the income tax, and then double the amount. The result will be owed on a joint return. Since the head of the household receives one-half the benefit afforded a joint return, divide the taxable income by 1.50, compute the taxes from the above table, and multiply the figure obtained by 1.50 to obtain the tax liability for the head of the household.

†*Source: Prentice-Hall Federal Tax Course* (Englewood Clifls, New Jersey: Prentice-Hall, Inc., Selected Issues).

The single proprietorship and the partnership do not pay federal income taxes in the name of the firms. Instead, the owner of a single proprietorship prepares a form showing income (or loss) from a business and includes it with his personal income tax return. Rates for an individual filing a separate return, a joint return, or as a head of a household for the years, 1960–1965 appear in the preceding schedules.

The partners in a partnership must include their proportionate part of net income and certain types of deductions (such as charitable contributions, interest expenses, and the like) on their individual income tax returns. The firm does not pay federal income taxes in its own name although it must file an information return. A partnership with fewer than 50 partners may

### DUE DATES FOR CORPORATE INCOME TAXES
### (CALENDAR-YEAR BASIS)

| Year | Percentage Paid in Income Year* | | | | Percentage Paid in Following Year† | |
|------|---------|----------|-----------|----------|---------|---------|
|      | Apr. 15 | June 15  | Sept. 15  | Dec. 15  | Mar. 15 | June 15 |
| 1955 |         |          | 5%        | 5%       | 45%     | 45%     |
| 1956 |         |          | 10        | 10       | 40      | 40      |
| 1957 |         |          | 15        | 15       | 35      | 35      |
| 1958 |         |          | 20        | 20       | 30      | 30      |
| 1959–63 |       |          | 25        | 25       | 25      | 25      |
| 1964 | 1%      | 1%       | 25        | 25       | 24      | 24      |
| 1965 | 4       | 4        | 25        | 25       | 21      | 21      |
| 1966 | 12      | 12       | 25        | 25       | 13      | 13      |
| 1967 | 25      | 25       | 25        | 25       | —       | —       |
| 1970 | 25      | 25       | 25        | 25       | —       | —       |

*Based on estimated income tax liability.
†Due date of tax on first $100,000 or underestimates.

### CORPORATE TAX RATES FOR SELECTED YEARS

| Year | Normal Tax (All Taxable) | Surtax (Taxable Income over $ 25,000) |
|------|---------|---------|
| 1955 | 30%     | 22%     |
| 1956 | 30      | 22      |
| 1957 | 30      | 22      |
| 1958 | 30      | 22      |
| 1959 | 30      | 22      |
| 1960 | 30      | 22      |
| 1961 | 30      | 22      |
| 1962 | 30      | 22      |
| 1963 | 30      | 22      |
| 1964* | 22     | 28      |
| 1965 | 22      | 26      |

*The special tax of 2 per cent on consolidated returns was repealed beginning in 1964.

elect to be taxed as a corporation, but this is seldom to the advantage of the partners unless the personal income tax brackets of the partners are extremely high and the firm is retaining a large percentage of the net profits.

Business corporations are taxed as separate entities, except for Subchapter S Corporations. Business corporations ordinarily receive exclusion of 85 per cent of the dividends received from another domestic corporation; however, SBICs and members of a control group which meet certain specifications may receive a 100 per cent exclusion. In order for the latter to qualify for a 100 per cent dividend exclusion, it must: (1) have made the election; (2) apply to dividends received from earnings of a taxable year ending after December 31, 1963; and (3) not have elected to receive the multiple-surtax exemption (explained below). The taxable income of the corporation is computed, the appropriate corporate federal income tax rates are applied (see schedule), and the payments are made on the appropriate due dates for corporate income taxes (see schedule). Beginning in 1964, collections of estimated income taxes were accelerated. By 1967 corporations will be on a pay-as-they-go basis. Corporations owing less than $100,000 in federal income taxes or owing for underestimates of tax liabilities make such tax payments in March and June of the year following the year of income (for calendar-year corporations). Tax loss carrybacks for three years and carry-forwards for five years are in effect for corporations.

A controlled group (80 per cent ownership of one corporation by another) may elect to take multiple surtax exemptions on separate returns and pay an additional tax of 6 per cent on each group member's first $25,000 of taxable income. They must forfeit the 100 per cent dividend exclusion. As an alternate, a consolidated return may be filed.

The 1958 income tax code permitted a small business corporation, if qualified as a Subchapter S corporation, to elect to be taxed similarly to a partnership—to pay no federal corporate income taxes in the name of the firm and instead to have each shareholder be taxed on his proportionate part of income. In order for a corporation to qualify as a Subchapter S corporation, it must make the election and must not: have any subsidiaries, have more than ten shareholders, have as shareholders anyone other than individuals or estates, have a nonresident alien as a shareholder, or have more than one class of stock.

A domestic corporation of any size may make the election during the first calendar month of a taxable year or the last calendar month of the preceding taxable year. Written consent of all the shareholders to such an election must be attached to Form 2553. The names and addresses of each of the shareholders, the number of shares owned by each as of the first day of the year for which the election was made, and the dates of acquisition of the stock must be filed with the District Director of Internal Revenue. The election terminates automatically: if a new stockholder does not make the election within thirty days of becoming a shareholder; by the consent of all shareholders; if the corporation ceases to be a small business corporation; if the corporation derives more than 80 per cent of gross receipts from sources outside the United States; or if the corporation derives more than 20 per cent of gross receipts from royalties, rents, dividends, interests, annuities, and net gains from sale or exchange of securities (except the latter is waived in the case of a small business investment company). Once the election is terminated, no new election may be made without the consent of the U.S. Commissioner of Internal Revenue until after the company has been taxed as a corporation for five years.